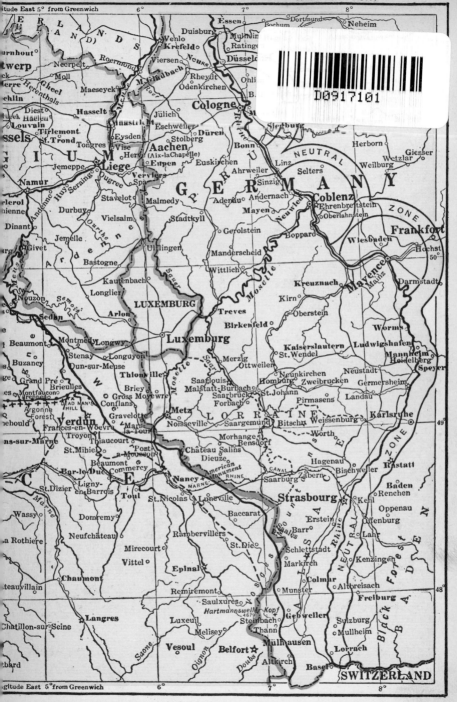

THE GRAND DUKE NICHOLAS

The Commander who led the Russian armies to their early victories in East Prussia and Galicia and afterward captured Erzerum and Trebizond in the Caucasus

THE LITERARY DIGEST
History of the World War

Compiled from Original and Contemporary
Sources: American, British, French,
German, and Other

BY

FRANCIS WHITING HALSEY

*Author of "The Old New York Frontier," Editor of "Great Epochs in
American History," "Seeing Europe with Famous Authors,"
"Balfour, Viviani, and Joffre, Their Speeches
in America," etc.*

IN TEN VOLUMES—ILLUSTRATED

VOLUME VII

RUSSIA'S EARLY VICTORIES—MACKENSEN'S BATTLE OF THE DUNAJEC
AND THE GREAT INVASION OF RUSSIA—RUSSIA'S SECOND OFFENSIVE
UNDER BRUSILOFF—THE REVOLUTION AND THE BREST-LITOVSK
TREATY—BOLSHEVIKI RULE AND RUSSIA'S EFFORTS
TO RIGHT HERSELF

August 1, 1914—July 20, 1919

FUNK & WAGNALLS COMPANY

NEW YORK AND LONDON

1920

CONTENTS—VOLUME SEVEN

IN THE EAST, NEAR EAST, AND SOUTH

CONTENTS—VOLUME SEVEN

PART IV—THE REVOLUTION, THE BREST-LITOVSK TREATY, AND ANARCHY UNDER THE BOLSHEVIKI

ILLUSTRATIONS—VOLUME SEVEN

FULL PAGES

TEXT ILLUSTRATIONS

ILLUSTRATIONS—VOLUME SEVEN

ILLUSTRATIONS—VOLUME SEVEN

ILLUSTRATIONS—VOLUME SEVEN

MAPS

IN THE EAST, NEAR EAST AND SOUTH

Part I

RUSSIA'S EARLY VICTORIES, AND HER DEFEATS AT TANNENBERG AND LODZ

1

RUSSIAN PRISONERS AND GUNS CAPTURED IN THE TANNENBERG BATTLE

I

IN EAST PRUSSIA: GUMBINNEN, TANNENBERG, AUGUSTOWO, OSOWIEC, WIRBALLEN

August 1, 1914—December 30, 1914

SO long as Austria cast her eyes eastward on Saloniki as the goal of her expansion, war between her and Russia had long been some day inevitable, for before reaching a port so far east, the Austrian Teuton had first to crush the Slav, and that meant a battle of great races. Hitherto Austria, in making progress eastward, had been able to avoid actual conflict with Russia, a notable example being her successful annexation of Bosnia and Herzegovina in 1908. She tried to make a peaceable advance in 1914 through Serbia, but circumstances were not then so favorable. Slavdom, in 1914, was not at the same disadvantage as in 1908; it was now ready to fight if that were necessary; for Austria mere bluffing, even with Germany back of her, would not be enough. Except for Greeks, Turks and a few Teutonic people, the inhabitants of eastern and southeastern Europe, numbering roughly 125 millions, were of Slavonic origin. They held their territories by right of original settlements dating from a time earlier than the coming of Teutonic peoples into Europe. Among them were people we now know as Bulgars, Montenegrins, Serbs, Croats, and Poles, at that time either self-governing themselves, or ruled by other Slavonic peoples. Many Slavs in the course of years had passed under Teutonic domination—for example, in East Prussia, where, besides Teutons, the Kaiser ruled over Poles, Kasubes and Serbs, and in Austria where the Dual Monarch had among his subjects several millions Poles, Czechs, Ruthenians, Serbians, Croats, Slovenicks and Slovaks.

Nevertheless, Slavs have been fervent nationalists, with an intense and unconquerable vitality. Like the Jews, they have maintained national traits distinct and unchanged in

3

spite of centuries of foreign domination. Conquerors who have ruled them have never been able to absorb them. This vitality has not been passive, as in the Jew, but active. When not actively hostile, the Slavs had commonly been waiting for an opportunity to become so, and to throw off their yoke. For nearly five hundred years Serbia was in subjection to the Turk, but Serbia never forgot that she had once been an independent empire; nor did she falter in her determination some day to be independent again.

Experiments in governing the Slavs, made by Germany and Austria, had proved scarcely more successful than the methods practised by the Turks. Neither country ever had real peace with its Slavonic subjects. Organized Pan-Slavist movements added enormously to their difficulties. Austria in particular had had many anxious moments. These movements had aimed at unity, if not at an actual union, among Slav peoples, and Russia had been in effect the natural head of the movement, the ultimate aim being to set up free Slavonic nations under the suzerainty, or protection, of the Czar. The immediate object meanwhile was to free themselves from the rule of foreign races. When Serbia in 1912 threw off the Turkish yoke, her object had been only half fulfilled. When she won back territory as a result of the Balkan War, there still remained millions of Serbs under Hapsburg rule. When in 1908 Austria, in a time of Russian weakness, seized Bosnia and Herzegovina, war for a time seemed inevitable, but the Powers stept in and Serbia, unable longer to get Russian help, was forced to acquiesce. She resented the indignity and her nationalist societies became more bitter and more bold, the chief of them the Narodna Obrava, which had an immense membership, drawn from all classes, in every town and village.

It was believed—at least in Germany and Austria—that on an evening early in June, 1914, five members of the Narodna Obrava had met in a house near the royal palace in Belgrade and taken the action that was destined to light the spark that kindled the European conflagration of 1914 by the assassination on June 28 of the Archduke Francis Ferdinand, heir to the Austrian throne, and his wife. Austria, influenced by Germany, a month later, presented

4

her famous ultimatum to Serbia, which made Russian intervention thereafter inevitable. Serbia at that time was exhausted in every way, because of her recent wars with Turkey and Bulgaria, and Russia was in the midst of a scheme of military reorganization which still required a couple of years for completion. War must have been the last wish to Russia; at any rate Serbia, acting on Russia's advice, made an almost abject submission to Austria. In spite of that Austria declared war on her. Proposals made for peace were dismissed and precautionary measures exaggerated into hostile acts, until on Friday, July 31, 1914, when Germany's military preparations had been practically completed, Baron von Pourtales, the German Ambassador to St. Petersburg, called on M. Sazonof, the Russian Foreign Minister, and formally demanded that Russia's partial mobilization cease within twelve hours. On the following day Germany declared war on Russia and Russia took up her task of defending the Slav from the Teuton.

The Eastern Campaign in this war was largely overshadowed for French, English, and American readers by the Western, especially during the first months. It was natural that this should be so. The Western Campaign, as described in earlier chapters, was made the more sensational and the territory was better known. The interest in it, moreover, was greater. To the western frontier the Kaiser sent his best forces and from there every day news was received. The storm in the east was comparatively slow in gathering and lacked, or seemed to lack, the spectacular element, in consequence perhaps of a press censorship even more severe than it was in the west. Only the barest details were published. Defeats were minimized as "local checks," victories were acclaimed as great triumphs.

Reports did emphasize the fact that not only Russia but all Slavdom was united against the Teutons, and that a new Russia was being built up as a result. When, on August 8, the Czar received the two Houses of the Duma at the Winter Palace in St. Petersburg and party quarrels, personal jealousies and political enmities were forgotten, the leader of every party came forward and announced that he and his followers would support the Government by every

5

means in his power. Even M. Purishkivich, the implacable leader of the Anti-Semite movement, praised his Jewish fellow-subjects. The Czar's speech, simple and direct, was significant because of the stress laid on the racial aspects of the war.

Russia from the start had not only Serbia and Montenegro for allies, but France, and within a few days she had England. While the terms of the Franco-Russian military convention had been kept secret for years, it had become generally understood—at least in diplomatic circles —that each partner was left free in the distribution of his forces and in the direction of his campaigns, subject, however, to the general purpose of the Entente itself, which was that it should be a defensive alliance against any attack by Austria and Germany. In compliance with this understanding, and having also in view the great difficulties of rapid mobilization in Russia, it was always regarded as a foregone conclusion that France would have to stand the first shock of an attack from Germany, but that Russia, so far as lay in her power, would assume a vigorous offensive at the earliest moment, in order to draw off and weaken the pressure against France. France was to continue to engage the enemy as long as possible, and at least long enough to enable the Russian hosts to carry out their concentration and assume a vigorous offensive along the whole line. It had long been assumed that neither Germany nor Austria-Hungary would engage in hostilities except conjointly and simultaneously.

The delay of 1914 in the declaration of war by Austria-Hungary against Russia was due not to military but to political causes. Austria-Hungary hoped first to goad Russia into offensive action along her borders, in order that the terms of the Austro-German treaty with Italy, under which Italy was to join Austria and Germany in a defensive war, might be invoked to compel Italy to join the Teutonic powers in hostilities. It was only when the Vienna Government clearly understood that Italy was determined at all costs to play a waiting game that the Austro-Hungarian Ambassador in Petrograd asked for his passports and the Austrian Government declared war. This, however, did not in any way affect preparations for war, for on both sides of the Austro-Russian border mobilization got into full swing. The Russian ukase of mobilization, as originally presented for the Czar's signature, included the whole army, but, for purposes of conciliation, the Czar put his pen through the words "general mobilization" and ordered only a partial mobilization—one confined to the four military districts confronting Austria-Hungary. Only on the following day, when the action of the German Government convinced him that Germany wanted war, did the Czar convert the partial order into a general one. That was

MOBILIZATION IN RUSSIA
The picture shows the entire population of a Russian village
responding to the call

July 30, the day of the bombardment of Belgrade. On the following day, Germany declared war against Russia and invaded Luxemburg, and the next day invaded Belgium.

It was believed that Russia could not possibly concentrate her vast forces within a period of less than three weeks, whereas Germany did not require more than ten days, France twelve days, and Austria-Hungary a somewhat longer period. As a matter of fact, the Russian concentration of armies, sufficient for the initial stage of war, was completed within sixteen days instead of twenty-one. Mobili-

zation in Russia was carried out in the face of more difficulties than in any other country involved in the war. The
undertaking had to be on so vast a scale that it would have
seemed impossible for human ingenuity to place it on a
systematic basis. The area of the Russian Empire is forty
times that of Germany, but its population is only three
times as great. The units to be concentrated were diffusely
scattered, and had to be gathered singly, while the aggregate length of the Russian railway system was only twice
that of the German lines. Moreover, few of the Russian
railways had been built with a view to meeting military
needs. The majority of the troops, when summoned to the
colors, had to traverse vast distances, and often to go on
foot, before they could reach a railway that would take
them to a mobilization center. Of the mobilization among
the Cossacks, a Government official in the Ural provinces
wrote a vivid account of scenes he witnessed. Cossacks supplied their own horses, uniforms, and equipment:

"On July 31st the village awoke to find a red flag waving before
the Government building, the sign that a general mobilization had
been ordered. Immediately everything was in a state of uproar.
Nobody knew who was the enemy and nobody cared. It was sufficient that there was war. Only the women made wild conjectures
as to whom it was against. There was no thought for work. Horses
were groomed, uniforms donned, rifles and sabers cleaned with enthusiastic vigor. Soon the Government veterinary surgeon took his
stand before the chief building and the work of examining the
horses began. Each man in turn brought up his horse and put it
through his paces. The test was most strict. Any animal showing
the slightest defect was promptly branded as useless. All day the
work continued, a crowd of women and children watching the proceedings. At night the red flag was pulled down and a red lamp
hoisted in its place. In the evening there was a great feast. A
whole ox was roasted and there was dancing among the younger
people, but owing to the new regulations there was practically no
vodka. All through the night men came riding into the village
from the outlying districts.

"On Sunday, when the preparations were almost complete, the
consecration service was held. The whole village assembled before
the little wooden church. It was a stirring sight to see these great
warriors in their full battle-array kneeling before their Maker and

8

solemnly asking His aid. At the conclusion of the service each man was blest by the priest and anointed with holy water. Then he led his horse away and received the blessing of his family. On the following day they set off on a journey of thousands of miles. Women, children and old men watched them. Their eyes gleamed with tears and their breasts heaved. Then, when the last man had disappeared from view, they turned away, walked to the fields and took over the labors which the men had left unfinished."

At no time during the mobilization was the religious

A GROUP OF COSSACK SOLDIERS

aspect of the war forgotten. Before starting on their journey, reservists knelt before their humble ikons. In every village the priest blest the troops as they passed. Ikons and sacred relics were often taken to the front. Petrograd—at that time still called St. Petersburg, but the change to Petrograd was soon afterward made—witnessed an impressive scene. There the most holy of all ikons, the famous Smolensk, "Mother of God," which is embellished with jewels enough to ransom the Czar himself, was carried in solemn procession to Kazan Cathedral. Hundreds of thousands stood in the streets while this ikon passed. Every head was bared, a muttered prayer was on every lip. During the services thousands were unable to gain admission to the cathedral and gathered outside, to the extent of fifty thousand, chanting responses and singing hymns. On the Sunday following the declaration of war, the Czar blest the Russian arms and those of his Allies. The flag of the nation was then placed on the altar before the Smolensk ikon. With all the Byzantine pomp and circumstance of the Greek ritual, the aid of the Almighty was invoked.

Russia had more men at her disposal for military service than any other nation. Every year about one million Russians attained an age when they were liable for service, but of this number only 365,000 were taken, for the reason that the State had no need for more. Those chosen were physically the best; Russia could not afford to keep weaklings in her army. In a country where conditions of life were so trying only men with the strongest constitutions could withstand them. According to Russian statistics, the total mobilized standing army and the reserves numbered six million trained men, or 20 per cent. of the population. In addition to this were the "Opolchina," or militia, numbering from 890,000 to 1,000,000. The "Opolchina" consisted of men averaging between 40 to 50 years of age who had served their time in the line and reserves. In spite of their age many were excellent soldiers, in some respects superior to the soldiers of the regular army.

On August 18 the Russian General Staff announced officially that an advance on the Prussian and Austrian frontiers had begun, and the Czar's armies expected soon to be in touch with their enemies. German anxiety over this situation became acute. Late in August, while fighting at Charleroi in Belgium, Germans heard that Russia had advanced into East Prussia and won several victories; that she had isolated Königsberg, and was moving forward toward the Vistula. At the end of the third week in August, therefore, it became necessary for Germany to deplete the armies she had sent against France. Two corps were ordered into East Prussia and yet the first great battle of the war in the West was unfought.

It was important, in understanding the offensive campaign in the East, to consider the configuration of that great Russian frontier district, for it determined the initial strategy. Russia was bound to assume the offensive against Germany, in order to relieve her Allies who were meeting the German onslaught in the West. Her natural line of attack was through Posen, that angle of her frontier being only 180 miles from Berlin, the salient of Poland going racially much farther west than the Warta, including as it did in the racial sense the bulk of the province of Posen and a considerable part of West Prussia. Germany had been unsuccessful in governing her Poles, schemes of Prussianization and land settlements having come to futile ends. By moving westward along the Posen route, Russia was moving among a race who, in spite of all they had suffered from Russia, preferred a Slav to a Teuton ruler. But this direct advance could not be made until Russia's flanks had been safeguarded by a conquest of East Prussia and Galicia— that is to say, until the Russian armies could be deployed safely on a front which may be defined by the Lower Vistula, the Warta, and the Upper Oder. Russia's first task, therefore, was to defeat the Germans in East Prussia and the Austrians in Galicia.

Actual hostilities in the East had begun in a small way long before Russia's army was fully mobilized. In the first days of August, at Prostken, in East Prussia, shots were exchanged between border patrols, and two squadrons of Russian cavalry invaded Germany, with Johannisburg as their objective. About the same time German troops crossed into Russian Poland and occupied the railway junction at Kalisz. Meanwhile, the German cruiser *Augsburg* invaded and bombarded Libau, the Russian port on the Baltic, where

RUSSIANS MARCHING IN WHAT WAS CALLED
"STEAM-ROLLER" FASHION

11

were stores of grain and naval supplies. As Russia had also threatened Galicia, a part of the Austrian offensive against Serbia had to be abandoned. At the same time numerous frontier raids were made by Germany, in order to harass the Russians while their mobilization was in progress. These German forces were chiefly Landwehr and comprised about twenty divisions of 20,000 men each, with thirty-one cavalry regiments and six batteries of artillery. This army, afterward commanded by General von Hindenburg, was mobilized on a line of about thirty miles, its right flank protected by the Masurian marshes, its left resting on Insterburg.

The Russians, after collecting considerable forces under General Rennenkampf, threw back the German cavalry which harassed them and made tentative advances over the Prussian frontier. Cavalry cut the strategical railway at Lyck, and pushed back German outposts toward the lakes. Having crossed the frontier at Suwalke and Wirballen on August 7, Rennenkampf attacked and defeated von François near Insterburg on the 16th, causing him to fall back on Königsberg. Meanwhile Samsonoff, advancing from southwest of the Masurian Lakes, attacked a German corps at Frankenau on the 20th, defeating it with heavy loss, and driving it in disorder toward Königsberg. Samsonoff entered Allenstein on the 25th and after deploying his army west of that town between the Thorn-Soldau and Thorn-Allenstein railways, sent out cavalry toward the Vistula. In these preliminary operations the Russians obtained a commanding footing in East Prussia, and the Germans penetrated Russian Poland. A Russian invasion of Galicia had meanwhile become significant. As early as August 8 a Russian army had crossed the Styr and obtained a footing, and two regiments of German infantry supported by cavalry occupying a position near Brody were attacked by Cossacks and took flight.

By the middle of August Russia was believed to have her army almost ready for serious war. From the most western Russian frontier the distance to Berlin was only 180 miles, and the Germans thus far had in the territory only Landwehr and Landsturm forces, second-rate fighting material, while Austria was too busy with mutinous soldiers to become a menace. Optimistic strategists said it might be only a matter of weeks before Russian legions would be close to Berlin.

East Prussia is a region much easier to defend than to attack, the greater part being covered with marshes, lakes, and forests. Moreover, it was strongly fortified. Königsberg was a first-class modern fortress, while on the line of the Vistula were Thorn, Graudenz, and Danzig, which were even more powerful. Königsberg and Danzig had the advantage of being ports as well as fortified towns, and so could be used for landing large supplies of men and material. Russia, however, might have made a sudden dash on Berlin at this time, and the dash might have proved successful. The country was favorable for a quick advance, the communications good, with well-made roads and direct railway connections with the Russian base at Warsaw.

GENERAL RENNENKAMPF

Rennenkampf commanded a Russian army under the Grand Duke Nicholas at the outbreak of the war and for several months after the Battle of Tannenberg

The capture of Berlin at that time, however, would no more have crusht Germany than the occupation of Brussels crusht Belgium, and such an advance would have been doomed to ultimate disaster. An invading army might have reached Berlin, but, sooner or later, it would have found itself cut off from supplies. It would have left behind it large forces of German troops in East Prussia and Austrian armies in Galicia, so that in time a Russian army around Berlin might have met with a greater and more disastrous Sedan than the French in 1870. Before Russia could set off on the 180-mile journey to Berlin, it was necessary for her first to remove all sources of danger in her rear. Germans had to be driven out of East Prussia or safely held there and Austrians swept from Galicia. The army of Rennenkampf now invading Prussia did not comprise the million men with which it was credited. It is doubtful if it comprised half a million. Russia had to guard a frontier about seven times as long as the one between Germany and France. The Grand Duke Nicholas, Commander-in-Chief, did not regard the invasion of East Prussia as of such paramount importance as the invasion of Galicia.

There was another route to Berlin besides the one through East Prussia, and it possest many obvious advantages, overlooked sometimes by strategists. It lies along the Oder, through Silesia and Saxony. If Russia could crush the military power of Austria in Galicia and drive the remnants of her armies across the Carpathians, pursuing them to Budapest and Vienna, or confining them to the Hungarian plains, she would be free to advance on Breslau and then on Berlin, This route, assuming that Austria had been thoroughly beaten beforehand, would then be. safe. The country was open and well provided with railways, had excellent roads, and contained only one fortress of any strength and this fortress could have been easily masked. An additional advantage was that Silesia was a busy mining and industrial province, with a population of nearly 6,000,000. An invading army could send in flight before it panic-stricken fugitives to impede defensive German measures and to strike terror in Berlin long before the menace of an invasion had seemed serious—so thought optimists among the Allies and their sympathizers.

The Russian offensive was thus divided into two parts—one directed against Austria, the other against Germany. The former was composed of twelve army corps, the latter, of perhaps fifteen. To meet the twelve, the Austrians had sixteen—that is, except those opposing the Serbians, those holding the Slavs in check in Austrian territory, and those protecting her coasts and the Italian frontier, for which work four corps at least were required, while two others had joined the Germans on the lower French frontier. Russia could therefore reckon on a numerical advantage of two corps. For penetrating Prussia and moving toward Berlin, she would ultimately have fifteen army corps avail-

14

able. The Germans in their Eastern territory had not more than five corps of the first line. To meet the difference they had to draw on their second line, but this could not be mobilized until the first was in the field and it was naturally inferior in equipment and in military value. Russia's advantage in this field, provided her regular army could be brought up, would thus be great.

The problem with Russia was to clear both her flanks, and then take Krakow. To that task she set herself again and again, and never really abandoned it, even when central and southern Poland were swarming with German troops and the people of Warsaw were preparing for flight. Throughout the whole of the first six months' campaigning, Krakow was the heart of the problem. While Krakow remained untaken, no advance on a grand scale into either Prussia or Hungary was possible, while the chance of reaching Vienna was too remote to be thought of. With Krakow in Russian hands the whole situation would have been changed. Roads through Silesia to Berlin, or through the Moravian Gate to Vienna, would then have been open and Hungary could have been raided to the gates of Budapest.

Russia soon found it was easier to mobilize her millions than to arm, equip and place them in battle-line. The perplexities and obscurities of the early months of the campaign turned on the difficulty of converting mobilized men into efficient combatants, clothed in uniforms, furnished with rifles and ammunition, and ready to fight. Her supply of clothing and arms, and above all of ammunition, was insufficient. The factories of Russia worked without ceasing, and the Allies did their best to supply her deficiencies, so long as there was any chance of getting supplies into the country. Japan sent great quantities of warlike stores and huge purchases were made from neutrals. Yet it was a long time before Russia was able to overcome her manifold needs. Lack of material, and not poor fighting qualities among her troops, was the chief explanation of such reverses as she encountered in the earlier stages of the campaign. She had to fight on an incredibly long front; her actual fighting line was at some points dangerously thin. She was particularly short of big-gun ammunition, a difficulty which soon hampered all the combatants.

The story of the first few months of fighting in the Eastern theater falls naturally into certain definite sections. First was the invasion of East Prussia, and the victory of Gumbinnen, followed by Hindenburg's retaliatory stroke, the famous battle of Tannenberg, and the unsuccessful attempt of the Germans to reach and cross the river Niemen. Then came, practically as a separate episode, the invasion of Galicia, and the first defeats of the Austrian armies, preceded by a brief Austrian invasion of Poland, after which followed the swift Russian advance; the fall of Lemberg; the investment of Przemysl, and all that confused fighting which carried the Russians to the crest of the Carpathians, and even enabled them to make short incursions into Hungary. These operations were as remarkable as the swift German invasion of France in 1870, and yet the world was slow to realize what Russia was doing and after it knew, was inclined to indifference to it.

The real Russian advance into Prussia began on August 16, the seventeenth day after mobilization began. On the 17th the advance forces encountered a German army corps and at Stalluponen fought a small action, stubborn while it lasted. The Germans claimed to have taken 3,000 prisoners before they fell back on Gumbinnen, where soon afterward was fought the first considerable battle in this Eastern campaign. The Russian advance covered a front of about 35 miles, from Pilkallen on the north to Goldap on the south. The center followed the line of the main road and railway from Stalluponen to Gumbinnen where the ground was flat and nearly featureless, in a country of rye-and potato-fields, with scattered farmhouses, little villages and windmills. The Russian left had to clear and traverse pine woods which stretch for miles east and north of the important railway junction at Goldap.

The main battle near Gumbinnen was fought on the 20th. Gumbinnen was a picturesque country town, with fine old gabled houses, dating from the early eighteenth century. Rennenkampf in this battle had a numerical superiority which suggested an enveloping movement, but he preferred

16

THE GRAND DUKE'S INVASION
OF EAST PRUSSIA
and the ensuing
operations against Warsaw

Railroads ————
Fortified places ✠

VII—16

a frontal attack on the center. The fighting began at dawn with an artillery duel, but the Russian infantry charged without waiting for much artillery preparation, and carried position after position by use of the bayonet and hand-grenade. The Germans counter-attacked with stubborn courage. Some of the ground changed hands several times in the course of the day. One German brigade was caught in a cross-fire of rifles and Maxims, and left 3,000 dead on the field. The fighting lasted fourteen hours. It was only at nightfall that the Germans withdrew. After six days the

© INTERNATIONAL FILM SERVICE, N. Y.

RUSSIANS RETURNING TO THEIR OWN COUNTRY FROM
THE UNITED STATES
The men are shown on arrival by rail in Jersey City, and had come from many parts of the country, after war was declared, to board ship in New York harbor

Germans retreated pursued by the Russians. Eight German regiments of the field army and six Landwehr regiments, with a total of 70,000 men and 200 guns, had taken part in the fighting during the first four days. Later reinforcements brought the number of Germans engaged up to perhaps 100,000. The total German forces then available in East Prussia, besides the independent cavalry division, were five corps of the field-army numbering 210,000 men; 540

17

field-guns, 180 howitzers, and a considerable number of siege-guns. The total German force in all parts of the East, not counting the Landsturm, was estimated at perhaps 500,000 men, with 1,100 field-guns and howitzers, and a large number of siege-guns.

The immediate result of Gumbinnen was to make Russia for the time being master of Prussia east of a line from Königsberg to Allenstein. When Insterburg fell into Russian hands it ensured for Rennenkampf ample supplies, and Tilsit being isolated, its capture became a matter of convenience. The whole region of the Masurian lakes was at the mercy of the Russians. Pursuing Cossacks caused a panic among the German civil population. From every village and town they began to fly, some toward Danzig, others toward Graudenz in the hope of reaching Berlin. They were said to number two hundred and fifty thousand. Germans told stories of Russian atrocities. Commerce came to a standstill and prices rose. No accommodations could be found for the refugees, most of whom were penniless.

The Russians reached Insterburg late on the 23d, and between the 24th and 29th occupied it. Thenceforward, Rennenkampf's advance was practically unopposed. His left wing prest on from Goldap to Darkehmen, and southward to Angerburg, on the edge of the lake country. Thence it followed the cross country strategical railway that runs from Nordenburg to Gerdauen and Allenburg. On the north it held Tilsit, and the Tilsit-Königsberg railway as far as Libau. On the main line to Königsberg it reached Tapiau. The northern portion of East Prussia was securely in Russian grasp as far as the River Alle. Rennenkampf's cavalry had pushed downward as far as Rastenburg and Korschan Junction. The claim was currently made for the cavalry that it had "invested" Königsberg. It hardly did that, for it left open the vital Königsberg-Danzig railway. But it threatened Königsberg, and might hope to press on toward Danzig and the Vistula.

It was not until after their defeat at Gumbinnen that the Germans took the danger to East Prussia seriously. Absorbed in their offensive in France, they had at first left only five corps of the active class to operate on the Eastern Front.

By the third week in August the General Staff saw that serious measures had to be taken, the German position in the east having been gravely imperiled. The story of how, within a week, they turned the tide, and how one of the few decisive, altho local, victories in the war was achieved, made a brilliant page in the military history of Germany. The reconquest of East Prussia was vitally necessary to the Germans. Without it, any advance from Posen would have been caught on the flank. East Prussia was one of the oldest provinces of the Prussian monarchy. Königsberg had been the capital of the dukes of Prussia in days when Berlin was an unknown fishing village among the swamps of the Spree.

Before the outbreak of the war, there was living in Hanover a General von Hindenburg, veteran of the war of 1870, who had been for some years on the retired list. He had spent much of his life in East Prussia, had commanded in succession two army corps at Königsberg and Allenstein, and often in mimic war at annual maneuvers had rehearsed the defense of that forest region against a Russian invasion. He knew every yard of the place as a Scottish gillie knows a deer-forest. After his retirement in 1911, he made the defense of East Prussia his sole hobby, haunted its forests and marshes, sometimes on foot, sometimes testing infrequent roads by motor-car, and sometimes experimenting with a field-gun from a neighboring garrison. Some of the lakes in this territory were wide and shallow stretches with hard gravel bottoms. By practical tests he found out where a gun could be driven through them. Others, tho shallow, had mud a yard deep below the water, and would be impassable for artillery. Year after year he explored the countryside and marked his maps with information as to every acre.

Before the war Hindenburg's military career had been one of regular, but not brilliant, advancement. Of genius no one suspected him. His powerful, square-cut face suggested resolution and method rather than inspiration. Called from his retirement and sent to this front, Hindenburg's strategical problem was, how with limited forces, and those largely second-line material, he could beat two armies nearly united, each equal to his own in numbers and possibly more than equal. Clearly he had to take them in detail. The essence of success was rapidity of movement and promptitude in assembling forces. So sure was he of his stroke that local superiority in numbers against one-half the enemy's forces contented him. He resolved to deal first of all with Samsonoff's army, and then, if that stroke should succeed, to deal with Rennenkampf, his chief strategical asset being the superb railway system of Prussia, which was worked night and day collecting his army. Hindenburg had the equivalent of about four full army corps, at most 160,000 men. Samsonoff had five corps, over 200,000 men, but they were somewhat scattered, and it was said that not more than three and a half corps (seven divisions) were actually engaged in the disastrous struggle among the lakes which came to be known as the battle of Tannenberg.

When Hindenburg arrived in East Prussia, two Russian armies had crossed the frontier and were moving in the direction of Königsberg, evidently intending to effect a junction there and capture that stronghold. Part of the Wilna Army had crossed in the region of Eydtkuhnen, on the main line of railway from Berlin to Petrograd. It had little difficulty, as it advanced westward, in pushing the small German Landsturm troops before it, but on a line some thirty miles east of Königsberg, Rennenkampf, its commander, grew cautious, intrenched himself, and awaited developments. The Second or Narew Army, under Samsonoff, had advanced from the South by way of Mlawa and Soldau, and occupied Allenstein; but he, too, growing apprehensive lest he should push ahead too vigorously, retired somewhat toward the south, and took positions among the western Masurian Lakes.

Hindenburg decided to attack Samsonoff's army at once by a double flanking movement. There was nothing novel in his strategy, but it was a daring venture against an enemy outnumbering the German forces, as Hindenburg himself assured us, by three to one. Another striking display of boldness and readiness to take big risks was seen when he drew away most of the troops that had been holding Rennenkampf in check, and brought them by forced marches to take part in the fighting against Samsonoff. This left Rennenkampf within striking distance of German columns moving to the east of Allenstein in order to turn Samsonoff's right wing, hold the northerly defiles between the lakes, and prevent him from saving himself by effecting a junction with Rennenkampf. The German main attack delivered from the south was thus able to crush in the Russian forces among the lakes and swamps, making it impossible for Samsonoff to deploy troops effectively. Hindenburg's columns making this movement became exposed to

RUSSIAN OFFICERS AT A GRAND ARMY REVIEW

the danger of attack from fresh Russian troops coming across the frontier, and had first to beat off an attack before effecting the destruction of Samsonoff's army.

As soon as Samsonoff had been disposed of, and before the immense booty had been fully garnered, Hindenburg began to move on Rennenkampf, following the best German strategy of unrelentingly pushing an advantage once gained. As it was not possible in this case to repeat an enveloping movement, Hindenburg directed a part of his forces against the Russian left and attacked vigorously. The main blow, however, was dealt elsewhere. The direct attack was only designed to veil it. While the fighting was in progress, another large force was sent swinging completely around the southern end of the lakes for the purpose of gaining access to the Russian rear east of Augerburg, a ruse that was successful; but Rennenkampf, seeing his danger, began a hurried retreat across the frontier, and succeeded in getting away with much less damage than Samsonoff had suffered.

The Russians had advanced against Hindenburg with little thought of peril. Easy successes had led them to suppose they had nothing worse to fear than a repetition of the same feeble opposition they had formerly encountered. They found, however, that they were dealing with larger masses, and that they were fighting against a well-conceived idea. Hindenburg, in his first strokes at the lakes, won the most complete victory which had so far fallen to any commander in any single battle of the war. His prisoners were as numerous as those taken at Sedan. On September 11 the Russians evacuated Insterburg, and in a general order dated from that town on the 15th, Hindenburg was able to announce that Prussia was free from the last of the invaders, and that German troops had penetrated Russia.

In this battle the Russians, believing a successful offensive was their only chance, had blundered forward, their center backed by a vast swamp. Hindenburg then struck his blow. An immense force was hurled against the Russian right, and a desperate encounter followed, with weight of numbers favoring the Germans, the Russians being forced back on the swamps. What followed was not a battle, but hideous slaughter. The Russian position was circular in shape. Outside this circle the land sloped up toward the surrounding enemy; inside was the network of swamp and lakes. On three sides stood the Germans; on the fourth side escape was only possible through swamps and boggy streams.

The Russians were unable to maneuver on swampy ground, while the Germans, in possession of solid higher ground, were free to move at will. From three sides they poured murderous fire into the helpless Russians, forcing them into the swamps. The carnage continued until nightfall. Rennenkampf then managed to escape with a remnant of his army, leaving three generals among thousands slain. Hindenburg had obtained ample revenge for the defeat at Gumbinnen, but, it was one of the most frightful of battles —a battle which was said to have caused officers to go mad from its horrors. The Germans closed in, concentrating a terrible fire on the Russians. Guns sank in the mud; horses and men were embogged. The nature of the ground caused the Russians to break up into helpless groups, many of them were forced farther and farther back into the awful swamps. The mists of evening added to the weirdness of the fray. Out of the blackness of night rang the wild neighing of

© J. RUSSELL & SONS.

CZAR AND KAISER TWENTY-FIVE YEARS BEFORE THE WAR

horses, mingled with the despairing shrieks of men sinking in the quicksands and the slime. Only the Sixth and half of the First Army Corps succeeded in escaping and recrossing the frontier. They had lost heavily. Germany was jubilant. Her people celebrated the battle of Tannenberg as their "Russian Sedan."

Hindenburg had taken up his position with unerring skill. His left was northwest of Allenstein, astride the railway from Osterode to Insterburg; his center about Gilgenburg; his right wing ran from Usdau to Soldau, and rested on the railway which runs from Eylau—the scene of one of Napoleon's famous battles—across the Russian frontier to Mlawa. All access to his front was barred by lakes and swamps, over which his artillery had a perfect field of fire. Between these obstacles he had dug trenches and felled trees, and had formed a line of improvised forest fortifications like those behind which the American armies fought in the Battle of the Wilderness.

When Hindenburg's troops had defeated the Russians he was not satisfied with having driven them into the swamps; but had tens of thousands of them who had surrendered and who tried to get out of the fen, pushed back with bayonets until killed or drowned. Such was his command to the soldiers. No quarter was given, for Germany had no use for so many prisoners. It was said in Germany at the time that "one could hear the cries of the poor Russians, that the thunder of cannon was drowned by their cries, and that many who had to hear the shrill sounds of desperation became insane.[1] " Ninety thousand prisoners were taken in that battle, but still more "were murdered when they were defenseless and begged for mercy and nobody uttered a word of regret. To the contrary, everybody in Germany approved the incident, saying that no other procedure would have been right."

On the 28th and 29th there was desperate fighting for possession of Passenheim, but the big guns from the Vistula fortresses made Samsonoff's position untenable. There remained only the defile toward Ortelsburg, and on the 30th the Russians were in full retreat along this narrow outlet. Hindenburg's left, not less than 60,000 strong, was well east of Passenheim, and the bulk of Samsonoff's forces were shut up in a tract of ground where, between clumps of wood, lay treacherous swamps and wide, muddy lakes. The Russian batteries, as they retired, found their guns sinking to the axle-trees. Horses struggled in vain through the bogs, and as the circle closed in on the beaten army, whole regiments were driven into the lakes and drowned in the water or choked in bottomless mires.

The last day of the battle, August 31, was an unrelieved

[1] Statement by Dr. Wilhelm Muehlon, a former director of Krupps, published in Switzerland in 1918.

disaster for the Russian army. Samsonoff had been lost with two of his corps commanders and several divisional generals and brigadiers had been killed or wounded. The Army of the Narew had been five corps strong at the beginning of the fight, but little more than one complete corps and a portion of another succeeded in gaining Ortelsburg, and retreating eastward by the line of the frontier railway. As to Samsonoff's fate, General Gourko,[2] at one time chief of the Russian staff, said that as night fell, Samsonoff, and five other staff officers, were guiding themselves through thick forests toward the Russian frontier. Amid a hail of bullets the party dismounted and continued their way on foot, into another belt of forest, when utter darkness surrounded them. Samsonoff, who suffered from heart trouble, finding his breathing more and more difficult, had lagged behind. Later, when everybody was called for, all answered except Samsonoff. His ultimate fate was never definitely cleared up, "altho little doubt remained that he died a lonely death during that melancholy flight through the darkened forest." Samsonoff, feeling it impossible to move a step farther, had probably sat down on a hillock. In the course of time in that locality an unknown soldier was found and buried. From his dead body a gold medallion was taken. It proved to be a portrait of Samsonoff's wife, which left little doubt that Samsonoff had died and been buried alone in that forest.

Samsonoff's defeat was due partly to over-confidence, partly to defective intelligence. He had won an easy victory on the 20th, and he trusted to luck rather than prudent generalship to take him further on his way to the Vistula. Up to the morning of the 20th he was unaware of the presence of a large German force on his front, and until Hindenburg seized Soldau he had no warning of impending danger. This was the fault of his airmen and cavalry, who failed to discover the German concentration till Hindenburg had got within striking distance of the Russian Army. When the facts of the situation were revealed, Samsonoff made the mistake of offering battle in a position which was neither defensible nor adapted for offensive tactics. The

[2] In his "War and Revolution in Russia" (The Macmillan Company).

rash strategy of the Russian commander, and his faulty decision to fight when he ought to have retreated, were the causes which led to this deplorable disaster at the opening of the campaign.

General Gourko attributed the disaster to the failure of certain corps to hold firm, to the imperfection of Russian communications, and to Samsonoff's lack of imagination in battle. The Russian flanks were prest back at the same time that the two center corps under Samsonoff were gaining a decided success; but Samsonoff failed either to hear of the retreat of the flanks, or to divine its possibility, and at the moment when he thought victory almost within his grasp it suddenly became evident that the Germans were not only at his side, but closing in behind him. Upon failure to supply the Russian armies with munitions, Gourko offered a large body of striking facts. In 1915 there was a much greater shortage than in 1914, the situation, to a certain extent, being remedied during the succeeding year. Foremost among the desiderata of the Russian armies were artillery and artillery ammunition. Russian batteries were sent to the rear simply because there were not shells for them, and this at periods when the Germans very heavily out-gunned the Russians. In 1914 the Germans were employing fourteen-inch guns, while throughout 1915 the Russians had nothing heavier than six-inch guns, few of these, and little ammunition for them. During 1915 there was such a shortage of cartridges that the troops were continually exhorted to be sparing of them, and in trench fighting the Russian rule was that no matter how heavy the German fire, the men were to use their rifles only in repulsing an attack. The most important cause of rifle shortage was the loss of great quantities on the field. When the war was well advanced units were formed especially for the collection of the equipment of the wounded and dead. As early as the spring of 1915 some of the reinforcements came forward unarmed.

Strategically, Hindenburg had outmaneuvered his opponent; tactically he had shown, not for the first time in history, that with skilful handling a smaller force may envelop a larger. Tannenberg was a vindication of the hobby of the old man's lifetime. The moral effect was lasting. Germany had anticipated great and immediate successes in the Western theater. No one had believed at the outset that much could be done in the East. But Tannenberg was decisive only as to East Prussia. In the larger aspect it was a local victory, since Hindenburg was unable at once to follow it up. Nearly a year elapsed before he could do that. Meanwhile he again and again made heavy efforts to capture Warsaw, and each time failed until a year later, when the Russians were short of ammunition and he succeeded. It was not until September, 1917, that the criminality of the old Russian government in withholding supplies from the Russian army then and afterward was demonstrated. In the trial for treason of General Sukhomlinoff, who was Minister of War when the conflict began, the jury rendered a verdict of guilty, and he was sentenced to life imprisonment. This verdict carried condemnation for corruption and treason almost unexampled in history. Sukhomlinoff's treason consisted in the betrayal of the Russian army into the hands of its German enemies, who paid him for his services. It was shown that he had received German money for allowing troops to serve in Galicia without supplies; that he had received German money for blockading railroads; that he had received German money for holding up at Archangel ammunition that had been sent to the army by Russia's Allies, and which might have given his country a triumph over Germany and Austria. Treachery for which he had received German money had cost tens of thousands of Russian lives. A jury in the new-born Russia found him guilty of all these things.

"This battle is terribly difficult for a civilian to understand," said a layman visitor [3] to the field of Tannenberg to a German officer, a year after the battle. "You can be sure," the officer replied, "that it is very difficult for an officer to understand. The truth is that, without maps, no officer could disentangle the details of the movement. The battle in one way was intricate; in another way it was not. Its large principle was simplicity itself, and that principle is as old as Hannibal's victory at Cannæ more than two

---

[3] James O'Donnell Bennett of The *Times* (New York).

thousand years ago." "And the old principle," said an American army-officer present, "is the principle of 'let 'em come, and then destroy them,' isn't it?" "Precisely," replied the German. "In other words, the principle of weakening your center, with attendant enveloping movements." "Luring them on, and bending them double," said the American. "That is near enough," replied the German. At Cannæ in 216 B.C. Hannibal, by the application of this principle, destroyed with his 50,000 Carthaginian mercenaries all of 79,000 Romans except 6,000, who broke through his enveloping lines.

A year after Tannenberg, soldiers were coming from remote parts of the world to study the field. Tannenberg, fought by a man 67 years old, who had served at Sedan as a lieutenant of three and twenty, had a terrain five times as large as the terrain of Sedan. At Sedan the Germans took 83,000 prisoners, including the Emperor of the French and a Marshal of France. At Tannenberg they took 90,000 prisoners and eliminated two of the foremost Generals of the Russian Army from participation in the war—one through death and one through resignation consequent upon discredit. Waterloo was fought and won in less time than it would take to cover the boundaries of the field of Tannenberg in a fast automobile. Tannenberg lasted almost as many days as Waterloo did hours. Waterloo began between 11 o'clock and noon of Sunday, June 18, 1815, and had reached a decisive stage by 8 o'clock in the evening. Tannenberg began on Sunday, August 23, and continued through Sunday, August 29. In extent it was as stupendous as it was unexampled in duration.

There were so many vital points in so extensive a field that it could not in strict truth be said that Hindenburg's victory was a battle of Tannenberg. It might have been called—and more accurately called—the battle of Mühlen, or of Gilgenburg, or of Hohenstein, or of Allenstein, or of Ortelsburg. Indeed, it was called by all but one of these five names for several weeks after it was won. Why Germany finally settled on Tannenberg was a matter of sentiment that had to do with a battle which Carlyle called "that fatal Tannenberg business" and "that terrible downcome of Tannenberg" that had occurred four centuries before. East Prussia was the cradle and stronghold of the original Prussian race. From its chill plains and dense forests sprang the nobles and rulers who, under the leadership of the House of Hohenzollern, eventually were to weld the German Empire into an organic whole. When, in the fourteenth century, the German tribes were pushed back from the Rhone and the Meuse, the tide of their migration swept eastward. German colonists crossed the Elbe and lower Vistula, and settled in the Eastern forests and marshes, already occupied in part by their own near kinsmen, tho still more by Slavonic tribes. The powerful Teutonic Order of Knighthood, that controlled this work of colonization, eventually came into conflict on this ground with Poland, and was overthrown by the Poles in the great battle of Tannenberg on July 15, 1510, a conflict which remains a landmark in the eternal struggle between Teuton and Slav, and finds a prominent altho sinister place in German history. The rejoicings over Hindenburg's victory were therefore more than the joyful reception of news of a great military triumph. The battle of Tannenberg seemed to Germany to efface a bitter memory, and to compensate her for the grief of four hundred years. But great as the victory was, Hindenburg failed in his efforts to follow it up.

The recapture of Lyck by the Russians afterward indicated that Germany over-estimated the results of her success. But Russia's route to Berlin *via* the north had now not only been barred, but her advance was turned into a

RUSSIAN ARTILLERY IN THE FIRST YEAR OF THE WAR

retreat and General Rennenkampf was forced back to Allenstein, altho every foot of the way was contested. Step by step he had to give up the results of his early victories. Finally Allenstein and Insterburg were in turn evacuated before the merciless pressure of the Germans and the troops investing Königsberg were recalled. Not until the frontiers were almost reached, when strong reinforcements came up, was a stop put to the German advance.

The worst piece of ground in all Europe for military operations lies along the Russo-German frontier in East Prussia. For days at a time the opposing forces fought in marshes, often up to their necks in water, while field-gun after field-gun was engulfed in the mud. Few could realize the difficulties and hardships encountered by the troops in marching through this maze of forest, bog, and water. In the face of such obstacles, Hindenburg's victory over the Russians was thought especially brilliant. It was more than that; it was a striking example of the manner in which Germany had prepared for war and of the value of such preparation.

As a consequence of defeat at Tannenberg, the whole Russian right under Rennenkampf had been compelled to evacuate East Prussia, and not until it passed the Niemen, did it recover from the effects of the disaster. Meanwhile, further German reinforcements reached the eastern frontier and important events were believed to be in store, heralding at no distant date another battle. Twenty-two German corps were concentrated in that territory, and the Kaiser arrived at headquarters. The obscure, retired soldier who had become in three weeks Germany's national idol was made a Field-marshal and entrusted with supreme command in the East. Hindenburg had achieved a brilliant success, but an under-estimate of the enemy was in some degree soon to neutralize it. The sequel to his East Prussian campaign restored for a time something of the prestige of Russian arms. When once on Russian soil the Germans no longer had at their disposal their own admirable system of strategical railways. They could adapt their rolling stock to the different gage of the Russian system, but of railways this region had few. German troops, fatigued with hard marching, once the frontier was crossed, discovered that only a few of the main roads were practicable for heavy motor-transport. Most roads were nothing but beaten tracks, which had never been macadamized, and in a wet autumn became impassable sloughs of mud. Such causeways as existed were often narrow defiles between lakes and swamps, where no army could deploy. To add to the misfortunes it rained heavily for three days, from September 27 to 30.

The struggle which went on during the next week is generally known as the battle of Augustowo, where the chief physical feature of the region is an immense forest, 30 miles long and 20 wide, on whose western edge lies Augustowo. Intricate chains of lakes stretch on either side of the road from Suwalki to Seiny, begin again southeast of Seiny, and are found on either side of the road from Surino to the Niemen. It is not a country for rash adventure, as the Germans were here to learn in a lesson which the Russians had learned amid the Masurian lakes. Above all, the Niemen itself is a formidable obstacle, more than 200 yards wide, too deep to ford, with bridges only at Grodno and Olita, and both fortified places. The right bank, which the Russians held, is high, and in some places might almost be called a cliff. The left bank, on which the Germans had to operate, is low, and, what was worse, in most places is swampy.

The attempt to cross the Niemen was made simultaneously at two points. The more northernly of these was Druskeniki, about 27 miles north of Grodno. Here on the morning of September 25 the Germans constructed a pontoon bridge. The Russians on the steep right bank reserved their fire until a dense column of men was already on the bridge. Then, from cleverly screened positions, the Russian field-guns and machine-guns fell to work, and the bridge was swept clean. German guns were soon brought into action and a long artillery duel followed. Thinking their artillery had at last silenced the enemy's fire, the German infantry crowded over the bridge, and met the same fate as their predecessors. It was said that thousands—but perhaps only hundreds—of Germans corpses floated down the river. A third attempt was then made, after an artillery duel, toward sunset, and with more determination and still heavier slaughter. The Cossacks crossed at nightfall and pursued the Germans over a distance of eight miles. Two divisions were engaged in this attempt, and they are thought to have lost fully half their effectives.

The rest of the operations which made up the Battle of Augustowo was little more than a German retreat along the few practicable roads, harassed by the fire of big guns, and pursued as occasion offered by cavalry. There was some hand-to-hand fighting in the forest, in which the Russians

PONTOON WAR-BRIDGE ACROSS THE RIVER NIEMEN

showed superiority with the bayonet and the grenade at close quarters. The decisive action was fought in the clear spaces around Augustowo, where the Germans had disposed themselves with considerable skill on three sides of a square, so as to command with cross-fire the exit from the forest. The Russians crossed the canal, executed a wide turning movement by the south, bombarded Augustowo from the west and northwest with heavy guns, and captured the town on the afternoon of October 1. Infantry prest on by the roads to Raczky and Suwalki, clearing the obstacles of barbed wire and felled trees as they went.

32

The stroke at Augustowo was well planned. A week of hard fighting and hard marching had sent the invaders back to their own country, their Tannenberg glory a little diminished and their numbers reduced. Some of the credit belonged to General Ruzsky, some of it to the swamps and forests of Lithuania, but the real hero was the Russian infantryman. The crowning exploit at Augustowo was a march of 30 miles, with a bayonet charge at the end of it. The Germans forfeited strong positions in the depths of forests, but the Russians captured them successively, aided by artillery. The fighting here in a number of narrow places through the woods and along the lakesides was a series of desperate encounters of necessarily small forces. The Russian heavy artillery shelled the German trenches with accuracy and effect, the ranges being well known to the gunners. The infantry completed the rout. The German losses were heavy, the ground offering but scanty opportunities for escape. Rennenkampf had driven the Germans out of Russian territory. He had extended the Russian front along the border nearly a hundred miles and repulsed German attempts to force a passage of the Niemen. Four army corps were engaged on both sides, the Russians reinforced from Vilna. Whole regiments of Germans were reported drowned in the Niemen, and to have lost their siege artillery. The Kaiser, who was present at this battle, was said to have escaped with difficulty. The weather was appalling—a continual downpour.

Forty-five miles south of Suwalki lay the Russian temporary fortress of Osowiec, which the Germans attacked with heavy artillery, but failed to assault successfully. The approach to Osowiec, by a narrow defile through impassable marsh and boggy forest lands, was peculiarly trying. The character of the ground compelled a frontal attack. The German retreat, therefore, lay solely through lands mostly undrained and boggy morasses which were practicable only in a time of heavy winter frosts. Through this awful region, under incessant and heavy rains, the Germans made their way for a dozen or fifteen miles before reaching any highroad. The railway embankment by which they approached Osowiec from the south was no longer available, since they were retiring hastily northward. Of the numbers involved there was no definite information, but they were very considerable, as the front extended from Mariampol to as far south as Vonzosh, which is about one mile south of Sczucyn and fourteen west of Osowiec. The points named as the extremities of the German front were eighty-four miles apart, so that an estimate made by experts probably approximated the truth, namely, that the Germans put into the field for all those movements eleven or twelve army corps. The subsequent fighting was largely of a guerilla character, owing to the broken features of the whole country. The German bombardment of Osowiec appeared to have been futile as regards the fortress, but it did considerable injury to surrounding buildings of a non-military character, and destroyed the wireless and overhead telegraph installations. The fortress itself, which had modern casemates and was bomb-proof, suffered little, and the losses of the garrison were infinitesimal.

Osowiec proved to the German a more formidable obstacle than Liége. A place with impassable marshes before it can not, in the ordinary sense of the word, be besieged, and an assault along a single causeway would be an almost impossible and a costly operation. The defenders further improved a natural strong position by opening the sluices of the Bobr. The attack earned a peculiar distinction from the fact that, while it was in progress, first the Kaiser and then the Czar visited the opposing camps. The bombardment lasted for four days and nights without a respite. The last episode in the siege was a brilliant sortie by the garrison. Bodies of infantry, by following paths over swamps known only to the inhabitants, contrived to get behind the advanced German lines, both from left and right. Another body charged up the causeway, and before the Germans had recovered from their surprise, contrived to capture three of the guns, while the rest went hurriedly northward. This was the last event in the siege, the date being October 1. The Germans now abandoned the attempt—not merely because Osowiec had proved so unexpectedly obstinate, but because larger German operations against the Niemen meanwhile had failed. A fortnight later the Russians were themselves pursuing a prosperous offensive over the road by which the Germans advanced, and were on German soil engaged in an attack on Lyck. It was just one hundred years since last the Russian Horse Guards had shed their blood on a battlefield—at Friedland, which lies only a few marches beyond the scene—Napoleon's Friedland, immortalized by Meissonier as well as Napoleon.

Hindenburg's movement to the Niemen was premature. When he crossed the Russian frontier he left his railways behind him, and got out of reach either of reinforcements or supplies. His force was insufficient for the invasion of

GERMANS BUILDING A BRIDGE ON THE RUSSIAN FRONTIER

Russia, while his adversary had fallen back on reinforcements which were awaiting his arrival on the Niemen. When he saw his error he was quick to correct it, his retreat being a masterly achievement, which secured him possession of East Prussia with time to prepare for a future offensive.

In the midst of the fighting around Augustowo, the name of St. Petersburg was officially changed to Petrograd. The whole Slav world hailed with exultation the decision that the capital of Russia should thenceforth bear a purely Russian name. To them the significance of the act was immense. It marked a deliberate breach with a tradition which had brought evil to their race. In spite of occasional quarrels, the Court and bureaucracy of Petrograd, ever since Russia first became a Great Power, had been largely under the influence of the Court and bureaucracy of Berlin. Each found its account in this relationship. Reactionaries on the Neva appealed to reactionaries on the Spree for countenance in oppressive features of internal policy, while the unprogressive Junkers looked to St. Petersburg for support. The alliance was based on a common desire to keep a people in subjection for the advantage of a small but powerful class, which arrogated to itself in both countries the exclusive privilege of rule. The step taken by the Czar was therefore a proclamation to the Slav race that this alliance was no more, and that his policy was henceforth a policy of "Russia for Russians," freed from any subservience to Berlin. When, at this time, the Czar issued his proclamation to the Poles of East Prussia he had already shattered the corner-stone of Russo-German friendship. That friendship had begun in the eighteenth century with the partition of Poland; it was nourished by Poland's oppression and abasement, but it now ended with an Imperial promise of her resurrection.

On October 8, after four days of constant fighting, the German army held a strategic and strongly entrenched position east of Wirballen, which lies north of Augustowo on the frontier behind Russia and East Prussia. That day a wave of Russian flesh and blood dashed against a wall of German steel, but the wall stood firm. The wave broke, was shattered, and then fell back. Broken bodies, wreckage of the wave, strewed the ground. A correspondent [3a] described how he was "startled out of his reverie by a weird tooth-edging, spine-chilling, whistling screech overhead." The shell was from 500 to 1,000 feet above him and probably another couple of thousand feet beyond. For half an hour the German battery paid no attention to shells that were passing overhead and out of range. The Russians attempted to carry the German center by storm. For two days artillery was hammering away at the opposing trenches. The marksmanship was bad. Twice under cover of field-artillery

[3a] This anonymous account was printed in many newspapers at the time.

the Russian infantry advanced in force, and twice were driven back to defensive positions. Again the Russian infantry came rushing forward and took up advanced positions, awaiting the formation of the new and irregular battle-line. Dozens of light rapid-firers were dragged along by hand. Other troops, reserves, took up semi-advanced positions. All the while Russian shrapnel was raining over the German trenches.

Finally came the order to advance. Hundreds of yards of the Russian fronting line leaped forward, deployed in open order and came on. One, two, three, and in some places four and five successive skirmish lines, separated by intervals of from twenty to fifty yards, swept forward. Some of them came into range of the German trench-fire almost at once. Then lines began to wilt and thin out, but others were able to make a considerable advance under cover. The smoke of a burning village gave a grateful protection to several regiments. But on they came all along the line, protected and unprotected alike, rushing forward with a yell, pausing, firing, and advancing again.

From the outset of the advance the German artillery, ignoring for the moment the Russian artillery action, began shelling the onrushing mass with shrapnel, which burst low above the advancing lines and tore sickening gaps. But the Russian line never stopt. For the third time in two days they came tearing on, with no indication of having been affected by the terrible consequences of the two previous charges. As a spectacle, the whole thing was maddening. The correspondent said he found his heart "thumping like a hammer, with no weapon more formidable than a pair of binoculars." He was "mentally fighting as hard as the men with the guns," and for the first time "sensed the intoxication of battle and learned the secret of smiles on the faces of the dead." On came the Slav swarm—into the range of the German trenches, "with wild yells and never a waver." Russian battle-flags—the first he had seen—appeared in front of the charging ranks.

Next day German artillery beat back the Russian advance. It was mostly an artillery encounter. The Russians did not have the German range. Their shells flew screamingly 1,000 yards to the Germans left. The effect on a hillock was exactly as if a geyser had suddenly spurted up. A vast cloud of dirt, stones and grass spouted, and when the débris cleared away a great hole was left. It was a queer sensation to peer through field-glasses and see Russian shells veer a few hundred feet to the right. The correspondent saw one strike a windmill, shattering the long arms and crumpling it over in a slow burning heap. On the right wing was witnessed the last of the Russian infantry advance. The wave of Russians had swept nearly to the German trenches, situated between two sections of field-artillery, and there been repulsed. Russians were lying in front of these pits, dead, dying or less seriously wounded, cut down by the terrible spray of German machine-guns. Strewn in the trenches were countless empty shells, the bullets of which had, as it appeared, slain perhaps thousands. There were hundreds of dead in the open field ahead.

Early in November the Russians attempted again to break into East Prussia by an old route south of Wirballen, but were met by General von Morgen and driven back across the frontier. Strong Russian forces entered the province at Soldau in the extreme southern part of East Prussia, and entrenched themselves twelve miles within the border. South of the Vistula from Hieshawa to Kalisch the Germans attempted a counter-attack, partly in the hope of checking the pursuit which was pressing their retreat, but also to draw off the Russians from an advance that was proceeding in the direction of Malva-Soldau. From Kalisch to Stalluponen, the distance is two hundred and eighty miles, and over the whole line fighting was in progress. This line portended a possible envelopment of East Prussia, the occupation of which was necessary for the development of further plans of the Grand Duke Nicholas.

Throughout October and the early days of November the Russians and the Germans faced each other in entrenched positions, which followed approximately the line of the frontier. The Germans dug themselves in elaborately, with all the paraphernalia of wire entanglements, concealed gun-pits and deep trenches. They attacked the slighter Russian trenches every night in a sort of habitual routine, with the aid of their searchlights, but they evidently had no thought of advancing. The real fighting on the Eastern Front was now to be in Poland, and it is probable that Hindenburg had transferred thither most of the first-line troops in East Prussia.

The Russians held the same area with some vicissitudes throughout December, and no serious effort was made to dislodge them. The fortunes of war in this region were now fairly balanced. Hindenburg had indeed destroyed a Russian army in a battle which was perhaps the most decisive

GERMAN CAVALRY IN FRONT OF A SOLDIER'S HOME

victory, as it was in a military sense, the most brilliant performance, of the war thus far, but his error of judgment in attacking the lines of the Niemen went far to neutralize that fine exploit. For the Russians the battle of Augustowo had wiped out the memory of Tannenberg. At the end of the year they could congratulate themselves that they had once more carried the war into the enemy's country.

Percival Gibbon[4] made a tour of the East Prussian battle-ground and of the Polish frontier in the middle of

[4] Correspondent of The *Daily Chronicle* (London).

IN THE EAST, NEAR EAST, AND SOUTH

October. His route was from north of Suwalki southward to Grævo, a stretch of country that had been in German occupation but in which no German outpost then remained. Mr. Gibbon wrote:

"It is stimulating to nerves troubled by a lack of news to see the Russian soldier in his habits as he lives and fights. I have seen many thousands of them camped in rain-swamped bogs or marching indefatigably over roads which are long quagmires of mud, always with an air of stolid contentment and a look of being bent on business. They include Baltic province men, speaking German with a strong flavoring, Jews from Riga-Libau brigaded with huge Siberians, whose marching must constitute a world record. The Cossacks were past counting, and with them were long-coated, tight-belted Circassians and Kalmucks, all representing a mixture of races and languages like that of the British Empire itself.

"Actually the whole line is a battle-front, from the north of Wirballen to well into Poland, and no day passes without contact with the enemy. This is an army in which every man has fought. Most of them have been in hand-to-hand conflict with Germans. There is no village which does not bear the mark of wanton destruction of life and property—houses burned, others pillaged, and the contents dragged into the streets, and there smashed. Churches have been invariably gutted and defiled."

At a time when the Kaiser in person was known to have command of the German army on this front, a Cossack one day came into a Russian camp, driving before him a plump but distrest Prussian captain whom he had captured during the day's work. "I've brought him," he announced. "I knew him by his mustache," and then produced an old picture postcard from his breast, showing the Kaiser with his characteristic mustache. He really thought he had captured the German Emperor.[5]

[5] Principal Sources: Marr Murray's "The Russian Advance," The London *Times'* "History of the War," *The Independent* (New York), The *Standard* (London), "Bulletins" of the National Geographic Society (New York), "Nelson's History of the War" by John Buchan, B. W. Norregaard in The *Sun* (New York), The *Daily Mail* (London); The *Times,* The *Evening Post,* New York; The *Morning Post,* The *Times,* The *Daily Chronicle,* London; William C. Dreher in *The Atlantic Monthly* (New York), Associated Press and United Press dispatches.

GENERAL VON HOTZENDORF, THE AUSTRIAN CHIEF OF STAFF
Hotzendorf directed the Austrian defense of Galicia and afterward the
operations in Italy

II

IN GALICIA: LEMBERG, RAWA-RUSKA AND PRZEMYSL

August 25, 1914—September 27, 1914

THEORETICALLY Austria, when the war began, could muster two and a half million men, and could invade Russia before Russia could complete her mobilization. To Austria had therefore been assigned the task of maintaining, for the first few months, the Teutonic cause in the East. Russian Poland was to be invaded, Warsaw captured and the Russian army kept at bay until the Germans, having conquered France, should arrive in the East and complete the work of overcoming Russia. The Czar had sent a relatively weak army into East Prussia, his strong force being sent against Austria, in order to crush Austria's forward thrust from Galicia. Had Russia been able to drive a shattered Austrian army westward through the Carpathians, and so out of the field of future operations, the great bulk of the Russian army could then have moved west and north toward Berlin, and such strength as remained to Austria would have had to be devoted to defenses eastward along the Carpathians and southward along the Danube. Therefore, in the east as well as in the west, a desperate game was played. While Germany was staking everything on success before Paris, Russia put all else in jeopardy, in order first to strike down an Austrian army that represented the full measure of Hapsburg strength, an army which was the sole sustaining bulwark for a nation composed of divided loyalties and speaking many tongues.

The war, as a contest between Slav and Teuton, was waged at first with Lemberg as the immediate and important objective. A victory there for Russia might prove as decisive for the Slav as Tannenberg four centuries before had been, when the Poles checked on that field the eastward march of the Germans. More vital to Germany for the

time was this eastern struggle, for neither France nor
England threatened Germany's actual existence, or sought
her provinces, save Alsace-Lorraine.   But Slav ambition
coveted East Prussia and Silesia, and Posen lay at the gates
of Berlin.   In a total population of 53,000,000 in the Austrian confine, one-half were Slavs.   With an army drawn
from all her racial sources, Austria sought to invade Russia,
the protector of Slavs, but as she saw a likelihood of trouble

AN AUSTRIAN COMMANDER WITH HIS STAFF

at home among her own Slavs, she took measures to meet
it, and so when outbreaks occurred in Dalmatia, Bosnia,
Croatia, and other Slav provinces of the empire, all men up
to the age of fifty were mobilized, hostile newspapers were
supprest, suspected clubs and societies dissolved, people for-
bidden to leave towns and villages, and leaders among discontented Slavs seized and held as hostages. These measures,
however, did not always crush the rebellious spirit.   In

Herzegovina some government officials were murdered and priests held as hostages were also killed. Acts of rebellion were everywhere followed by acts of reprisal. In the army, Slav regiments were kept separate from Teutonic ones, but thousands were said to have mutinied rather than fight against their brother Slavs. In some cases whole regiments refused to serve and were promptly punished. The mutinous spirit extended to Poland and Bohemia, where stern measures were resorted to and became effective, but at one time it caused the mobilization almost to break down, and this was when time was valuable to Austria, because Russian mobilization was pressing forward to completion. An Austrian invasian of Russia and a capture of Poland became daily less likely of accomplishment.

GEN. VICTOR DANKL
Austrian commander on the Galician front early in the war

In spite of these difficulties the concentration of the First Army under General Dankl was sufficiently advanced by the second week of August to enable him to take the offensive. On the 10th his advance guards crossed the Galician frontier, and deployed on the right bank of the middle Vistula. No serious resistance was at first offered. Austria was allowed to advance almost to Lublin. At one time she came within 11 miles of the place. Meanwhile, on the line from Lublin to Kholm, Russia was massing an army—or two armies cooperating as one—under command of Generals Ewarts and Plehve, with General Ivanoff in supreme direction of the combined force. The Russians had two railways behind them, one leading to Warsaw, the other to Kieff and Odessa. Every day, as the Austrians drew nearer, the Russian strength increased until, by the first days of September, it probably amounted to upward of 400,000 men.

Dankl now became aware that he had in front of him a worthy opponent. It was not in the Russian program to strike on this line—at least, not yet. The Austrians saw themselves checked; they were definitely held up by forces at least as great as their own; meanwhile the Russians under Ivanoff bided their time.

General Ruzsky, however, had developed a rapid offensive movement against the Second Austrian Army, which was covering Lemberg under General Auffenberg. On August 14 Ruzsky occupied Sokal, and continuing his movement, succeeded in placing his own army between the two Austrian armies, while General Brusiloff, advancing up the left bank of the Dniester, reached the Tarnopol-Halicz line on the 28th, and effected a junction with Ruszky, who was already threatening Lemberg from the northeast. Russian forces were soon to achieve successes which seemed at the time practically to eliminate the Austrian armies as serious factors in the war. On September 1 two of the Russian generals attacked Auffenberg simultaneously, rolled up both wings of his army, and on the 3d forced him to evacuate Lemberg and fall back on the Grodeck position a few miles west. On the same day Ruzsky entered the town. General Ivanoff, his concentration now completed, attacked Dankl on the 6th, and after a six-day battle defeated him near Rawa Ruska, taking 100,000 prisoners and an immense quantity of war material. Both Austrian armies fell back behind the San, and the Russians invested Przemysl. By September 15 the whole of East Galicia was in Russian occupation, and Russian armies were threatening Krakow north and south of the Vistula.

The Russian plan had been simple; with superior numbers, it aimed at enveloping the Austrians on both flanks. While Brusiloff, who in 1916 was to lead the great Russian offensive of that year, prest on Auffenberg's right, Ruzsky hammered his left and center. After crossing the frontier between Brody and Sokal, Ruzsky had spread out on a wide front, his center pushing straight toward Lemberg, while his right, advancing almost due west, aimed to drive a wedge in between Auffenberg and Dankl, pressing with all his might on Auffenberg's left. Meanwhile Ruzsky's own left felt its way southward in order to effect a junction with Brusiloff, the Austrians falling back slowly in all directions, but resisting gallantly. On Ruzsky's right and center the fighting was severe with heavy losses on both sides. In his army were some of the best of the Russian first-line troops. Narratives of those who took part showed that the Russians attacked with recklessness and that the Austrians, altho continually overpowered, fought desperately. The attention of the western world was at this time engrossed in stirring events in France and Belgium, and little was recorded of operations in Galicia beyond mere statements of successive steps in the Russian advance. The impression created was that this advance had been easy, which was far from the truth. Ruzsky had a week of such stern fighting as at another time would have fired the world's imagination. He finally drove the Austrian center back to the Bug at Krasne and across the railway at Zlota.

This was the preliminary stage of the Lemberg campaign. Auffenberg's Army as yet was not only not beaten but hardly shaken. It fell back into a strong and carefully prepared defense in front of Lemberg, stretching over a front of 70 or 80 miles, from near Busk in the north to Halicz on the Dniester in the south. To Brusiloff and his corps commander, General Radko Dmitrieff (the Bulgarian hero of Lule Burgas and Kirk Kilisse), belongs the honor of a brilliant operation by which the outcome of the battle was determined. After forcing the crossing of the Zlota Lipa on August 26, while his right wing made connection with Ruzsky in the north, Brusiloff's left swung wide to the south as far as the valley of the Dniester, making an extraordinary march, the country being rough, devoid of railways and almost destitute of roads. On August 30 the main body of this flanking force arrived before Halicz and on the following day the assault began with a furious and irresistible attack concentrated on a point near the little village of Botszonce. The condition of the field afterward, the ground being ploughed everywhere with shell-fire and strewn with fragments of projectiles and equipment, showed how desperate the struggle had been. The Russians seem to have carried through the final assault with the bayonet under cover of a torrent of shell-fire. By nightfall on August 31 a breach some kilometers wide had been made. Once the line had been pierced, the entire Austrian right gave way. A last stand seems to have been made in Botszonce which was quickly reduced to a heap of ruins, and the retreat of the Austrians became a flight. The road, strewn with abandoned guns, transports, and all the impediments of a defeated army, afterwards gave ample evidences of their haste. Around Botszonce and Halicz the Russians were said to have buried 4,800 Austrian dead, and captured 32 guns, some of which had been mounted in positions where they never came into use.

The general misery attendant on war was now intensified by a succession of storms with drenching rains, by which much of the country was flooded. The Russians suffered tremendous losses in two days of reckless charges against the Austrians, but appeared to have taken perhaps 60,000 prisoners. Their lowest estimate of the Austrian losses, including killed, wounded, and prisoners, was 130,000. The Austrian army of defense had formed a semicircle facing north and east, with Lemberg in the center. After pushing his right wing toward the west, Ruzski formed another outer semicircle. When the Russian semicircle began to contract, it forced back the Austrian line with vise-like pressure in a battle lasting seven days in which the fighting was most stubborn. Every inch of ground was contested, the losses on both sides enormous. As days passed, the superiority of Russian artillery began to assert itself, and the Austrian fire weakened. At all points the Russians were successful and on the seventh day the main Austrian force, five army corps, was driven back on the town itself with heavy losses.

At half-past two in the morning the actual storming of the town began. The Austrians attempted to form again, but were thrown into confusion by repeated artillery and cavalry attacks. With their left driven in, their whole army was in danger of being surrounded. A searching fire was then directed at the center, which lay before the town, the object being to impede the retreat of the Austrians, now beaten on the right flank, and, if possible, to surround the town completely before its garrison could withdraw. In the hope of checking the Russian advance, the Austrians threw out a rear-guard screen of Slav troops with a backing of Magyars (Hungarians). The Russian commander, at the critical moment, opened a terrific artillery fire over the heads of the advancing Slavs and upon the retreating Austrians. This hail of projectiles set up a panic in the ranks of the Austrians, who, abandoning guns, ammunition and stores, broke into disorder, and fled along the road to Grodek. This was the decisive stroke of the battle.

There was criticism at the time of the Austrian commander for failing to hold Lemberg. While the position that had been so stubbornly defended was over twelve miles to the east, the town itself, after the Austrian line was once broken, became indefensible. Brusiloff's pursuing army was sweeping to the west of the city and Ruzsky was already closing in from the north. Lemberg's inner defenses were not such as to enable it to resist for long. To have attempted to hold out would only have been to meet bombardment and to sacrifice whatever troops were left to defend it. No defense of Lemberg being attempted, few retreating Austrians passed through the city. On September 3 the Russians entered it without disturbance or excesses on the part of the troops. The Slav inhabitants received the Russians with demonstrations, shouting "Long live the army of our Russian liberators!" The progress of the Russian regiments through the town became a kind of triumphal procession.

Russia here achieved her first real triumph in the war. She had accomplished the first step on her desired route to Berlin—the crushing of the military power of Austria. In addition she had taken 637 guns, 44 quickfirers, several flags, and 60,000 prisoners, with stores of ammunition and provisions. These stores lightened considerably the strain on the Russian transport and commissariat departments. Lemberg, being the capital of Galicia and the chief Austrian military center north of the Carpathians, contained an arsenal, railway, and other works useful to invaders. Rolling stock was perhaps the most important of all things captured. Important also were the strategic results. At Lem-

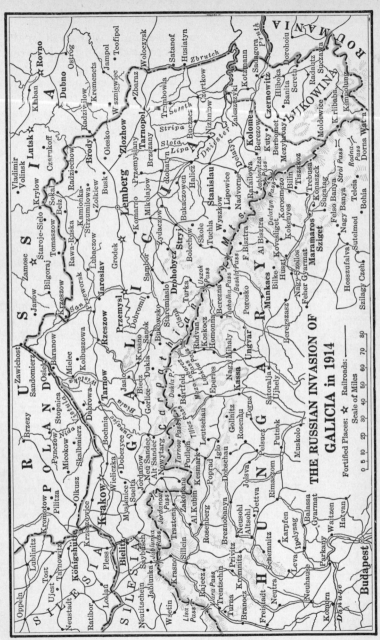

THE RUSSIAN INVASION OF
GALICIA in 1914

Fortified Places: ☆   Railroads: ——

Scale of Miles

0 5 10   20   30   40   50   60   70   80

berg all means of communication converged. Eight railways and as many roads connected it with every point of civil and military importance north of the Carpathians. Thus it was an ideal base for operations in Galicia. It commanded approaches to Przemysl on the west and to passes over the Carpathians leading to Vienna and Budapest on the south, and had railway connections with four points on the Russian frontier, which allowed direct communication

AUSTRIAN PRISONERS TAKEN BY RUSSIANS

with the military centers of Kief on the east and Warsaw on the north.

These operations in Galicia and Poland were fought on the same vast scale as those in western Europe. They extended along a front of 200 miles. In point of numbers engaged also the Galician and Polish operations were equal to those in France. Conditions in the east and west being therefore more or less equal, Russia's victory was the first and only decisive engagement thus far won by any of the Allied armies—preceeding as it did by a few days the battle of the Marne. The fall of Lemberg was announced on September 1, when 60,000 Austrians were said to have been captured, and 50,000 killed or wounded. Five of the eight non-Slav corps which made up the Austrian army were said to have been crusht. The Austrian left, which had been moving on Lublin, was "in the air," and had to turn back fighting, in order to get to cover at Przemysl and Jaroslav, but it, too, met with disaster.

At Lemberg, anciently, and now to be called by the Russians Lvov, the fighting lasted over a fortnight, of which the last eight days were an uninterrupted action, extending over a front of nearly 300 miles. The city had more than 200,000 inhabitants. Many private houses were filled to overflowing with Austrian sick and wounded, who had been abandoned to the Russians. The Russian attack was so swiftly pushed home that everything was found intact. Over 200 guns were taken. The Russian force not only commanded the roads, railways, and waterways, in all directions, but was strongly established in the rear of the main Austrian armies. Galich, or Halicz, on the Dniester, which the Russians also occupied, was only second in importance to Lemberg. It commanded another series of roads, railways, and waterways, and was defended by thirty forts. Some of the hardest fighting in the conflict took place around Halicz. The Austrians here tried desperately to turn the Russian left flank. At Halicz, in 1917, the Russians, under Korniloff, won their last victory over Teutonic forces.

The establishment of Russian authority in this region was facilitated by the native population, which, being Slav, welcomed the Russians after they had made good their advance. The whole region, like Eastern Prussia, was anciently Slav. Practically all the names were still Slav. Prisoners, the number of whom did not become known, guns, including mitrailleuses, the number of which was first stated as 2,000, then as 1,200, but later stated officially as 2,000, and 30,000 rations for one day, were only parts of the booty taken at Lemberg and Halicz. The Russians had entered Lemberg while the Austrians were still in flight, leaving the ground in places strewn with abandoned equipment, clothes, rifles and ammunition. Some officers had thrown away their swords. Wounded were abandoned on the field of battle. Hospitals and houses in the town became full of them.

Ambulances were used as vehicles to escape in. The Russians now had 2,000,000 men actually in the field, and their huge, machine of mobilization was grinding out fresh brigades.

As the story of the fourteen days' battle shaped itself, its outstanding feature was the high quality of the Russian infantry. For two weeks they had thrust themselves at the Austrian line, which extended from Komenka to Halicz, Ruzsky being in command on the north, and Brusiloff on the south. The latter had for his objective the junction of the Guile Lipa, and Dniester rivers, where the Austrians held a bridgehead which presently became the key to Halicz. It was here on September 3 that the great diffused battle narrowed itself down to a real struggle. This was almost entirely a battle of infantry, who advanced across low-lying levels in which lay the big Galician village of Podhajeco, against a huge body of Austrians strongly entrenched and covered by forces of artillery. The dispositions of the latter had already been disturbed by the previous day's artillery attack. The discipline and steadiness of the Russian infantry under terrific fire were spoken of by observers as beyond praise. Witnesses of their behavior, in Galicia or in Prussia, remarked on their sobriety, their level bearing, and their equanimity of temper. In the earlier forward movement, with a massed attacking force in wooded lands east of the river, they lost heavily, but, in spite of this and of the fact that they had already been in action almost continuously for two weeks, their first actual assault carried them into the Austrian position.

With the loss of Lemberg the position of the Austrians became critical. Their left directed a hot attack between Lublin and Kholm, but they were beaten back. The Tenth Corps lost 5,000 prisoners in this attempt to break through the Russian defenses, and the rest were compelled to retire. Great was the Russian estimate of losses (more than 35 per cent. of the Austrian armies participating), but this was considered extravagant, even when keeping in mind the fact that the battles in Galicia covered three weeks. History, however, records greater proportionate losses in other campaigns. At Borodino, where Napoleon met them in 1812, the Russians lost 50 per cent. of their men. All the roads in the Galician field were congested and blocked by commissariat trains abandoned by the Austrians in their flight. Thousands of wagons were captured and hundreds of gun-limbers taken.

Victories on the Marne in France at the beginning of September had checked the German advance on Paris, and made necessary the shifting of German troops. It was in the same eventful week that Lemberg fell. Galicia was soon described as "a Russian province," save only for Jaroslav and Przemysl, toward which fortress the shattered Austrian armies of Auffenberg, Dankl, and their German allies had fled. Dispatches from Austrian sources denied Russia's success and claimed notable successes for Austrian troops, altho they were known to have been greatly outnumbered. Count Berchtold, the Austrian Foreign Minister, explained that the Austrian retreat before superior numbers had been made for the purpose of securing a more favorable position, preparatory to new actions; headway had really been made against both the Russians and the Serbians. The *Neue Freie Presse of Vienna* was quoted as saying, after the fall of Lemberg, that "the high moral quality of the Austrian and Hungarian troops must eventually prove victorious." Despite those assurances that the Austrian retreat was merely tactical, outside observers were almost unanimous in regarding Austria's position as desperate. Rumors of financial troubles and internal dissensions gave color to this view, as did vague intimations that Austria was ready to discuss peace terms independent of her ally, Germany. Within ten days optimistic military observers predicted that Cossacks and Serbian cavalry would "meet on the plains of Hungary and move on Budapest."

Meanwhile, during the last days of August and the first of September, there had been some confused fighting between detached forces on the northern frontier of Galicia forty miles from Lemberg. In Berlin and Vienna official claims were made to successes, which a semi-official statement from Petrograd declared untrue. Out of a mass of claims and counter-claims, all that emerged clearly was that the Russian wedge had been successfully advanced to Tomaszow, where the Austrians suffered a defeat, contemporary reports asserting that among the slain were two generals. From here the Austrians seem to have fallen back westward to the swampy country about Belgoraj and on Tarnogrod. The situation became so critical that it was necessary for Dankl either to break through the Russian defense or fall back. A desperate effort to pierce the wall of resistance in south Poland between Lublin and Kholm was made, the Tenth Austrian Army Corps leading the attack against a weaker portion of the Russian line. It had reached

TRANSPORTING AMMUNITION IN GALICIA

to within eleven miles of Lublin when beaten back. In the retirement some 5,000 prisoners were left in Russian hands.

While Auffenberg's army was holding its position before Lemberg, there had, indeed, been prepared a new line of defense in its rear, which ran from Grodek to Rawa-Ruska, and thence, apparently, along the railway line toward Narol. It was a fine achievement on the part of an army which had been handled as roughly as this had been, to pull itself together at once after a precipitate flight and resolutely take up this new position. Immediately after the capture of

Lemberg, fighting was resumed first around positions into which the Austrians had retreated, or been driven, at Grodek. The extreme north of the line began first to give way. The Austrians were unable to make any prolonged stand here. Russians, besides attacking furiously from in front, proceeded to envelop their left. Fighting went on confusedly over a wide area, in a broken and marshy country. At several places considerable numbers of Austrian prisoners were taken. Long afterward Russians found Austrian guns and batteries entangled in swamps. The upper part of the Austrian line was forced back, fighting desperately as it went, until the whole line became doubled back on itself at an acute angle from Rawa-Ruska where the fighting became terrific.

It was not often on the vast, extended front of a modern battlefield one could put a finger on any point and say: "Here the battle was decided," but in this battle on the Grodek line Rawa-Ruska was such a point. One could even pick out a bit of land, only ten acres in extent, which was the key to the entire position. As the battle developed the importance of this small area became accentuated. It is probable that, in the whole war, there had been no more bitter and furious fighting in so small an area. The defense did not have a front exceeding six, or at most eight miles, and yet it was said that for eight days, perhaps as many as 250,000 men fought on that ground continuously night and day. For eight days Russian infantry assaulted and stormed against the heights that defended the angle. In a single mile the Austrians made stands at eight distinct points. Some of these were taken and retaken several times before they were evacuated, but evacuation then meant only a retreat of a few hundred yards to be followed by a more determined resistance.

Once it became evident that this was the strategic center of the whole conflict, the Russians, day after day and inch by inch, drove back the Austrians until they got them into a deep trench on the slopes of the crest of the final ridge of hills defending the town. The last trench was not above 400 yards in front of their own guns. The Russians had been quite unable to make any headway against it until they massed there a number of batteries of heavy field-howitzers. Then they slowly destroyed with their big shells the entire front. It was possible to read the evidence of this operation afterward, not in the trenches, for it was hard to see where they were, but in an unbroken line of shell-holes, each ten foot across and five feet deep, which extended for hundreds of yards along the former Austrian line. A man could walk for nearly half a mile, stepping from one crater to another, while the ground in and between and all around was strewn with shreds and patches of blue uniform, fragments of equipment and relics of humanity. Here was a clenched hand, there a foot sticking out of a boot, and, again, a soldier's overcoat ripped into ribbons.

The result of these operations awakened sympathy for Dankl's army and admiration for it. In some ways its fate was compared to that of the British when falling back from Mons. The spectacle of the retreat was made the more dreadful because of its size. The front, on which lay an army of something over 300,000 men, extended approximately for 80 miles. As it fell back, with the left wing hemmed in by the river Vistula and the right subject to continuous pressure from Russian forces on the east, this front continually contracted. By the time it reached the San, the crossing of which, so far as the bulk of the force was concerned, had to be made on four or five bridges at different points, the front had contracted to less than 40 miles. Such a movement might easily have degenerated into a panic, accompanied by slaughter, until the whole army was either obliterated or had surrendered. Dankl received credit for escaping a final catastrophe, however serious his losses may have been.

As the Germans, after the battle of the Marne, went north until they secured firm ground on the Aisne, so the Austrians, after their defeat at Lemberg and Rawa-Ruska, seeking a defensive field, found one behind the San, some seventy miles west of Lemberg. Flowing north from the Carpathians to the Vistula, straight across the whole province of Galicia, the San, which is a large stream, supplied them with a good barrier. Both flanks of their army standing behind the San were protected—on the south by the Carpathians, on the north by the Vistula flowing east from Krakow. Not only was this position on the San naturally strong, but in the center were two fortresses, surrounded by detached forts, Jaroslav and Przemysl. Retreating from Rawa-Ruska, Lemberg, and Halicz, the Austrians, on finding reinforcements at these points, could hope to make a second and more successful fight, provided the morale of their armies had not been too much shaken. But the ensuing fall of Jaroslav (on September 23) was to demonstrate that Russian descriptions of the Austrian reverses had not been wholly exaggerated.

By September 20, the Austro-German armies had been rounded up in an area enclosed by the double turn of the San at Przemysl and its confluent, the Vislok. The area is rectangular in shape, extending thirty-two miles east and west and sixteen north and south, the corner points being Przemysl, Jaroslav, Rozozoff, and Dynow. In theory, the passage of the San by an army invading Austria should have been almost impossible. The Austrians had spent immense sums in an endeavor to make it so. The upper, or southern, part was protected by Przemysl and Jaroslav. Thence a light railway, built purely for strategic purposes, ran parallel and close to its left bank almost to its confluence with the Vistula. At various places, as the Austrians fell back, they had destroyed bridges behind them. Had they destroyed all the bridges, the first army would have had at least a few days' rest. But the Russians, in their pursuit, were too swift. By a brilliant stroke they rushed, captured, and made good their hold on the bridge of Krzeszov, a few miles west of Tarnogrod. In the figurative words of an official *communiqué* from Petrograd, the Russian soldiers "leapt across the river on the very shoulders of the retreating enemy."

As early as September 17 a Russian official statement had put the Austrian losses, since the taking of Lemberg, as high as 250,000 killed and wounded, and 100,000 prisoners, with 400 guns, many colors, and a "vast quantity of stores." The rifles captured were said to number nearly half a million. What the total losses on the Austrian side were in the whole campaign there was no way of knowing. In all, the Austrians probably put into the field, including later reinforcements, both Austrian and German, from 1,000,000 to 1,200,000 men. · They may have lost in killed, wounded, and prisoners, somewhere near 400,000. Official Russian estimates placed their losses at from 35 to 50 per cent. of their total force. The Russian losses were also heavy, but Russians said that, in the whole campaign, they did not much exceed 100,000.

The Russians now undertook to bombard Jaroslav with

AN AUSTRO-HUNGARIAN ARMORED TRAIN

siege-guns and to invest the fortress of Przemysl. The latter had been cleared of all its civilian population, an exception being made only of such as proved themselves in possession of three months' food supplies. Three German army corps, or rather the remnants of three, minus most of their artillery munitions and equipment, were enclosed with the Austrians in a triangle between rivers. Jaroslav was put under bombardment and the town reported at one time to be in flames. It fell on September 23. The Austrians then gave up, not merely the line of the San river, but the railroad from Krakow to Przemysl. They had not recovered sufficiently to defend a position ten times as strong naturally as that which the German army in France had been able to hold six days after they withdrew from the Marne to the Aisne. Having possession of Lemberg, Jaroslav and some other towns of importance, and all the railways operating between them the Russians were masters of eastern Galicia. They controlled the oil-fields and the agricultural output of the rich Galician plains. Cavalry were already inspecting approaches to the Carpathians, from the Dukla Pass to Bukowina. Przemysl alone held out, but they moved forward slowly. If Krakow could be reached they would be at the frontier of Germany; for Krakow was the sentinel of Silesia and Krakow was almost in sight. Even if Przemysl should hold out for a time longer, its fate seemed as certain as that of Maubeuge in northeastern France had been earlier in September. Once Przemysl had fallen, the Russian left flank would have been solidly planted on the Carpathians and the march to Berlin could perhaps have begun.

Well into December Przemysl held as firm as a rock. The place was apparently impregnable, and promised never to be taken, except after a terrific struggle and the sacrifice of thousands of lives. Not only was Przemsyl prepared for an extended siege, but the Austrians on the frontier were intrenched in the best possible positions. There was incessant firing from Austrian batteries. The terrible roar of heavy guns never for an instant ceased. When, at daybreak, the Russians began to shell the Austrian defenses, and rained steel throughout the day, they were answered shot for shot. Reports that the morale of the Austrian army was broken and that its ranks were being thinned by the ravages of cholera, were untrue. Everywhere their determination to hold Przemysl to the last man was evident. It did not seem that the powerful fortifications could be taken, "except after an extended siege."

Besides its strength as a fortress, Przemysl was a veritable garden city, set round with orchards and flowers, with a history reaching back into the tenth century. In the town and its environs, in 1914, was a civil population of about 50,000, chiefly Poles and Ruthenians, who lived together in amity and with religious toleration. In September, when the victorious Russian advance swept all resistance before it, there was said, in official reports from Vienna, to be an army of 80,000 men based on Przemysl, under command of one of the best Austrian generals. The Russians took it for granted that the stronghold eventually would fall. Allied newspapers around the world said that its fate was sealed. But stores of all kinds had been poured into it, and preparations made for

HUNGARIAN INFANTRY IN BUDAPEST

a long resistance. It was said to have provisions enough to last until May, 1915, and in General Kusmanek a commander who had no inclination to leave the place. The first investment was made complete by September 26. When the Russians called on the fortress to surrender, Kusmanek replied that he would not even discuss the subject until all powers of resistance had been exhausted. An effort was then made to carry the place by storm, but it was a costly experiment. The Russians finally gave up that attempt and settled down to a regular investment until such time as heavy siege-guns could be brought up and the way prepared for a more vigorous assault. The real bombardment did not begin until early in March, 1915.

The struggle in Galicia and the Bukowina had resolved itself, from the Russian point of view, into two objects— the first to reach Krakow, at the western extremity of Galicia, possession of Krakow being an imperative prelude to an invasion of Silesia and Posen, or to march southward through the Moravian Gate upon Vienna; the second, to secure the passes of the Carpathians, which would give access to Hungary. The Russians were anxious from the outset to bring pressure to bear on Hungary, hoping thereby to force Austria to conclude a separate peace. This possibility was widely entertained in England, in quarters where conceptions of the Magyar attitude were based on romantic and quite misleading impressions that had come down from the days of Kossuth. After the war had been in progress for some time, it was more generally realized that the Magyars were largely responsible for the Austro-Hungarian policy, and that their inclination probably was to stand or fall with Vienna. The steady growth in the influence of Count Tisza, the Hungarian Prime Minister, who was soon to become the most powerful man in the monarchy, confirmed this conclusion. Tisza, at the end of the war, was assassinated.

The real reasons why Przemysl was able to offer so prolonged a resistance was that the Russians were at first short of heavy siege-artillery, and still more so of shells. Their ultimate objective was not Przemysl but Krakow, and that city was surrounded by a ring of six powerful forts on both sides of the Vistula. The total length of the perimeter, however, was comparatively small and so it was not believed that Krakow could withstand a prolonged siege. Early in December the Russians were driving near the city from the north. Their cavalry had been actually within five miles of it on the south, when Hindenburg's second fierce rush on Warsaw compelled a hurried shortening of the Russian line. When Hindenburg fought his way to the Bzura river and dug himself in, he was aiming, among other things, at the salvation of Krakow, and, therefore, of Silesia. Krakow is the heart, soul, and nervous center of Polish life. Many cherished souvenirs of Polish history are preserved in its museums. Its ancient university and its Academy of Science are twin centers of Polish thought. Polish literature, music, and decorative arts have taken their inspiration from Krakow. There are any number of historic buildings within the inner, or old, city which link the Pole intimately with his past and keep him saturated with nationality. Kings and heroes of his nation are buried there in the Stanislaus

AUSTRO-HUNGARIAN SOLDIERS RESTING IN THE USSOK PASS
IN THE CARPATHIANS

cathedral, a heavy structure of the sterner Gothic style, which, from a rocky eminence, dominates the city.

After Russia's extraordinary success in conquering so much of Galicia, Germany sent large forces to her Silesian frontier in order to save Krakow. The routed Austrian armies were in flight toward Krakow, and had lost all semblance of an effective military force. The Russians had gone in pursuit, adding to the disorder in which not only divisions and brigades but even individual regiments, were mixed up. In fact, the forces of Austria had been reduced to such disorganization that almost every man seemed to be seeking safety for himself. Captures of prisoners, guns, and military stores were still being made. The garrison of Przemysl was said to be in a state bordering on mutiny; at any rate, it contented itself for a time with an attitude of passive resistance, but finally attempted a sortie, which, however, was beaten back.

It was sixty-six years since the last Russian force had crossed the Carpathians and descended into the rich plains of Hungary. But on that occasion Russian armies entered Hungary on a friendly errand, and in response to a personal appeal, made in his youth by the Emperor Francis Joseph, who had journeyed to Warsaw to meet the Czar Nicholas I in furtherance of this purpose. Russian armies soon crusht the Hungarian revolt, and saved to Francis Joseph his throne. Now, under another Nicholas, Russian armies were threatening to enter Hungary to free it from the yoke of Austria, to overthrow the same throne and dynasty that Russia had saved in the revolution of 1848. The Russians expected again to enter Hungary by the same passes and the same roads as those followed by the Czar's armies sixty-six years before.

Russia's success endangered Germany's province of Silesia, an invasion of which from Krakow would have presented few difficulties. Silesia, half the size of Ireland, is the largest province in Prussia. It contained, in 1914, a million Poles, mostly settled near the frontier, and was the greatest manufacturing and mining district of eastern Germany. Silesia was thrust out like a wedge between Russia and Austria. While one of the richest divisions of Germany, its industrial advantages did not compare with those of lands along the lower Rhine. Wealth was not so evenly distributed there as in many other parts of the country. Silesia had vast estates, rich mines and great factory plants, owned by a few wealthy men, while the laboring classes were composed of the very poor. This was in part accounted for by the enormous seasonal influx of pauper labor that took place from Russian Poland and Galicia. Especially did Polish men and women compete in Silesia for work as agricultural laborers. They regularly swarmed across the border in seed-time and harvest and in a few cents of daily German pay found an opportunity for better living.

A glance at the map would show why Krakow should have played a vital part in the war. A hundred miles west the mass of the western Carpathians, the High Tatra, breaks down into the plains through which the river March flows to the Danube. These plains, between the Carpathians and the Bohemian mountains, constitute the famous Gap of Moravia, the old highway from Austria to north Germany. Through this gap the army of Kutusof had marched in 1805 to find its doom at Austerlitz. Through this gap runs the railway which connects Silesia with Vienna. The general who could master Krakow had a clear and easy road before him to the Austrian capital. Not less was it the key to Germany. Forty miles west of Krakow is the Silesian frontier. Seventy miles from the city flow the upper streams of the Oder. An army which could enter Germany by that route would turn the line of the frontier fortresses of Thorn and Josen, the system of lateral frontier railways, and the great defensive position on the Warta. It would have before it only Breslau, which had limited defenses, and the old second-class fortress of Glogau. The capture of Krakow would have meant more than an open road to Berlin and Vienna. It would have involved an immediate blow at the heart of Germany through one of her chief industrial centers. That was why so much importance was attached to the Russian movement.

After the disaster of Rawa-Ruska there had been a drastic overhauling of the Austrian commands. Dankl and Auffenberg were under a cloud. The supreme command could no longer be left in the hands of the Archduke Frederick. The Chief of Staff, Hoetzendorff, was also out of favor at German headquarters. Accordingly all the Austrian forces were placed under Hindenburg, with the Archduke Frederick as a kind of sub-generalissimo; and German staff officers were assigned to the Austrian armies. The Teutonic movement had been everywhere slow till Hindenburg arrived from East Prussia to take command, which fact was sufficient to convince the Grand Duke Nicholas and his staff that they would soon have to meet the long-awaited German offensive in Poland. The curtain was rising on the great second act of the Eastern drama, when battle between the Teuton and the Slavs was to reach the very gates of Warsaw.[6]

[6] Principal Sources: Marr Murray's "The Russian Advance," The London *Times'* "History of the War"; *The Literary Digest, The Independent,* New York; The *Morning Post,* The *Daily Chronicle,* London; *The Times,* The *Sun,* "Bulletins" of the National Geographic Society, New York; "Nelson's History of the War" by John Buchan; Associated Press and United Press dispatches.

A CORNER OF KRAKOW

III

THE BATTLE OF THE VISTULA—HINDENBURG'S DRIVE FOR WARSAW FAILS, BUT HE FINALLY SECURES LODZ—POLAND'S DEVASTATION WORSE THAN BELGIUM'S

September 27, 1914—December 30, 1914

DURING the last week of September the Russian advance in Galicia, after almost incredible exertions, but with its immediate objective achieved, had spent itself in momentary exhaustion. For a few days the Russian tide stood at flood—or until September 27 when the first movement of an Austro-German counter-offensive began, the object aimed at being the reduction of Poland—its isolation and lopping off from the main body of Russia, from which it boldly projected itself into Prussia and athwart Galicia, "like a fist thrust into a pillow." Had the early Teutonic northern operations by Germans from East Prussia, and the southern by Austrians from Galicia, succeeded, the Teutonic armies should have effected a junction somewhere on the eastern border of Russian Poland in the Litovsk-Bialystok region, and so, having all Poland in their hands, would have had, as a base for further advances, a continuous front on a straight line from the Baltic to the Carpathians. But these operations did not succeed; they failed in the north after Tannenberg and they had now failed in the south. With her right hand and her left hand Russia had held two enemies at bay. The next Teutonic move took the form of a direct thrust in the center of the line. This meant a thrust at the heart of Poland, which was Warsaw.

The alternative which confronted Poland when the war began was critical. To have remained true to Russia and resisted a Teutonic invasion, could have meant only desolation to her land and people; hostile armies would have overrun her and made her a vast battlefield. Had the Poles consulted their immediate material interests, they would have thrown themselves into German arms. To Poland came the same dilemma as to Belgium, and like the Belgians, the Poles chose what the Allies regarded as the loyal part. The weight of Polish opinion had already been strongly against giving aid to Austro-German forces, when on August 14 there came from Russia the proclamation which definitely crystalized Polish sentiment in loyalty to Russia. From a private telegram coming through Copenhagen news of the Czar's offer of autonomy to Poland reached western Europe. It took the form of a manifesto issued by the Grand Duke Nicholas.

Even among patriotic Poles the hope of recovering national independence had up to that time been faint and visionary. War, however, had always presented for Russia new necessities, if not new opportunities. The Crimean War led her to emancipate the serfs; the Japanese War to establish the beginnings of parliamentary institutions. When the Russian advance on Austria and Germany began, it was inevitable that the Poles, from the Baltic to the Carpathians, would receive from Russia inducements affecting their destiny and, as Horace has put it, the word once spoken spread abroad and "could not be recalled." It set millions of weary hearts beating anew. The act was in some quarters regarded as one of the great master-strokes of military history. Unspeakable joy reigned, especially in the Polish colony of Paris, where family groups of Poles gathered to celebrate the news and many pious Polish women went to their mission-church to offer up prayers. The action of Russia was in line with those natural and racial aspirations which had been at the basis of most European wars since the map of Europe was reconstructed on a dynastic basis after Napoleon's fall. From the Congress of Vienna in 1815 to the Treaty of Bucharest in 1913 wars in Europe had been provoked by the longings of men of the same race to achieve national unity. As the French Revolution carried the gospel of democracy and equality from Madrid to Moscow, so each succeeding European conflict after 1815 exprest the aspirations of men who spoke the same tongue, shared the same culture, and were born to the same racial unity. Serbia, Greece, Belgium, Hungary, Italy, Roumania, Germany, Bulgaria, have each acquired a place on the map

only after wars which have made up the martial history of
Europe in the nineteenth century. Danzig, Königsberg and
all Prussia east of the Vistula, might logically be included
in a new Poland, together with half of that Silesia which
a Prussian King appropriated from Austria a century and a
half ago.

What Napoleon promised, and could not quite bring himself to do, Nicholas II now undertook to achieve. Obviously
his Polish proclamation was intended to assist in disrupting
Austrian armies and to stimulate treason in Prussian forces.
Poland restored, even with its frontiers confined to areas

ALLIED MILITARY ATTACHÉS WHO FOLLOWED RUSSIA'S
OPERATIONS IN THE WINTER OF 1914-15

where the Polish language was spoken, would give Europe
a new state with nearly 25,000,000 inhabitants. It would
take from Germany three provinces and deprive Austria of
half her population, if to the freeing of the Poles there
should be added the logical work of liberating all Slavs, so
that a large part of the Austrian Empire, if not the whole
of it, would disappear from the map of Europe. There
would then appear at least three new Slav states, Poland,
Bohemia, and Serbo-Croatia. To Slavdom would be added
not fewer than 30,000,000 Slavs, bound by ties of race, re-

ligion and common hatred of Teutonic governments. Such in its wider aspects was the meaning of the rescript of the Czar. In it was found much warrant for the German assertion that at bottom the present war was a struggle between Slav and Teuton.

On October 4, the Czar, with a small suite, embarked for the theater of war on the Galician front. Russian Emperors on other great occasions had joined their armies in the field. The Japanese war was not an exception, inasmuch as it hardly ranked for Russia as *dignus vindice nodus;* even the Russian Guard took no part in it. Now, however, matters were different, and Nicholas II following the traditions of his house, greeted his gallant troops amid actual scenes of action. Whatever might be said for or against a sovereign's presence in a theater of war, resolved itself finally into a question of how that presence, so inspiring to every soldier, could be utilized in the cause for which the nation fought. Nicholas II took no court with him. He went as the supreme head of Russia's fighting forces to mark with imperial approval deeds of the past and to encourage men to greater efforts in future. He had not been exactly a "War Lord," tho he commanded the largest army on earth; nor would his appearance on the scene of conflict alter one jot of the strategic schemes of war specialists were engaged in devising. But it was known that, after seeing in person their "Little Father," every Russian soldier would be doubled in fighting power, and every commanding officer assured that his efforts would not go unnoticed. The imperial visit, made as it was without ceremony, but with a business-like eye to essentials, stiffened confidence in the Russian army.

Hindenburg, seeing that a stalemate had been reached in East Prussia, which might continue through the winter, and conscious at last that that province was a self-contained area, in which no amount of German success would affect the critical Galician position, resolved to stake everything on a blow at the Russian center. If he could take Warsaw before the autumn ended, he would have ideal winter quarters; a base pushed far into the enemy's territory from which he could advance in the spring. His advance became slow and deliberate, more like the occupation of a territory already won than an attack against an unbroken enemy. As he made progress, he constructed roads, which were destined to exist for a few weeks only. Great stretches of forest were cut down, and the felled trunks used to make corduroy paths over marshes. In the worst places artillery causeways were built, but they were soon blown to pieces by the Russians. The gage of the Kalisz-Lodz-Warsaw railway was altered and many new miles completed each day.

The fight for Warsaw began on October 16 and continued till the evening of the 19th. Hindenburg had probably five army corps massed for the attempt, and was present in person. The brunt of the Russian resistance fell to the Siberian corps, who had just arrived by rail from Moscow. The Grand Duke Nicholas was also much assisted by batteries of heavy guns—some said as many as thirty—served by Japanese gunners, which Japan had sent across by the Siberian railway. During the first day the issue hung in the balance; but the Russians established an unshakable trench position a few miles beyond the outer forts, and next day the attack died away. The reason was soon apparent. The Grand Duke Nicholas had swung his right across the Vistula under cover of the guns of Novogeorgievsk, and was driving in the German left center. Meantime the attempt to cross the Vistula had been vigorously pushed forward. One effort was made in the section between Ivangorod and Warsaw; but since the Russians had a railway line on the eastern bank, they were able to bring up guns and blow German rafts and pontoons to pieces.

Next day the Russians crossed the river at Novo Alexandria and, having established gun positions, prepared to advance. The following day they landed parties of Caucasian troops north of Ivangorod, and these held their ground till the river could be bridged. So began the battle south of the Pilitza, the fiercest part of the great engagement, the chief fighting taking place near the village of Glovaczov, on the river Radomka. The Russians drove the Germans from open country beside the river into great woods of spruce, ten miles deep, which made a screen between the Vistula and the Polish plain. Among trees were hundreds of separate engagements, desperate hand-to-hand fighting in cranberry mosses and forest glades. Ultimately the Russians forced the Germans into the open on the west side, where their guns completed the destruction. At Kozience they buried 16,000 dead, their own and Germans. A correspondent who visited the scene after the battle thus described it:

"The forest for miles looks as if a hurricane had swept through it. Trees staggering from their shattered trunks, and limbs hanging everywhere, showed where shrapnel shells had been bursting. There was scarcely an acre that was not sown like the scene of a paper-chase, only the trail here was bloody bandages and bits of uniform." [7]

The Germans fought desperately, struggling to save their guns or render them useless to the Russians. By the 25th the Germans were at Radom, and Ruzsky's right was moving so fast that it got between them and the Pilitza. The next stand of Hindenburg's army was at Kielce; but, after an engagement lasting a day and a night, the Russians, on November 3, drove them from the town, along the southern railway, with a loss of 2,500 prisoners and many guns. By the beginning of November the long German front had been broken into two pieces, with the Pilitza between—the southern fleeing southwest toward Czestochowa and Krakow, the northern retiring westward toward the line of the Warta. Ruzsky's victory in the south determined Rennen-kampf's success north of the Pilitza. Grojec and Skiernie-wice were taken, and then Lowicz and Lodz; for, with both flanks turned, there could be no resting-place for Hindenburg short of the frontier. The Germans fought with extraordinary gallantry, thousands of men being sacrificed for the safety of guns and transports. As Hindenburg retreated he left a desert behind him, the roads he had laboriously made being mined and destroyed, as was the new gage of the Kalisz-Lodz railway. He "chess-boarded" ordinary highways, blew up railway stations, water-towers, and bridges, and was said to have used a machine which turned steel rails into shapes something like corkscrews. Half his rear-guard actions were fought to enable this work of destruction to be completed.

[7] Stanley Washburn in his "Field Notes from the Russian Front" (imported by Charles Scribner's Sons).

The area of conflict was on a front of some sixty miles along roads leading eastward to Warsaw and Ivangorod. When the Germans met the Russians on the left bank of the Vistula on October 10, the fight promised to continue for weeks, and possibly for months. The Germans, in an attempt to break the Russian line around Ivangorod, were at first driven back. Here the fighting reached a desperate stage. A great battle, rivaling in the strength of the opposing forces and the importance of the conflict the battle

GERMAN TROOPS ADVANCING ON WARSAW

of the Aisne in France, began to develop on a front that stretched along the Vistula and San rivers from Warsaw to Przemysl and thence south to the Dneister. Hard fighting was soon reported from all points along this line. In the south the Austrians, rehabilitated by their new German commanders, assumed the offensive and made attacks in conjunction with strong German forces. Below Przemysl Russian cavalry were in conflict with a strong force of Austrians and Germans. Before Warsaw the Germans sent aviators to drop bombs into the city of Warsaw. A Zeppelin flew in full view of hundreds of citizens, but before the airship could drop its missiles it was brought down by a shot from one of the forts. An aeroplane which dropt a bomb later was captured a few miles up the river.

Warsaw was defended by nearly twenty detached forts. Altho it had lost in political status, it had increased its prestige in other directions, and was still the gay, active metropolis of a land whose literature and arts it dominated. It was also the great industrial and commercial center of Poland. Machinery, carriages, food products, animal products, and woven goods were among its many and varied productions. There were nearly fifty book-printing establishments in Warsaw. The inhabitants numbered 909,491 in 1913, about one-third being Jews. Germans formed a considerable part of the population. The Russian garrison had over 30,000 men. It was the residence of the medieval dukes of Masovia. As early as the seventeenth century it had supplemented Krakow as the capital of the kingdom, altho Polish kings continued to be crowned at Krakow.

On October 14, when there was fighting at various points between Sandomierz and Ivangorod, an official statement from Berlin announced that "the whole of Poland, with the exception of Warsaw, is in our possession." If the statement had also excepted a small area round Ivangorod, it would not have been an exaggeration, for the Germans were within ten miles of Warsaw and on the 16th penetrated to within seven miles; and there was then no adequate Russian force in sight for the city's protection. Apparently the Russians had been slow to realize how serious was the threat against Warsaw, with forces of such magnitude converging upon it from all parts of the west and south; tho actual force engaged in the immediate attack does not seem to have exceeded from five to seven army corps, only a small portion of whom were first-line troops. Plans had been made for its occupation on or about Octber 18. Its value as a base for future operations against Russia was obvious, and its capture at that time, just a week after the fall of Antwerp in the west, would have had great moral effect.

The thunder of German guns was first heard in Warsaw

HINDENBURG AND LUDENDORFF

This picture was taken when the military operations of Hindenburg and
Ludendorff had been confined almost wholly to the Eastern Front

VII.

on the night of October 10–11. From that time it drew gradually nearer, while hostile aeroplanes paid daily visits, and something like panic began to spread. Accounts of the happenings in the next few days inside of Warsaw are confused. A decision to evacuate Warsaw was probably taken as early as October 15 or 16, when trains were provided for officials and others who wished to leave. Practically all the British colony and many others who did not care to fall into German hands departed in haste. Outside the fortifications Russian troops were holding the Germans back stubbornly, tho outnumbered two or three to one. By day and by night windows in Warsaw shook with the detonation of distant guns, while from the roofs of buildings the population could see shells bursting to west and south. Wounded men were pouring back into the town and still there seemed no sign or hope of relief. For a day or two the Poles gave themselves up to an unhappy conviction that, in spite of their professions, the Russians had abandoned them. On October 17 great shells from six-inch field howitzers were exploding just beyond the town.

Opposed to the German advance in one direction outside of Warsaw was part of a division of one of Russia's choice Siberian corps. It was to this band of men that Warsaw became indebted for remaining nine months longer in Russian hands. For a period of seven hours it was believed that the Germans might have entered Warsaw unopposed, had they made the attempt. The Siberians had then been fighting all day and were cut almost to pieces; their artillery had withdrawn, and they were virtually in retreat, offering scarcely any semblance of rear-guard action, while the Germans were believed to be actually entering the town as resistance had apparently been abandoned. From the Radom road streamed into Warsaw the shattered fragments of regiments and for four hours or more there was said not to be in one direction a gun or effective unit to oppose a German advance.

Just at that critical moment, however, the Germans ceased their attack. Through Warsaw, from street to street and from house to house, spread news leading to an uproar of rejoicings. "Warsaw," it was announced, "is to be held at any cost; the Grand Duke has said so and reinforcements are actually on the way." Reinforcements were in fact coming as fast as steam could bring them. The first to arrive were one of several units from Siberia whose soldiers almost leapt from box-cars into company formation and without a moment's delay swung out over the Vistula through the main street and on by the Jerusalem road to the front. People who saw this entrance into Warsaw and the march through its main street and out for a new campaign (in which these men fought for eighteen consecutive days and were then decorated by the Grand Duke with the Order of St. George), spoke of the scene as extraordinary. With a brass-band blaring, soldiers poured through the town, unshaven, dirty, haggard and warstained from the campaign in Galicia, but marching with the swinging stride of veterans.

All Warsaw seemed to go wild with joy. Women and children wept. Flower stores were stript and every sort of blossom was thrown among the troops, while men and women alike ran beside the soldiers tossing them cigarets, fruit, and bits of bread—anything and everything that a population, frenzied with delight, could offer to men who had come to save them. Tears even came to the eyes of men who witnessed the scene and said they could never have believed that they would live to see the Poles giving such a welcome to soldiers of the Czar. Behind this first regiment came another and another and then guns and ammunition caissons. Behind them were more regiments, more guns, more cavalry, and still again more divisions and more corps, until at last there seemed to be no end to the hordes of troops that Russia was pouring in. From the day of their arrival Warsaw was safe. By October 21 the Germans were in retreat.

There had been before this occurrence severe fighting in the region of Lyck on the East Prussian border, each side claiming the advantage, while in Galicia the Russians had been compelled to retreat from a line hardly sixty miles from Krakow to a line that followed the San. But like the Germans in France, the Russians had kept their armies intact. Their forces between Warsaw and Ivangorod faced an army of about 600,000 Germans. South of Ivangorod, and facing the Vistula, was an Austro-German force of another 600,000, while in Galicia the Austrians, with a few German corps, were operating some 300,000. The total strength of the German armies in Poland and Galicia was estimated at about 1,200,000, and the Austrian force might bring the figure up to 1,500,000. The Russians were believed to be employing not fewer than 2,000,000, which did not include Rennenkampf's force in East Prussia, estimated at 400,000.

On October 22 it was announced from Petrograd that the Russians had won, and that the Germans were in retreat. Some of the Germans, however, operating toward Warsaw, between the Bzura and the Pilitza, confluents of the Vistula, and other Germans south of the Pilitza river, were still holding their positions. German shells had reached parts of the outlying suburbs. The hardest fighting was with forces outside the railway from Skernievive, within a few miles of Warsaw. The Germans apparently made their last stand between Bloni and Pasechno, the former sixteen miles west, the latter twelve miles south, of Warsaw. It was by sending cavalry round to the rear of the German left and infantry to their left flank from the fortress of Novogeorgievsk, while other forces which had crossed the Vistula eighteen miles south of Warsaw increasingly threatened their right, that the Russians compelled the Germans to retreat.

A DIFFICULT MILITARY ROAD IN POLAND

When the main object of the Russian plan—namely, to crush the German active force, while leaving the second-rate troops of the German reserves and the Austrians to be dealt with later—had been achieved, the Russians had moved forward along a line some two hundred and sixty miles in length, from the Carpathians to the Vistula west of Novogeorgievsk. This advance quickly drove the Austrian forces back from the San. Here, and south of Przemysl, the Russians had only to deal with Austrian corps, broken remnants of which had been drawn into formation again and put under German command, but their fighting value was not increased. The German main armies had now been overcome and were retreating on fortified lines along the Polish frontier.

The Grand Duke's strategic plan showed how he relied on his soldiers, both as fighters and marchers. Several corps had had to cover something like 150 miles in order to take up positions. The marching was done under never-ceasing rain, over roads cut up into sloughs, with the enemy's heavy artillery attacking them from a distance. They had to cover the whole front with a thick screen of cavalry and operate far to the west of the Vistula, beyond the reach of Germans, until they were ready to take up their final positions. They then crossed the Vistula, fought for enough space in which to deploy, and entrenched themselves on the left bank.

On October 23 a Russian official announcement said the Germans were in full retreat from before Ivangorod. It was on October 21 that the Germans had begun to fall back from Warsaw. By October 22 they had gone so far from the city, and the Russians were so vigorously pressing the pursuit, that the chief fighting was on the Bzura beyond Sochaczew in the neighborhood of Lowicz. On the 24th Dankl's Austrian army was forced back to Radom. On the 25th the Russian official *communiqué* spoke of the battle as raging along a front from Radom to Skierniewice. On the 28th Radom, at one end of the line, and Lodz, at the other, had been reoccupied by the Russians.

The chief lines of German retreat were along the main railway from Warsaw by Piotrokow and Novo-Radomsk to

Czestochowa, along the railway from Lodz to Kalisch, and northwesterly from Lowicz toward Thorn. The Austro-German forces fell back on the route by which they had come, by Kielce to Olkusz and under shelter of Krakow. The retiring armies did their best in destroying bridges, wrecking railways, and plowing up roads in order to delay the pursuit. German official accounts of the operations, published three months later, declared that by these measures the Russian advance had been rendered slow, so that Teutonic forces had time to retire in good order.

The center of the Austrian line was in a village about ten miles east of Kielce. In the village was a walled-in graveyard, the whole of which had been flanked with gun-positions and protected with wing-trenches and hurriedly erected barbed-wire entanglements. This graveyard was the strongest position on the whole line of defense. It had a little white church in the middle of the field. Before the Austrians were fully alive to what was going on, the Russians were pouring over the wall, over-running barbed wire and wing-trenches, with an impetuosity which crumpled the Austrian center as an incoming tide dissolves a sand castle on a seashore. The little graveyard, where for centuries the dead of the village had been laid beneath overhanging trees, was transformed into a shambles. The only outlet was a single gate, and Russian soldiers took this in their rush, effectively closing the compound within.

Here, in the darkness, men fought hand to hand, stumbling over graves and wakening the echoes with rifle shots and shoutings and with the groans and moans of the dying. It would be no fiction to speak of the ground as soaked with blood. A correspondent [8] who visited the spot soon after the action found great clots of coagulated blood, "like bits of raw liver," lying everywhere. The Austrians, taken by surprize, had fought with desperation and stubbornness, but as hundreds of dead were crumpled up under trees and among tombstones they became no match for the Caucasian soldiers when they came to hand-to-hand fighting with cold steel and clubbed with rifles. When morning came the Austrian center had disappeared and the whole line of the army left

[8] Of The *Times* (London).

to screen the German retirement was in retreat. At one o'clock the Russians poured into Kielce—horse, foot, and artillery—while on the flank their infantry were sucking up stragglers among the enemy, and, on the extreme left were entering Sandomierz, which had to be taken by storm against a triple line of defenses.

It was not until October 28 that news came to Western Europe of Russia's victory over Hindenburg at Warsaw. The German and Austrian armies, operating well south of the River Ilianka, had been broken in two, altho the northern part, defeated a week or more before in an attempt to march into Warsaw, was still fighting desperately north of the Pilitza. South of that river the Grand Duke Nicholas had inflicted a defeat on the enemy, who were in retreat, leaving a gap between the two main groups of armies equal to about one day's march.

This victory had been won after several days of severe fighting, extending from Bialobrzegi on the Pilitza, twelve miles west of the Vistula, southeastward through Glovachey and Politchna, to Inavetz, on the left bank of the Vistula opposite the village of Kazmierz. The total length of this front was forty-two miles. The two theaters of the main struggle were divided by the Pilitza, which flows into the Vistula from the west, twenty-eight miles south of Warsaw, a considerable river over a hundred miles in length, with a width from a hundred yards to twice that extent, with a marshy tract about its confluence with the Vistula. As the Germans had not bridged the river the main battlefield resolved itself into two separate theaters of war. In both severe fighting was in progress for a week. North of the Pilitza the Germans were driven from fifty to seventy odd miles from the line of the Vistula. South of the Pilitza they were one march further forward in the immediate neighborhood of the river.

The armies opposed to the Russians had their base at Mekhov, north of Krakow; the Staff was at Radom. From Radom to the Vistula runs the only railway in this theater of war, its back parallel to and twenty miles south of the Pilitza. From Radom to Kozenitze, forming a very narrow "V" with the railway, ran the only good road to the

Vistula. The greater part of the area of this theater was covered with thick forest, traversed in all directions by tracks which at that time of year were clay sloughs. Only three considerable open spaces of nearly level country were available for army operations amid the forests. One, about Kozenitze, running fourteen miles along the Vistula, was only six miles in its widest part. This the Grand Duke Nicholas selected as a *place d'armes* for the deployment of his forces when the time should come to cross the Vistula. The Kozenitze entrenchments were held, with a valor never exceeded in this war, by a small force against desperate

GERMAN DISPATCH-RIDERS AWAITING ORDERS

assaults for over a week. Two other open spaces were each about fifteen miles by ten. Glovachev was the most considerable township near the center.

The fighting in the forest was of savage character, bayonets being most effective in the hands of Russian troops. Artillery and maxim surprizes also accounted for a good deal of the slaughter, which ranked with the heaviest experienced on this front. The German losses were thought not to be under a hundred thousand. The Germans appeared to have somewhat the best of the battle at the outset, the Russians being the attacking party and unable to use their guns with the freedom enjoyed by the Germans. From batteries in open spaces they were able to keep up a heavy shell-fire on the Russians, who, as they advanced through the woods, drove the Germans back with the bayonet. This work lasted overnight, the Germans shelling the forests incessantly behind fighting lines, which were engaged in hand-to-hand struggles with bayonets, alternating with hurried entrenching work and rifle-fire. The fighting largely consisted of bayonet charges. After some twenty-four hours of hard fighting the Russians emerged from the woods, which they had cleared of the enemy. The battle then assumed a more regular appearance, but bayonet-fighting and the persistence of the Russians slackened the Germans.

In a northern open space the Russians emerging from the fringe of a forest, established themselves in strong entrenchments which they had dug during the night under a ceaseless fire. These by degrees gave them a fighting front of some five miles between the villages of Adamoff, Severinoff, and Marinoff, which commanded three of the best tracks through the forest behind them, and served to secure direct communications with the rear. Glovachev and the whole line northward from that township to the Pilitza was taken by a direct attack after extremely severe fighting against some of Germany's best corps. In the night the Germans began their retreat. The Russians prest them hard during a whole day and by nightfall German-Austrian armies south of the Pilitza were in retreat on the Edlinsk-Radom-Ilsha line, and guns and prisoners were falling into Russian hands. The chief significance of the Russian victory lay in the fact that these armies had been cut off from the Pilitza base. There was no longer before the advancing Russians on the Vistula a front of one German grand army, but two entirely isolated fronts. The victory was strategic.

Over the whole Vistula front, the German armies were now in retreat, pursued by the Russians. Ezhov, south of Skerniewiece, had been seized by the Russians, as also Strykoff, which was within ten miles of Lodz, the terminus of railway communication, on the German gage. Novomiasto, the most forward point occupied on the Pilitza by the German armies, was also in the hands of the Russians. Russian cavalry had reached Lodz in the northern theater, and Radom in the southern. The Teutonic armies, both now in retreat, were hourly widening the space between them, as the armies north of the Pilitza were retiring westward and those to the south of that river almost due south. An interval of at least forty miles separated the two parts of Germany's army.

Of the fourteen bombs which the Germans before this retreat had dropt over Warsaw, two altogether failed to explode. The dozen others inflicted damage that was futile from the military point of view, and without effect as a threat, even on a civil population. One fell in a street frequented for evening promenade, hit the corner of a house occupied by a popular café, but did no harm, notwithstanding the crowded state of the street. Another fell in a municipal garden-space which was closed for the evening, and therefore empty at the time. Two fell in the Jewish quarter, one in the courtyard of a Jewish hospital. Others were dropt in the neighborhood of the railway-station and the field beyond. The total score for fourteen bombs dropt during the flight of an hour and a half by several aeroplanes was seven killed and forty-six wounded. The populace, unscared, joked about the German bombs as a characteristic form of German greeting. Their missiles were called in derision "Germany's *pour prendre* cards." [9]

Of the part borne by the Cossacks in this fighting it may be said that they did not hesitate to attack any odds. Cossacks never leave any of their dead or wounded behind—but pick them up without dismounting. Comrades generally get a dismounted man away. Even when a Cossack happens to get left behind, he is rarely caught. One so left in this battle arrived in camp on a German officer's horse behind its legitimate rider. His own horse, it seemed, had been shot dead just as his party were off again, after having inflicted a blow upon an enemy outnumbering them. As the German officer rode up to cut the man down, the man ducked under the officer's charger, leaped up behind from the other side and, giving a Cossack yell in the officer's ear,

[9] In allusion to the French phrase, *Pour prendre congé*—To take leave.

so startled him that he dropt his sword. The Cossack then got control of the horse and made him move in the direction of his own lines, where he arrived unhurt with his German prisoner.

The Germans became eloquent over the "hideous barbaric yells" of the Cossacks. There was something about this yell which appealed to the equine species, whatever the effect was on a man. Cossacks owned their horses. If they lost their mount, they had to provide themselves with another. It was a favorite sport with them to obtain remounts from the enemy's camp by stalking at night. They rarely failed to turn up with one, two, or three selected mounts, and never said anything about how many of the enemy they had killed to get the horses. The Cossack thought only in horses; men hardly counted. Of course, they had to ask their officer's permission to make such raids, but they were rarely refused. A Cossack without his horse, tho still a fighter and good shot, was a miserable man.

Out of the fog that surrounded operations in Poland for several weeks afterward emerged a solid bulk of Russian achievement. The great German invasion under Hindenburg was for the time over, the invading army was flowing back steadily, and by the end of October was held on German territory and was still retreating. Examined with reference to its purpose, the German advance meant that the Germans had thrust their troops east from Posen and Breslau in order to relieve the pressure on the Austrian armies, which, after a series of defeats in Galicia, seemed to be breaking up. From this point of view, the German invasion was measurably successful, but only in a limited degree. Merely for the moment had the advance into Poland helped the Galician campaign of Germany's ally. Fresh Russian corps, flung from Warsaw upon the German right, had outflanked it, Cossack regiments reaching beyond the flank and frontal attacks making the advance. The offensive had reached only the suburbs of Warsaw, but from there, after fierce fighting, was sent back seventy miles. Lodz and Radom were reported in Russian hands. These cities were half-way points between the Vistula and the Silesian boundary.

The main thing to note was that the Russians, after a tremendous defeat at Tannenberg, had in turn defeated and almost destroyed Austrian armies in Galicia, had driven Hindenburg's German armies advancing from East Prussia into Poland, back across the frontier, and pursued them after a long and desperate battle. Russia had demonstrated that she was not the Russia of the Japanese war. The Battle of the Vistula proved that there were Russian generals who, having retreated, could advance. More than

RUSSIAN SOLDIERS CAPTURED BY GERMANS

this, the manner in which the troops were moved, concentrated and sent north and south to the decisive point, proved that the Russian high command was skilful.

By November 10 the Russians had not only forced the Germans out of Poland, but between Kalisch and Thorn some of their detachments had penetrated 20 miles into Prussian territory, while others were within 20 miles of Krakow. Silesia was again threatened. There was some justification for a Russian claim, voiced in a telegram from the Grand Duke Nicholas to General Joffre, that the Russians had gained "the greatest victory since the beginning of the war." By this the Russian commander-in-chief referred to the great conflict which began within cannon-shot at Warsaw on October 14, and ended with the occupation of Jaroslav. During these three weeks of fighting, the Russians beat at least three armies—Germans who advanced through central Poland against Warsaw; Austrians who advanced through southern Poland against Ivangorod; another Austrian army which advanced in Galicia against the river San, driving the Russians from Jaroslav, virtually compelling an abandonment of the siege of Przemysl, and at one time threatening the evacuation of Lemberg, which the Russian armies had won in the first month of the war. The Austro-German forces thus defeated may have numbered a million men. Probably at that time no such battle had been fought since the beginning of the war on either front.

Meanwhile, on the East Prussian frontier, the Russians had prest forward till they were once more on German soil. The completeness of their victory was rivalled only by the full round of German successes in Belgium and France during the third week of August. Russia had been able to take the full measure of Austria. One could only wonder at the future value of the Austrian armies. Only strenuous German efforts could brace them to action after such defeat. Austrian successes against the Russians were made possible only by the German drive against Warsaw, and when that army was turned back the entire Austrian battle-line cracked, first at Ivangorod, south of Warsaw, then in the great bend of the Vistula, around Sandomir, and afterward around Jaroslav and Przemysl. Even German aid and guidance had failed. The way seemed open for a formidable Russian thrust from the Baltic to the Dniester.

In Poland and Galicia war had kept its dramatic aspects— rapid marches, heavy engagements, decisive results, swift retreats, surprize-attacks, flanking movements, sharp rear-guard actions. Thus, in Galicia the battle-line swayed back and forth, not hundreds of yards at a time as in the west, but twenty-five, fifty, or a hundred miles at a time. By the middle of September the Russians had crossed the San and were pressing on Krakow. Three weeks later they were back of the San in full retreat. Early in November they were once more across the river, moving on Krakow. The most dramatic change of all occurred in central Poland. On October 20 the Russians had been battling to save Warsaw, but in the first week of November the Germans had retreated nearly 150 miles, and the Russian vanguard was across the Silesian frontier. This Russian war-tide, after a

A MITRAILLEUSE IN USE BY RUSSIANS IN POLAND

short ebb, had been carried back to within cannon-shot of Warsaw, and was now sweeping forward again with a momentum that, for a time at least, overwhelmed the German and Austrian offensive and cleared Russian territory of the foe. Moreover, the interrupted invasions of East Prussia and Galicia, were resumed with increased strength. For the first time, Russian troops had crossed the boundary into the province of Posen and were within 200 miles of Berlin.

IN THE EAST, NEAR EAST, AND SOUTH

By these achievements Russia seemed to have preempted the center of the stage. Such rapid developments in the eastern field afforded a vivid contrast to the titanic deadlock that now existed in northern France and Belgium in what is known as the first battle of Flanders. Operating on a battle-line aggregating hundreds of miles, the Russian armies had driven back Hindenburg's invading forces, estimated at 1,000,000 men, the retreat being forced at a rate of fourteen miles a day. Following are parts of a letter written in the midst of these events, by a Russian officer to an English friend.

"How do I live, you ask? No two days alike. To-day pure joy, anyhow; clear sky; cool, not cold; nothing to do; some milk for chocolate they sent me from home; in the distance heavy cannonading just makes a piquant addition to the idyllic scene. I have 'Faust' in my pocket, and a volume of Jules Verne in German. The latter I grabbed in a looted house in Austria. What more could you want? I get on well with the soldiers, tho you have to speak to them like children, and, goodness knows, I am a poor pedagog. During the past month we put in three weeks in Austria, and then turned against the Germans, and did it all on our flat feet, altogether over six hundred miles' marching in two months. And the rain! What rain! Roads washed out, men and horses sticking fast in the mud, altogether about like Dante's Third—or is it Fifth?—Circle in Hell. But don't think I am whining. On bright nights, near the Great Bear, we make out our comet—of course, ours—and when I look on it I am a fatalist. Surely it is a link between heaven and earth, or if you will between God and humanity. You gaze at this long-tailed visitor and feel that something tremendous is happening, something catastrophic in the world of physics and psychology."

For more than two weeks Russian armies were moving west over a whole battle-front from the Baltic to the Carpathians. And every German and Austrian effort to make a final stand had failed. The Russian advance had almost reached Posen; it had passed the Wartha River and driven the Austrian army back on Krakow. But there had been no rout of the Germans. They would unquestionably prove to be as strong on the defense in Silesia and Poland as they had been in the Champagne and Flanders. Bloody and terrible checks were therefore the natural thing to expect, now that Russia was again on the border of Germany. The real value of the Vistula campaign to the neutral observer lay in the fact that Hindenburg had failed. His efforts thus far to crush Russia were quite analogous to German failure to dispose of France. Russia, like France, had emerged from a supreme test unshaken. The German High Command, in official bulletins, explained the defeat by saying they were unable to operate because of bad roads. Russians replied to this by asking how, after forty years of preparing for war, it came about that German commanders failed to know that Poland was not provided with the same splendid highways as Germany?

By the middle of November Hindenburg's plans for a second invasion of Poland were getting into shape. While his Austro-German Army had been pushed back to the frontier, pursued by the Russians, the retreat was by no means a rout; indeed, before the defeated army reached the frontier, it had managed to shake off its pursuers, partly by destroying railways, roads and bridges, partly by putting up strong rear-guards to cover the retirement. Detaching themselves from their Allies, the Germans fell back in two main groups, one making its way down the left bank of the Vistula to Thorn, the other crossing the Warta at Sieradz, and in due course reaching Kalisz. The Austrians, who had been fighting on the Ivangorod-Sandomier line, fell back slowly along the right bank of the upper Vistula to Krakow, where they were joined by the Austrian Army of Galicia, which had retreated from the San, in conformity with the general withdrawal from Poland.

It was soon found that Hindenburg had not yet been disposed of. Leaving his army to find its way to the frontier he hurried to Thorn, summoned General von Mackensen to his aid from Danzig, who had thus far been unemployed in the war, due, rumor said, to severe criticisms he had made of the Crown Prince's pretensions to knowledge of war, and formulated another plan of campaign by means of which he intended to carry the war back into Poland. Mackensen, being reinforced, was ordered to remain strictly on the defensive in the entrenched positions he had taken up guarding the eastern approaches to Thorn. The new troops were partly composed of those who had fallen back from Poland, partly of new formations brought rapidly up to the rendezvous by Germany's admirable railway system. The Russian War Office estimated this army as composed of twelve corps, and gave it an approximate strength of 500,000 men. It intended to move rapidly up the left bank of the Vistula, and, by threatening Warsaw, force the Russians to concentrate between the Vistula and the Warta, by this means taking pressure off the Silesian frontier.

After placing Mackensen in executive command of the Thorn army, Hindenburg went down to Kalisz, and there, with equal promptitude, collected another army, destined to operate against the left flank of the Russians opposing Mackensen's advance. Holding the defensive on the Czestochowa-Krakow line, the commander received similar orders to those given to the general on the frontier of East Prussia. He was not to attempt an offensive movement, but was to hold on to his entrenched position with as few men as might be found necessary. Hindenburg aimed to reconquer Galicia, and safeguard Krakow. The plan covered the whole eastern theater of war, and was so conceived as to neutralize the initial strategical advantage which the Poland salient conferred on Russia.

On November 14, at Thorn, a German counter-offensive was noticed across the border in Poland in the direction of Wloclawek. It was pushed with great violence along the left side of the Vistula and toward Kutno and Lowicz. The Russians do not appear to have had available here more than three army corps. Hindenburg, in Poland, was now attempting what Napoleon tried to do in eastern France in 1814. Napoleon, with a small army, admirably led, endeavored by successive blows to hold back three armies— Prussian, Russian, and British—that were moving toward Paris. Each in turn he defeated, but while he was fighting with one, two others slipt forward, until he was compelled to turn and deal with both before he could destroy the one he had beaten before. So when the Russian Army in East Prussia had been assailed and defeated, the armies in Galicia and Poland advanced. Later, when the Army of Poland had been attacked and was withdrawing, armies in Galicia and East Prussia stormed forward. Hindenburg displayed some suggestion of Napoleon's genius, but numbers were against him. Napoleon was finally crusht because Marmont surrendered Paris to one of the invading armies while Napoleon was battling with the two others. For Hindenburg, the Austrians seemed to be playing Marmont's rôle.

GEN. VON LINSINGEN

Linsingen was twice commander of a German army opposed to Brusiloff on the Russian front

Hindenburg, interviewed on the frontier in those days, said he did not doubt of his ultimate success. He thought that Russia was already "getting stale." All signs pointed to her soon being "at the end of her tether." She was beginning to lack arms and ammunition, and her soldiers "were going hungry." Even the officers were short of food. The country, too, was suffering from distress; Lodz was starving. That was regrettable, he said, but it was "a good thing, for one can conduct no war with sentimentality; the more brutal the conduct of war, the more charitable it really is, for the sooner it will be ended." One could observe, "even by the way in which the Russian troops fight, that soon they will be able to fight no longer." Two of Hindenburg's staff were General Ludendorff, afterward to meet with a decisive failure in the west, and Lieutenant-Colonel Hoffman, one of the discredited heroes of the treaty of Brest-Litovsk. The latter observed: "We have a feeling of absolute superiority over the Russians; we must win and we will." Ludendorff, who was already well known in Germany as the "monosyllable general," merely said, "We'll do it."

But Russia's power in recovery and in renewing an attack was to be illustrated further in this campaign. The Grand Duke's way was to take a front sufficient only for the purpose of his strategic plan. Behind and within easy reach were men ready to fill gaps in the line. These constituted practically a second army, while far away in distant provinces still another army was being made fit. Ever since the beginning of the war a continual flow of Russian troops in regular sequence had taken place. The fighting front was always kept at full strength. The influx of new material was gradual, but thereby it kept soldierly qualities and a knack of campaigning at high-water mark. Russia at this stage of the war had large categories of disciplined men still available who had not even been summoned to serve. In fact, she had not drawn upon half the total available resources of the Empire, and there was no intention of drawing upon them except as they were required.

So rapid was the new German advance into Poland that by November 16, from its base on Thorn, it had reached a line running from Plock to Leczica, some 50 miles inside the frontier, or about half way to Warsaw. The force under Hindenburg was divided into two armies—the left, or northern one, commanded by Morgen, and the right commanded by Mackensen. On November 15-16 the Russians, in spite of their inferiority in numbers, ventured a delaying action against Morgen in the neighborhood of Kutno, but were driven back. Hindenburg announced the result as a victory, claiming to have taken 28,000 prisoners. The news was received with enthusiasm in Berlin, and Hindenburg was made a Field-marshal. On the following day, Mackensen's right successfully engaged the Russians between Dubie and Leczia, driving them northwest along the Bzura toward Lowicz. The Germans opened a gap in their lines, into which, between Strykow and Zigerz, they drove a wedge. If they could have penetrated the Russian line effectually at this point, and could have forced troops through, the Germans believed they would have had Warsaw in their hands. New troops were hurried up from Breslau, and on November 18 fighting was in progress at Lodz nearer Warsaw, and on the 20th at Lowicz and Skiermewice, which were still nearer. On the 23d the Russians claimed a success near Strykow. From that date to the end of the month, the Germans gained no advantage.

The Russians had been heavily reinforced, not by weakening armies in the south, but by bringing up new troops from the east. In the following fortnight Hindenburg beat in vain against the Russian line along the Bzura to and beyond Lodz. Besides killed and wounded the Russians tcok many prisoners. It was said that 5,000 were taken on one day, and 6,000 the next. A few days later Warsaw was full of them. Apparently two corps lost almost all their guns. News of the German reverses, even in a modified form, brought depression in Berlin, where a brilliant victory by Hindenburg had been anticipated. In importance, as in numbers lost, the result outweighed the German success achieved at Kutno. Both, however, were only incidents in a great struggle which, on this front, went on unceasingly and on a gigantic scale, and the issue of which by the end of November had turned in favor of Russia.

Russia for the third time had checked a considerable German offensive and, temporarily at least, transformed it into a retreat. In similar ways a German thrust at the Niemen was repulsed in October and one at Warsaw in November. The invasions failed because, after considerable success and some real progress, the Germans were unable to retain the advantage of superior numbers at the decisive point. As their armies proceeded into Russia, the Russian armies increased until no advantage in equipment, generalship, or training could counterbalance the ponderous bulk of the Slavs, whose armies presently became overwhelming on the German fronts and began to overflow on their flanks. In the east, German armies seemed unequal to their task, in the sense that they were too small to make a victory decisive. The German campaign in Poland more and more gave the impression of a magnificent use of a few men to do the work of many. An undoubted success won by the few gradually became circumscribed.

The incident which stood out most conspicuously in December was the occupation by the Germans of Lodz, of which they had not had possession since October. Lodz was the second city of Poland. The Germans celebrated its capture as a great triumph. They had taken a large number of prisoners and much booty. Russians said its evacuation was a strategic move only, that it would enable them to take up a shorter and more advantageous line and they "did not lose a single man" in the operation. For fifteen hours the Germans shelled empty trenches from which the Russians had retired on the preceding day. The truth probably was that the Russians would not have given up the place, if only for the moral effect of the loss, unless they had been obliged to do so. Its surrender was a reverse, and the Germans were justified in claiming the acquisition of it as of some importance. Threatened with destruction, the Russians had swept back in a half circle away from Warsaw. When attacked in front of German troops advancing from Kalisz, the enormous resources of Russia had saved her from disaster. Gathering up the garrison and the reserve troops in Warsaw and nearby fortresses, Russia sent out from Warsaw a new army which took in the rear the Germans, who, by a sudden turn of fortune, after having half surrounded the Russians at Lodz, found themselves caught between Russian troops at Lodz, and others coming along the Warsaw railroad and operating south of Lowicz and Skiorniewicz.

While Berlin claimed a decisive victory, Petrograd talked of a German "Sedan" in Poland. German military skill had, however, met a crisis that was the gravest Germany had thus far met. While her troops cut their way out of the Russian net in the north and west, new troops, apparently brought hastily from Flanders and France, covered her broken corps as they emerged from the Russian gap. Some of the most desperate and costly fighting of the war took place at this stage. When it terminated, Russians and Germans faced each other in a double line across Poland from the Vistula to Galicia, and the campaign had resolved itself into a deadlock.

About the middle of December the German attacks appreciably decreased until the last week of the year saw little fighting of any importance in this region. Between December 20 and 25 the Russian line, as a whole, fell back a little, not so much under pressure as for the purpose of taking up a better position on a straighter front. Both sides were content to dig in and entrench themselves. Southward confused fighting continued along the Pilitsa to the neighborhood of Novo-Radomsk, and thence on the Nido, where, in the last days of the year, the Russians claimed some minor successes with the capture of considerable numbers of prisoners.

The conduct of the campaign by the Grand Duke Nicholas was marked by a combination of caution and resource which repeatedly saved the situation when it seemed well-nigh lost. He acted throughout the operations with a cool and calculating judgment which never allowed his adversary to profit by the initial advantage which he possest of being able to take the offensive. It was a duel between two strategists, one of whom was always attacking, and the other always defending, meeting thrust with counter-thrust, refusing to take risks, and never accepting battle at strategical disadvantage. Never once did the Russian generalissimo place his men in a false position, or make demands on their services to which they were unable to respond. Surprized by the sudden irruption of Mackensen into Poland, he ordered his troops to fall back till reinforcements could arrive in sufficient numbers to assure success. Surprized a second time by Hindenburg's movement from Kalisz, he withdrew his left wing to save his communications. Keeping an eye on both his flanks he was ever ready with a counter-stroke before there was time for his opponent to deliver his intended blow. On his side, the German commander also played his cards with consummate skill, and altho he committed errors he speedily rectified them.

Along the Carpathians fighting continued through the first week of December. The Russians found that their opponents at many points in this region were no longer Austrians, but Germans. Advices from Petrograd to London said the Austrian armies around Krakow had "ceased to exist as an independent force and were all mixed up with Germans." So long as Przemysl held out and Krakow stood firm, it was impossible that the Russians should entertain any idea of invading Hungary in force. To push an army any distance across the mountains would have been almost tantamount to giving it as a hostage to the enemy. The Russian position in Western Galicia and in Poland would have to be much better assured before any real invasion could be undertaken without great risk. Before that time arrived there was to come a long winter, with terrible fighting in deep snows and bitter cold on the mountains.

For five months fighting such as the world had never seen had now raged over a front of more than 700 miles, or from the Baltic to the frontiers of Roumania. On the two sides not fewer than perhaps 5,000,000 men had been engaged. At the end Russia was believed to be stronger than ever, while Germany had suffered reverses at least as heavy as any she inflicted on the enemy. The combined losses of Germany and Austria were probably heavier than those which Russia suffered; and Russia was much better able to stand losses than either of her opponents. At the end of the year it was announced that the prisoners in Russia included 131,737 Germans, with 1,140 officers, and 221,447 Austrians, with 3,186 officers, or a total of 4,326 officers and 353,184 men.

The saddest feature of all was the devastation that had been wrought in Poland. The Polish people had paid a terrible price for loyalty to Russia. For five months contending armies had swept backward and forward over Polish lands. The country became one vast battle-field. Farms, villages, and towns were almost obliterated; provinces laid utterly waste. In their first advance, the German armies behaved with restraint and on their retreat they did not seem to have committed such outrages as were perpetrated in Belgium, at least not in such numbers. But they ruined the land, not only by the destruction of railways, roads, buildings, and bridges, but by plundering and carrying away supplies of food and clothing. The condition to which such of the population as remained in devastated regions was reduced was, as winter came on, pitiable beyond description. The world at the time heard less of the sufferings of Poland than of those of Belgium. Nor did Poland find such ready hands to reach out to succor her. Nowhere did Belgium suffer such starvation and frozen misery as, during that winter, stalked through Poland.

In Belgium the sweep of war was swift and final, while in Poland it was a matter of being swept now in one direction, now in another, by rival armies for weeks and months. The area and population affected in Poland were more than ten times those of Belgium—that is, considering both Poland in Russia and Austrian Poland as equally devastated by the war. Of eleven provinces in Poland only one, Siedloe, escaped invasion. The devastated territory amounted to more than 40,000 square miles—nearly as great an area as New York State, New York's land area being 47,000 square

THE CLOTHES OF CAPTURED RUSSIANS BEING DISINFECTED

miles—in which 200 cities and towns and 9,000 villages were partially or entirely destroyed. Five thousand villages were razed to the ground. Railroad tracks for a distance of 1,000 miles were torn up. The soil was rendered unfit for tilling by innumerable trenches and big holes bored into it by heavy projectiles. The agricultural production, representing $500,000,000 a year, was stopt in its entirety for lack of funds, seeds, farmhands, and cattle. The agricultural population of 7,000,000 people were virtually starving. The people hid themselves in forests, or under the ruins of their former villages, having as food only roots, bark, rind, and decaying carcasses of horses killed on the battle-fields. The fate of cities and industrial regions was no better. Some of them suffered depopulation, some were flooded by a tremendous wave of refugees who deserted the fighting zone. Eighty per cent. of this class of refugees were Jews. Kalisz, capital of the provinces of the same name, which before the war had a population of nearly 80,000, numbered afterward only 10,000.

© AIME DUPONT.

EDOUARD DE RESZKE

The de Reszke estate in Poland, which was a large one, was much overrun and parts of it ruined in the early operations of the Germans in Poland

Warsaw, the capital of the kingdom, twice as large as Brussels, harbored over 200,-000 refugees. The city of Lodz, with 50,000 inhabitants, twice captured by Russian and German armies, looked like a cemetery. Important industrial centers like Chenstochova, Sosnovioc, and the coal basin of Dombrova shared the same fate. An industrial output valued at $400,000,000 a year was annihilated. Three millions of people who had earned their daily bread in factories and mines were starving. Coal mines, altho not in the fighting zone, had been flooded by the Germans for strategical reasons, and all the costly machinery destroyed as was the case in cities of northern France. The total material loss was estimated as high as $700,000,000. On all sides were hunger, disease, and ruin. Out of a total of 1,500,000 horses in one part of Poland, 800,000 had been requisitioned by fighting armies. Not less than 2,000,000 cattle were confiscated. Milk was scarce and the mortality among infants showed a terrific increase. In Przemysl, Rzeszow and Jaroslav people were dying from hunger. The counties of Cleszanov and Dovromil in Eastern Galicia and Lancut, Prze-

worsk, Nisko, Tarnobrzeg, and Krosno in Western, were
so thoroughly devastated that they looked as if they had
been destroyed by an earthquake. Among heaps of ruins
dogs ran wild with hunger. Flocks of crows and ravens,
in search of food, were digging with their beaks into the
shallow graves of Russian and Teutonic soldiers. Of the
total area of Galicia only 7 per cent. was untouched by
war, 23 per cent. partially and 70 per cent. totally ruined.

The devastation of Poland was the worst between Lodz
and Warsaw. After Warsaw, probably the most interesting
of all Russian Polish cities was Chenstochova, which lies south
of Lodz and half way between it and Krakow. Not far
from this city was the De Reszke estate, the home of Edward
and Jean de Reszke, the famous opera singers of a former
decade. Previous to the war, which made the country about
their estate one of the grounds of conflict, the estate numbered 12,000 well-cultivated acres. Back of the villa was
forest-land, really a small game reserve, in which the brothers with their guests often hunted deer, partridge, and
hare. Most of the land was given over to potato raising,
from which an annual supply of vodka was made. Happily
employed were 400 peasants with their allowance of proven-
der, their little homes, and a dependable yearly wage. Of
the spacious De Reszke home only the cellar now remained
to shelter Edward, who was almost destitute, Jean being
in Paris. It had been a beautiful, peaceful domain. The
homes of peasants on this estate were interesting. Married
men had individual huts, but bachelors lived in long low
buildings of simple lines. Near the entrance to the estate
stood a very old church, which, because of its distinctive
national architecture, the De Reszkes allowed to remain. An
adjoining estate contained an ancient underground hermi-
tage which had been used in the seventeenth century as a
retreat.

In measuring the Eastern campaign, which in December,
as in November, attracted the attention of the whole world,
it was necessary to note that, for the first time in the
war a German army had been brought near to destruction,
and that it had escaped. German generalship and German
courage had risen to their highest level in those months of

conflict, but the moral effect was not to be mistaken. To Germany and her Austrian ally were lacking sufficient numbers to meet on equal terms the Russian forces arrayed against them. On both fronts east and west they were outnumbered. In the west the Germans still held most of Belgium and a slice of northern France, but in the east Russian soldiers occupied a corner of East. Prussia and Austria had abandoned all of Galicia save the territory about Krakow, and had again evacuated the Bukowina. Upward of 35,000 square miles, with a population of 10,000,000, had thus been temporarily or permanently lost to the Teutonic emperors—a complete set-off, for the time being, to the conquests Germany had made in August in the west. But the western world, and especially America, knew little of this.[10]

[10] Principal Sources: The London *Times*' "History of the War," The *Daily Chronicle* (London), *The Literary Digest,* The *Times,* The *Sun,* New York; The *Times* (London), The *Evening Sun* (New York), The *Standard* (London), "Nelson's History of the War" by John Buchan, *The Fortnightly Review* (London), Associated Press dispatches, The *Morning Post* (London), The *Evening Post,* The *Evening Sun,* New York; The *Daily Mail,* The *Daily News,* London; The *Neue Freie Presse* (Berlin), "Bulletins" of the National Geographic Society (New York).

IV

HINDENBURG AGAIN FAILS TO TAKE WARSAW, BUT THE RUSSIANS TAKE PRZEMYSL AND THREE CARPATHIAN PASSES

January 1, 1915—April 15, 1915

BEFORE the end of December Hindenburg had brought up new forces, including stiffened remnants of the Austrian armies, and had reorganized the whole in a manner creditable to German recuperative powers. The Grand Duke Nicholas, meanwhile, had abandoned temporarily his main objective and drawn his armies together. Krakow, and everything around Krakow, had been abandoned. Wholesale withdrawals of Russian troops from positions before held, except those in front of Warsaw, indicated tactical movements to secure better positions. The whole Eastern area of war, like Cæsar's Gaul, was still divided into three parts, the East Prussian, Polish, and Carpathian zones, By New Year's Day the position in the Polish zone was regarded as favorable to the Russians. They held an advanced position in front of the Vistula, and were using, as an additional artery of communication, the great river which, during Hindenburg's first invasion, had served the Russians so well as a defense. Should the line of Russian trenches ever be pierced, the army could fall back on the Vistula. But any retreat in that zone would merely be used to strengthen their position on their chief railway junctions lying east of the Vistula, on a line parallel to the river-front on its eastern side, but well out of reach of guns from the western bank.

Hindenburg resolved to make one more effort for Warsaw by a frontal attack. He had good cause to believe that the defenses of Warsaw had been weakened, for he knew the limitations of the Russian equipment, limitations which later in the year became the chief cause of Russia's downfall.

Moreover, Hindenburg recalled that the fifty-sixth birthday of his Imperial Master was approaching. Warsaw had been the objective of his winter campaign—Warsaw by a frontal attack—and it was the merit, as it was the defect, of the veteran field-marshal that an idea once implanted in his stubborn German mind was hard to uproot. There was a disposition in the West to regard his third assault on Warsaw as a feint intended to cloak this massing of men in East Prussia. On January 31, Mackensen had concentrated masses of artillery along the front of the Rawka, and down the Bzura as far as Sochaczev, and made a great artillery bombardment on a wide front, in order to puzzle the Russians as to the direction of his main attack. In the meantime he was getting together his strength of men and guns on a line of seven miles in front of Bolimov. Here, on the evening of February 1, he had not less than seven divisions—140,000 men—including various units of the Prussian Guard brought up from Lowicz, which gave him a strength of something like ten rifles per yard.

Mackensen did not propose to repeat the mistake he had made before Lodz of driving into the Russian front a wedge too narrow to be effective. He realized that the breach must be wide enough to move about in so that he could operate against broken flanks. His plan almost looked like succeeding, but the place he had chosen for his assault happened to be the place of all others which the Grand Duke Nicholas could most readily reinforce, because he had two railways and two good roads over which troops could be hurried from Warsaw. Through driving snow supports came in, and on February 4, late in the afternoon, the German advance was checked. But it had got over the crest of Barzymov, and advanced nearly five miles along the Warsaw railway until in another day the Rawka front might have been fatally breached.

Around Barzymov the slaughter was so great that German dead formed material for redoubts and embrasures. When the advance reached its furthest point, it became weak, and yielded to a counter-attack. By the 18th the Germans were back on the Rawka flats, and the Russians crossed the Bzura at Dachova near the mouth of the Rawka. An advance had been won which for a moment threatened the whole front, but the counter-attack shattered it. This action was the last of three frontal attacks on Warsaw. The Bzura-Rawka lines were found too strong to give such immediate results as Hindenburg had sought.

It looked as if the Russians might again expel the invaders, and carry the war into their country. In central Poland, Mackensen's repeated attempts to break through had failed, and the lull which followed the fighting had led to a belief that he was waiting for an opportunity to retire from a position which appeared to be daily growing more untenable. Then occurred another of those dramatic transformation scenes, witnessed so often during this war, which once more set back the hands of the Russian clock. Apparently not disheartened by his failures, Hindenburg determined to make fresh efforts from fresh plans. A large Austro-Hungarian army, reported to be 400,000 strong, had been concentrated in Hungary ostensibly for the purpose of invading Serbia, but really to reconquer Galicia.

Four or five corps, composed partly of Bavarian, Saxon, and West Prussian troops, and including a brigade of Prussian Guards, had been hurried to the Danube, and thence sent to reinforce the Austro-Hungarian Army, which was being concentrated on the Theiss river. Leavened with German troops, this army was divided into three main groups, the right group being intended to advance into the Bukowina, the left to effect the relief of Przemysl, and the central group, which was the strongest, and composed largely of German troops, having for its object to pierce the center of the Russian line of resistance and re-occupy Lemberg. The plan of campaign for giving effect to these intentions had been carefully worked out by Hindenburg. Owing to the secrecy with which it was launched the initial conditions favored its success.

Simultaneously with this movement the left column of the Austro-German Army, advancing along a sixty-mile front from the west of Kassa to Ungvar, and making use of the three railways, which converged on the Galician frontier in this locality, pushed its way through the Dukla, Lupkow, and Uszok passes, the Russians, according to their wont, falling back before the Austrian advance to prepared positions behind the crest of the mountains. On January 26 and 27 the Russians turned on the invaders, and after a hotly contested running fight compelled all the Austrians to fall back through the Dukla and Lupkow passes to positions which they had in their turn fortified for use in case of retreat, on the Zboro-Mezo Laborez line, where a seven days' battle was fought, ending with the Austrians being driven out of their entrenchments with a loss of 170 officers, 10,000 men, and a quantity of guns and war material. The Russians now were eight miles or so south of the Galician frontier.

This Austrian invasion of Galicia was made with a large force acting on a concerted plan. Every pass over the Carpathians had been brought into use, and every railway leading from the interior of Hungary had been made available for bringing up troops and supplies. Altho the movements took place along a front extending for more than 200 miles from the Dukla to the Kirlibaba passes, the three main columns kept in touch with one another throughout the advance. The conception of the undertaking was doubtless the work of Hindenburg, but the executive direction must also have been in good hands, for there was no hitch to the strategical arrangements which led to the deployment of a force amounting to something like 600,000 men along so extended a front. Strategy did its work, and did it well; but the main fact here was the stolid, stubborn, enduring Russian soldier never seen at his best till standing on the defense, when full scope was given to his virile fighting qualities. Then he was hard to beat. In attack he was less successful, not from shortcomings on his own part, but because of difficult conditions under which he had to fight, with scanty communications available to keep men supplied with ammunition, of which the expenditure with modern quick-firing weapons was so enormous.

In order to prevent troops from being detached from Central Poland while the invasion of Galicia was in progress, Mackensen was instructed to make another determined attempt to break through to Warsaw, no matter how great the cost might be. Owing to the difficulty in making a way across the Bzura river north of Sochazew, where the country between the river and Warsaw alternated between dense forests and impassable marches, the German Commander abandoned further effort in this direction, and, after leaving enough troops to hold on to the German trenches on the left bank, moved the bulk of his force down to the Rawka river, and then crossed over to the right bank for the purpose of attacking the Russians, who there were strongly entrenched. Finding the Russian position strong, and the defense well-

TYPES OF RUSSIAN SUBJECTS CAPTURED IN POLAND
Among these were Tartars, Bashkirs and Kirgises

organized, Mackensen sent back for reinforcements, and by the end of January had concentrated as many as seven divisions. Then began a long and sanguinary battle, lasting from the 29th of January to the 5th of February. One of the most determined of all the German attacks was made on the 31st of January, when as many as twelve regiments were sent against the Russian lines at Humin.

Further south on the frontier the German offensive had failed. A series of battles of secondary importance had followed, but, as a net result, after three months of effort, the Teutonic position was hardly better than it was on New Year's Day. The Germans had gained ground in East Prussia and reconquered strategical backwaters in the Pruth valley, but they were eventually to lose Przemysl. For two weeks full reports came of fighting on the Bzura and Rawka rivers. In its main outlines the fighting resembled that in Flanders. There was plenty of mud; more work for picks and spades than for rifles; continuous shelling and sniping. These rivers (more especially the Bzura, which is lined by marshes on either bank) offered a splendid field for firing, but made rapid advances impossible. Such advantages were lost as soon as frost came, when the river ceased to be a serious obstacle, and so the tactical situation was radically changed.

Early in February was reached a culmination of siege-warfare that had been carried on for six weeks. Since January 30 the ground had been as hard as a rock. On a front of not quite seven miles the Germans deployed seven divisions, supported by the fire of one hundred batteries. During a single hour these batteries dropt 24,000 shells on Russian trenches. The Germans attacked in close formation, with a depth of from ten to twenty-one men, and gained some ground, only to lose it. The concentrated fury of the German attacks came to a climax when, from a confusion of bursting shells, point-blank slaughter by rifle-fire and bayonets, and an overhanging mass of poisonous chemical smoke, the Russians charged across three lines where the Germans had intrenched themselves after a tremendous fight. Mackensen made his crucial effort by swiftly forcing a picked army of 100,000 men, backed by nearly 600 guns of all calibers, pouring shells without pause, into a comparatively open gap of country six miles wide, which had for its main features a deserted distillery on the north, near Gumine, and in the south, near Bolimow, in a woody park, the large manor house of Wola-Szydlowiecka.

The Germans maintained a hurricane of shrapnel over well-concealed Russian shelters. Many guns fired shells charged with suffocating gases. But the Russians remained unshaken even when the Prussian Guards were brought up

FIELD MARSHAL VON HINDENBURG AND HIS STAFF

Hindenburg stands with both hands in the pockets of his white overcoat. To the left of him is Ludendorff; to the right General Hoffmann, who figured conspicuously in the Brest-Litovsk treaty of 1917

from Lowicz. When the German supreme effort was spent, the Russians rose up through the smoke and doubled forward on the low, broken walls around the distillery, where the Germans had been working fifty machine-guns, and captured fourteen of them, while a desperate close-quarter fight ensued. The Russians, at the southern end of the battle, found a weak position in the German line, and through this poured into the park at Wola-Szydlowiecka. About an hour later the Germans were driven back from the mansion, leaving, it was said, thousands of dead. Russians declared that the Germans lost about 30,000 killed in this six-mile battle. Many fell before the bayonet.

On February 7 began a Russian counter-stroke. From the right bank of the Vistula was directed a cross-fire against the Germans on the left bank of the Bzura, near its confluence with the Vistula, and subsequently attacks were pushed home around Kamien and Vitkovice. On the same day the Russians made progress in the angle between the Bzura and Rawka, and then the Germans settled down on the Bzura Rawka front. During one week they were said to have suffered 40,000 casualties, but German and Austrian papers gave no hint or suggestion of this fierce fighting in front of Warsaw. A month later, the Russian army fell back on the Rawka and Bzura, where, during the whole of that time, fighting was almost incessant. The Russian line, save for readjustments of front and small strategic variations at certain points, remained the same as on December 19. Neither army succeeded in gaining territory.

The whole long line began to have the appearance of a stalemate. The Germans continued their efforts, but they no longer made terrific attacks on twenty or thirty positions at once. As far back as January a Russian army of unknown strength and accompanied by a large force of cavalry had begun to move up the right bank of the lower Vistula, advancing at first between the Skwra and Wka rivers, and then gradually extending its line east and west toward the frontier of West and East Prussia. The advance was slow, as the roadways were blocked with snow, while away from roads the country was cut up by marshes and numberless small tributary streams which fed the two rivers on their way down to the Vistula. No serious opposition was encountered till within some twenty miles of the frontier, when Russian cavalry came up against detachments of German troops who were watching the approaches to the frontier from the south. Successful actions then took place, the German troops falling back before the Russians, who pushed their cavalry patrols close up to Lipno, only eighteen miles from Thorn, and to Chorzele, about ten miles north of Przasnysz. Simultaneously with this movement, the Tenth Russian Army, which had been marking time for three months in its positions east of the Masurian Lakes, began to retake the offensive from Pilkallen on the north, and Lyck on the south. The troops at Pilkallen crossed the Niemen, destroyed the railway-station at Pogegen, and threatened Tilsit.

The German Emperor had transferred his headquarters from the West to the East, where Hindenburg, undaunted by his failures, was preparing a new offensive movement against the Russians in East Prussia. Hindenburg had brought from the west the Twenty-first Corps, which had been with the Bavarian Crown Prince, and three reserve corps. From elsewhere he got the Thirty-eighth and Fortieth Corps, which were new formations and borrowed the equivalent of three corps from other parts of the Eastern Front, including the better part of a Silesian Landwehr corps and a reserve corps of the Guard. He had thus accumulated a total force of nine corps—over 300,000 men—to hurl upon General Sievers' 120,000. The force was organized in two armies, the northern, commanded by General von Eichhorn, operating on the Insterburg-Lotzen line, and the southern, under General von Below, on the Lotzen-Johannisburg line. The German advance was prest along the whole Tilsit-Johannisburg line. According to custom the left wing swept in an enflanking movement east of Tilsit in the curve formed by the Lower Niemen. The Russian right, in front of Pilkallen and Gumbinnen, was compelled to retire to avoid envelopment. The natural line of its retreat was along the railway to Kovno.

A bare outline gives little idea of the difficulties of the

operation. For an army to fall back seventy miles under the pressure of a force three times its superior and based on a good railway system, would be a difficult feat at any time. More than half of Sievers' army had no railways to assist them, but had to struggle with their guns through blind forests choked with snowdrifts. The Russian losses were large, but in the circumstances moderate. The Germans claimed 75,000 prisoners and 300 guns. The chief Russian loss was in General Bulgakov's Twentieth Corps, that the Germans asserted they had completely destroyed. But during the fortnight which ended on the 20th, at least half of that corps, and more than two-thirds of its guns, safely made their way through the Augustovo and Suwalki woods to the position which had been prepared for the Russian defense.

The battle of Augustowo Wald began on February 7, after Hindenburg had transported German troops from Poland to East Prussia, and new troops had been brought up from inner garrisons. His total reinforcements were

GENERAL VON BELOW

five corps. Concentrating around Gumbinnen, this German army advanced simultaneously with another army, which had made preparations behind Lyck. The Russian line zigzagged across East Prussia, south of the Memel, east of Ragnit, to Gumbinnen, wedging forward along the line of the Angerrapp and back through the Masurian Lakes to Lyck. Since mid-November the Russians had held this line. A third of the rich East Prussian farmlands was behind their line. Not able to advance with their cannon, the Russians came up with them, forcing their way through a storm of snow. They tried with carbine-fire to cover the retreat of their guns, but the Germans proceeded to shoot live horses that were standing in their traces and piled them up, the dead and the living, to block the road of escape. Supported by captured cannon, the Germans rushed on. A battle followed in the streets of Eydtkuhnen, and by midnight the Germans had driven the Russians into Wirballen. Captured cars were found filled with boots and fur-lined garments, and Russian field-kitchens filled with food, a welcome capture, since, for two days, the Germans had lived on knapsack rations. North of Ragnit, as far as the Baltic, the Russians were driven back across the frontier. Thus the battle went on from February 10 to the 21st, the crumbling Russian Army of East Prussia, under Ruszky's command, being pushed from the north against the troops of Below on the south. Russians, pouring out of East Prussia, attempted a stand at Suwalki, fighting as they ran down the road to Augustowo, where they were met by Eichhorn's army, which had marched from Augustowo, 120 kilometers, through the snow in two days. Below, coming across from Lyck, made a junction with Eichhorn, and pursued the Germans into forests and a frozen swamp.

Hindenburg then attempted to strike at Warsaw by sending an expeditionary army down the Narew river. Leaving only a containing force to face the Russians, he detached the bulk of his troops and before the concentration was complete sent three corps across the frontier with orders to seize Przasnysz, a great road center, and to link them up with a German army, which had been moving slowly for some weeks up the right bank of the lower Vistula. Przasnysz was captured on February 25, but the German success was short-lived, for the Russian position on the Narew was stronger than anywhere else in Poland on account of three railway lines which converged on Ostrolenka. After a two days' battle, Przasnysz was recaptured on February 27 and the Germans, who were caught between two fires, were driven back toward Mlawa and Chorzele. The battle of Przasnysz restored prestige to Russian arms, and came as an opportune set-off to the defeat of the Tenth Russian Army earlier in the month.

Early in February the Russians made a swift move in the Bukowina east of Galicia and west of Roumania. Three towns were captured. The political effect of this success, as affecting the participation of Bulgaria and Roumania in the war and the subsequent relations of the Balkan States seemed then important. The Russians occupied Cypot, Kameral, and Illischestie on the direct route from the Bukowina to Transylvania. The Bukowina was a Duchy and Crownland of Austria, sandwiched in between Galicia and the northwestern frontier of Roumania. The name means the country of beech trees. A great portion of it is forest clad. It lies among the southern spurs of the woody Carpathians. Czernowitz, its capital, had about 70,000 inhabitants. The population of the whole country was some three-quarters of a million, of whom about 40 per cent. were Ruthenians and nearly another 40 per cent. Roumanians, the remainder being a Balko-Hungarian mixture of Magyars, Germans, Poles, Jews and gipsies.

The Roumanian people in the Bukowina and in Transylvania were not settlers who had come across the Roumanian frontier, but people whose roots lay deep in their history. Roumania herself was a geographical anomaly. It was curious to find here in Eastern Europe a Latin enclave surrounded by Slavs and Hungarians. Not only did Roumanians speak a Latin tongue resembling Italian but, in spite of all mixtures with Slavs, Turks, and Greeks, many retained strong evidence of Italian blood. Roumanians are descendants of Trajan's Roman colony of Dacia. The explanation for the survival of a Latin people in the Bukowina and in Transylvania lay in the fact that Trajan's original province included both districts and was much larger than modern Roumania. Apart from this ancient tie, Roumanians had set up a more modern claim to the Bukowina. Roumania was created a Kingdom in the 19th century by a union of the two provinces of Moldavia and Wallachia, which were formerly Turkish, and the Bukowina was once a part of Moldavia, Suczava in the Bukowina having been once the Moldavian capital.

About February 24, the center of operations shifted to the sector of the Russian "barrier" facing the southern edge of East Prussia. A German advance in force against Przasnysz began on February 20, when the Russian forces in that region consisted of only one brigade of infantry and small bodies of cavalry. By a wide turning movement, which passed east of Przasnysz, the Germans totally out-flanked the Russians until they surrounded them. On February 25 the Russians had to evacuate Przasnysz with little hope of escaping destruction, but just then relief came. The Germans were unable to prevent the Russian reinforcements from crossing the river, and in the battle of Krasnosielec, some Germans who had surrounded Przasnysz from the south were in turn enveloped. It was a confused and desperate battle that ensued on February 26 and 27. On the 28th the Germans began to retreat, leaving perhaps ten thousand prisoners in the hands of the Russians. Eight to ten German army corps were said to have been gathered on the Willenberg-Soldau line for this new attack on Przasnysz, but this was perhaps a fantastic exaggeration of their numbers. The Germans again advanced by parallel progress along the valleys of the Orzec and Omulec, and fighting occurred on the entire front.

The German winter campaign in East Prussia, which at first seemed to offer unusually good chances of success, had thus ended. After marked success in the first week it closed with practically aimless fighting. It was doubted whether a comparison of the losses suffered on both sides during the entire campaign would give an advantage in their favor. The Russian "barrier" on the Vistula had been tested once more and found equal to its task. The fortress of Osoweic had withstood attacks such as no western fortress had as yet survived. The Russian retreat from East Prussia may have been only a "strategic retirement," but it had seemed a substantial German victory, altho not a decisive one. To Germans this repetition of Hindenburg's earlier success in the Masurian Lakes region meant, first, in the Kaiser's words, that "our beloved East Prussia is free from the enemy"; and, in connection with a reported Russian evacuation of Bukowina, portended a general advance along the whole Eastern battle-front from the Bukowina to the Baltic, with the Russians already "rolled up in many portions of the line." Petrograd, however, was said to be taking it all very calmly, considering that the German forces had failed to deliver the crushing blow that was intended. Successful in the Carpathians and before Warsaw, the Russians fell back before the German advance in East Prussia only to take up a strong defensive position within their own borders.

The fighting about Warsaw had been one of undoubted disappointment to both sides—to the Russians, because they had been forced time and again to cancel their plans of invasion in the north and south, in order to reinforce their center and yet had been unable to gain a firm upper hand even before the Polish capital; to the Germans, because, at a cost of perhaps some hundreds of thousands of men, they had gained nothing but the temporary possession of a tract of snowy waste. The whole winter campaign of Warsaw showed a stubborn conflict, long drawn out, but it had given little help to either contestant.

By the beginning of March, the Russian counter-attack had set in and from Kovno to the Narew the Germans were being pushed back. On March 5 the German attack on Osoweic ended, and their big howitzers were shipped back on railway carriages. Hindenburg, after announcing that he had never meant to cross the Niemen, gave orders for a gradual retreat to the East-Prussian frontier. On March 8 there was desperate fighting about Seyny and Augustovo, and the Russians made captures of German supplies. By the middle of March, Hindenburg had drawn back his left and left center to a position some ten miles inside Russian territory, and covering his own frontiers. Not only had the Niemen line proved impracticable and Osoweic impregnable, but further south on the Narew a great battle had been fought and lost.

On the 22d the Germans captured Przasnysz, taking a number of guns and about half an isolated brigade. The Russians were now hard prest for munitions and arms. At Przasnysz soldiers were flung into the firing-line without rifles, armed only with a sword-bayonet in one hand and two bombs in the other. That meant desperate fighting at the closest quarters. The Russians had to get at all costs within range in order to throw their bombs, and then they charged with cold steel. This was berserker warfare, a defiance of all modern rules, a return to the conditions of primitive combat. But it succeeded, and the Germans gave ground before numbers who were not their equals. The battle of Przasnysz decided the fate of Hindenburg's new bid for Warsaw, which had been made by a flank movement. About the same time when the siege of Osoweic failed, the Twenty-first Corps falling back from the Niemen, the whole movement languished. As a result Hindenburg merely had his northern front inside the Russian frontier.

The Germans in the East had now to make choice from several possible lines of action. They could press their gains in East Prussia at one extreme of their frontier line, or in Galicia at the other, or they could stand on the defensive and wait. By means of their railway facilities they might move their forces rapidly for a succession of blows north and south alternately; or, by abandoning the east for the time being, and leaving only a minimum of troops for its temporary defense, they could throw the bulk of their armies from the Eastern to the Western Front. One thing alone they could scarcely hope to accomplish unless conditions at other points underwent some favorable change. That meant to resume, with success at an early day, their attacks on Warsaw, but before the summer was over they were able to accomplish this in a way that startled a world ignorant of the great Russian weakness in material equipment. Looking back, however, on the campaign which had been carried on so strenuously on the Eastern Frontier for six months, there was as yet little to show for the fearful wastage caused. The Russian invasion of Germany had been checked, but the menace was still there, and nothing which Hindenburg had yet done had been able to remove it.

Przemysl, which fell on March 22, was the chief fortress of the Austro-Hungarian Empire, and one of the greatest fortresses in Europe. Its fall involved the surrender of a garrison of nine generals, ninety-three superior officers, 2,500 subaltern officers and officials, and 117,000 men of the rank and file. Thus was lost to the Teutonic Allies an army equipped with a train of artillery, including guns of the modern type. The forces within Przemysl exceeded the number required for an effective defense. Their original strength must have been about four army corps—at least so it appeared after a siege of four months and a series of desperate sorties with 120,000 men still remaining in the fortress. A garrison of sixty-thousand would have been sufficient for its defense; a greater number merely hastened the day of surrender. The excessive size of the garrison and the deficiency in supplies were alike due to one cause— the unexpected turn in the course of the war which had set in after Tannenberg toward the end of October.

POLISH PEASANT WOMEN BEING FED BY GERMAN SOLDIERS

The Russian siege of Przemysl had originally begun as early as September 16, and was then temporarily raised on October 14, when the Russian troops fell back to the line Medyka-Stary-Sambor, their retreat effected in good order. Before retiring they blew up bridges and destroyed large sections of railway and roads, so that it was not until October 23 that another train from the west entered Przemysl. The siege was renewed on November 12. Experience at Port Arthur had taught the Russians many lessons concerning modern fortresses. They did not try to take Przemysl by storm. With inadequate siege-artillery at their disposal, any attempt on their part to rush the forts or trenches would have been difficult and expensive. For years Austrian engineers had been preparing it for a possible siege. Austrian artillery men knew the exact range of every point around it. The Russian siege-army was commanded by General Selivanoff, who constructed his own defense works.

Przemysl was a fortress with a circumference of twenty miles, surrounded now by an outer ring of Russian counter-fortifications, so strengthened as to offer effective resistance to any attempts on the part of the garrison to break through the Russian lines. While the Russian ring was being fortified, Russian troops were approaching the forts by means of saps—slow and weary work, but sure to be more effective than direct attacks, and to cause far smaller loss of life to the besieging army. The fall of Przemysl rendered available for further operations in the Carpathians a Russian army of more than 100,000 men. What was more, it secured for the Russians full freedom in using an excellent system of railways covering the quadrangle between Lewow, Stryj, Jaslo and Rzeszow.

There was vain talk now of a Russian capture of Krakow, of overleaping the Carpathians, of the roads to Berlin and Vienna being open, of the elimination of Austria as a factor in the war, and of the probability of Austria concluding a separate peace. Vain as were these expectations, the result was of substantial value. In itself the Austrian defeat was on so vast a scale—not less than 2,500,000 fighting men being engaged from first to last—and the battles for it were so gigantic that, judged by any standards in history, the campaign around this fortress ought to rank as one of the war's greatest events. In comparison with this, and with battles that had been fought around Lemberg, Grodek, Rawka-Ruska and Tomaszow, most of the famous earlier battles in history were trifling.

The fortresses of Belgium that fell in August, 1914, had fallen swiftly, before the most effective machinery of attack that ever approached a fortified place, and before the most efficient organization that ever carried on a siege with the rapidity of a bombardment and the precision of clockwork. Przemysl was reduced slowly, with infinite patience, and without the use of heavy howitzers and a clockwork system which were all on the side of the defenders. Its fall was evidence that persistence and courage still could work against the most perfect fortress defenses possible to the whole art of war. The siege was remarkable in that throughout its duration the Russian commander had to wage a double war—that within the fortress zone, and that against four successive relief attempts from German and Austrian armies from without. It was twice interrupted,

AUSTRIANS LEAVING PRZEMYSL AND RUSSIANS ENTERING IT

and once entirely broken off. It thus became difficult to compare its duration with that of other sieges. Altho the place was first attacked in the opening days of September, it was not systematically bombarded till September 20; its complete investment did not take place until later, and then for a month nothing like a state of siege existed. Its defenders, meanwhile, had been able to replenish their stores. During December pressure from within and without brought a pause in the operations, and for a while the Russians, without actually loosening their grasp, were on the defensive. The final operations began in January and led slowly up to the capture of the outer forts on March 19.

As an achievement, the capture of Przemysl in three months of unhindered effort, in the depth of winter, by a force inferior to the besieged in armament and technical ability stood out as evidence of Russian military virtue. Until Przemysl fell, there could be no safe Russian advance southward into the Carpathians for fear of an advance on the fortress from Krakow, eighty miles to the west. Likewise, any Russian plan to move on Krakow was held in check by fear of an Austrian advance over the Carpathian passes. But with Przemysl taken, the Russian point of weakness was turned into a point of strength from which the Czar's armies could move safely west against the Germans and south against Hungary. The Russians were gainers by much more than the release of the 100,000 or more men employed in the operation, for at least twice that number were freed from the duty of bolstering up the Russian line. In addition the Russians gained storehouses and a distributing point for munition, more favorable in some respects than Lemberg, and possession of an uninterrupted line of railroad from Tarnow in the west.

Przemysl was founded in the eighth century, and rose to some importance in the Middle Ages. Most of its population was annihilated in the seventeenth century by inroads of Tartars from the south, Cossacks from the east, and Swedes from the north. Its population in 1900 was 46,000, one-third of whom were Jews. The town is picturesquely situated on the San about 140 miles east of Krakow. On a hill above it are ruins of an old castle said to have been built by Casimir the Great. The Austrian Government from 1890 to 1900 spent over $5,000,000 on its twelve permanent forts, with double that number of lunettes looking toward the north and east.

Around the northern plain of Hungary from Pressburg, on the Danube near Vienna, to Orsova, on the Danube facing Roumania, stretch the Carpathians in a widespread arc. East and north of the Danube for about 800 miles they form for that region the boundary of Hungary. The hollow of this arc, and the most favorable points of approach into these mountains, lie south toward Hungary. Troops from the north, or from the convex side, the side from which the Russians had to come, faced the least favorable passes, and operated with the least shelter from biting winds. While the average height of the Carpathians is low, they are lofty enough to check blizzards and ice-winds from Russia and so to deflect them from Hungary. Warm southern breezes are caught and broken among these mountains and so prevented from reaching into Galicia. The Carpathians form the eastern wing of the great central mountain system of Europe. Steep and craggy along their northern expanse, they fall away toward the south in lesser groups with broken, sloping plateaus. Except for parts of their eastern ramifications, which belong to Roumania, the range lies within Austro-Hungarian territory. They attain their greatest height in the Hohe Tetra group, near the center of the range, just east and south of Krakow. Here also they have their greatest width. The passes vary in length from 7 to 230 miles. Peaks rise to 8,000 feet; the Gerlsdorfer, the highest, reaching to 8,737 feet.

The Carpathians have no formations to compare with Alpine groups, or with our own Rockies, but there are innumerable peaks, which vary in altitude from 5,000 to 7,000 feet. Because of the involved character of the passes, they have been for ages effective barriers against invaders. They separate Hungary from other States—Moravia, Silesia, Galicia, Bukowina, Moldavia, and Roumania. Some of the most destitute people in the world live in this mountain range and on its forest-covered sides, mostly Polish Slavs with homes on bleak, northern exposures, a people almost in subjection to the Magyars of the south. The Carpathians are richer in metallic ores than any other mountain group in Europe. Gold, silver, copper, iron, lead, coal, petroleum, salt, zinc, and other minerals are mined there.

Along the Galician front of the Carpathians the position of the Russians about the first of the year 1915 was one of distinct advantage. The lines of the San and Dniester, in themselves would have been sufficient for mere defense, or for a war which aimed primarily at attrition. But instead of that, the Russians were holding in Galicia all the passes leading to Hungary. From the eastern part an invasion could be contemplated only in cooperation with Roumania.

For a purely Russian invasion the natural route was further west on the road followed in 1849 when Hungary was saved to Francis Joseph I by Russian intervention. That road leads through passes around Dukla. Prolonged siege-warfare is impossible in the Carpathians. Trenches could be used for the protection of particular positions, but there could be no continuous lines of trenches.

About January 23 Teutonic forces began an advance on the passes along a front of over 200 miles, from the Dukla to the Kirlibaba. After the Teutonic failure in front of Warsaw, attacks round the Dukla and the Lupkow Pass lost their intensity, but an offensive by Teutonic forces in the east was being prest with vigor. One Austro-German army advanced through the Uzsok toward Sambor, a second through the Vereczke and Beskid passes toward Stryj, a third across Wyszkow toward Dolina, a fourth across the Jolonica toward Delatyn and Nadvorna, and a fifth across the Kirlibaba and Dorna Vatra passes into the Bukowina. Only the last two succeeded in reaching their objectives; the others, despite desperate efforts, failed to get north beyond the crest of the mountains. The eastern groups reached Stanislau on February 21, and followed the railway toward Kalisz, pressing in a northerly direction toward the Dniester.

In the Uzsok Pass late in January snow lay several feet deep, while in the valleys roads were covered with mud and slush. Heavy transports had so broken up the roads as to put them almost beyond repair. Only severe frost could save them. Caterpillar-wheels could do good work on muddy roads, but could not be used on snow. Instead sledges had to be put under wheels, guns taken off and transported on other sledges. Sometimes an army would get on to a piece of ground where neither sledge nor wheel would work—for example, on a steep slope where the road was under ice, and neither nailed boots nor "roughed" hoofs would obtain a foothold. Men had to crawl round such places while leading horses after them. When they reached some higher level they had to pull the transport wagons up with ropes.

Under such conditions transporting even small guns was an arduous task, and shells could not be fired at the rate of thousands a day, as they sometimes were in other theaters of this war. Infantry attacks were in most cases difficult. It was almost impossible to remain unseen in the snow. Against white backgrounds men made excellent targets, whatever the color of their uniforms. Nights, even when there was no moon, were bright from the light reflected by the snow. Where there was no snow, entrenching was difficult, because, even if the surface was soft, the earth below was frozen. When the Austro-German campaign in the Carpathians began, each pass was practically an isolated theater of war; lateral connections had to be established between troops operating in various passes. Because of the great danger of becoming isolated and encircled, each corps had to follow carefully the general trend of events in its own neighborhood.

The Austro-German armies opened attacks against the passes along a line of over two hundred miles. Between January 26 and February 6 Russian corps operating in the Lupkow were said to have made prisoners of 170 officers and 10,000 of the rank and file, but the Austrians still retained their hold on heights round Wola Michowska, east of Lupkow, and it was not until March 11 that the Russians took Smolnik and Lupkow. After a three-days' battle (January 23–26), the Austrians had captured the Uzsok, the ground round the Uzsok being such that it could not be held against a numerically superior enemy. Practically any position could be turned. The pass itself rises over 2,500 feet, and is closely surrounded on all sides by mountains between 3,000 to 4,500 feet high. The slopes were covered by thick woods, under cover of which it was not possible to advance, even in the snow, without being seen. Positions on the southern side did not offer to the invader favorable fields of fire, the road and railway both following a winding, narrow depression, which was steep toward the Hungarian plain. In about twelve miles the road drops almost 1,500 feet. The Austro-German attack on the Uzsok was prest with greater insistence than were the attacks made afterward on passes west of it. From the Uzsok the forces could threaten railway communication by way of Sambor between Lemberg and Przemysl.

IN THE EAST, NEAR EAST, AND SOUTH

On February 6 one of the most desperate battles yet fought in the Galician zone began in front of the Russian positions at Kozlowa. The Teutons tried to take the position by storm. On February 7 no fewer than twenty-two attacks had been delivered. Whenever the Teutons gained a footing, they were dislodged by furious counter-attacks with the bayonet. Attacks of this sort were repeated for the next few weeks. The last to be made before the fall of Przemysl had changed the whole character of the fighting in the Carpathians.

FIELD-MARSHAL VON EICHHORN, MURDERED IN KIEFF IN 1918

Eichhorn was one of Hindenburg's lieutenants in the east. He was made military governor in the Ukraine in 1917. Exercising his power arbitrarily, he was assassinated by a Russian who threw a bomb at him while he was going home in Kieff

Meanwhile, the district of the Pruth in the Bukowina, or the Pokuce-Bukowina sector, had acquired significance. Hardly any Austrian troops then remained in the Bukowina. In January Russian troops advanced in the southwestern corner and at the same time toward the Transylvanian frontier. From Gora Humora they marched toward Kimpolung over passes rising to 2,000 feet and between mountains ranging above 5,000 feet. The advance ceased about January 21 when an Austrian army of 50,000 men was heard of as approaching from Transylvania. The Russian garrison of Czernowitz, altho it numbered not more than a few thousand, sent help to their retreating comrades, and next day the whole Russian division withdrew from Czernowitz eastward. During six days a desperate battle raged between Nadvorna and Kolomea—the Austrians having brought by railway across the Jablonica a powerful train of artillery. The Russians threw fresh troops into the town, but were not able to hold it long and then a battle began

120

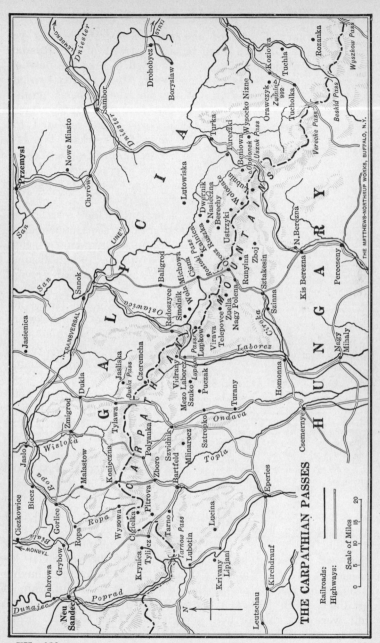

THE CARPATHIAN PASSES

Railroads:
Highways:

Scale of Miles

THE MATTHEWS-NORTHRUP WORKS, BUFFALO, N.Y.

in the broad valley between the two Bystrzycas and the Dniester. Between February 21 and March 4, the Russians captured 153 officers and 18,522 of the rank and file of the Austrian army.

With the coming of March a much more important engagement was developed in the west. As soon as Przemysl fell the investing troops were sent to reinforce the Russian army threatening Hungary from across the Carpathians. The surrender became the signal for a rigorous offensive along the Dukla-Turka line, where the Grand Duke had concentrated a powerful army destined to secure possession of the Central passes, and then descend into the Hungarian plain. This offensive had in fact existed all through the month, the battle-line having been advanced as far as the line extending from Regetow to Stropko, and thence to Wolosake and Bukowiec, four miles north of the Uzsok Pass. During the first week in April the right wing, advancing more rapidly than the center and left, pushed the Austrians back through the Dukla Pass, and reached the valley of the Ordava at Stropko, large captures of prisoners being made on the way. The advance down the Laborocz river for more than ten days was slow. Severe fighting took place round Meso Laborcz, the Austrians trying to hold the Russians from the railway which follows the valley down to Homona. But their counter-attacks were repulsed, and the Lupkow and upper Laborcz passes were soon in Russian hands.

Further east, after dislodging the enemy from fortified positions on the upper San, the Russians fought their way slowly to the Rustoki pass. By the middle of April they secured Carpathian boundary summits and southern slopes, from Regetow to Wolosake, but had still ground to cover before they could reach the valleys of the Ung and Latorcza and so make use of railways leading to Ungvar and Munkacs. The Uzsok, Tucholka, and Beskid passes still remained in possession of the Austrians, whose troops in this direction had been reinforced by Germans from East Prussia, and Hungarians from the reserve army at Temesvar. The Germans were reported to have ten army corps on the Orosz Rusky-Kosziowa line with an equal number of Austrian corps.

IN THE EAST, NEAR EAST, AND SOUTH

The Grand Duke Nicholas and Hindenburg had much the same object in view—to strike at each other's communications, and paralyze their respective offensive movements. The Russians were striving to reach into the Hungarian plain, and by seizing Ungvar and Munkacs cut the Austro-German line of retreat to Budapest. The Germans, operating north of the Carpathians, sought to make their way down the Stryj valley and turn the Russian left flank. Large forces had been massed by both commanders, for they saw the battle might have decisive results. Elsewhere on the extended Eastern Front the opposing forces were awaiting results in the Carpathians. Petrograd, Berlin, Vienna, London, Paris, all saw the meaning of the conflict. The operations at the Dardanelles for a time lost the world's stage to the Carpathians, because the possible downfall of Austro-Hungary seemed a larger thing than the final exit of the Turk from Europe.

In Vienna and Berlin it was well recognized that the battle in the Carpathians marked a crucial point in Teutonic fortunes. More important than the military were the political issues involved. The capture of Przemysl, the attack on the Dardanelles, the far less considerable but apparently distinct, British success at Neuve Chapelle—the cumulative effect of these had been unmistakable in dispatches from Rome, Bucharest and Athens. A decisive Austrian defeat in the mountains would have meant an invasion of Hungary and would have made necessary the evacuation of Transylvania and Bukowina, and the opening of them to Roumanian invasion. An Austrian defeat in the Carpathians would have compelled an immediate withdrawal of Austrian troops from Russian Poland, for Krakow was the gate to Silesia and Berlin.

One mass of the Austrian army was then holding the line before Krakow, not, however, as a protection for Vienna or Budapest, but rather as the first line in the defense of Breslau and Berlin. Hence, if Russian armies could penetrate into Hungary and threaten the Magyar capital, it was almost inevitable that Austrian troops east of Krakow would be recalled and the task of covering Silesia be left to Germany, which would have meant an end to German attacks on Warsaw. Indeed, it would probably have meant the withdrawal of Germans from the Bzura-Rawa line, to the Wartha, the evacuation of Lodz, the relinquishment of Germany's Polish conquests, and would have led to an eventual evacuation of East Prussia, provided pressure from the Allied armies in France and Belgium had created fresh need for German reinforcements in the west.

Once the Russians reached the Hungarian plain, with three railroads and a national highway at their service, and

A VILLAGE ON FIRE ON THE RUSSIAN FRONT

a level plain a hundred miles broad on their front, they could have deployed masses and resumed the tactics which won in Galicia. The key to the whole operation was the Dukla pass, a narrow isthmus between the Galician and the Hungarian plain. Bartfa or Bartfeld, the first Hungarian town the Russians occupied, was only about ten miles south of the watershed which separated Galicia from Hungary. The storm center was on the crest of the Carpathians, where the Russians exerted every effort to gain a passage that would make it safe to invade in force the Hungarian plain. The activity of the Germans in Poland had slackened, partly it was presumed because a considerable force had been drawn off for Hungary. Four army corps, or about 160,000 men, chiefly Bavarians and Saxons, had been brought around by way of Budapest and sent north by rail to Ungvar, opposite the Uzsok pass. This became the chief point of attack. Fighting of the most desperate character went on in this region for a fortnight. A total of 33,000 Austrians had been taken during the last week in March. But the Austrian War Office announced that the Russian attacks had been repulsed and that during March Austrian troops captured 183 officers, 39,042 men and 68 machine-guns.

When the Russians gained the Uzsok in addition to the Dukla and Lupkow passes, they had possession of the Carpathian ridge for over twenty miles, a sufficient base from which to project a triangle of invasion into Hungary. From these passes railroads led down the valley to the Hungarian capital which was less than a hundred miles to the southwest. Such was the high tide of Russian fortunes in the Carpathians that was so soon to ebb at the Dunajec.[11]

[11] Principal Sources : *The Tribune, The Independent,* New York ; *The Morning Post* (London), *The Times* (New York), The *Times* (London), The London *Times'* "History of the War," *The Daily Chronicle* (London), The *Sun,* The *Evening Sun,* "Bulletins" of the National Geographic Society, New York; *The Fortnightly Review* (London), *"Nelson's History of the War"* by John Buchan, The *Daily Mail* (London).

IN THE EAST, NEAR EAST AND SOUTH

Part II

MACKENSEN'S GREAT THRUST AND THE GERMAN INVASION OF RUSSIA

FIELD-MARSHAL VON MACKENSEN

I

MACKENSEN'S BATTLE OF THE DUNAJEC AND THE GERMAN RECAPTURE OF PRZEMYSL AND LEMBERG

April 22, 1915—June 22, 1915

BY the end of April the scene of interest—a scene with portentous outcomes—was transferred from eastern to western Galicia, where the German Staff had concentrated a large Austro-German army, with the object of striking a sudden blow at Russia. The plan had been carefully concealed, the concentration being carried out with the utmost secrecy. Until the storm burst over his head, these preparations for it had been unknown to the Russian commander. Some six weeks had intervened between the fall of Przemysl, on March 22, and the opening, in the first days of May, of this great Austro-German offensive. The Russian invasion of the Carpathians had so far succeeded as to have compelled the Germans to direct against Russia the new forces they had accumulated during the winter. Russia's activities up to this time had provided her Allies in the west several months in which to complete preparations for an offensive of their own. Russia in the Carpathians had helped the Allies, in the same way that Russia in East Prussia had helped them in 1914.

Hindenburg, with Mackensen as his chief support, had conceived this eastern campaign, which began on April 22 and led on August 4 to a success which he had sought in vain in the east for almost a full year—the occupation of Warsaw. Army after army had been organized, concentrated, and launched for Warsaw, but he had failed until now to obtain the results he expected. This was not the fault of his strategy, but was due to the skill of his Slav antagonist, who always knew when to stand and when to retire. Falkenhayn, at this period, had succeeded Moltke as Chief of Staff.

Eight separate armies, collected in three groups, each

group under its own command, were now put to use in another attempt to gain the much-sought prize. The first group, which Hindenburg took under his own direction, consisted of Below's army in Courland, Eichhorn's on the Niemen, and armies commanded respectively by Scholtz and Gallwitz, to whom the Narew River region was given. By the middle of July these armies were deployed on a 300-mile front, extending from the Windau, in Courland, to the lower Vistula, between Thorn and Wloclawek. West of Warsaw, in the salient formed by the middle and lower Vistula, was the group commanded by Prince Leopold of Bavaria, who, besides his own corps, had command of the Austrian army under General Woyrsch, which was operating toward Ivangorod, on the left bank of the river. The third group was under Mackensen, whose army, chiefly composed of Prussian corps, was linked with that of the Archduke Joseph Ferdinand. The sphere of operation of the latter lay between the Middle Vistula and the Bug, the Archduke taking charge of the country west of the Wierpz, while Mackensen's army was deployed east of that river. Further south were the armies of Linsingen and Pffamzer, watching the Russians on the left bank of the Zlota Lipa and Dniester rivers. The length of the entire front occupied by the opposing forces approximated 700 miles, while the strength of the forces engaged was believed to have been not less than two millions on either side.

Mackensen, who was in executive command in the southern region and was now to become a great German military hero, launched his attack from Neusandec against Dimitrieff's left, which was driven out of Gorlice toward Jaslo in an initial success that was followed by an overwhelming attack directed by Mackensen in person, with the Archduke Frederick looking on, against the Russian center at Cziezkowice on the Biala river, the infantry attack being preceded by a heavy bombardment to which the Russians had no guns with which to reply. Driven out of their entrenchments by an artillery bombardment, the Russians fell back behind the Wisloka which, rising in the Carpathians near the Dukla pass, flows nearly parallel to the Dunajec (from which the battle took its name, tho it has sometimes

Territory of

THE BATTLE OF THE DUNAJEC

Railroads
Highways
Heights in Meters
Scale of Miles

THE MATTHEWS-NORTHRUP WORKS, BUFFALO, N.Y.

been known as the battle of Gorlice), till it reaches the Vistula at Ostrowek, about thirty miles above the confluence. Mackensen gave his troops no rest, but sent them promptly as a phalanx after the Russians, who lost heavily in prisoners on their way back to the San. On May 7 the German advance guard crossed the Wisloka at Jaslo, and pushed the retreating Russians ten miles further back across a tributary of the San.

On May 10 the Austro-German army was deployed along this line, a remnant of the Russian army still clinging to the right bank of the Vistula, and yielding ground slower than the center and left wings which were exposed to the

RUSSIANS IN FLIGHT BEFORE GERMAN CAVALRY

full force of the enemy's attack. Another Russian army in the neighborhood of the Lupkow pass began to fall back on the upper San in order to save its communications, which were being threatened by Mackensen's advance. A further advance was made on May 11, Dynow and Sanok being occupied on the 12th, and Dobrovil on the 14th, on which day Mackensen's left wing reached the left bank of the San at Jaroslav north of Przemysl, the latter place being stormed by the Prussian Guard on the 15th. The whole of western Galicia was now in Teutonic possession, and Przemysl in danger of being invested. On May 11 the Austrians crossed the lower Vistula near Mielec and on May 12 reached Kolbuszova. During the next few days the Russians continued their retreat to the north, toward the confluence of the Vistula and San, fighting continuous rear-guard actions. Between May 15 and 17 a battle developed on this front, which was one of the few in this war fought thus far in the open without trenches. In any other war it would have been called a good-sized action. More than 100,000 men and perhaps 350 to 400 guns were engaged in it.

Such were the conditions in the middle of May, so soon after the great Russian forces had seemed about to possess themselves of the plain of Hungary. When the Russians fled east from Jaslo, they uncovered the rear of their Carpathian troops now facing Austro-Hungarian troops at the entrance to the Dukla Pass. Caught thus in a trap large numbers of them were captured, but at least one division cut its way through with heavy loss. A similar fate threatened the Russians in the Lupkow Pass, for the Austro-German advance pushed rapidly east toward the San. The broken Russian forces were approaching their last defensive positions in western Galicia, which were on the line of the San from Przemysl to Jaroslav and from Przemysl to Dubromil in the Carpathians. On May 15 the Austro-Germans had crossed the San north of Jaroslav, penetrated the defensive line at Dubromil, and were close to Przemysl. As yet the pursuit had not slackened. The victors had regained control of both ends of the Dukla and Lupkow passes and the Teutonic armies, which had been fighting on the Hungarian side of the mountains to hold back the Russian advance thus automatically released, were pouring through the passes into Galicia to support armies which had swept east from Tarnow. Thus had ended the Russian campaign in the Carpathians. Only north of the Uszok Pass did the Russians still hold any strong positions in the mountains. Retreat was inevitable.

Meantime, a second Austro-German operation claimed the attention of the Russian command in Galicia. Could this offensive be pushed further with equal success the Russian hold on Galicia would be narrowed to a strip of territory between the Carpathians and the Russian frontier. At first the Austrian forces were brought to a temporary halt south of the Dniester and driven back behind the Pruth. Gathering all their reserves, the Russians had launched a vigorous counter-offensive and the Austrian line was rapidly prest back, so that all danger of an envelopment of the Russians, of a cutting of the life-line in Galicia, was ended. Only the failure of the Austrian offensive in the extreme east saved the Russians, whose hold on central Galicia had become very slight. All of western Galicia, and much of the eastern portion, had been completely lost. In a military sense the Teutonic victory was tremendous. Austrian conditions were now ameliorated and all chance of a Russian invasion of Hungary was ended. The explanation was found primarily in the superiority of German artillery, discipline, and command, combined with a shortage of Russian ammunition. The disaster was evidence of facts demonstrated at Lodz, and the Masurian Lakes—that neither Russian generals, nor Russian soldiers, were a match for the Germans, except in defensive fighting in trenches where the artillery of the two was approximately equal in effective power.

After April 28, when Mackensen first swooped down unexpectedly on the army defending the line of the Dunajec river, the Russians met with nearly unbroken reverses. Mackensen had compelled the Grand Duke Nicholas to withdraw, first from one position, then from another, until nearly the whole of the territory he had conquered in September was won back. Mackensen, directing the Austro-German offensive from its first inception, then determined to break through the Russian center at Przemysl, and, by threatening Lemberg, force the Grand Duke to give up the Dniester line, and withdraw his armies behind the Bug. With this purpose he ordered a demonstration made all along the Dniester, in order to draw away Russian troops from the center, where, astride the Jaroslav-Tarnow railway, he concentrated ten German corps from the flower of the German army. These ten corps were massed in close formation, one behind the other, and formed a phalanx practically irresistible. This phalanx was sent across the San between Sieniawa and Jaroslav, but suffered severely on the way. The Russians for a time held up its advance on the Lubaczowka river, where indecisive trench-fighting proceeded for more than a fortnight. The Austrians crossed the San, midway between Sieniawa and Przemysl, and attempted to march up the Wisnia river to Mosciska, while Mackensen completed the investment of Przemysl on three sides by detaching a force to attack the north forts.

The next few days marked the beginning of one of the most desperate battles of the war. A Russian counter-offensive along the entire line opened on May 21, its aim not to save Przemysl but to render possible the evacuation of the place. Przemysl could not be held, most of its forts having been destroyed by the Austrians before its surrender in 1914. Those which had survived were too well-known to the Germans to be of much value to the defending Russian forces. The new works constructed by the Russians could not be compared in strength with those on which the Austrians had worked for many years. Whatever there was of the fortress of Przemysl was bound to fall before the heavy Teutonic artillery. Its defense now was meant merely to retard the advance of the enemy. The Russian counter-offensive of May 21-25 was therefore planned as an enveloping movement against the envelopers of Przemysl. In face of the superior artillery of the enemy, the Russians were unable to cross the San, so that the advance of the enemy north of Przemysl was not long delayed.

By the end of May only a zone about ten miles wide, running eastward from Przemysl past Mosciska toward Grodek, separated the Sixth Austro-Hungarian Army Corps from the Prussian Guard. Except for that the fortress was surrounded on all sides by the enemy, and on May 30 even the railway line from Przemysl to Grodek came, near Medyka, under fire of heavy Austrian batteries. As early as May 17 Przemysl had been invested from three sides. On May 30 the Bavarians captured Russian positions near Orzechovec, which covered the northern sector of the outer rings of forts. On the same day a violent bombardment was opened and infantry attacks were delivered against the entire northern and northwestern front. On May 31 the Bavarians concentrated again the fire of their heaviest batteries against the forts round Dunkoviczki. The bombard-

ment was continued till 4 P.M., when the fire stopt, and the
enemy's infantry, consisting of one Prussian, one Austrian,
and several Bavarian regiments, proceeded to storm the
forts, which by that time had been changed into mere
wreckage. Their garrison, decimated by the bombardment,
could not resist much longer, and withdrew beyond the
road which runs behind the outer ring of forts round
Przemysl. On the night of June 2-3 the Teutonic allies
entered the village of Zuravica, which lies within the outer
ring of forts.

The evacuation of the fortress occupied the Russians several
days. The only part which they held with considerable
forces was that which covered directly their line of retreat
toward Grodek and Lwow. During the night of June 2-3
the last of their forces withdrew to the east, and early in
the morning of June 3 Bavarians and Austrians entered
Przemysl. Its fall had been unavoidable from the very
moment when the superiority of the Austro-German artillery
and the enormous concentration of their troops had broken
the Russian defenses on the Dunajec-Biala line. In anticipation of the exhaustion of their ammunition supply, the
Russians either destroyed or carried off all serviceable guns
and war material before evacuating Przemysl, which was
now only the shadow of the fortress it had been. No booty
was left behind, and no prisoners were taken. None the less
its fall was a heavy blow to the Russian cause. Inability
to keep what had been conquered two months before could
not fail to have a bad moral effect on an army already de-
jected through defeat. Strategically the fortress in its dismantled condition had ceased to have value. Its fall, however, released the investing Teutonic troops and removed
a menace to Teutonic communications.

On May 27 General Irmanoff, with a Caucasian corps
which had been holding the line of the lower San from the
Vistula to Rudnik, crossed the river, captured Sieniawa,
and threw the enemy back behind the Leg. This movement,
aimed at Teutonic communications, was immediately checked
by Mackensen, who brought up reserves by rail and compelled Irmanoff to re-cross the river. Meanwhile Linsingen,
with the original German army, moved up, and on June 5

captured the bridgehead at Zurawno. Next day a large part of his troops crossed the river, and turned their faces toward Lemberg. The Galician capital was now threatened with a converging attack by Mackensen marching down the Lubaczowka, by Marwitz moving along the Przemysl-Lemberg railway, by Bohm-Ermolli from the direction of Hussakow, and by Linsingen.

The Grand Duke saw his danger, and met it with decision. Concentrating against Linsingen, he attacked on June 8, and after a three-days' battle drove him across the Dniester with heavy loss—15,000 prisoners and a quantity of war material being left in Russian hands. On June 10 the Russian army was successful in a series of engagements along the line of the Dniester and on the Przemysl-Lemberg railway it thrust back a strong attack by von Marwitz. The tide seemed to be turning in favor of the Russians, but on June 13 Mackensen, always alert and ready to pounce, began a fresh attack with reinforced troops on a forty-mile front and the Russians, after an obstinate resistance, gave way. The primary cause of the German success was numerical superiority over the Russian artillery. The Germans and Austrians had probably brought into the field as many as 4,000 guns, while the Russians seemed not to have had more than a third of that number. Without guns and ammunition the rifle and bayonet were powerless. The fire of big guns decided the battle before the infantry advanced.

While these astounding events had been taking place in western Galicia, the Russian army had retired from the Bukowina as the Austrian right wing invaded it, but now it suddenly resumed the offensive, crossed the Dniester in force near Zalesczcki, attacked and defeated the Austrians in the neighborhood of Horodenka, and drove them back to the Pruth, capturing, it was said, 20,000 prisoners on the way, and reoccupied Nadvorne. Thus Mackensen's victory, disastrous as it was to the Russian plan of campaign, was not yet decisive. The Russians had been defeated but not beaten. As their armies were still "in being" this reverse could do little to relieve the pressure on Germany from the Allies in the west. If German troops were to be detached from the east to the west, or if Austrian troops were to be sent to the Italian frontier, this could only be done by weakening the line of defense in the east at some point where troops were necessary to oppose another possible Russian invasion. Herein lay the significance of the intervention at this time of Italy (May 25, 1915), which promised also, it was believed, to bring Roumania into the war-arena as soon as her crops were gathered. Between them the two powers could place and maintain in the field a fighting force of a million and a half of men. So great a reinforcement, thrown into the scale at such a time, could not fail to weigh heavily on the side of the Allies.

There was something colossal in this battle of Galicia, of

A VILLAGE FIRED BY GERMAN SHELLS

which the western world heard little in detail at the time, and which came usually to bear the name of the battle of the Dunajec. Germans and Austrians had thrown a million or more men into it, and so had the Russians. Each had been bringing forward fresh units daily, Germans transferring troops from the Western Front. The Kaiser himself was on the San, urging his soldiers and preparing to change the disposition of his armies, as soon as Italy should reach a decision. The battle had raged for days with great intensity. The Germans, during a fortnight, fired two to three million shells. German prisoners declared that the plan was to expel the Russians from Galicia at any cost, and then fling the new Teutonic force across Europe to pierce the Allied front in the west. Hindenburg was reported actually to have been on the Western Front preparing for an attack to be made there later. In spite of the success, the Teutonic losses had been heavy. During the first four days of a three weeks' battle, they were said to have averaged about 10,000 a day, some days amounting to 30,000 and even 40,000 were named. In several regiments not more than one company was left. In all they may have lost a quarter of their infantry, including 40,000 prisoners.

Until the first week in June, the battle continued with undiminished vigor between the Vistula and the Nadvorna region. On the left bank of the lower San, Russian troops pierced German lines and captured a position. But they had lost Przemysl. As a result of four weeks of vigorous offensive, the Germans had cleared the whole Carpathian barrier, driven the Russians into the Dniester plain, and behind the San, regained the entrance to passes on the Galician side of the mountains, and won back something like 10,000 square miles, and so had completely wrecked the Russian campaign in the Carpathians. Germany had saved Austria, turned back a Russian host on the point of entering Hungary and retaken an area about as large as Belgium. Austrian and German reports claimed the capture of 175,000 prisoners. All things considered, Russia could hardly have lost fewer than a quarter of a million men, an enormous amount of artillery and arms, and quantities of other military material. She had lost the hard-won fruits of nine months of fighting.

The German troops in this offensive were new formations who had been trained all winter and were just taking the field, stiffened by veterans of the Lodz and Mazurian Lakes campaign. The Germans used artillery in greater quantities than ever before in the east. To face this storm Russia had little artillery and less ammunition. There was even a suggestion that in many cases ammunition had failed her entirely, that threatened hostilities between Japan and China had held up shipments Japan was to send to Russia. For months Archangel had been icebound. The Russian High Command seemed to have attached too much importance to forcing the Carpathians and too little to protecting the flank facing Krakow. German commanders had waited until Russia had sent her available reserves into the mountains and then they struck. The whole blow was well timed and instantly effective.

What was most interesting now was whether Germany would send some of her victorious troops against the Italians or would continue her drive in the east. When Przemysl surrendered to the Russians two months before and the Russian van pushed through the middle Carpathian passes and threatened the Hungarian plain, Vienna had begun to count Galicia as a sort of Lombardy and Venice—another pearl taken from the crown of the Dual Monarchy. But now Galicia was almost redeemed and Przemysl had been evacuated before the Teutonic allies isolated it.

Soon Lemberg also fell, the Russians evacuating it, so that the Austrians might obtain no booty; but the evacuation had been made inevitable by the general retirement of the Russian line. Great rejoicings took place in Berlin and Vienna. Lemberg was by far the largest city that had been captured by the Allies since the war began. Its military importance was chiefly that of a great railway center. No fewer than eight lines radiated from it and connected it with parts of Galicia and adjoining territory. Just as its capture by the Russians had enabled them to conquer two-thirds of the province, so its recapture promised to carry the fighting back to the Russian frontier. The Germans and Austrians had been abundantly supplied with ammunition; they literally sprayed the Russians with shells.

The recapture of Przemysl and of Lemberg had apparently been assured when Japan at this time made new demands on China, accompanied by an ultimatum. Up to the middle of February she had sent to Russia over the trans-Siberian railway more than $40,000,000 worth of munitions, but when China demurred to her sudden and extreme demands, there rose unexpectedly the possibility of a second war in the Far East, and from that time the exports to Russia of guns and shells from Japanese factories were suspended since Japan had to make provisions for her own needs in the contingency of a war with China. The Chinese Government yielded and then, that danger passed, the export of munitions to Russia was resumed, and apparently in large volume, but they arrived too late to save Russia. Dispatches from Tokio told of great accumulations at Vladivostok of munitions for Russia. Shipments arriving at that port were, in fact, in excess of the forwarding capacity of the trans-Siberian railway.

That Russia could not be disposed of by her antagonists until her armies had been beaten and exhausted was a lesson that had come down from the Napoleonic wars in eastern Europe and especially from the ill-fated expedition to Moscow. Russia's territory was too vast and her chief centers were too far apart and too isolated to give any decisive character to an invasion. Warsaw might be abandoned under pressure from the line of Brest-Litovsk, behind which the mobilization of August, 1914, was effected, but that would not have meant the elimination of Russia as a highly influential factor in the military situation. The Teutonic success on the whole could not yet be said to mean much in solid advantage. A longer line had been gained, a weaker front, a wasted province, and a ruined city, but for those gains a heavy price had been paid in lives sacrificed, stores of ammunition consumed, positions undermined or sacrificed on the French and Italian fronts. Moreover, the stubborn Russians were certain to return. But Germany was exultant. "Calais will follow," said some of the notes dropt into French and British lines by German airmen. In Berlin the popular enthusiasm was shown in the cry, "On to Paris!" which was heard everywhere, while Herman Ridder in his *New Yorker Staats-Zeitung* declared that "the way to London lies through Lemberg." It appeared that these wild rejoicings were due, less to the value of Austria's recovered province, than to a belief that this was only a prelude to more decisive events.

Russia had now surrendered about all the territorial advantages she had gained since the beginning of the war. Altho far from eliminated, she was reduced to a position where her forces, for the present at least, were of less strategical value than they formerly were to the Allies in the west. Russia's shortage of ammunition was in due course to be repaired. For months she had had no new supplies, but there were new supplies on the way from America. By June 25 twenty thousand American freight-cars and four hundred American locomotives were due at Vladivostok from the United States. These would relieve the congestion at that port caused by supplies sent to Russian armies at the front. Vladivostok would now supply the needed guns, rifles, and ammunition. Armored cars were needed, hundreds of them, but Vladivostok would supply these also. The Russians needed dynamite, cotton, and food, and

A RUSSIAN BRIDGE ON THE KALISH-WARSAW LINE DESTROYED
IN THE RUSSIAN RETREAT

Vladivostok hoped to see them get all these. Guns, rifles, and ammunition were arriving from Japan and the United States and armored motor-cars by hundreds, mostly by way of Seattle, on vessels sailing direct to Vladivostok. Cotton was coming from New York by way of Panama in such quantities that, more than anything else, it had caused that condition of congestion at Vladivostok which had forced Russia to place rush orders for more locomotives and cars. Cotton in bales was long piled high on the hills back of the city, waiting to be forwarded to Moscow for manufacture into blankets and uniforms. From Great Britain came guns, from France ammunition, from the United States nine-inch guns, and an amazing quantity of barbed wire to protect trenches. Ships had been arriving at Vladivostok in such numbers and with such rapidity that they could not be accommodated at docks, and a temporary enlargement of the port had been effected. Huge gangs of men were put to building pontoon-piers and making shift-docks. Vessels, unable to squeeze into piers, were forced to tranship cargoes to lighters, but a shortage of lighters made even that method of discharging slow and the Russians had to build more lighters. Vladivostok, the Russians thought, would save the day for their armies.

The Russians claimed, and perhaps with truth, that in the months of May and June the Germans lost more than 250,000 killed and wounded men, besides prisoners who fell into their hands. Russia for the moment had lost Galicia, but the Germans had gained no Sedan. Their battles seemed like Pyrrhic victories. The Grand Duke Nicholas always avoided decisive contests; he held on to positions long enough to compel his adversary to deploy his forces, and then retired protected by rear-guards. He repeated these tactics, not once, but continuously, during this year's campaign. The skill with which he maneuvered his armies was beyond praise. There is no more difficult task for a commander than to withdraw his army from the battle-line without committing it to a decisive encounter, but this was what the Russian generalissimo did with unfailing success.

The Germans were no nearer their goal in August, 1915, than they were twelve months before, but day by day were receding from it, for a fifth ally, Time, was beginning to assert its influence, and promising in another year to be the dominant factor in the gigantic war problem. Mackensen's success on the Dunajec, and his advance through Galicia, were due to his having brought up an overwhelming mass of heavy and light guns against positions occupied by the army of Demitrius. Without those guns, and the ammunition required for their service, his "phalanx" would never have hacked its way to Przemysl and Lemberg.

As the Germans pursued their advances, the Russians

THE GERMAN INVASION OF RUSSIA

continued to retire. Rear-guard actions cost the Germans heavy losses, with no appreciable gains. There was a set purpose about this steady Russian retirement. Retirement had never in history brought failure to Russia, but quite the contrary. The Russian spirit differed from that of western nations. It was not blunted by apparent retrogression, but consolidated and confirmed. Russia laughed at the Germans whom they now drew steadily on, who dared not go back, and who had to fight, when, how, and where it pleased Russia to have them fight. This had been the fate of all invaders of Russia from Charles XII of Sweden to Napoleon. Such was the philosophy with which many Entente observers found comfort at this time. They did not know—no one knew, and few dreamed—that before another year had passed all calculations deduced from past experience would be thrown to the winds by a revolution, in which the Czar was to be dethroned and put to death, and men called Bolsheviki were to come into power.[1]

[1] Principal Sources: *The Fortnightly Review*, The *Daily Chronicle*, London; The *Times*, The *Tribune*, The *Literary Digest*, New York; The *Times*, London.

POLISH PEASANTS IN RETREAT
The period illustrated is the summer of 1915, after the fall of Warsaw

II

THE FALL OF WARSAW

August 4. 1915

WHILE the Germans were making almost uninterrupted progress in Galicia, Mackensen was preparing to strike the third German blow at Warsaw. He determined to move northward into Poland between the Vistula and the Bug with the intention of reaching Warsaw on the right bank of the middle Vistula. Russian Poland in this war had often been described as like a nut held within a cracker, one jaw of which was East Prussia, the other Galicia. In a military sense, Hindenburg was the upper, Mackensen the lower jaw. Germany's gigantic movement in the east had thus far been an effort to bring these jaws together, and so crush Russia's military force. Had Germany been wholly successful, the plan would practically have destroyed the Russian military power; Russian troops west of the Bug, defending Warsaw and holding the railroads to Moscow, Petrograd, and Kiev, would either have been pounded to nothing or been captured. Little hope could then have remained to France or Great Britain of ultimate victory, for should Hindenburg and Mackensen then go west, little chance would have been left of freeing Belgium and liberating northern France.

Such was the German view and it pointed to what the Germans really expected. Germany was more confident of success in July, 1915, than she had ever been since before the battle of the Marne. Should the Grand Duke be able, however, to escape from the jaws of the cracker; should his army elude destruction as Joffre's had done in August, 1914; should he get his main forces safely behind the Bug, then, while the Germans would win a considerable advantage and much territory, their hope of a real decision would have been shattered, for once behind the Bug, the Russians would have been beyond the peril of an envelopment. The very vastness of Russian territory precluded a successful operation. Only complete Russian disaster could satisfy German necessities.

The weakness of the Russian position in Poland had revealed itself as a precarious salient, which depended on the integrity of two long railway lines which connected Warsaw with Petrograd, Moscow, and Kiev. In front of each lay the enemy—from Mlaw to Shavli in the north, from Sandomierz to the Dniester in the south. At the apex stood Warsaw, the key of the Vistula. German armies were already pressing northward against the southern line. It was Hindenburg's business to balance this movement by a descent from East Prussia upon the northern sector. What had happened on the Dunajec, the Wisloka, and the San would happen on the Narew, the Niemen, and the Bug, once the railways were cut, and troops in the point of the salient were isolated, for it would be a marvel if they should be able to extricate themselves from such a trap. Warsaw would have to fall, and then would no longer be a Russian city, but a German rear-guard one.

But Falkenhayn, then chief of the German Staff, to whom Hindenburg was chief executive officer, aimed at more than the conquest of a capital or a river line, or the occupation of a few thousand more square miles of Polish ground. His business was to shatter the Russian armies. To this end he fell back upon Germany's favorite enveloping strategy. His scheme was not over-confident. Germany had behind her all the advantages of speedy transport. Her shell supplies were still enormous, she had lost few guns, and the gaps in her ranks had been filled up from reserves. The reinforce-

WARSAW BRIDGE WRECKED BY THE RUSSIANS BEFORE THEY
EVACUATED THE CITY

ments necessary for the great movement were obtained in some degree by drafts from the Western Front, but mainly by means of four new corps raised in Pomerania, Schleswig, and North Prussia and concentrated at Thorn. The German army which faced Russia after the fall of Lemberg was probably the most formidable yet launched against the Allies. The great onslaught involved every army on the Eastern Front, from the Baltic to the Bukowina; but for the moment the really vital attacks were made against the two lateral railways.

Mackensen, who was soon to be made a field-marshal, had proved himself one of the ablest of the German generals. A Saxon by birth, he had risen, like Kluck, to high command by sheer merit. He had been responsible for the great offensive of November, 1914, which gave Germany western Poland, and gravely threatened Warsaw. Hindenburg had accustomed the world to look for sledge-hammer blows, and much of the new offensive was after the true Hindenburg fashion; but there were elements of ingenuity which were not in his manner, and credit for these and for skilful tactical handling belonged to Mackensen. Germany never played her traditional game to more brilliant effect than in the movement now begun. It was more dramatic than her great sweep on Paris in August, for then she was working in the heyday of a first enthusiasm, whereas now she was stemming a hostile tide after long months of drawn battles. An army composed of forty-five corps opened battle on a front stretching over perhaps a thousand miles. In the extreme north a group of six army corps began on July 13 a second offensive against the Baltic provinces, while on the southern flank four army corps advanced against the line of the Niemen. The operations west of the Kovno-Grodno line were, however, at this time of only secondary importance.

At least three army corps stood in front of Warsaw, between the Vistula and the Pilica. Toward the end of the month they were reinforced by three more German and three Austro-Hungarian divisions, these six divisions being not included in the estimate of forty-five army corps. Between the Pilica and the Roumanian frontier stood the "southern armies," which had borne the whole brunt of

© PAUL THOMPSON.   THE KAISER AND HIS STAFF OFFICERS ON THE EASTERN FRONT

The General at the right is Field Marshal von Mackensen

VII.

battle between May 2 and July 9. The strength of these six armies was put at not less than twenty-four army corps. The advance in the Baltic provinces took place in the second half of July and had for its aim to tie up Russian forces in that region and to prepare the ground for an enveloping movement from the north against the line of the Niemen. But the course which events assumed in the south deprived operations in Lithuania of immediate importance.

It was soon apparent that, if Hindenburg forced the Russian defenses on the Narew, and Mackensen reached the Ivangorod-Cholm railway, the Warsaw salient would become untenable. The Grand Duke would have no alternative but to abandon the Polish capital, give up the line of the Vistula, and draw his army back behind the Bug. Threatened by an all-around enveloping movement, which had been carefully prepared and was being energetically carried out, Warsaw was in greater danger than it had been at any time during the campaign. Vigorous counter-attacks might save the situation, but it was doubtful if the Russian troops, after their recent reverses, were in a mood to resume the offensive. What was more probable was that the Grand Duke would sacrifice Warsaw to save his army.

Before an Austro-German advance coming from the region south of Warsaw, the powerful Russian fortress of Ivangorod interposed itself midway between the metropolis of the Poles and the north Galician frontier—a stronghold of the first class, and forming the center of a defensive line guarding the southern approach. Especially important was it since it stood at the junction of railways from Warsaw south, one of which ran southeast to Lublin, and the other southwest to Kielce. Ivangorod was 143 miles north-northwest of Przemysl, more than 60 miles from the Austrian border and about 60 miles southeast of Warsaw. It was situated at the confluence of the Wieprz and the Vistula—the Vistula there of sufficient size to be navigable for large boats. Nine permanent works stood on the right bank of the Vistula and three on the left. Ivangorod, with Brest-Litovsk, Novo-Georgievsk, and Warsaw, formed the celebrated Polish quadrilateral, the kernel of the Russian scheme for the defense of their frontier lands.

The skies soon darkened for Russia along the whole front. General Kirchbach, commanding a mixed Moravian, Silesian, and Galician corps in Boehm-Ermolli's army, forced a crossing of the upper Bug at Sokal, altho a few days later General Brusiloff managed to clear most of the right bank as far up as Kamionka. In front of Warsaw, where the enemy's strength was lowest, the Blonie line was still held, but events south and north were speedily making it a position of danger. The advance of Mackensen and the Archduke Joseph was bound very shortly to make Ivangorod untenable, and the shortening of the Bzura front turned the flank of the Radom position.

Far in the north there loomed up now a peril more remote, but not less deadly. On the 14th the left of Below's army crossed the Windawa near Kurschany, and was sweeping round toward Tukkum, the half-way house between Windau and Riga, while his center was in front of Shavli, with the great guns of the East Prussian fortresses in support. Tukkum and Windau fell on July 20, and the advance on Mitau began, while the center was now east of Shavli. Farther south, on the Dubissa, the Russian line was forced, and Eichhorn's left wing advanced on Kovno. The factories and depots at Riga began to move their goods and plants to the interior. Below was within twenty miles of Riga, and Eichhorn within sixty of Vilna. To extricate great armies from a narrowing salient along three railways, two of which might any day become impossible, in the face of an enemy so amply equipped, might well seem to demand a miracle for success. It meant that wearied troops must hold for a space of weeks the sides of the salient while the front retired. The easier path seemed to be to trust to fortresses, and hold out in the triangle, in the hope of some sudden gift of fortune such as even strong men sometimes flatter their souls may come.

On July 19 Below began to move from the Dubissa toward the Aa and Swenta, his right and left flanks covered by large bodies of cavalry. On this day Gallwitz crossed the Narew near Pultusk, which was the signal for the Grand Duke to begin an evacuation of Warsaw. Next day reports showed that a general retirement of the Russian forces was in progress all along the front. On the 21st Russian troops, covering the western approaches to Warsaw, fell back to the Blonie-Nadarzyn line, and on the same day a division of Woyrsch's army crossed the Vistula at a point fifteen miles south of Ivangorod. On the 23d, after storming the bridgeheads of Rashan and Pultusk, Gallwitz crossed the Narew in force. On the 25th, Below in Courland reached Ponievitz, and Scholtz, coming into line with Gallwitz, crossed the Narew near Ostrolenka. On the 26th and two following days the Russians made a series of determined counter-attacks against the whole line of German troops on the left bank of the Narew, delaying their advance and inflicting heavy losses.

In these last days of July some reassurance came to those who for weeks had lost all hope of saving Warsaw. The resistance shown by the Russian troops in the south and north alike started fresh courage, but suddenly there came a dramatic end to these hopes and in a way least expected. The Vistula had seemed to offer sufficient protection against the west, but, with the exception of districts around the bridgeheads of Warsaw and Ivangorod, it was held by comparatively weak forces. Permanent bridges spanned the river between those two towns, the river being between 600 and 1,200 yards wide and from 10 feet to 15 feet deep, its banks fairly high, the eastern higher than the western. The valley was only a few miles wide. Wooded hills approached in many places close to the river. Both the roads and the railway which connected Warsaw and Ivangorod avoided the immediate neighborhood of the river. Few villages lay on the eastern bank for the fifty miles which between Warsaw and Ivangorod formed the western front of the Russian salient in Poland.

The unforeseen event occurred in the success of the Germans in crossing the Vistula about twenty miles north of Ivangorod, the German commander having decided to force the Vistula by crossing in the neighborhood of the mouth of the Radomka. By the evening of July 28 his preparations were completed, everything having been arranged secretly for a night attack and arranged down to the smallest detail. Next day troops were ordered to reach the shore of the Vistula at 1.30 A.M. at all points, in order to begin a crossing at once. The Vistula in this region has an average breadth of 1,000 meters. What were the positions of the Russians behind the river, in what strength they stood, and how their forces were divided, were facts unknown to the Germans. As it was necessary for them to strike in the dark, one could appreciate the tension of the situation to the Germans.

At 1.30 A.M. German troops everywhere broke out from their last lines of cover on shore. Heavy pontoons were quickly brought forward, the water entered, and they pushed off, with everything quiet, when suddenly heavy artillery-

THE PUBLIC SQUARE IN WARSAW

fire set in, the attention of Russians on the other shore having been attracted to the boats. German artillery standing in readiness, took up the fire, giving effective protection to the German infantry crossing. The crossing having been effected, battalion following battalion, the dawn came and then the German artillery showed themselves the decisive factor in the fight; they broke the last resistance of the surprized Russians. But heavy fighting still lay before the Germans. Protecting troops close to the shore had thus far been the only ones in force; it still was necessary to defeat the Russian reserves who lay further to the rear. After battles lasting four days, possession of the bridgehead was fully assured, the Russians thrown back from position to position, and their power of attack broken.

In the meantime, Austro-Hungarian troops standing under command of General von Koevess had won a successful battle before Ivangorod. By July 23 the Russians had been driven back on Ivangorod, and on the 24th Koevess was ordered to invest and capture the place, while the Germans advanced on the north wing and forced the passage of the Vistula. The special strength of Ivangorod consisted in the marshy land which protected it on the west and the advanced positions which the Russians had taken up in other parts. The attack was ordered to begin on August 1. Artillery-fire prepared the way. Regiments from Transylvania made a bayonet-attack, and, in spite of a counter-attack, succeeded in holding their ground. Then came the hardest part of the task. The advance had to be carried through the woods to the south where heavy losses were inflicted by machine-gun fire. On the night of August 2 the Russians were driven from points south of the railway line back of the Vistula. Meanwhile, preparations for moving up heavy siege-artillery proceeded. On the 3d Koevess ordered the second advanced position and the inner belt taken with one effort. The troops pushed on and pierced the line. The western part of Ivangorod was taken, and before the heavy siege-artillery could be brought up the Vistula was reached.

As early as July 28, when the Kaiser was holding a council of war to the west of Warsaw, Russian trains bound for Moscow became crowded with Russian refugees. The Grand Duke Nicholas fully recognized the wisdom of allowing Warsaw to be occupied by the Germans in order to avoid subjecting it to the ravages of a siege. Hundreds of thousands of Russian soldiers passed through Warsaw, sometimes to the music of a military band, but more often not, the men well fed, well clad, and the horses in first-rate condition. Peasantry, fleeing before the Germans, appeared in picturesque Polish costumes, giving touches of brightness to scenes which previously had lacked them, charitable people providing public kitchens to supply them with food. In a few days some 350,000 citizens, or more than one-third the entire population, including nearly half of Warsaw's Jewish inhabitants, departed eastward, in ceaseless procession, day and night, moving toward the frontier. Tired, dust-whitened, peasant families, with cattle and portable goods, thronged all roads leading away from Warsaw. Tens of thousands of homes were thus instantly broken up. Men who had believed themselves worth some hundreds of thousands of dollars in June found themselves in July nearly penniless.

Factories were feverishly stript of machinery, owners having been granted free transport eastward for what they could save. Day and night could be heard the roar of dynamited plants, embedded in concrete and too cumbersome to be dismantled and transported. Every fragment of metal was taken away. Newspaper linotype-machines among others were ripped up from floors and carted to Moscow and other towns. Hardly a ton of copper fittings was left in Warsaw. All copper stocks in pipe-factories and plumbing-shops; all the copper used in household ware; all copper of every kind wherever found, was removed and so were stocks of hardware dealers, hospital supplies, and officers' kits.

Warsaw knew no stoppage of activities during that last week-end. Endless columns of laden carts and lorries converged on bridges that crossed the Vistula. Millions of rubles in paper-money and the irreplaceable records of law courts were piled on wagons, guarded by a handful of soldiers. Day and night gangs of soldiers worked briskly stripping mile after mile of copper wire from telegraph-poles. Church doors were flung open and their interiors crowded with weeping and praying Poles and Russians. Among them passed ministering priests in gorgeous robes. Aloft in church-towers huge bronze bells were unslung and then carted away to prevent them from being used as ma-material for Krupp cannon. All church-bells, archives, and treasure; all gem-studded altar pieces; all screens, vest-ments, and icons went across the Vistula and were sent to Moscow. The vault of the Church of the Holy Cross in Kravoski Street was opened and the Sacred Heart preserved there removed. The telephone exchange was dismantled. Dynamos supplying power to street-cars were removed, and so were all wheels and detachable fittings of cars. Crops around Warsaw were destroyed and villages razed to the ground. Two thousand hackney-carriages were driven by their owners across Russia to Moscow, nearly a thousand miles distant.

During the first week of August, the Russian retirement became more pronounced. In Courland, Below, moving on a front of seventy miles, occupied Kupischki, on the

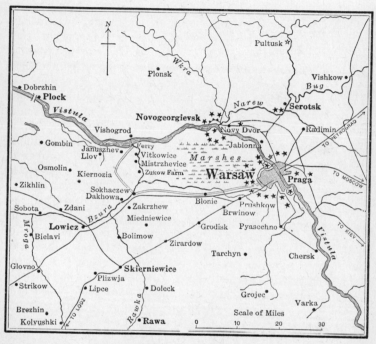

WARSAW AND ITS SURROUNDINGS

Ponievitz-Dwinsk railway. His cavalry reached the neighborhood of Schonberg to the north of the Aa and Swenta rivers from Mitau down to Wilkomir. About this time reinforcements arrived and the Russian commander, taking the offensive, turned on Below, reoccupied Kupischki, and threw the Germans back across the Aa and Swenta. Meanwhile, Gallwitz and Scholtz, advancing from the Narew, and continually pushing back the Russian rear-guards, made further defense of the Warsaw salient impracticable, and on August 3 the Russian army, covering the approaches through the town to Praga, left Prince Leopold of Bavaria free to enter Warsaw on the morning of the 4th. The evacuation had for some time been practically completed.

The final retreat of the Russians was a masterpiece in strategy. It began during the night of August 3-4 and at the northern end of the Blonie lines, the Russians crossing the Vistula on pontoons. By August 4, at noon, there was probably not over one corps left on the west side of the Vistula. Probably the last division left about midnight. At 3 A.M. on August 5 the bridges were blown up. At 6 A.M. the Germans arrived. They had not even been in touch with the Russian rear-guard. There was therefore no last battle before Warsaw.

The capture of Warsaw became for the German soldier another station on his long pilgrimage eastward. He now had before him the prospect of exchanging quarters on the Bzura, which he had occupied in the preceding winter, for some still more desolate place in the plains, forests or marshes of Russia proper. The capture was regarded in England more as an incident than as an event, and from a military point of view was not considered important in a campaign which had for its object, not the occupation of territory, but the destruction of the Russian armies. Hindenburg's plan was to envelop Warsaw by a rapid movement of Gallwitz from the Narew and of Mackensen from Galicia. If these two generals could have met together on the Bielostock-Brest-Litovsk line, while Prince Leopold was playing with the Russian army to the west of the city, the Grand Duke would have been locked up in Warsaw as Marshal Bazaine was locked up in Metz. Here was Moltke's strategy over again. If it had succeeded, it would have meant the doom of the Russian army. Its failure was due to the Russian infantry, who fought with their backs to the wall with magnificent courage. They had little help from artillery, for their guns were overwhelmingly outnumbered, as well as outclassed; while their ammunition supply began to fail just when the pressure of Hindenburg's attacks became most pronounced. In spite of these adverse circumstances, the Grand Duke's rear-guards, fighting with stubborn tenacity, so delayed Gallwitz on the north and Mackensen on the south as to give time for the orderly withdrawal of the army out of the threatened salient, and for the evacuation of Warsaw. Admirably conceived and precisely executed tho it was, Hindenburg's plan failed in the main purpose for which it had been undertaken. Altho Warsaw itself was taken, the Russian army was not.

For the moment Germany had cleared her frontiers and seemed free to turn many army corps westward again to deal with new French forces and the advance guard of

THE SAXON GARDEN IN WARSAW

Kitchener's new men in the spring campaign. She had won a triumph which deserved admiration as a military achievement. But she had settled nothing and a new Russian force was already beginning to gather. As a single performance, the German victory passed all qualification; but what fatally lessened its appeal to the imagination of the world was the fact that after it there came no promise of peace, of truce, or even of parley. For this the Germans held Great Britain's sea power responsible. The German gain was the fact that the winning of Galicia had bound Austria-Hungary closer than ever to the German

Empire and so had banished all hope among the Allies of enticing Vienna or Budapest into a separate peace. Fully as important was the culminating influence of these events on the Balkan countries which were believed then to be about to enter the war. The diplomatic work essential to maintaining neutrality in Roumania, Bulgaria, and Greece had been causing many sleepless nights at the German Foreign Office. If Germany had dispersed, or captured, the bulk of the Russian army, her victory would have surpassed anything in modern history, and would have constituted the gravest defeat the Allied cause had known.

Looking back in August at the course of events since April, it was easy to discover Russia's mistakes. She had been holding an impossibly long line, and her Carpathian advance had made it daily longer and more vulnerable. The Russian front was not the same continuous series of entrenchments as existed in the West. There were gaps in it, such as that between the Niemen and the Narew. In many parts it was terribly thin. The Russian army suffered from lack of mobility. Troops could not be brought up quickly to a threatened point. Each regiment was in effect left alone to repel any attack that might be made on it. The Germans in an advance, by means of admirable railways, could weaken remote parts along the front to strengthen the operative part, but the same tactics were not open to the Russians. Moreover, the Russians lost the advantage of internal lines, while the Germans could operate against a convex front and so had far greater powers of local concentration.

Russia's total of heavy guns was far lower than Germany's. Her field-artillery, excellent in pattern and efficient in gunnery, was poorly supplied with shells and at various times, in the course of the retreat, munitions gave out altogether, and no attempt was made to cope with the fire of the Germans. The Russians were terribly short also of machine-guns, having at most perhaps one to the Germans' four. Many new recruits took their places in the firing-line without rifles. Men often had to wait in trenches under heavy fire till they could get arms from wounded comrades. One entire Siberian division had to face shrapnel attack without a single rifle among them. Field-artillery in one division was limited to two shells a day. When Irmanov's Caucasians fought at Jaslo they were compelled to refrain from a counter-attack because they had only twenty rounds of rifle ammunition per man. In the words of a Russian private: "We had only one weapon, the breast of the living soldier." That this force, which had lost incredibly, and was short of every munition of war, was able to hold the Germans firm, and after the first week to fall back at its own pace, with stubborn rear-guard actions and many successful counter-advances, astonished neutrals. There were no sweeping losses. The few Russian guns taken testified not only to the scarcity of arms, but to the orderliness of

THE GRAND OPERA HOUSE IN WARSAW
This great building, erected in 1833, contains, besides a large theater in which grand opera is presented, a smaller theater for the production of comedies

the retreat. Observers bore witness to the absence of panic or signs of excitement. "If we only had guns," said Russian soldiers, "we should be marching the other way. As it is, we shall soon return."

From the moment when they began their attack on the Dunajec line in early May, until their entrance into Warsaw, almost exactly three months later, the campaign of the Germans represented one continuous attack. Every detail seemed to have been arranged, and once the movement started, men and munitions were fed into the maw of war without intermission until their objective—Warsaw—was attained. The determination and bravery of the German soldiers in those three months of ghastly sacrifice never faltered. But the Germans probably had five shells to the Russians' one. Except for this great superiority, they would not have pushed back either the line of the Narew or the Cholm-Lublin. The situation was that Russia could not convert her resources into ammunition and Germany could. To this fact Germany probably owed her capture of Warsaw. Russia stayed until the last minute and the last shell, and then extricated herself from an extremely dangerous position.

As to responsibility for the defeat, the Russian nation soon passed judgment when radical changes were made in the administration. The aim in these changes was a change of system. At a meeting of the Duma in August, during the time of Russia's worst reverses, sentiment promised the mobilization of the entire national strength. Hardly had the Duma come together when it passed an order affirming an unshakable resolution to "continue the struggle with our faithful Allies until final success is attained and not to conclude peace before victory is complete."[2]

[2] Principal Sources: *The Fortnightly Review* (London), The *Tribune* (New York), The *Daily News* (Chicago), The *Vossische Zeitung*, The *Berliner Morganpost*, German High Command report printed in The *Frankfurter Zeitung*, Associated Press dispatches, The *Economist* (London); The *Evening Post*, The *Journal of Commerce*, New York; The *Times*, The *Morning Post*, London; United Press dispatches, The *Berliner Tageblatt*, The London *Times'* "History of the War," "Nelson's History of the War" by John Buchan.

III

KOVNO, BREST-LITOVSK, AND VILNA FALL—
THE PATHOS OF THE GREAT CIVILIAN
RETREAT—THE GRAND DUKE RELIEVED
OF THE EASTERN COMMAND

August 6, 1915—September 18, 1915

HINDENBURG now transferred his movements from
the Vistula to the Bug, apparently in the hope of
setting another trap at Brest-Litovsk, which lies on the
Bug about 150 miles east of Warsaw. Leaving Below in
Courland, he increased the area of his enveloping movement
by first capturing Kovno east of Warsaw, and the key to the
Russian line of defense on the Niemen. On August 6
Eichhorn, who had been facing the Niemen for six months,
and had now been reinforced with siege guns and material,
arrived before the western defenses of the fortress and
began an attack. Bold advances made by infantry were
first employed to secure observation stations for artillery.
Then followed the installation of guns, which was a very
difficult matter in a country of pathless forests. Fire was
opened with artillery, and, meanwhile, infantry and pioneers worked their way forward in hotly contested battles
lasting night and day: Not less than eight advanced works
were taken by August 15, each a fortress in itself and constructed after months of work. Exceedingly strong counter-
attacks by the Russians against the front and south flank of
the attacking troops were repeatedly repelled, with heavy
losses.

On the 16th the attack was carried close to the line of
permanent fortifications. By artillery-fire, raised to the
highest degree of intensity, and directed with help from
observation-balloons and aeroplanes, the defenders of forts,
connecting lines and intermediate batteries, had been so
badly shaken that a forward assault could be initiated.
Infantry first broke through and then, rolling up the front,

157

stormed the entire line in both directions between the Jezia and the Niemen. Artillery, which was quickly brought up, now undertook the reduction of the main defenses of the west front. After their fall, on the 17th, the artillery attacked the Russian forces retreating on the east bank. Under protection from artillery brought close to the Niemen, the river was crossed under hostile fire, at first by several small detachments and then by stronger forces. Soon the Germans succeeded in getting two brigades across to replace those destroyed by the Russians. In the course of the 17th, the forts on the north front fell, then those on the eastern, and finally those on the entire southern front. In addition to more than 20,000 prisoners, the Germans said they had captured "an incalculable amount of booty," more than 600 guns, including a large number of the heaviest caliber and of modern construction, great masses of ammunition, numberless machine-guns, search-lights, war material of all sorts, automobiles, tires, and provisions "running into millions in value."

Kovno was a first-class fortress, commanding the railway from East Prussia to Vilna, and one of three fortresses which barred the passage of the Niemen, the others being Grodno on the south and Olita in the center. For the time being, the Germans had confined their attention to the northern fortress. The forts encircling Kovno were eleven in number and situated at a distance of two or three miles from the center of the town itself. Three guarded it on the east, one covered the Vilna bridge, and seven protected the southern approaches. Apart from its military importance, Kovno was a large town with a considerable *entrepôt* trade in timber, grain, and other commodities passing from and to Prussia. It had a population in 1913 of nearly 92,810 people, of whom about one-half were Jews. It was founded in the eleventh century, and possest some fifteenth-century churches.

The fall of Kovno was a greater military disaster than Warsaw. Not only had the line of the Niemen been turned, but the road to Vilna was opened. Another German army could therefore be let loose to act against Russian communications with Petrograd and Moscow. But Eichhorn's army had for its objective Vilna, which, when occupied, could be used as a fresh starting-off point for an advance to Minsk, for the purpose of getting behind the Russian Army covering Brest-Litovsk in the south, and so cutting off its retreat to the Dnieper. The Field-marshal had paid dearly for the capture of Kovno, but in a military sense the prize was worth its cost. By taking Kovno he had seriously compromised the Russian second line, the so-called Niemen-Bug line, which extended from Kovno on the Niemen to Brest-Litovsk and the Pinsk Marshes east of Kovel. The Kovno

KOVNO

army, now in close cooperation with the Germany army operating south of Riga, was farther east than the main mass of the Russians, who were still in retreat from Warsaw. The two armies were in a position to strike south and east, cutting the Petrograd-Bielostok railroad at Vilna and the Moscow-Brest railway at Minsk. But the distances were great, the country difficult and the possibilities for Russian resistance unmistakable and serious.

The natural expectation was that the Russians would retire from the Brest-Litovsk position and that the German advance would then cut still deeper into Russian territory.

It seemed probable that the German High Command now realized the extent to which their attempt to envelop the main Russian mass had failed. While, with Kovno, the whole system of Russia's permanent defenses on her Western frontier had fallen, the meaning of events in the east seemed rather to be that the Russians had been able to make another successful retreat, had got themselves clear of the enveloping net of Hindenburg and Mackensen and were retiring in good order on Brest-Litovsk, losing few prisoners and next to no equipment.

Back of the Russian retreat from Kovno were said to be nearly 3,000,000 refugees. The reason was that for a while the retreat had been so rapid that the fleeing civilians could not keep up with it. Kovno was evacuated suddenly and in a panic, houses and stores being left in a dilapidated condition, so that when their owners and families returned afterward they could have been seen standing about broken-hearted in their empty, dirty shells of buildings. Barefooted women hovered about at the station, or lay down in straw, frightened and shivering with cold, their black or vari-colored shawls drawn tightly about them. Here some woman with barely enough clothes to cover her body might have been seen carrying a sewing-machine, or there, a boy and his father carrying a sack that contained their only possessions, including a pet kitten. Left behind were pitiful old women and men who could not undergo the hardships of miles and miles of traveling afoot, and so had stayed behind during the bombardment when shells were flying thick as blackbirds down streets and over roofs. No cellars or bombproof trenches were there in which to hide. Afterward those forlorn people could be seen wandering about the city, barefooted and leaning on old hand-made canes, or on Sundays might be seen in churches, walking up to kiss the feet of statues of Christ, or kneeling and sitting in deserted confessionals. Along cobbled streets rumbled peasant-wagons, with perhaps a mother and her family lying in the straw and a giant father walking alongside. Further back would appear a family group driving a cow. Everywhere were German soldiers and groups of Russian prisoners marching from one part of the town to another. Large auto-trucks, in constant communication with the front, meanwhile, hurried through the city. Big touring-cars bearing officers were seen everywhere.

Before the end of August Brest-Litovsk fell. Its fate had been settled with the capture of Kovno the week before, and its evacuation was inevitable. Since the decision to leave Warsaw, the Russians had embarked upon a policy of retreat to which they had rigidly adhered. If the purpose of the Germans had been solely to acquire territory, the

THE RUSSIAN CHURCH IN GRODNO

taking of Brest would have been the culminating circumstance in a campaign successful beyond all parallel in the history of this war. But it was the Russian Army, not a mere military position, that was the true object of Austro-German strategy—and this object had not been reached.

At Novogeorgievsk, which fell on August 19, the Germans claimed to have taken 85,000 prisoners and at Kovno 20,000 —each estimate an apparent exaggeration. But the Russian garrison at Novogeorgievsk was sacrificed, in order to delay German transports on the Vistula, just as the French in September, 1914, sacrificed 40,000 troops at Maubeuge in order to control the Liége-Paris trunk railroad. The siege of Novogeorgievsk was entrusted to Beseler, who had fame in Germany as the conqueror of Antwerp in October, 1914. The Staff had assumed that a lengthy defense would ensue with a consequent hold-up of German communications, but the great cannon which had battered down Liége in a week, and Namur in less time, carried Novogeorgievsk, altho it took them something under three weeks. Twenty thousand of the garrison were captured, and over 700 guns, most of which had been rendered useless. When the Germans entered Novogeorgievsk, the Russian armies were already some 80 miles away. The Kaiser held a review, described as follows in a German newspaper in that comic German literary form which had been exposed to Entente smiles so often in this war:

"With gigantic, mighty strides he advanced upon the parade ground, with a thick stick in his hand. The Kaiser comes close in front of me. He looks at me sharply. I know the look. To-day there is something immensely joyous, almost humorous, in the keen eyes. Oh, you stupid Quadruple Ententists! If you only had an idea. His Majesty went with the same powerful strides from battalion to battalion. In his customary short, sharp tones he thanked his troops in the name of all Germany, and distributed Iron Crosses."

The Russian loss of 200,000 in prisoners in rear-guard actions in a period of three weeks, was not regarded by the Allies as an unduly heavy loss. It rather indicated how deliberate and successful had been the Russian retreat, which, as a military operation, equaled in success the German offensive. Brest-Litovsk, which was to become the scene of the famous, or infamous, German treaty of 1917 with the Bolsheviki, lay at the junction of navigable rivers, the Bug and Mukhovets. At the point of confluence stands the city fortress on the right bank of the Bug, sharply outlined where the river turns from north to northeast. Railways from Odessa, Kiel, Moscow, Warsaw, Vilna, and East Prussia intersect at this point. Here also is an inland waterway connecting the Baltic with the Black Sea, the course of which connects with a canal beyond Brest, between the upper Mukhovets River and the Pripet. The city is thus served by a well-nigh perfect system of communications, reaching north, east and south, and points toward the northwest, west and southwest. Brest had a population of about 63,579 in 1913, more than half of whom were Jewish.

While the armies of Prince Leopold and Mackensen were converging on Brest-Litovsk, the Germans made an attempt to capture Riga from the sea. After clearing a channel through the mine-fields, a fleet, chiefly light cruisers and gunboats, entered the Gulf of Riga on August 19. After four days, the German fleet was beaten by the Russian

A STREET SCENE IN RIGA

Admiral, who turned on the enemy's ships after he had drawn them into the Gulf, and compelled them to retreat to the Baltic with the loss of two cruisers and eight torpedo boats. The Russians lost only the gunboat *Sivoutch*, which was sunk in Mohn Sound by a German cruiser. The German fleet endeavored to seize control of the Gulf. The success of such an endeavor would have had an important bearing on the military situation in that region, since it might have made possible the transport by sea of reinforcements to the invading army of Below, and so perhaps turned the Russian flank. Abandonment of the enterprise, coming as it did during the great Allied depression due to the German military advances in the Eastern theater of war, had a reassuring effect. Exaggerated stories became current. One of these was that four barges full of troops wh ch had attempted to land at Pernau had been annihilated. The fact was that these vessels were empty steamers sunk by the Germans in order to block navigation; so at least the Germans said.

When on August 25 Brest-Litovsk fell, it had held out long enough to enable Ewarts to get away with guns and supplies. His armies were soon well into the tangle of the Pripet Marshes, with Mackensen following from the south, and Prince Leopold's group fighting their way on the north through the great forest of Bieloviesk, which had been the last sanctuary of the aurochs or ancient European bison. On August 28 Below began a great attack on the line of the Dwina. On that river, from Riga upward, there was no crossing till the little town of Friedrichstadt was reached, some fifty miles from the coast. Below were great stretches of marshy forest which lined the left bank of the stream. On one side was the main Riga-Vilna railway. At Friedrichstadt, on the left bank, a road reached the river. Five miles south was a single-line railway. So long as the Russians held Friedrichstadt they controlled the only practicable crossing of the Dwina between Riga and Jacobstadt, and protected communications of the port with Dvinsk and Vilna. When Below moved on Friedrichstadt he aimed, not at isolating Riga, for there was still the northern line to Petrograd, but at cutting it off from Russian armies to the south. On the Dwina there was a desperate struggle for the Friedrichstadt crossing. Below issued a special order to his troops:

"After the brilliant campaign on the Russian front, and the occupation of many cities and fortresses in Poland and Lithuania, you must make one more effort to force the Dwina and seize Riga. There you will rest during the autumn and winter, in order to march on Petrograd in the spring."

On the night of September 2 the Russians, who held the left bank of the river below Friedrichstadt at Linden, made a gallant assault on Below's flank. But on the morning of the 3d the Germans attacked the position at the bridgehead with incendiary shells, and forced the Russians back to the east side from Linden to Friedrichstadt. Below had cleared the left bank for a space of ten miles, but he had not won the bridgehead.

The German eastern campaign had now entered its third period. The first had come in Galicia, when the sudden drive by Mackensen threatened the envelopment of the Russians in the Carpathians. The second was about Warsaw, when another enveloping effort was made. Now had come the third, which was not to be an enveloping operation, but an attempt to crush in detail beaten trooops no longer protected by permanent defenses and withdrawing through difficult territory. Twice thwarted in a primary purpose, Germany still had a third. Success could come only with the destruction of the enemy's main armies. That would probably have opened the road to Petrograd and Moscow, and to a separate peace. But, with the Russian army intact, Germany's chance for a real decision in the east promised to disappear, and with it all chance of an early peace. Except for isolated positions on the Niemen and west of that river, as at Grodno, all the nine provinces of Poland were now in the hands of the Germans. In addition, the greater part of Courland and Kovno had been overrun, and Austro-German armies were pressing forward into Volhynia and Grodno. The immediate aim of the Germans in the invasion of Courland was to occupy the Dubissa line, and to seize Libau, the Russian port from which, before the war, a regular line of passenger-ships ran to New York. Only along a narrow slip of Galicia east of the Zlota Lipa river, did any Russian army now stand on German or Austrian soil. In just four months Russian armies had been driven from the crest of the Carpathians, from Poland, and from the East-Prussian frontier, in a campaign which, for sweep of operations, the armies engaged and the sustained energy of the offensive, had no parallel.

In order to ensure the evacuation of Grodno, which by September 3 was blown up, strenuous fighting had been necessary. After the place was taken, the Russians retired from all posts west of the Niemen. A German threat to cut the railway was one of the last events that led to the evacuation of Grodno. Grodno was a stronghold on the main railway from the west to Petrograd, and one of the most powerful links guarding the line of the Muscovite frontier. It lay on the line of advance from the lake region in East Prussia, and was about fifty miles from the German border, 540 miles southwest of Vilna, and 160 miles northwest of Warsaw. About 110 miles south of Grodno was Brest-Litovsk.

Before Vilna fell on September 18, the battle of Melsgowla was fought, one of the most desperate encounters of the war in the East, Ewerts and Eichhorn having command of their respective forces. The Russians had half a million men distributed in the Vilna sector, among whom were two divisions of the Russian Imperial Guards, sent by General Ruszky from Petrograd to stiffen the front. These divisions bore the brunt of the fighting in the first line. It was only when they were broken up that Ewerts ordered a retirement. The retreat from Vilna ranked as one of the most brilliant exploits of the Russian armies. The Germans had not only encircled most of the city, but, by throwing off masses of cavalry, followed by light infantry, had pierced and swept round from the far north into the rear of the Russian communications at Molodetchna and Lebedevo. The withdrawal of the Russians from Vilna began not a moment too soon. Further delay would have enabled the Germans to drive a wedge into their rear. Part of Hindenburg's efforts were directed toward compelling the Vilna group either to fight till surrounded or to retreat in a southerly direction. The latter course would greatly have confused the withdrawal of Ewerts' other armies north of the Shara. In order to avoid such confusion, the Vilna group moved eastward, but in taking this course it had to fight to overthrow the enemy's enveloping columns. Thus it came about that the right wing of the Vilna group had to face the Germans coming from the east. The engagements at the crossings of the river partook of the strange character of men turning their backs on Vilna, in order to clear the line of retreat before them.

THE GERMAN INVASION OF RUSSIA

Hamilton Fyfe,[3] a war correspondent, described the retreat from Vilna as a tragedy which none could understand who had not seen it. The roads were filled so full of people, horses and wagons, that, from a balloon, "you could not have seen any road." Had one wished to get along more quickly than the fighters who filled the road, he would have found it impossible to do so unless he had driven into the throng and forced a way through—as one does on a country road filled with cattle. On the surface of roads moved solid masses of men, horses, wagons, light carts, guns, cais-

GERMAN OFFICERS OVERLOOKING VILNA FROM THE
ROOF OF A CASTLE

sons, and motor-vehicles. Adding to the confusion were throngs of frightened and miserable refugees, who carried their most treasured possessions in their arms, wheeled them in perambulators, or stowed them in farm-carts. One had a clock, another a bird-cage, another a picture, and many clung to sewing-machines. Others had mattresses and sheets, but had left behind such clothing as they owned. All roads running in the direction which the retreat had to take were thus turned into living streams of men, women, and chil-

[3] Petrograd correspondent of The *Daily Mail* (London).

dren, flowing carelessly and chattering as they went by, but with furrowed brows and grim eyes.

The lot of troops in the main army was easy compared with the perils that came to the rear-guards. Upon them was laid the duty of securing ultimate safety. A rear-guard could continually fight a losing battle. At best, it hoped only to delay the enemy, to thin his ranks, to throw his advance into confusion. Its business was to hold the enemy back in order to give the main army time to get away. But it had always to keep in touch with the main army, and always to give way step by step, so as to be able to make good its own escape when its difficult and dangerous task was done. The rear-guard had another task: it had to leave a trail of destruction behind it. All stores and grain, whether garnered or standing, everything that could be carried away, all shelter even, had, if possible, to be demolished. In consequence, the track of the rear-guard was marked by devastated cornfields and haystacks, often burning and sending skyward red ashes and smoke which only a few hours before had been provisions for man and beast. So, also, had railways to be torn up, bridges to be broken down, and roads made difficult for troops to march over, for wheels to run on. This war in the east produced a countryside silent, ruined and bare.

On these rear-guards was laid the burden of saving the Russian army from defeat. What the Germans sought was a resounding victory. They planned to strike a blow of which the noise should echo around the world, and which would bring Russia to her knees, and after Russia the Western Powers. Against the threat, Russia opposed a policy of retirement which was adopted as much for the sake of the Allies as for her own. Her generals, her army, and her people would have preferred a more desperate strategy, would rather have risked a bold throw, but by the other method Russia for five months detained the Germans in the East, and also prevented them from massing in tremendous force in France and Flanders.

In retreating from Vilna the Russians were confined to a corridor, with the enemy on either side. But the corridor widened as they went back, and so the struggles of the

THE GERMAN INVASION OF RUSSIA

Germans to throw themselves across the path of the Russians became steadily more difficult. Never before, however, had the Germans been so near the fulfilment of their one ambition and desire—the gaining of a great victory by an enveloping plan. Obsessed as they had been for more than forty years, by the elder Moltke's stroke at Sedan, they never once in this war had a success with plans that followed his. They did actually block one of the roads on which the Russians were moving, at a place called Lebedeff, but fresh Russians were sent against them with the bayonet, and they

JAPANESE GUNS AT BREST-LITOVSK

were pitchforked out, leaving everything behind them. So escaped the Russian army from this most nearly successful of all the German strategical designs, and it owed escape to rear-guards. Vilna was important because its capture and retention by the Germans threatened the Russian communications and crippled the second line of Russian defense, along the Bug, on the Brest-Litovsk line.

The combined retreat from Vilna, Eastern Poland and Galicia has sometimes been considered the greatest operation of its kind in the annals of war. Never before had numbers so immense been withdrawn from so extensive a front and for such great distance in the presence of an enemy so active and enterprising. The mere withdrawal of a million or more men spread over several hundred miles of front without confusion, or the interference of contiguous bodies of troops, would have been a high test of proficiency, but the execution by Russia of this operation while in contact with a powerful enemy elated by an extraordinary success, involving as it did a continuous rear-guard action and the maintenance of an unbroken front, must have taxed to the utmost the coolness and resolution of the Commander-in-Chief and his Staff. The credit was due in full measure to the Russian troops, for, had their valor and determination failed, the most perfect staff arrangements must have proved abortive. And, throughout the whole ordeal, the troops were short of rifles and ammunition, and exposed to the ravages of German artillery, with which their guns were powerless to cope. An Austrian officer who went through much of the fighting in July and August, called the great retreat a masterpiece of terrifying and systematic devastation. The invaders in their progress found little more than black deserts. There was not a human being in sight, nor a roof, nor a grain of corn.

Of that long Russian retreat, Stephen Graham [4] collected interesting notes at the Kief railway-station in September. He sat long in an immense waiting-room thronged with people, all terribly hot, noisy, and deprest. Children were crying everywhere, babies at the breast, babies on all fours crawling among bundles, children of all ages—terribly hungry and sleepy. Parents sat about, with careworn faces and strained eyes, curling themselves uncouthly about bundles of quilts and clothes. So it was elsewhere on that frontier. Thousands of fugitives were waiting at every station platform, barracks, or camping-ground. Twenty thousand fugitives might arrive every day, and none might stay, having been assigned to provinces in the depths of Russia, given free passage on trains, and hurriedly moved away, so as not to impede the oncoming rear of the Russian Army, and so as to relieve towns of tremendous destitution

[4] Correspondent of The *Morning Post* (London).

and give the unfortunate wanderers some better chance of starting life afresh. From the banks of the Dnieper one saw a never-ending procession of slowly moving cart-tilts; carts wandering along endless roads and lanes, all a peasant's goods in one cart, his chairs, tables, ikons, with a cow tied by a rope following behind. The peasant, as often as not, could not tell where he was going.

There were splendid faces among these people, broad, calm, potent faces. There were fine peasant families seen. Great was the pity that they had thus been rooted up. All had the same expression—that of people who had given up everything and now stood on the threshold of a new life, with all the money they had collected in one purse, all their material possessions in bundles. There were unwontedly large family groups, with old aunts, grandmothers, and grandfathers, people who ordinarily never stirred abroad, now walking or sitting with dishevelled gray hair, their eyes unnaturally excited and sad. They had barely slept for five days and were worn-out, heavy-eyed, silent. No one grumbled. Everyone asked for his neighbor's story, tried to calm children, gave food, said their prayers, and had farthings with which to buy candles to burn before station altars. Even Jews, secretive in their devotions, could be seen saying prayers.

Kief had one central station which had become a vast terminus, with rows of platforms which ordinarily looked bare and uninhabitable, but in August and September, trains came into the station at Kief to find the platforms piled as high as the roof with all manner of packing-cases and bundles. As a train slowed down, astonished passengers on board heard a great vocal hubbub and saw throngs of multi-colored fugitives, with all the pitiful details of broken-up homes—beds, cradles, chairs, tables, sofas, perambulators, packing-cases enclosing sewing-machines, red boxes innumerable, and corded baskets. Across the Dnieper safe from the Germans stood trains laden with all imaginable things— huge boilers, cisterns, tanks, cylinders, receivers, separators, broken, torn, twisted, and rusted. They could not be packed together, because so variously shaped. There were innumerable samovars, kettles, agricultural machinery, wheels on trucks laden with nothing but wheels, church-bells on trucks laden with nothing but church-bells. Some of these bells were little tinkling bells, others huge bells that could sound loud over a great city. Many were ornamented with representations of Jesus, or of Mother and Child, but now scrawled over in white chalk, or colored paint, with the name of the church and town whence they had been taken.

Besides the migration of people came the removal of factories, universities, academies, schools, hospitals. All in the official phrase had been "evacuated," that is, removed from western Russia to the interior. The University of Warsaw went to Rostoff; Urieff University to Yaroslaff. Factories went in all directions, and, aided by the Government, started again. Even far-off Omsk advertised in the newspapers for refugees factories, and gladly afforded them facilities. With the peasants were long-haired village priests, looking woebegone, harried, away from their parishes. Many found refuge in monasteries. The famous Petchrrkaya Monastery at Kief had several thousand guests, including "evacuated" monks, priests, and fugitive peasants. At this great settlement, which stands high above the Dnieper, all things seemed to have been turned into holiday activities. Scores of minstrels, fortune-tellers and beggars beguiled the crowds assembled there. Every altar and shrine gleamed with candles. The sacred music died down only at meal times, when multitudes sat down at tables in open courtyards. Stalls stood about laden with peasants' wares. In caves and along galleries, where lay long dead saints and priests in coffins, were seen constant crowds. Jews turned up at this and other monasteries seeking food or refuge and were not refused.

Stanley Washburn [5] believed the greatest tragedy of the war was not seen on battlefields. Tragedy and pathos in their highest form were seen over the main arteries of travel running from west to east along which there flowed in September that endless stream of refugees fleeing before the German advance. He had observed refugees on the Western Front for a year, and had imagined he could not see them in greater numbers than during the early summer of 1915, but after two days of travel westward on the Warsaw

[5] Correspondent of The *Times* (London).

road he felt as if he had never seen such maneuvers before. In two days he saw probably 100,000 men, women and children, fleeing from the Teutonic invasion. In one town alone whose population was normally 25,000, there were 83,000. They were everywhere, camped in streets with all their household belongings, and spread out along the countryside for miles in every direction. Their fortitude was something incredible. They were typical of two millions or so of refugees who were then on the roads in Russia, and had been on roads for weeks or months. Nearly all had left villages in ashes. Crouching at roadsides round little fires made of faggots were dozens of groups. Endless lines of carts were strung out with small tired horses dragging huge loads of household effects. In every wood were camps of hundreds and the roadside was already dotted with little white crosses which marked where unhappy and homeless exiles had at last found rest.

The failure of the Russian defensive campaign had a noticeable effect on Russian national feeling. It shook that constitutionally stolid and unemotional country from one end to the other. The change, however, was not one of fatal discouragement or submission. It moved no one to talk of ultimate defeat, or of the possibility of Russia's undertaking separate peace negotiations. Russia's reaction took the form of an intense indignation at Government officials who were responsible for the tragic shortage of ammunition. The full meaning of that shortage was known only to men at the front who, with empty gun-caissons, helplessly faced the concentrated artillery attacks of the Germans and watched the progress of German and Austrian trench-builders directly under their own positions, without being able to stop them. These soldiers were determined and experienced fighters—Russia's best troops—who were crippled and finally demoralized by insufficient ammunition and a knowledge that this lack had caused their continued retreat from one position to another.

The most rigidly censored press in the world failed to check the avalanche of criticism that followed. For once, expression of opinion in Russia was unhampered. No attempt was made to conceal the reproaches leveled against the methods of bureaucrats accused of having crippled Russia's fighting strength and materially delayed the end of the war. It was not voiced alone by men of revolutionary inclinations, or opposition tendencies, nor uttered in hushed voices, or secret places, but clamorously current everywhere among men of all parties and classes. In these proteststs there was no disloyalty. A common view was that the evil was due to the residue of German influence which still existed in various departments of the Russian Government. The spirit of revolt against a German element in Russia had caused terrible riots in Moscow in the early months of 1915, when as the order expelling all Germans from the city had not been enforced, the mob decided to take the matter into its own hands and expel them forcibly by destroying their homes and business. The allegation was made that Russian officials who superintended the purchase of war munitions had insisted on such large commissions on all contracts that the business of buying war materials had to wait until a purchasing commission had adjusted the commissions satisfactorily.

Whenever there was a chance to fight, the Russian soldiers fought with great obstinacy, but in the majority of cases the tempest of German artillery attack so far accomplished its aim that a charge was superfluous. Sometimes as many as sixteen German guns concentrated upon one Russian position, tore up every sign of the Russian entrenchments. When the Germans advanced on trenches there was no opposition.

A RUSSIAN ICE-BREAKER AT WORK OFF ARCHANGEL

THE GERMAN INVASION OF RUSSIA

In many cases not a single Russian soldier was found alive. The Russians, before making a retreat, actually expended the last shell they had. Caissons laden with ammunition were rushed up at full speed to battery positions, then unloaded and vainly spent. Two days before Warsaw was abandoned, ammunition had begun to arrive in large quantities, but the Russian forces, threatened with being completely cut off by the encircling movement, could no longer gamble on the chance of an eleventh-hour arrival.

Archangel, where most of Russia's ammunition arrived

OCCUPATION BY THE GERMANS OF THE RUSSIAN PORT OF
LIBAU ON THE BALTIC

Libau was the port used by a Russian passenger line which, before the war, made regular trips to New York

during the summer of 1915, had had at that time probably the greatest trade expansion ever reached by any seaport in so short a time. Previous to the war its trade was confined to exports of timber, fish, furs, and other local products of northern Russia, and a relatively small return movement of goods was required for local consumption. Now, however, Archangel was the only port of European Russia open for foreign business by direct sea communication, and, except

Vladivostok, in eastern Siberia it had in that sense no rival in the Russian Empire. It thus suddenly became one of the most important ports in the world, rivaling even New York in the number and tonnage of ships arriving and departing. Between early May and the close of ice-free navigation, as many as 120 large steamers could at one time have been seen in this port, while an immense number of smaller boats and barges were engaged in river and canal navigation, many of them carrying 2,000 tons. These had been diverted largely from the lower Volga river traffic. In front of the main part of the city were about thirty-five large piers, as against only three or four a year before. Over 100 warehouses had been built within the year, and yet there was still an insufficiency. Ships sometimes had to lie out in the stream for weeks before they could unload. One American steamer took five weeks in discharging its cargo.

The Russians had had no choice except to avoid a decisive engagement. Under the Grand Duke they had done all that from May to September. But the Grand Duke had failed to bring home a great triumph. News of his deposition and enforced departure for the Caucasus came as a great surprise to the Allies, from whom he had received constant praise for extricating his armies from the Teutonic grip. It was believed that, with a shortage of munitions and other difficulties, he had accomplished all that was humanely possible in the circumstances. But in Russia the inclination was to give credit in this war only to the peasant soldier. The Commander-in-chief's strategy had, from the beginning, been regarded with doubt by a large element of military opinion, including some of the Grand Duke's lieutenants. The collapse of his plans was cited as proof of their essential unsoundness. The invasion of Galicia was considered to have been a perilous adventure. It became common rumor in Russia that Ruszky and Brusiloff, who had won the battle of Lemberg and overrun Galicia in 1914, had been acting against their own better judgment in obedience to the Grand Duke. Apologists for the Grand Duke argued that his views were justified by the necessities of the general situation on both fronts, for even in her defeat, Russia had served the Allied cause by saving France and Great Britain from defeat. The first Russian disaster in East Prussia, at Tannenberg, in this view, had compelled the withdrawal of German troops from the west, and so had decided the battle of the Marne. The Russian advance from Warsaw in October, which ended in defeat at Lodz, had served in the same way to relax German pressure against the British around Ypres.

Nothing in September, 1915, created so much comment as the action of the Czar in superseding the Grand Duke. Allied capitals feared this step might foreshadow a lessening of Russian effort, but the Czar formally pledged himself to continue the war until Russian soil was free. It was apparent that dynastic reasons had compelled him to this course. The war had become a national war, both for racial and religious reasons, and was supported by the sentiment of the Russian people. Altho popular with the army, the Grand Duke had been unpopular with the ruling classes. His strictness as a disciplinarian and his stern rule had roused opposition. Outside of Russia his military skill was everywhere conceded. He had conquered Galicia and the Bukowina. The world believed his ultimate defeat was due to corrupt and blundering officials charged with organizing the machinery for supplying her army.

Stanley Washburn thought the Grand Duke Nicholas in one way the greatest man Russia had produced since Peter the Great, but not in the way a reader might think. Nicholas had not brought to the war enormous sagacity, or extraordinary military capacity, and probably was not responsible for more than a fair portion of the strategies evolved in the campaign. What he did contribute was "a great personality and an extraordinary character which at the beginning of the war was a far greater asset than mere brains." In the beginning, when bureaucracy was frantically trying to direct and control the elemental forces which the war let loose, the Grand Duke towered above every single figure in Europe. He was "a moral force replete with patriotism, sincerity, courage, and the iron will that swept from his path intrigue and petty quarrels." Men of more finesse might have been found to conduct the strategy and tactics of the campaign, but "there was no man in Russia who could have held that great cosmopolitan army together as a cohesive unit through the first chaotic year of the war save only the Grand Duke Nicholas.'' Leaving the western Russian front in what was an official disgrace only, the Grand Duke, before that winter of 1915-1916 was over, had won, perhaps, the most spectacular victory of those first war years—the taking of Erzerum and Trebizond.[6]

[6] Principal Sources: United Press dispatch from Carl W. Ackerman, German High Command report printed in The *Frankfurter Zeitung,* The *Morning Post* (London) ; The *Times,* The *Tribune,* New York ; The *Daily Mail* (London), *The Literary Digest* (New York) ; The *Economist, The Fortnightly Review, The Quarterly Review,* London ; *The Evening Post* (New York), The *Statist* (London), "Bulletins" of the National Geographic Society (New York), "Nelson's History of the War" by John Buchan ; The *Times,* The *Manchester Guardian,* London ; Stanley Washburn in *The Review of Reviews* (New York).

IV

THE CHECK TO THE GERMAN ADVANCE

September 21, 1915—December 1, 1915

IT had been a commonplace with military historians that a successful invasion of Russia was impossible—that is, in the sense that it could be attempted without disaster to the invader. Such views dated back at least to the fate of Charles XII of Sweden at Pultowa, to which Samuel Johnson, in his poem, "The Vanity of Human Wishes," made familiar references:

> "On what foundation stands the warrior's pride,
> How just his hopes, let Swedish Charles decide,
>
>   *   *   *   *   *   *   *
>
> He left a name at which the world grew pale,
> To point a moral or adorn a tale."

and to that of Napoleon, in his enforced retreat from Moscow, when his army suffered as much from the rigors of a Russian winter as from the harassing onslaughts of Russian troops. It was in May, 1812, that Napoleon, collected 400,000 men for this expedition from Eastern Germany. Having crossed the Niemen on June 23, the invasion of Russian Poland was readily accomplished. It was only when his army entered Russia that his difficulties began. Roads being bad, his transports broke down, and excessive heat and a failure in supplies caused disease to spread. Before he reached Smolensk, which was burned on August 17th, he had lost 100,000 men.

Battle was offered to Napoleon on the Borodino, where after terrible losses the road was opened to Moscow, which he entered on September 14, only to find it bursting into flames and deserted. For five weeks the French remained in Moscow, vainly waiting for the Czar Alexander to accept terms which he never accepted. It was not until mid-October that the order was finally given for the great retreat, the horrors of which live in many familiar pages.

The army which on December 14 crossed the Niemen and entered Prussia, was a ragged remnant of the mighty host that had set out for Russia seven months before. Some 200,000 men had perished. Almost as many more had been captured.

Since 1812, however, a revolution had taken place in methods of warfare, and, above all, in means of communication and transport, so that, if the Germans in 1915 could have controlled the trunk line to Petrograd, held Courland, and commanded the Bay of Riga with their fleet, an attack on Petrograd might have been possible. The blow delivered at Moscow in 1812 was a blow at the political center of the Czars; but since then Petrograd had outdistanced Moscow in population and become the political capital, and hence any such blow would now have to be delivered at Petrograd. Some of the vital factors in the problem, however; had scarcely changed at all in the course of a century—for example, the psychology of the Russian people, and the topography of Russia, both of which remained integral parts of the situation the Germans had to face.

On August 5 the German troops had entered Warsaw, and on September 18 came the fall of Vilna. The intervening forty-four days practically embraced the great Austro-German offensive against Russia which, having virtually been begun in May with the battle of the Dunajec, remained throughout the summer of 1915 the main, if not the absorbing, concern of Germany. Four weeks after the fall of Warsaw, Austro-German armies were in possession of the entire Bug-Niemen line. After the fall of Brest their offensive showed no sign of slackening, but the skilful retreat of the Russian armies had deprived the Teutonic commanders of that "crowning mercy," that they had hoped for and were seeking. Thus they had failed to achieve in the east a sought-for second Sedan which, having failed to get in 1914 in France, they had planned to get the next year in France on an infinitely larger scale, and again had failed. Had they succeeded in the East, the event would have settled the war in so far as Eastern Europe was concerned; but, since they could not capture the Russian army, they still hoped to reduce it to a state of practical impotence by

THE GERMAN INVASION OF RUSSIA

forcing it to abandon the railway-line across the Pripet Marshes, the most impassable area of morasses in Europe. Had Russians been forced to abandon that railway, their armies would have been cut in two by swamps. All direct communication between troops operating in the north and those concentrated in the southern area would have ceased, because no other railway crosses from north to south over those 180 miles of dreary marshland.

The occupation of Vilna was the high-water mark of the

A CORNER IN RIGA

great German invasion of 1915. After its fall, the German offensive began to slacken. General Scholtz reached Lida on September 20, but Eichhorn found the roads to Minsk blocked by fresh troops, brought up from Polotzy and Bobruisk to relieve Russian corps defeated at Meisdagowla. Prince Leopold of Bavaria reached the railway junction of Baranovitche on the 28th and called a halt. Mackensen, after struggling for more than a fortnight with the Pripet Marshes, withdrew his troops from behind the Originski

Canal, dug his right wing into defensive positions around Pinsk, and then handed over his command to Linsingen. If the Germans had had any intention of marching further eastward to the Dnieper, they gave it up when they discovered that the Russians had been reinforced with men and munitions and were resuming the offensive. As for Mackensen, he had other operations to look after in Siberia, that great drive which forced an entire population out of their homes.

German armies under Eichhorn and Below strove to complete the success they had achieved in the neighborhood of Vilna, by an advance to the east. In Lithuania, a country of lakes and forests, operations on a large scale were limited almost entirely, especially in autumn, to the lines of main roads and railways. In the region of Svientsiany, the Germans tried to follow up their original piercing movement by an advance towards Polotsk, with five cavalry divisions and strong infantry support. The struggle lasted unabated for about a fortnight, during which all their attacks were repulsed. For two more days the Germans made onslaughts west of Vileika, where their offensive developed into a pitched battle. One attack followed after another, and fighting never slackened. On September 27, 10,000 heavy shells were fired on a sector held by a single Russian regiment. As the result of about a week's fighting between the Dubisca and the Niemen, the Russians extricated their advanced detachments, straightened out their front, cleared their lines of communication of enemy raiders, and by a counter-offensive prest back the Germans at several points. Further south the German enveloping movement made no progress at all, attempts to cross the Niemen east of Novogrodek ended in failure, and in the first days of October the offensive in the northern center began to "fizzle out." Withdrawals to the Western front and for service against Serbia had depleted the German reserves, and soon autumn rains and bad roads hampered them more and more.

The capture of Dvinsk would have been a decisive success for the entire German offensive east of Vilna. Once the Germans could be firmly established there and threatening an advance against Polotsk by roads and railway which ran along the right bank of the upper Dvina, the position of the

Russians in the northern center opposite Svientsiany and Vilna would have been practically untenable. As a strategic center Dvinsk was equal in importance to Vilna, Brest-Litovsk, or Rovno, and second only perhaps to Warsaw. It formed the junction of two of the most important Russian railways, the Petrograd-Vilna-Warsaw and the Moscow-Smolensk-Riga lines. Moreover, a branch line connected Dvinsk, by way of Ponevesh and Shavle, with the Baltic port of Libau; and at Shavle it was met by a narrow-gage railway from Taurogen, which the Germans had constructed since the summer. Dvinsk was also the center of a network of roads. It was a mistake, however, to think of Dvinsk as a fortress;

RUSSIAN CAVALRY IN RETREAT

in a strategic discussion one ought to speak rather of the Dvinsk district as a fortress.

Less than a week after the fall of Vilna, and when any moment was expected to bring news of the fall of Dvinsk and the breaking of the line of the Dwina, there was apparent a stiffening of the Russian resistance and a slackening of the German advance. On their left wing, in the south, the Russians seemed actually to have brought the Teutonic advance to a standstill, and to be exercising pressure on the German's left in the Riga-Dvinsk region where they had slowly given ground. In the center, the Teutonic advance had been most rapid. On October 31 the offensive against Riga entered on its last stage. The main interest during the first half of November centered around attempts to break through in the Shlock region, between Lakes Kanger and Babit.

There come moments in many campaigns when the high tide of an advance appears to have been reached and the ebb begins. At the time it is imperceptible to combatants on both sides. By early December, looking to conditions on the Eastern Front, after four of the most tempestuous months that ever armies endured, there might have been detected a real clearing of the skies in Eastern Europe. Salients had gone, the line was nearly straight, the wings hard prest, but they could still hold out. Waves of confidence now surged through the Russian Command. The Emperor had put himself at the head of his soldiers' in place of the Grand Duke, who for more than a year had borne perhaps the heaviest burden carried by any single man in the war. That the Czar should follow the example of Peter and Alexander and take command of his armies, was to the whole Russian people a sign that the war was to be waged to the bitter but successful end. It was regarded as their answer to German efforts for a separate peace.

Finding that he could make no progress in the center, Hindenburg now renewed his efforts to capture Dvinsk, but the topographical conditions were unfavorable for the attack, the town being approached from the south and east by an intricate maze of shallow lakelets and bogs, which precluded the maneuvering of artillery, and so enabled the Russians to keep the German heavy guns out of decisive range. Below, who was formally charged with the direction of the operations against Dvinsk, began by launching a direct attack along the road from Vilkomir, but finding the Russians strongly entrenched, changed the frontal attack for an enveloping movement directed against both flanks of the Russian positions covering Dvinsk.

This movement failed when, early in October, Ruzsky brought up a large force of reserve troops from Petrograd well supplied with artillery, and began to develop a powerful offensive all along the line from Vileika to the Drina, pushing back the Germans west of the Dreswiata Lake, while lower down the line he threatened their retreat from

Koshiany. Then Below, reinforcing his left under Lauen-
stein, directed an attack against Russian positions between
Jacobstadt and Lennewaden; but this attempt to get across
the river met with no better success than others elsewhere.
Not to be outdone, Below then shifted his attack further
up the river, and a three days' battle of great activity took
place at Garbunowka, two miles south of Illut, and some
ten miles or more northwest of Dvinsk. In the course of
this battle the village of Garbunowka repeatedly changed

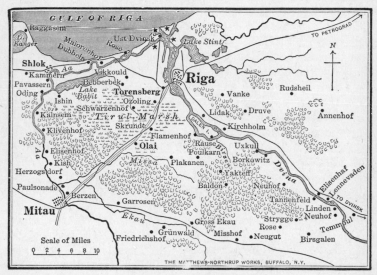

RIGA AND ITS SURROUNDINGS

hands, but on October 11 was finally captured and held by
the Russians.

In these conditions the Russian retreat came to an end.
Russian commanders were attacking the whole 700-mile front
from the Dwina to the Dniester, their offensive on the flanks
being particularly observable. In spite of heavy losses during the summer campaign, they had been rapidly recovering
from the effects of their reverses, and were reinforcing their
troops with daily increasing supplies of men, guns, and am-
munitions. The division of troops to the Serbian frontier
had visibly weakened the German strength, and opened up

opportunities for Russian commanders to break through lines opposed to them. The general commanding the German forces before Dvinsk had expected to enter the town by the end of September; a month later he stood still in approximately the same position, having lost something like 40,000 men in attacks against Russian lines. After a short lull the fighting began again, and on October 23 the Germans scored their first marked success in the Dvinsk region where, after long and vigorous artillery preparation, they attacked the Russian trenches west of Illuxet. At first their attack was repulsed, but toward the close of the day they succeeded in breaking through, and, after a desperate battle in the streets, occupied the town. It seemed as if that success was to open up a new chapter in the battle before Dvinsk. Again on October 27-28 the Germans broke through the Russian front near the village of Garbunovka and south of it, and reach the western outskirts of big forests which extend between the Illuxet-Shiskovo road and the Dwina. Here, however, their advance was brought to a stop. The Dvinsk front was held by an army deemed one of the best disciplined among the Russian forces, and was abundantly supplied with artillery and ammunition. In ten days of fierce fighting in the region of Lake Sventen and Illsen, which ended on November 11, it had justified its reputation.

On October 31 the offensive against Riga entered on its last stage. The main interest during the first half of November centered around attempts to break through in the Shlock region, between Lakes Kanger and Babit and the sea. The offensive began with attacks near Kemmern and Tchin, at the western extremity of Lake Babit. Fighting continued for several days, spreading to Raggasem at the northeastern end of Lake Kanger. As the battle continued it turned slowly to the advantage of the Russians, and culminated on November 10 in a battle in which the Russian fleet coöperated effectively with land batteries. The Germans attempted to assume the offensive, but were beaten back by a counter-move. The Russian advance was attended with incredible difficulties, troops going forward over thawing snow in swollen marshes, and with a German maxim posted on every mound and elevation. The men were obliged in many places to wade waist-deep in icy water. Off Riga, the Russian fleet rendered support. Its shells, bursting far into German lines, blew up trenches, dismantled batteries, and cut off connection with reserves, until finally the Russians surged into Kemmern. Eleven days of almost uninterrupted fighting had resulted in a German defeat, and all attempts against Riga along the sea were thereafter given up. Isolated attacks in the neighborhood of the farm of Bersemunde, opposite the islet of Dalen, became late in November the end of the German offensive against the line of the Dvina.

By November 25 the Germans had entered upon the difficult operation of withdrawing from the Riga territory. Mitau, their forward base, had already been evacuated of everything bulky or valuable. Over a great part of the two hundred mile section artillery-fire was now almost the only form of their activity. They devoted their main energies to the construction of a fourfold line of trenches, with a formidable series of wire-entanglements extending over scores of miles. In their remote rear they were kept busy building field-railways and tram-lines. These were made to work regularly from the interior of Germany as far east as Bausk and Poniewitz, which were the termini of trunk lines. Wireless telegraphy was installed along the rear of the whole extent of the German front. Light metal buildings were provided with steam heaters and so were some of the trenches. Supplies of sleeping-sacks were procured and provisions made for quantities of spirits, strict orders being issued that soldiers should rub themselves all over with the spirits daily.

Quantities of calico, linen, holland-cloth and other white materials were sent to the front, the whole region held by the Germans being pillaged of such material. The object was to cover with it uniforms, trenches and supply-carts, in the hope that they would thus be made as invisible to the Russians as snow fields were. Special tripod supports, able to carry a large expanse of white material, were provided, under which soldiers could bivouac unseen by aeroplanes. About Kemmern and Olai were prepared well-built dugouts with portable stoves and beds. These were destroyed twice by long-range artillery-fire, and finally taken by the Russians, German attempts to recapture them being unsuccessful. By December 2 in the Vilna region the Germans had completed an unbroken line of winter trenches from Smorgen to Novo Svientsiany, and as far south as Dieliatitchi. In anticipation of a spring offensive from Russia the Germans were fortifying the line of the Bug, for which work they requisitioned large companies of French and Belgian prisoners—some 30,000 in all. Three rows of fortifications with concrete emplacements for heavy artillery were completed on the right bank of the river. On the opposite bank were deep trenches and mine galleries.

Russian officers meanwhile, snugly ensconced themselves in dugouts, simply but cleanly furnished with camp beds, collapsible tables, stools, ikons, and lamps, with the latest magazines, papers, and maps. These austere surroundings were in contrast to the rather luxurious quarters of German officers at the rear of the Mitau front, which were said to be provided with electric lights, soft couches, carpets, bells, and innumerable toilet articles. The cold told especially on the aviation service in this region. German aeroplanes went up less and less often. Owing to the rapid increase in the cold with every hundred yards of altitude aeroplanes were compelled to fly comparatively low, which, having regard for the Russian artillery, was often a fatal risk.

It might well have been asked why Hindenburg's plans for the subjugation of Russia had miscarried. It began with advantages all in his favor. The Germans had greater mobility in all that concerns routes of transport and transport appliances. Their munitionment was many times better than that of the Russians. They had the mechanical devices —limitless motor-transport, skilled gangs of road-makers—to overcome the pathlessness and roadlessness of the country. Nor was there anything wrong in the plan itself, and there certainly was no lack of energy in carrying it out and yet armies, superior in numbers, in guns and in every scientific aid to the prosecution of modern war, failed to destroy and cut off any considerable part of the Russian force which for nearly five months had been involved in the intricacies and discouragements of a retreat.

BERLIN'S WOODEN STATUE OF HINDENBURG

The unveiling occurred in the summer of 1915, after the great victory over Russia. Subscribers to war loans were allowed to drive nails into the statue—for each five marks one iron nail

Much could be set down to the tenacity and skill of the Russian resistance, and to the fact that German armies as they rolled eastward began to lose their initial advantages. Large numbers had to be absorbed in garrison duties and in guarding lines of communications, for the country was hostile, and security had to be fought for. The fighting remainder meanwhile lost its elasticity. Many units had been advancing since May, and while they occupied great tracts of land, they had never received that inspiration which comes from inflicting indubitable defeat on an enemy in the field. The Germans were weakened by their own strength. Under the best of circumstances their great guns and large supply-trains had to travel slowly. Any section of the Russian front could be driven in, but the fruits of the resulting salients could not be reaped. Before their bases could be cut, the Russians slipt out of the noose and straightened their line.

The end of September had seen a definite check in the German advance. While Vilna and Grodno had fallen the Germans had not made good on the line of the Dwina. With winter almost upon them, they had found no suitable place for quarters; they had still to struggle on through the rains of autumn and the first snows. While the Russian armies were clearing themselves against further threats of danger, news came of a new aspect in the winter campaign. On September 25 was begun the long expected Allied offensive in the west, the French in the Champagne, the British in Artois.

On their southern wing the Austro-Germans had been doing badly. Along the Austrian right and center the advance had slackened and in places had stopt, even when Hindenburg's armies were fighting in the north for possession of Dvinsk and Riga. At both ends of the Teutonic line in Russia, weakening of the offensive was directly traceable to the nature of the country. The Austro-German line showed a big gap in the region of the Pripet Marshes, the Austrians were, for the moment, out of touch with their allies in the north. The history of the war had repeatedly shown that, once the Austrians lost the aid and skill of German troops, they were hardly a match for Russians, especially when it came to widespread operations with much cavalry fighting, as now was the case in the Volhynia district and along the Galician border.

To a minor degree, but still to an important degree, this was also the case along the Dwina front, and with Prince Leopold north of the Pripet Marshes, where the great mass of rivers, lakes, bogs and forests mark a country unadapted to that symmetry of operations which in this war and other wars had been one of the main reasons for German successes. Given a lake and marsh country, well provided with railways, and the Germans would have had the game in their own hands, as Hindenburg had twice had it in the Tannenberg country; but given swamps, lakes and rivers, without railways or roads, and the Russians were on a level with the Germans.

For almost two months a desperate battle went on on the middle Styr, in which the Austrians and German forces under Linsingen met the Russians under Brusiloff, commander of the Eighth Army, who, in the summer of 1915, had carried out a skilful retreat from the central Carpathians to Volhynia. A battle on the Styr had begun on September 27, with a German offensive in the southern areas. For weeks the fighting continued to oscillate east and west. Attacks and counter-attacks followed one another with that almost monotonous regularity which was characteristic of regular trench-warfare. About October 25 Austro-German forces assumed a counter-offensive on the Lisova-Budka line and round Komaroff. During the following week, every day each side reported heavy fighting and big captures of prisoners. The Russians had to fall back before overwhelming numbers and then in turn, on receiving reinforcements, they advanced. Meantime the late autumn was rendering operations more difficult, and, when the enforced lull set in, the Austro-German forces still stood on the western banks of the Styr, far away from Rovno.

On October 30 the Austrians assumed the offensive north of the Dniester. Holding the belt of forests and canons on the left bank between Butchatch and Zaleschyki, they had a distinct tactical advantage, and the initiative lay with them, but before the movement had time to develop it was checked by a vigorous Russian counter-offensive which was opened on the following day in the sector of Siemikovitse. Seriously threatened from that quarter, the Austrians had to relinquish for the time being all attempts at flanking movement from the south. This was, however, only the beginning of the fighting at Siemikovitse, one of the most peculiar battles fought in the war. Forces amounting on either side to nearly an army corps contested a front about a mile and a half wide, while batteries of all calibers developed hurricanes of fire from the opposite banks of the lake and marshes. Making use of broken ground and of the cover which it afforded, the Austrians attempted on November 2 an attack against Siemikovitse. At first they succeeded in penetrating the Russian front, but a Russian counter-offensive cut off the advanced body which had entered the village. During the next few days the Austrians regained most of the ground on the western bank of the Strypa. Then a lull set in, but it was again broken toward the end of the month, when the Austrians attempted to regain a foothold on the eastern side. By a skilful counterattack the Russians managed to drive them back and pin retreating columns to the river. A fearful struggle ensued; in preference to surrendering, the Austrians threw themselves into the water, where they were either drowned or perished under the fire of Russian batteries.

Toward the end of November a complete lull in the fighting set in along the entire Eastern Front. The opposing forces were still facing one another practically on the same lines which they had held two months earlier, at the conclusion of the Russian retreat from Vilna. The German plan of gaining a front in the East, which, owing to superiority of communications and the possession of a lateral connection across the Marshes of the Pripet, could have been held by forces inferior to those of the attacking side, had failed. On the Dwina and everywhere south of the Marshes also, the Russians maintained themselves in positions in which they had the use of equal, if not superior, systems of roads and railways.

After a successful advance of five months, during which, with comparatively few reverses, the Austro-German armies had been making progress on an average of about two miles a day, their offensive had broken down in front not only of Riga and Dvinsk, but of Rovno and Tarnapol. This final breakdown in the East failed, however, to strike the imagination of the outside public, as had the collapse of the German advance in France in the early days of the war, and yet the two events seemed at the time comparable in intrinsic values to the Allies. In either case the Teutonic forces, by their previous advance, had conquered a country they could exploit and oppress, but in both cases they failed to reduce their opponents to a state of strategical and military impotence. Both failures seem to have been due in part to similar causes; an exaggerated estimate of the re-

COSSACKS CROSSING SNOW

sults first achieved and an under-estimate of the recuperative power of the enemy, which in turn led to a premature withdrawal of forces from the area in which a decisive victory had been almost gained.

Winter weather was soon to impose inactivity in all parts of the Russian Front, but the Russians in winter would be able to do many things which the invaders could not. Immense reinforcements could be forwarded, and when spring came Russia not only would be well provided with munitions, but would have so completed her preparations that she might be in force superior to her Teutonic enemies. No Russian probably had expected to meet an army powerful enough to invade Russian soil and Russian cities. Proof from the Germans and Austria to the contrary only called out the fortitude and determination of the Russian people, who in 1915 had shown the fortitude which their great-grandfathers had shown when Napoleon advanced on Moscow. Fresh armies were being organized at Petrograd, Smolensk and Kief, in preparation for a spring campaign. Russia's resources in men were known to be practically inexhaustible. Allowing for a permanent loss already of four million killed, disabled and prisoners, there still remained from seven to eight millions between the ages of twenty and forty-four who were either in the fighting line or being trained in depots. Then there was the Opolochenie, or Imperial Militia, the final Russian reserve, which had not been drawn upon at all, but which could yield 10,000,000 men of fighting age when required. As far as men were concerned, Russia was in position to continue the war long after attrition had done its work among the armies of the two Central Powers. If the Russian Government could cope with the equipment difficulty during the winter months, she could look forward with confidence to the results of another year's campaign—that is, provided the morale of her people could be maintained, provided also that a revolution did not nullify every kind of forecast.

Russia expected by that time to have vast numbers of new men available for service out of the millions she would summon. All were to be under strict military law, but the majority were intended for use in perfecting services on which the success of the fighting forces at the front depended. Within a brief period of time all Russia that winter was turned into a military camp. Factories, ironworks, and engineering shops were taken over for the manufacture of everything needed for the armies in the field. The railways were served by men under military discipline. Russia was thus doing what Germany did at the outset of war. All the able-bodied men in the nation were serving her, some with rifle and bayonet, some with gun and maxim, some with pick and spade, but many others with the tools of peace which had now become the necessary tools of war. When properly supplied with rifles, Russia expected to have at least 2,000,000 additional soldiers. In due time her army would be well supplied with heavy guns and munitions, and her infantry with thousands of machine-guns and rifles. Thus optimistically ran the Russian news all that winter.

Russia was not to depend for another year on Archangel for an outlet in the west. Before 1916 she would have ready a still better port on the Arctic Ocean called Novo Alexandrovsk, which was the only port in the Arctic not absolutely closed to Russia at any season, either by the exigencies of war or by the rigors of winter. It lies well within the arctic circle. Through the winter of 1915-1916, munitions and supplies poured into it. Its importance became so great that a new and regular passenger-service was established from it to England and Sweden. Novo Alexandrovsk lay on a sort of eastern continuation of the Scandinavian peninsula. It was further north than Archangel, and, unlike Archangel, was not sheltered by land from arctic winds. Nevertheless, it was free of ice all winter long. The reason was the presence in its harbor of water from the Gulf Stream which there reached the last stage of its journey eastward and so warmed the arctic sea that with the air 22 degrees below zero, there was not a particle of ice in the harbor. The sea-water in this harbor, as a matter of fact, made snow along the water's edge continually melt.

It was not until the war revealed to Russia the urgent need of an ice-free port that certain old plans for a port at Novo Alexandrovsk and for a railway leading to it from the south, first made in Count Witte's time, had been disinterred, and thousands of men employed to put them into execution. By the latter part of 1915, a section of the line running south from the coast as far as Kandalaksk was ready. Meanwhile, communication from that point with Archangel over the ice of the White Sea was established for the winter by means of sledges and motor-wagons, while another line of sledge and motor-wagons was opened westward from Kandalaksk to Rovenieme, the nearest railway-station, with relays at intervals of from twenty-five to thirty miles. Some of the Finnish railroads were worked overtime while carrying supplies from Russia's new port. Meanwhile preparations were made to hasten forward a double-tracked line from

Novo Alexandrovsk to Petrograd, some 650 miles in length, as soon as the spring thaw of 1916 should set in.

This port stood out as one of the most important constructive results of the war. Finns, Lapps and Russians, alike labored unremittingly on the railway line between Petrograd and Semenowa, the latter city far beyond the arctic circle. The work was pushed feverishly in order to overreach the blockade by land and sea that had isolated Russia in the west. It meant the building of a road through an unfavorable country, in many places water-soaked by low-banked rivers, filled with countless lakes, and, through a great part of the year, frozen and buried under feet of snow. The line, in leaving Petrograd, ran east around Lake Ladoga, then turned to a northern course, until it reached its terminus on the Polar Sea. Novo Alexandrovsk was formerly a small collection of fishermen's huts. With its large docks and other harbor improvements, it was now to become a thriving port. While not such a warm-water port as the Muscovite had sought for years, it was on ice-free water, and navigation was possible all the year long around the North Cape. It gave Russia a new city on open, western waters, and a naval station beyond molestation by a rival Power. Thus, as stated, it probably formed the most important constructive effort put forth, at least by Russia, during the course of the war.

[7] Principal Sources: The *Times,* The *Tribune,* New York; The *Times* (London), The London *Times'* "History of the War"; The *Economist, The Fortnightly Review,* London; The *World,* The *Evening Sun,* New York; The *Daily Chronicle,* The *Morning Post,* London; "Bulletins" of the National Geographic Society (New York), Associated Press dispatches, "Nelson's History of the War" by John Buchan.

IN THE EAST, NEAR EAST AND SOUTH

Part III

RUSSIA'S RENEWAL OF THE OFFENSIVE

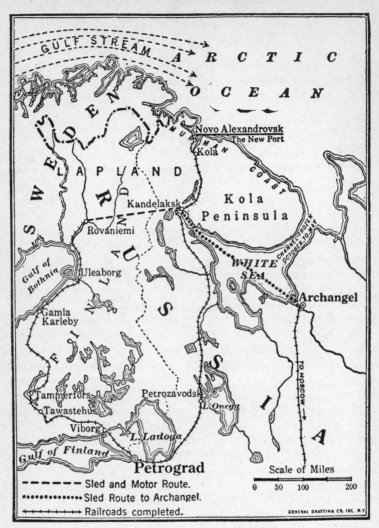

RUSSIA'S NEW RAILROAD TO AN ICE-FREE ARCTIC PORT

What came to be called Russia's Murman Railroad, its termini being Petrograd and Novo Alexandrovsk, a port on the Arctic Ocean, was completed in the third year of the war. Novo Alexandrovsk is ice-free all the year, owing to its exposure to the water from the Gulf Stream, whereas the more southern Russian Arctic port, Archangel, is closed from October to May for want of such water. At Novo Alexandrovsk vast supplies for Russia from Entente countries were arriving when the revolution eliminated Russia from the war

I

LUTSK, CZERNOWITZ AND KOLOMEA RECOVERED BY THE RUSSIANS UNDER BRUSILOFF

December 23, 1915—July 5, 1916

O N the Eastern Front the Russians, taking the offensive in the late winter and spring, assaulted German entrenchments at four points on the 700-mile line between Riga and Roumania, which now represented the high-water mark of the German advance of 1915. This line, except for local irregularities, ran almost straight north and south from the Dwina to the Pruth; that is, it followed the shortest route between the two points. It was shorter by a third than the line which the Germans and Austrians would have had to defend if they had stayed within their own national boundaries. Thus by their invasion of Russia, which had eliminated the Polish salient, they had shortened their front, instead of lengthening it. But they had assumed new obligations on the lower eastern frontier—that is, obligations to defend Serbia and Bulgaria from Allied drives that now were expected to take place later from Saloniki, Mackensen having conquered Serbia in an easy drive.

While the line along which the Germans had maintained their winter-quarters was well adapted for defensive purposes, they had failed at two points to secure strategic positions; these were near the two ends of the line. At the southern end, the Austrians had not been able to free their country altogether from the invaders: the Russians held on stoutly to a corner of Galicia north of the Dniester and to the fortress of Rovno, just inside the frontier. At the northern end, the Germans had not been able to capture Riga and Dvinsk, where their front made a curve around the two cities, between which it extended to the Dwina at Jacobstadt and Friedrichstadt. What the Russians now did was to strike at these two defective sectors in the Teutonic line. If they could succeed in the south, they might be able to reinvade the Bukowina and Galicia, in which case Roumania might join with them in an attack on Hungary. If they succeeded in the north, they might compel the Germans to evacuate the Baltic provinces.

The mildest winter in decades had been an important factor in rendering futile Rusian efforts thus far to gain lost territory. Every mile of the front fairly bristled with deadly machine-guns. With a multitude of rapid-firing guns, the Germans, with a small number of men, were able to hold a line definitely. Millions of running feet of barbed-wire entanglements had transformed each village and house into a fortress. Swamps from two to ten miles wide, in the region of Pinsk, were not once frozen over entirely during the winter. Not only was every yard of this front fenced in with entanglements, but there were supporting points at short intervals which, in themselves, became veritable fortresses surrounded by star-shaped barricades of wire. Each was subdivided into barricaded sections, with bomb-proof shelters, and machine-guns along both sides of each point of the star. Supporting points were surrounded by wire, stretched knee-high on which were hung pairs of empty bottles which would clink an alarm the moment a wire was touched.

On December 23 fighting had been unexpectedly renewed at the southern end of the front. Here the Russians were the attacking side. For months news had been current of the massing of Russian troops in southern Russia. As far back as the middle of February, the fall of Erzerum had made it clear to the world at large how considerable a portion of the Russian army was operating in Asia, and yet another portion had been ready for an offensive on the Bessarabian frontier toward the end of December, the purpose being to distract German attention from the Balkans, and to cover up the Russian preparations for the master-blow that was to come in the Caucasus. The most natural line for this Russian offensive against the Teutons, because the most threatening, led through a gap between the Dniester and the Pruth. Here an advance could be effected on a limited front. Broken ground offered scope for skilful maneuvering and enfilading fire from well-placed batteries. Sapping and mining devices were used. A much-contested ridge between two villages was carried, and important heights dominating the approach to Czernowitz were captured. Tales were told of heroic deeds, suffering and death by Tcherkiss fighters from the Caucasus, by patient Russian muzhiks, by Slav peasants from Moravia and Croatia in Austro-Hungarian uniforms, as well as by Magyars and Germans, the two master races of the Hapsburg monarchy.

Late in January, along the Dniester and in the corner where meet the frontiers of Russia, Austria and Roumania, the Russian offensive attracted close attention. For several weeks progress was made. Once there were heard from Petrograd unconfirmed rumors that Czernowitz had fallen and that Russian troops were about to penetrate the Bukowina. Further to the north, about Tarnopol and east of the fortresses of Dubno and Lutzk, which had fallen to the Austrians in the summer offensive, the Russians were approaching the Styr river between the fortresses of Lutzk and the Pripet Marshes. Fighting here was severe. The Russians made material progress in Galicia, and passing the Sereth approached and crossed the Styrpa at certain

GENERAL SUKHOMLINOFF

Sukhomlinoff served first as Chief of Staff to the Grand Duke and afterward as Minister of War. He was accused of treason, formally tried and sentenced to imprisonment with loss of rank

points, pushing up-stream along the Dniester at several points north and west of Czernowitz. After moderate progress this offensive in the last days of January had apparently been checked.

In February, however, it was announced that the Russians had captured Usciezko in Galicia. Usciezko was a natural stronghold, on a high ridge between the Dniester and its tributary, the Zurin, near the point of confluence. Here the Teutons dominated a wide stretch of country on the east bank and poured a galling fire into Russian positions. The precipitous slopes of the ridge, covered with dense undergrowth under the guidance of German engineers, had been converted into a miniature Gibraltar. The Russians not only stormed this strong German position, but crossed the Dniester, altho the opposite bank was equally precipitous and strongly fortified. By driving the Teutons west of the Dniester, they achieved a notable tactical success and one which favorably influenced the minor strategy of the campaign in Galicia.

The Russian operation in all this territory bordering on the Bukowina and Roumania was an effort to retake certain valuable positions in order to make more certain their hold there, and to strengthen their line against a possible spring offensive by regaining towns and hills that possest strategic or tactical value. There were now distinctly hopeful signs of an Allied success on the Eastern Frontier because of this recuperation in the Russian armies. Under these circumstances the Russians in the last days of March renewed the war, assuming the initiative at first south of Dvinsk, where they aimed at driving a wedge into the German lines. The extent of the battle-front indicated the employment of large forces, but they felt able to take advantage, and perhaps to take chances, from the absorption of German energies at Verdun, where the great assault had begun on February 21. The resumption in the north was coupled with an offensive in the lake-country south of Dvinsk, where the Russians engaged the Teutons on a fifty-mile front between lakes Drisviaty and Narocz, and must have brought into play well over 100,000 men with an expenditure of ammunition to correspond. Simultaneously the Austrian bridge-head at Usiesko, one of the two positions on the north bank of the Dniester that remained in Teutonic control after the January fighting, fell into Russian hands. The importance of the struggle then going on around Verdun naturally overshadowed in all the war news the contest on the Eastern Front, but on the evening of March 19, more than 50,000 shells, chiefly of heavy caliber, fell over a small section in the east near Postavy. At night the Russians attacked in thick waves, the first two of which were mowed down before they reached the German entanglements. The third only pierced the German position on a front of less than 100 yards, and by a counter-attack the Russians were ejected from it. At dawn they made a fourth attack, but it was smothered in the initial stages by German artillery.

Four divisions participated in these movements, which were finally developed from isolated encounters along a ten-mile front into a general engagement that extended over more than thirty-five miles. The Russians forestalled the Germans by cutting into the German front between

RUSSIAN DUGOUTS

Augustinov and Epkun, and by a southward advance toward the railway. This German sector projected in a horseshoe-shaped line toward the east. Despite fierce counter-attacks the Germans were not able to recover what they lost. The Russians also pushed out in the neighborhood of Lake Sventen. Climatic conditions hampered movements on both sides, but all along the front some fighting was in progress. In the neighborhood of Kolki the Germans abandoned their first line defenses because they were flooded out of them, but they held their second line. They did a large amount of aviation work, but some of their aeroplanes were brought down. Tremendous expenditures of ammunition on the Uxkull bridgehead did not bring them results. For weeks they failed to penetrate the Russian line in frontal attacks.

May brought an Austrian eruption into Italy, but General Alexeiev made no sign of further movement in the east, which aroused criticism because the Italian commander, Cadorna, was sorely tried, and it looked as if the Archduke Karl might reach the Venetian plains. The fact was that Russia had her own plans and they needed time to mature. She was making ready for a great combined Allied offensive which was due as soon as Germany had spent her strength at Verdun and British troops and guns were ready for action on the Somme in northern France. It had taken Russia all the weeks of a long winter to make her preparations, to drill her reserves, to improve communications, and collect munitions. Ivanov's Christmas attack on Czernowitz and Ewert's spring offensive toward Vilna had been only local assaults with a local purpose. The real advance had been conceived on a far greater scale, and with a wider strategic purpose. At a given signal, in conjunction with her Allies, Russia finally swept forward, when that device of Germany's which had hitherto checked Russia—the power of moving troops at will by her great internal railway lines —was defeated. The Teutonic power when fighting everywhere at once would have no troops to move.

With the coming of early summer, Russia resumed the offensive, vigorously now and for weeks successfully. Her task had been in a way similar to that of Great Britain. She had found herself in the midst of an unprovoked war in a condition where she had to build up new armies and devise means for supplying them with war-material. Russia, however, unlike Great Britain, was favored in having highly trained officers, and in possessing, in the widest sense of the word, the tradition of a great national army; but she was handicapped in matters of industrial development and of communications within her border, and with the outer world. In spite of this, Russia thus far accomplished results and surpassed even the hopes of Russia's Allies. All this should be kept in remembrance when reflecting on Russia's collapse in March, 1917.

RUSSIA'S RENEWAL OF THE OFFENSIVE

The summer of 1916 found Russian armies between the Baltic and the Roumanian frontier grouped in three main divisions. Kuropatkin, who by an Imperial ukase dated February 19, had been appointed Commander-in-Chief of the Northern Armies in place of Plehve, was in charge of the Riga Dvinsk line. The center facing Vilna remained under command of Ewarts, who, by skill displayed in the retreat from the Niemen, had enhanced a reputation earned in the Russo-Japanese War. The armies south of the Pripet Marshes were under command of Ivanoff, but in the first days of April that old soldier was recalled to Imperial Headquarters to act as military adviser to the Czar, and his place at the front was taken by Brusiloff, who had hitherto led the Eighth Army. At the beginning of the summer offensive, Brusiloff's command included four armies. Toward the end of June, when Volhynia had become the main battle-ground of Europe, the army commanded by Lesh was transferred to this theater.

It was in the southern area, and especially in the spheres of operation of the Eighth and Ninth Russian Armies, that the chief battles were fought during the opening stages of the new offensive. There were two separate regions within that area, the Russian district of Volhynia and the Austrian territories in East Galicia and the Bukowina. It was in the country between the Dniester and the Carpathians that the advance was pushed most vigorously during the first month. Here it was possible to exploit to the full an initial advantage without danger of sudden reverses.

There were three stages in the Russian offensive. The first began on June 4, with the piercing of the Austrian lines in the district of Lutsk and in the Bukowina. The following month saw these tactical achievements developed into strategical victories. Two Austro-Hungarian armies, one in Volhynia and the other south of the Dniester, were involved in irretrievable disaster, and the parts of the front held by them caved in. The second phase was mainly concerned with three Austrian armies holding the line between the Pripet Marshes and Roumania. The problem here was whether an approximately straight line was to be regained by the flattening out of Russian salients or by a completion

205

of the Russian advance. By the middle of August, when the troops of Bothner evacuated the last remaining sectors of the original front, this question was definitely solved in favor of the Russians. The problem of the third phase was whether it was possible to make any further advance at this time in the Podolian center; that is, between the Lvoff-Krasne-Tarnapol railway in the north and the Dniester in the south. Considerable tactical success was gained toward the end of August and in September, but no strategic advance was achieved and meantime the center of the fighting on the Eastern Front shifted to the Roumanian theater. Management of the Eastern Front had now passed into German hands, which had provided large reinforcements to fill gaps in the depleted ranks of Austria, and the entire front was put under Hindenburg.

It was after some advances by the Germans at Verdun, after their capture of a village from the British in Picardy, and after Austrian captures of Alpine peaks and passes from the Italians, that brief bulletins came from Petrograd announcing the taking of some thousands of Austro-Hungarian prisoners and the occupation of regions some square miles in extent. By June 4 the Russian drive extended along a line of 250 miles, or from the Pripet River to the Roumanian frontier. No such ambitious attempt had been launched since the Austro-German advance in the spring of 1915 on a line stretching from the Baltic to the Carpathians. It eventually effected the collapse of the Austrian line along the Styr and Ikwa rivers, with results in the Pripet Marshes and in Galicia. Such was the news that now came from the eastern frontier that for a time it overshadowed the land-fighting in any other territory, even that at Verdun. Russia apparently was to prove herself the savior of the Entente. She had once been beaten, but it had taken Austria, and all the men Germany could spare, from February to October, 1915, to do it, and during all that time the lines in the west were practically free from attacks. But now, with Italy in straits, Russia once more was coming forward. Austria's advance in the Trentino had proved that her concentration was far greater than the Allies knew or had imagined, and yet the Russian front was the only

place from which Austrian forces could have been drawn.
Russia at the same time was fighting desperately against the
Turks in the Caucasus and in Mesopotamia and was apparently making every sacrifice, in order to maintain her
eastern army at a maximum of offensive power.

The military objectives of the Russian drive were
essentially two. The first was the town of Kovel; the second
Lemberg. The railroads from Kovel and Lemberg were the
life-lines of the Austrian army north of Galicia. If Kovel

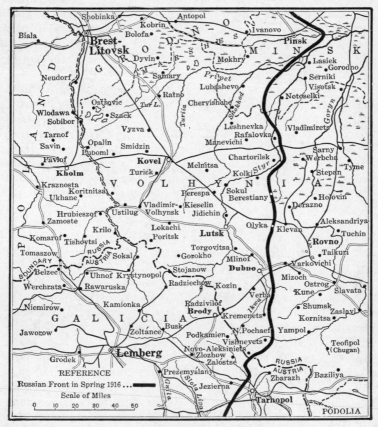

BRUSILOFF'S SECOND OFFENSIVE IN TERRITORY EAST OF
BREST-LITOVSK

fell there would be a section of line more than a hundred miles in length without railroad transportation, in a country that was one vast swamp, and through which it was almost impossible to construct roads with any of the paraphernalia

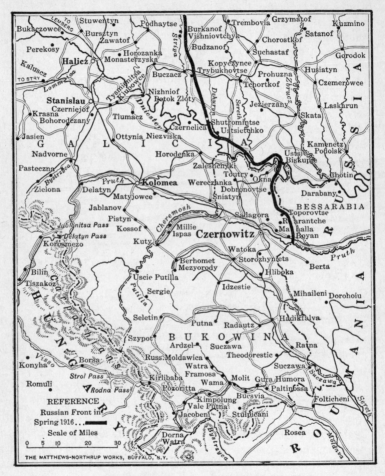

BRUSILOFF'S SECOND OFFENSIVE IN THE SOUTHERN PART

The advance began on practically the whole eastern line, but was most notable in the parts shown in this map and the map on page 207. The towns most concerned in it were Lutsk, Dubno, and Kovel in the map on page 207, Kolomea, Stanislau and Czernowitz in the above map

carried by an army. This offensive could not be compared to any of the offensive movements in the west. Here it was not a question of storming a first-line trench and then resting. The Russians had first to sweep through whole networks of trenches that the Austrians had constructed for several miles in the rear of their lines, but they now had them in the open and did not give them time to dig in.

Events seemed to be moving favorably for this project. The Serbian army, reconstituted under French protection at Corfu, had been brought to Saloniki, and was about 100,000 strong. Turkey had lost Erzerum and Trebizond and been forced to send her best troops away from the Balkans. Italy had resisted the Austrian attack, not brilliantly, but sufficiently to reassure her Allies. Austria had lost in the late winter an important position at Usziesko on the Dniester. It was small wonder that the Bulgarians became alarmed and seized Greek forts on the Macedonian border in an effort at any cost to strengthen their southern front; small wonder that the Crown Prince redoubled his efforts to break the French front at Verdun because the danger to the Teutons in the southeast had become immediate.

On June 4, Russian guns began slowly and methodically to throw their shells on previously selected points of the German line. It did not appear that any attempt was made to wipe out the German trenches; the object was rather to cut avenues in wire-entanglements through which the Russian infantry could proceed to attack German positions. The artillery action in the different sectors lasted from twelve to thirty hours. Then followed a bayonet attack. As soon as the Russians entered Austrian front trenches, artillery developed a curtain of fire which precluded all communications with the rear, and the Austrians were trapt. Their deep trenches, covered with solid oak timbers, fastened with cement, and surmounted by thick layers of earth, once the Russians reached them, became cages, and death or surrender was the only alternative. During the first hours the Teutonic infantry, especially the Hungarians, fought furiously, and thousands were killed. Then their resistance slackened and they began to surrender. One day alone the haul of Austrian prisoners amounted to 13,000. On the third day, by noon, the armies of Brusiloff had taken as prisoners 900 officers and over 40,000 of the rank and file, had captured 77 guns and 134 machine-guns, 49 trench-mortars, searchlights, telephones, field-kitchens, and a large quantity of arms and material of war, with reserves of ammunition. A number of batteries were taken intact with all their guns and limbers. As ammunition-magazines are usually stationed about ten miles behind the front trenches, the enormous hauls of the first days in themselves gave witness to the swiftness of the Russian advance. The shortness of the bombardment preceding the attack and the simultaneous character of the operations along a front of about 250 miles, were novel features of the offensive. The most important fighting and the most signal victory of these opening days occurred within the triangle of the Volhynian fortresses.

The Austrians probably never dreamed of being turned out of their positions. Their works ran along the edge of a wood, with trenches constructed elaborately from great unhewn logs, heavily covered over, and so connected up with reserve- and support-trenches winding in every direction through the woodland that the occupants must have considered themselves absolutely secure. At a safe distance from rifle-fire behind the lines, Stanley Washburn [1] came on officers' quarters which seemed like a veritable park in the heart of a forest. He found a beer-garden "with buildings beautifully constructed from logs and decorated with rustic tracery, while chairs and tables made of birch stood in lonely groups about the garden, just where they were left when the occupants of the place suddenly departed." In a sylvan bower was erected "a beautiful altar of birch trimmed with rustic traceries, the whole surrounded by a fence through which one passed under an arch neatly made of birch-branches." Mr. Washburn thought the Austrians must have had an extremely comfortable time there. Everything was clean and neat, and, no matter how humble the work, it was always replete with good taste. One of the advancing corps captured a trench which had a piano in it.

[1] Correspondent of The *Times* (London).

Everywhere Mr. Washburn found signs of the Austrian intention to make their stay as comfortable as possible.

The attack against the fortress of Lutsk was conducted along concentric lines. On the first day it cut clean through the lines and cavalry poured through the gaps. Large bodies of Austro-Hungarian troops between Olyka and the Ikwa were cut off from all possibility of retreat before they even knew that their front had been broken. By June 6, the Russian forces had advanced more than twenty miles from their original positions and were approaching Lutsk from two sides. Lutsk itself, in a strong, natural position, covered on both wings by the deep and tortuous valley of the Styr, had been changed in the course of the war into a regular fortress. Defenses of enormous strength covered its approaches, but the Austro-Hungarian troops were unable to offer serious resistance. Their lines were broken through near Podgaytse and near Krupy, and on June 6 the first Russian detachments entered Lutsk. Considerable artillery-stores fell into their hands. The Austrians, having had no time to clear out the hospitals, had to abandon thousands of their wounded.

Not only did the Russians gain the banks of the Ikwa and Styr, but they crossed those streams. In the region of Kovel, midway between Lutsk and Brest-Litovsk, and near Rovno, southeast of the fortress, they extended their lines, and in Galicia captured along the lower reaches of the Stripa heavily fortified positions. Considerable activity at the same time was shown by the Germans on the northern sections of the Russian front, where German guns bombarded the line along the Dwina to the lake region south of Dvinsk and threw infantry attacks against Russian positions south of Smorgon. By June 10 Petrograd reported that 1,143 officers and over 64,700 men had been made prisoners since the great drive began. The advance was notable for prisoners taken and machine-guns, ammunition, and other war-stores captured. The Russians reported that they had forced back the organized lines of their antagonists from the region of the Volhynia fortress triangle as far as Roumania.

Having captured Lutsk, the Russians retook Dubno, the

second of the fortresses in the triangle. Here the work was not as easy as it had been at Lutsk. The picturesque old town, in consequence, had to suffer severe damage. Simultaneously with this advance another Russian detachment captured the Austrian *point d'appui* at Mlynoff, on the Ikwa, and then crossed the river and occupied the Demidovka region. During the next few days they forced the enemy from the forests which cover this region, thus securing the Lutsk salient from a sudden counter-offensive from the south. On June 13 they reached the village of Kozin, eighteen miles southwest of Dubno and nine miles west of the old battle-front on the Ikwa. Lutsk and Dubno, when the war began, constituted Russia's second line of defense in Poland.

Due west of Lutsk the advance, meantime, was pushed forward at considerable speed. On June 12 the Russians reached Torchin, eighteen miles west of Lutsk. Next day fierce fighting occurred near Zaturtsy, more than half-way from Lutsk to Vladimir-Volynsk. By June 16 the sweep of the tide westward had attained high-water mark. Outposts occupied a wide semicircle round Olyka, with a radius of about forty-five miles, which stretched from about Kolki, on the Styr, to the north, then followed the Stokhod from near Svidniki to Kisielin, and reaching its farthest extension west in the Lokatchy-Sviniukhy-Gorokhoff sector bent back to the east toward Kozin. It was on the two wings of that salient that the last considerable gains were effected during the first stages of the offensive.

The Germans were certain soon to start a counter-offensive. They were bringing up fresh troops, not merely from the northern area, but from France also, for they had to defend Kovel at any price. Its loss would have meant the cutting of direct communication between the northern and southern armies. A violent battle developed in the narrow sector where the courses of the Styr and Stokhod approach within some six to eight miles of one another, and by June 10 the Russians entered Radzivloff, the frontier-station on the Rovno-Brody-Lcoff railway.

Twelve days of the offensive in Volhynia had resulted in an advance of thirty miles to the southwest of the recaptured fortress of Dubno, and a similar distance to the northwest of Lutsk. The entire Volhynia triangle of fortresses was again in Russian hands, while their outposts approached within some twenty-five miles of Kovel and reached the northeastern border of Galicia in front of Brody. In the course of those twelve days, the Cossack army of Kaledine alone had taken as prisoners 1,309 officers, 10 surgeons, and 70,000 soldiers; it had captured 83 guns, 236 machine-guns, and quantities of other war-material.

About the middle of June the pressure of the new German concentrations was beginning to make itself felt in

A GERMAN WAR-BRIDGE IN RUSSIA

Volhynia, and resulted in about a fortnight of fierce, but more or less stationary, fighting on the entire front. German operations, which had Kovel for their base, were directed mainly against the Stokhod-Styr sector, while the Austrians, supported by German troops, fought in front of Vladimir-Volynsk, Sokal, and Stojanoff, and attacked the Lokatchy-Sviniukhy-Gorokhoff line. Before these violent German onslaughts the Russians found themselves obliged to withdraw their troops from the western bank of the Stokhod near Svidniki. A furious battle ensued on the front extending from Sokal by way of Gadomitche, Linievka and

Voronchin to Kieselin, and on June 19 this fighting resulted in success for the Russians, who captured considerable numbers of prisoners. No less violent was the German counter-offensive against the apex of the Lutsk salient. The similarity between Brusiloff's advance and the Russian drive against the Austrians at the beginning of the war was generally commented on. One difference, however, was pointed out; Brusiloff's initial blow in 1916 was considerably more effective, the retreat of the Austrians this time being more precipitate than in August and September, 1914.

There were no official reports printed of the Austrian losses. Optimistic estimates at Petrograd placed them as high as 200,000 men. Kovel, next to Lemberg the most important railroad center behind the eastern Austrian line, with Lemberg and Czernowitz, was an immediate objective of the Russian drive. With its capture the Russians would have been in complete control of the railway system serving that wing of the Austro-Hungarian front. They were squeezing the southern Teuton armies between two flanks, forcing them to retreat further and further toward the Carpathians. With Kovel taken the Teutonic right wing would have been completely cut off from their armies in the north. Kovel, a town of 30,000 people at the beginning of the war, owed its strategic importance wholly to the fact that it was the junction point for railroads which radiate, like the spokes from the hub of a wheel, in five directions. To the northwest, 77 miles distant, was the strongly fortified city of Brest-Litovsk, with a population in 1913 of 63,579, over whose possession there had been a terrific struggle when the Germans were driving the Russians back through Poland early in the war. To the southeast, 84 miles away, was Rovno, a fortress with a population of 34,923 in 1913, and at that time the headquarters of the Eleventh Russian Army Corps. Lublin, with 69,972 inhabitants in 1913, was 100 miles due west, on the railroad running to Warsaw, 209 miles away. Then to the south was Vladimir-Volynski, 35 miles distant. To the east ran the line which passed through Sarny on its way to Kief.

By June 19 Czernowitz was in the hands of the Russians, and the Austrians were in retreat towards the Carpathians.

Hard fighting took place for the capture of the Czernowitz bridgehead, but finally the Russians gained the right bank of the river and the Austrians evacuated the capital, leaving 1,000 prisoners and some guns in the hands of the Russians. Altho Czernowitz had changed hands many times in this war, it still remained a point of interest and importance. It was the capital of Austrian crown-lands, forming one of the richest parts of Galicia. It was, moreover, the strongest bridgehead along the Pruth. Once taken, the entire Austrian position along the Pruth could be turned, and the Austrians compelled to retreat to the Carpathians. A large section of the Austrian army would by such a maneuver be cut off from the main army and placed in a precarious position. With a population of 94,000 in 1914, Czernowitz was the most easterly city of importance in the Austro-Hungarian empire.

It was now beginning to appear that the rejuvenation of the Russian forces had been so complete that the whole aspect of the war might change. The real advance on Czernowitz had been held in abeyance until the capture of Lutsk and Dubno could be accomplished, so that the final assault awaited the moment when Brusiloff was sure of his gains in the Lutsk region, 150 miles further north, and when he might cut off the defenders of Czernowitz from their natural line of retreat, westward through Sniatyn, thus forcing them southward into the Carpathians. The capture of the place was in this manner subordinated to a greater purpose. As soon as the offensive had made fast its gains beyond Lutsk, and had provided against a withdrawal of the Austrians from Czernowitz toward Lemberg, the assault moved forward and forced its way into the city.

The reoccupation of Lutsk meant not merely the collapse of the Austrian line along the Styr and Ikwa, but produced results immediately perceptible north in the Pripet Marshes and south in Galicia. Victory in the neighborhood of Czernowitz had similar importance. Elements of surprize largely entered into news of this advance. Vienna spoke of incredible stores of ammunition which the enemy had at his disposal, and of unceasing attacks in solid formation. Russian resourcefulness apparently had been equal to the gathering of vast reserves without their being discovered. It was plain that, if the seriousness of the menace had been recognized at Vienna, there would have been no diversion of troops to the Italian frontier. The new Russian commander's strategic plan seemed to have absolutely deceived the Austrians. Whatever might be the furthest reach of the advance, the harvest of prisoners was bound to mount rapidly.

Lutsk and Dubno not only offered the military facilities which such places always give, but in addition were selected strongholds, forming an integral part of the old Russian defensive organization. Their capture brought the Russian strength on this part of the front back to what it was at the outset of the war, for it reintegrated the fortified triangle. This first chapter of the offensive exceeded in results all that the Germans had to show for nearly four months at Verdun, or that the Austrians could boast for their three weeks' offensive in northern Italy. Obtained by tactics of suddenness, the successes were won without any expenditure comparable to that which a slower method would have involved. The fortresses fell without a siege, and with them was taken a huge aggregation of Austrian troops. The number of prisoners reported had a parallel only in the earlier stages of the war.

Russia's defensive problems, however, were north of the Pripet Marshes, not south of them. A victory against Hindenburg would strengthen her defense more than any other success. Her lower successes were brilliant but secondary. Their chief importance lay in their relation to further plans for which they formed the preliminary. By June 13 heavy fighting was in progress over virtually the entire Eastern front from the Gulf of Riga to the Bukowina, a distance of between 600 and 700 miles. From Riga to the Jasiolda River, northwest of the Pripet Marsh region, the Germans had taken the offensive probably in an effort to divert Russian attention. On all sectors the Russians successfully withstood the onslaughts; they even gained ground north of the Tirul Marsh, southwest of Riga. Altho the Austrians vigorously counter-attacked, the only place where the Russians were forced to give ground was near Robulintze, north

GEN. ALEXIS A. BRUSILOFF

VII.

of Buczacz, in Galicia, where the Austrians had been reinforced by German troops. The total of men made prisoners by the Russians since their offensive began had now grown to more than 114,000.

Russia's restoration to a state of military efficiency, as shown by these events, was in no small degree due to the opening of her new port on the Arctic Ocean and the building of the Murman railway which connected that port with Petrograd. In less than a year Russia had laid and set in operation four-fifths of this line, which put her out of all danger from future isolation by the Teutonic powers. By late spring in 1916 the last 150 miles were completed, so that Russia thenceforth became accessible from the ocean at all times of the year. Endless and seemingly bottomless bogs were crossed; piles and pile-drivers more than once disappeared in bogs; miles of bald rock were levelled' and smoothed out by use of dynamite. Thirty thousand men worked to carry out the project. The line was a broad gage, single track route, fairly free from heavy grades and sharp curves. Forests supplied wood for fuel, wood being the customary railway fuel in Russia.

General von Linsingen, in battles from June 15th to the 18th, not only checked the Russian forward movement on his front, but at some places forced a retrograde movement countering on the wing. He advanced on the line between Vladimir-Volynski and Lutsk from Boronzowicz to Cholinowka. The turning point was near Novomosor. In this movement he took 3,500 Russian prisoners. Brusiloff at the same time was increasing his pressure on the center of the middle sector, but this movement was apparently affected by the counter-pressure against the Russian line in the northerly part of Volhynia. Brusiloff was recognized as the first Russian strategist who had proved himself worthy of the mettle of the German strategists matched against him. By June 21 it was seen that the Germans and Austrians in Volhynia were vigorously on the offensive and seemingly had stopt for the time being the Russian drive westward. Along the Stokhod River, west of the Styr, in the region of Sokul, and still farther west around Mylsk, sanguinary engagements were in progress. In some of these encounters the Germans and Austrians were repulsed, but on both sides of the Turia River and southward from Sviniauki and beyond the Russians were driven farther back, and northeast of Lutsk their attempts to dispute German successes were without result. On the Stripa in Galicia the Russians took portions of trenches near Gaivironka and farther south in Bukowina drove their forces southward and captured Radautz, thirty miles below Czernowitz, where they took more officers, men, and guns. North of the Pripet Marshes, in the region of Riga, the Germans opened a rather general offensive, heavily bombarding Russian positions, or making violent infantry-attacks against them. The Germans vigorously bombarded the Ikskull bridge-head and drove their infantry against Russian positions around Dvinsk, near Dubatowka, south of Krevo and on the Oginski Canal.

Fierce fighting, with the Germans generally aggressors, was now in progress along the Stokhod and Styr rivers and in the region between Lutsk and Vladimir Volynski. Russians who had crossed the Styr and reached Gruziatyn, west of Kolki, entered that town and captured eleven officers, 400 men, and six machine-guns. The town changed hands several times, but under a concentrated German artillery-fire the Russians finally were driven back with the loss of 1,000 men made prisoners. Along the Stokhod, near Bajmiesto, the Germans delivered a heavy attack, which resolved itself later into hand-to-hand fighting, in which the Russians, according to Petrograd, forced the Germans to flee. Near Kisel'n another heavy onslaught was checked by the Russians and the Germans put to flight. Near Lokatchi, southeast of Vladimir-Volynski, Vienna reported the capture of 1,300 Russians. North, west and northwest of Lutsk vicious encounters ensued. Across the frontier in Galicia a stalemate in the region of Buczacz persisted. In Bukowina the Russians continued to drive the Austrians west and southwest. Petrograd announced that the prisoners taken by the Russians in Volhynia and Galicia up to June 15 aggregated 172,484.

Radautz, in the southern Bukowina, eleven miles southwest of the Sereth, fell to the Russians on June 22. Radautz lies

a little more than nine miles west of the Roumanian frontier. Its capture put the Russians in possession of thirty
miles, or one-half of Roumania's western border, thus isolating the northwestern part of that country from the Central
Powers. The fall of Radautz further placed the extreme
left wing of Brusiloff's invading armies in full control of
the railway running vertically through the Bukowina, from
Zalesczyki to Radautz, and threatened the southern prolonga-
tion of this line running through Suczawa into the interior

REPAIRING A DAMAGED RAILWAY-BRIDGE ON THE
DUNAJEC RIVER

of Roumania. Thus the Russian commander had now, in
the line from Tarnopol in northwestern Galicia down to
Radautz, an excellent base-railway for the continuation of
his offensive.

Moreover, the new advance into southern Bukowina had
dealt a blow to the commercial relations recently established
between Roumania and the Central Powers by the conclusion of a trade-agreement under which the three powers
were to export to one another surplus quantities of foodstuffs. Much of the grain shipped from Roumania to Aus-

tria and Germany under this compact went via the Bucharest-Budapest-Vienna-Berlin railway. The Russian drive in the south assumed a new aspect in that it threatened a tightening of the food-blockade of the Teutonic countries. If pushed further to the south on the Danube, on which river the bulk of the commercial exchange was carried on, the new trade-pact would be reduced to abrogation. Roumania would be isolated and virtually blockaded from the north, northwest, and east, while the Teuton-Bulgarian Macedonia army would be placed between the Russians and the Franco-British forces.

The fall of Radautz compelled the Austro-Hungarian troops in southern Bukowina to retreat before the Russians to the foothills of the Carpathians. From Radautz a railway line runs due west as far as Frasin. When the Austrians reached that point in a mountainous region, they would be practically cut off from rail communication and would have to work their way through hills to the northern lines which in turn were menaced by the Russians driving toward Kolomea. The ferocity of the fighting in Volhynia was indicated by a sentence in the Russian official report to the effect that "no quarter was given, as the enemy used explosive bullets." The scene of this particular occurrence was in the region of Voronchin, east of the Stokhod.

Meanwhile Pfanzer's demoralized Austrian army was preparing to abandon all southern Bukowina to the Russians, and the Russians were throwing large forces across the Sereth, aiming to cut off the Austrians. The Russian advance on the Kovel sector had now been checked by heavy Austro-German counter-attacks, but the Russians were overrunning the Bukowina and making a dash for the Carpathian passes as they had done eighteen months before, when they reached Kirlibaba Pass that overlooked Austrian Transylvania. The Russians had already taken possession of two railways leading from Roumania into Bukowina. By forced marches along the Roumanian frontier the Russians reached the extreme south of the Bukowina by June 24, and at Kuty on the north and Gurahumora on the south approached the thickly forested spurs of the Carpathians where a good road, roughly about 100 miles long, runs through narrow valleys and gorges by way of Kimpolung and Dorna Wastra to Bistritz, Hungary, offering Russian guerrillas an excellent opening into the country. The Russians in their pursuit of the Austrians thus far had crossed four rivers— the Dniester, Pruth, Sereth and Suczava. Two days sufficed to cover the fifteen miles between the Sereth and the Suczava. The objective had been Radautz, where the Austrians were expected to offer a stubborn resistance, owing to the fact that the river forms a natural defensive line to the north and northwest of the town, but they failed to make any serious stand. Radautz is only five miles southwest of the important railway junction of Hadikfalva, close to the Roumanian frontier, which also was in Russian hands.

Lemberg was now imperilled. Once it was recovered, the Russians would be in a position to repeat their offensive of 1914 against the Carpathian passes. The Austrians were far less strong than they were sixteen months before, and besides they now had to guard Serbia and oppose Italy, while Germany had fewer troops to send them in an emergency. The chain of Teuton dependencies could be cut at Budapest as well as at Sofia or Constantinople. The Russians were convinced of Austrian exhaustion and that they could force the fight into Hungary, and carry the warfare into Bulgaria as well. With the occupation of Czernowitz the Russians had completely severed connections between the Teutonic northern and southern armies. This stroke had enabled the Russians to establish direct connections from the frontier to Sniatyn by the shortest and most convenient route which greatly facilitated Russian progress toward Kolomea, and, by obviating further the necessity of a turning movement, allowed the Russian southern forces to advance solidly from the Czernowitz region westward.

It was not true, as often stated, that the fall of Czernowitz was more important in its diplomatic implications than in its military results. Czernowitz had changed hands before and yet Roumania had not taken action. Russia, more than a year before, had stood at the gateways of the Carpathians, and Roumania still held off. Complete Austrian disaster alone could have forced Roumania from her position of obstinate neutrality. The fall of Czernowitz and the forcing of the Pruth were important military events. The advance of Russian forces from Czernowitz northward toward Kolomea and Stanislau was a threat against the rear of the German army under Bothmer, whose obstinate stand on the Strypa had been one of the conspicuous incidents of the campaign. It was only the Germans who could make any head against Brusiloff—in the south under Bothmer, in the north under Linsingen.

Each time a change was made in the possession of Czernowitz, the question raised was: What of Roumania now? When the Russians first took Czernowitz in the Autumn of 1914, all the world expected Roumania to declare her adhesion to the Allies. It seemed the most natural thing for her to do, whether considered politically or morally. Russia would have been willing, no doubt, to give Roumania the conquered province of the Bukowina, but Roumania remained neutral. It was well for her that she did so, for the Austrians eventually recovered the Bukowina, and the political odds in that part of Europe were suddenly, but not permanently, altered. During the German Balkan campaign, which engulfed the neutrality of Bulgaria, Roumania a second time was in a position to make a handsome bargain, for the Allies would have promised her almost anything in reason for her accession to their cause, as a counterweight to Bulgaria, which had gone the other way, but, again, Roumanians knew what their own interests were, and so kept a tight hold on their neutrality, and went on trading at great profit with belligerents, and especially with the Germans.

Roumania accordingly grew rich, while her relative strength steadily mounted. She had the largest army in the whole Balkan peninsula, more efficient troops than Bulgaria and Greece combined, and held the balance of power in that theater of war. With the man-power of the great belligerents diminishing constantly, her importance increased, until it seemed able in itself to determine the fate of the peninsula. Apparently she could, either herself or in coöperation with Russia, close to the Germans the corridor running through Serbia and Bulgaria to Turkey, and so could close again the iron ring around the Central Powers and cast Turkey out of the fighting world, all by one stroke. But Roumania, with all this apparent good fortune, found herself in a dilemma. She knew she had to come into the war some time, or she would lose her position and influence in the Balkan peninsula. To take part with the Allies, however, was to stop the stream of German gold pouring in for her products, whereas to go the other way was to part with her neutrality prematurely, and in addition make perhaps a wrong guess.

JAPANESE GUNS CAPTURED BY GERMANS FROM THE RUSSIANS

After these successes Brusiloff was asked to explain why he had achieved such results. He declared that they were not the product of chance, or of Austrian weakness, but represented the application of all the lessons learned in two years of bitter warfare against the Germans. Russia, in 1914, lacked the preparation which the Germans had been making for forty years. Personally, he had not been discouraged, even in the summer of 1915, for he was convinced that, given munitions, the Russians could do again exactly what they had just been doing in June. The main element of his success, he said, was due to the absolute coordination of all the armies involved. On the entire front the Russian attacks began at the same hour, so that it was impossible for the Germans to shift troops from one quarter to another. The most important fighting was in the sector of Rovno, where their greatest advances were made. Could the Russians take Kovel, there was reason to believe the whole eastern front would be obliged to fall back. Asked how he was able to take so many prisoners, Brusiloff replied that while modern trenches, with their deep tunnels and maze of communications, were difficult to destroy, they became a menace to their own defenders once their position was taken in rear or flank, for it was impossible to escape from them quickly. Russians in this offensive, for the first time, had sufficient ammunition to provide a curtain of fire that could prevent the enemy from retiring save through a scathing zone of shrapnel-fire, all of which made surrender imperative.

By June 21 the Russians had crossed the Sereth southwest of Czernowitz, and occupied Zadova, Stroginetz, and Gilboka. The Austrians in this region, with their army cut in two, were declared by Petrograd to be in a disorderly retreat, the Russians pursuing them toward the Carpathians. But uncertainty rose as to the situation between the Pripet River and the Galician frontier. Divergent reports came from Russian and German War Offices. Both claimed successes. Northeast of Kiselin, which lies between Lutsk and Vladimir-Volynski, Petrograd said an Austrian attack, supported by Germans, had been repulsed, while Berlin asserted that the Teutonic Allies were victorious in fighting their way forward against the Russians. The Russians claimed a defeat of the Teutonic Allies southeast of Lakatchi, while Berlin declared that, between the Kovel-Lutsk railroad and the Turia River the Teutons had broken down the Russian resistance or repulsed their attacks. In Galicia, Austrians and Germans were resisting Russian attempts against Lemberg. Six German divisions (120,000 men) had been hurried eastward. Two German divisions were en route for the Lutsk-Kovel front where the Austrians, supported by Germans, were counter-attacking with great vigor on this northern flank of Brusiloff's armies. Four German divisions were being rushed into action on the thirty-mile front from Brody southward to a point east of Przemysl, where the Russians had opened a heavy artillery-attack, evidently in preparation for a smash toward Lemberg.

During the last ten days of June fierce fighting took place between the Styr and the Stokhod, neither side being able to gain any decided advantage. Then it was that Brusiloff brought a fresh army into the field north of the Sarny-Kovel railway with the intention of moving across the lower Stokhod and attacking Kovel from the north. This army was under command of Lesh, who began to develop his attack on July 4, and, after fighting a successful battle which gave him possession of the railway-station of Manievitchi, succeeded in carrying German positions covering the passage over the Stokhod, and in securing that river on the right bank down to its junction with the Pripet. During the course of his advance he captured 12,000 prisoners and took 45 German guns with a large quantity of war-material. Meanwhile, Kaledine had been supporting Lesh's attack with a cooperative movement south of the railway west of Chartoriisk and Kolki. This was successful in forcing the Germans back behind the upper Stokhod, which the Russians crossed at several places after recapturing the bridge-head at Svidniki. Between them, Kaledine and Lesh were said to have captured during this drive more than 650 German officers and 22,000 men, with 50 guns and other war-booty. Linsingen rallied his beaten army on the left bank of the Stokhod, and put up a stubborn resistance on this last line of defense east of Kovel.

The sudden first success of this Russian attack had so startled many persons in sympathy with the Allied cause as to impair their sense of proportion and relative values. Some saw the rapid disintegration of the entire Austrian army; others saw an immediate capture of Lemberg; one went so far as to predict for the Germans a retirement from Belgium and France. Nothing, however, had happened on the Russian front to give reasonable ground for belief that any one of these things was pending. The Russian offensive by the end of June had not made progress far enough to stamp it either as a success or a failure. A military movement is successful only when it achieves the object for which it was undertaken. We can only speculate as to the Russian offensive having had its genesis in the influence that its success would have on Roumania; or having aimed at relieving pressure on Italy, or on Verdun, or having had, for its express purpose the beating of the Austrian army and so removing protection from the German flank, and forcing the German line to retire. If the capture of Czernowitz had induced Roumania to take a step which would line her up squarely with the Allies, the Russian movement would have been an unqualified success, even tho nothing further had been obtained. If the object had been to relieve the Trentino situation, it was already a success, but if it had been undertaken with the object of destroying the Austrian power, the decision was still in the balance.

It had been part of the history of this war that, whenever Austrians and Russians met, the Czar's troops were invariably the victors. But there was a great difference between conditions as they were in June, 1916, and as they were when Austria called on Germany for help in the Spring of 1915, on the occasion of the Russian pressure in the Carpathians. Then Germany was not herself seriously engaged on any other front. She had men to spare and surplus ammunition. Now the help that Germany could give seemed comparatively small. On the Russian line she had had all she could do to hold the Russians in their trenches north of Poliesse. She had been able to send aid as far south as Kovel, but no further. Austria, in addition, was herself in a bad way for men. Of all the belligerents she was the most nearly exhausted. The disasters that followed her footsteps in the early days of the Russian successes of 1914 had placed a serious drain on her resources, while the latest Russian success had taken from her almost a half million men that she could not replace.

It was plain that the situation in the Galician and Volhynian regions was approaching a crisis which might involve the safety of the whole front of the Central Powers from Riga to Roumania. When the attack began, the eastern front followed the Dwina River from the outskirts of the city of Riga to the Dvinsk, approximately an east and west front; then it turned sharply south through Pinsk, which the Germans held, through the Pripet Marshes, along the Styr, east of Lutsk and Dubno, which were Austrian, along the Sereth, just west of Tarnapol, which was Russian, to 'he Dniester, and thence to the Pruth, just west of the Roumanian frontier.

From the Gulf of Riga to the Pripet Marshes and to the southern border of this swamp, the line had been long undisturbed, but a little south of the marshes there began a wide, deep curve which the Russians had now driven westward. This curve was almost a semicircle drawn about Dubno, with a radius of perhaps thirty-five miles, and represented the extreme penetration of the Austrian front. Going south there was a second semicircle of perhaps twenty-five miles' radius, from the point where the Dniester reaches the Russian frontier. The northern curve extended toward Kovel and Vladimir-Volynski, the southern extended southwest of Czernowitz and approached Kolomea. The two were the wedges the Russians had driven into the Austrian lines, after breaking the trench-front. War in these sectors thus had become a war of movement as contrasted with trench-operations. The two circles represented breaks in the dike which the Central Powers had erected against the Slavonic flood. Russian waters were pouring through them and extending not only westward, but tending to swirl round the ends of the dike. Exactly what happens when there is a break in a Mississippi levee was taking place along the Eastern Front. In putting up a defense, the Germans and Austrians had tried to build a temporary dike behind these waters and to circumscribe the area of inundation. Great concentrations of troops had taken place behind the line that was broken, and in front of Kovel and Vladimir-Volynski, while Austria made a new stand between the Dniester and the Pruth west of Czernowitz.

The Germans were still bringing up reinforcements from the French front and Austrians from the Italian front. Their number was said to be about 200,000, but since the defense of the Bukowina had been practically abandoned, the bulk of these reinforcements were evidently to be concentrated against the armies of Kaledine and Sakaroff on the northern half of Brusiloff's front. Prisoners from German regiments, brought over from Verdun, declared the violence of the Russian fire reminded them of the French fire at Verdun. The dispatch of troops to the Kovel sector had not, however, involved a relaxation of the German offensive against the French fortress. The Germans were merely shuffling their cards; they were maintaining the fighting energy of their troops by a change of service, not by a cessation of work. Apparently regiments badly battered at Verdun had been replenished and then sent to the danger zone on the Russian front, their places at Verdun being taken by regiments that had not yet gone through a terrible ordeal. Since the forcing of the Pruth nothing had checked the Russians. The center and right of Pflanzer's army had become practically non-existent as a fighting force. There remained his left, forced by the Russian capture of Kuty to retreat along narrow mountain-roads up the valley of the Black Tcheremosh. The Austrians were now threatened with a fresh invasion of Hungary from the east instead of from the north. The result would have been an immense lengthening of the German line, if the Germans expected to give support to the Austrians. Russia, with new reserves of the same quality as her first troops, could afford to lengthen her line, but her Teutonic enemies could not afford to lengthen theirs.

After the elimination of Pflanzer's army in the Bukowina, Brusiloff's forces were directed upon Kolomea, the key to the defense of Lemberg. The occupation of Kimpolung and Kuty opened the way. The Teutonic forces appeared to have been able to stop to some extent the breaching of their front in the Kovel region, where a large force of German troops had stiffened the Austrian line. It was evident that preparations were being made for a desperate stand at Brody, on the southern wing of that position. Nevertheless, in the face of stiff counter-attacks, the Russians by June 26 were able to push the wedge in the direction of Vladimir-Volynski to a point which threatened that town and endangered Brody, the gateway to Lemberg. According to a military expert, the Germans had taken full charge in this region and had filled up the ranks of Archduke Ferdinand's broken army.

By June 28 the Germans in Volhynia had captured the village of Liniewka, west of Sokul, and Russian positions south of that point. The announcement indicated an important German success, but gave no indication of the fighting which had been of the hardest kind yet seen on this front. It lasted for three days and three nights. Tens of thousands of hundredweights of lead and iron had been thrown; hundreds of wounded had dragged themselves toilsomely to field-hospitals or been carried there, and many had closed their eyes forever. Slow progress and hard fighting occurred in swamps with an overwhelming superiority of the Russians in numbers. In one night they put into action nearly two entire divisions against a couple of German regiments. In an attack over a front of twenty-five miles, extending eastward from Kolomea, in Galicia, the Austrians were compelled to retire on a part of the front in the region of Kolomea and southward. They valiantly attempted to hold back the oncoming Russians, but were compelled to give way before superior forces. In this fighting, and also in battles near Kuty, in the Bukowina, the Austrians suffered heavy casualties. In addition 221 officers and 10,285 men were made prisoners, and heavy guns, machine-guns and stores were lost. On June 27, an official statement issued by the Russian War Office placed the number of prisoners captured by Brusiloff's army between June 4 and June 23 at 198,972 officers and men. The number of heavy guns, machine-guns and bomb-throwers taken was said to be more than 1,000.

The main difference between Russia's present drive against Austria and the Austro-German drive of 1915, which compelled Russia to yield so much of her territory, lay in the fact that the Russians in 1916 broke through the Austrian lines, while, in the Russian retreat in 1915, the Russian lines retired intact. This difference was considered of much importance by many military critics. The capture of Czernowitz at this time no doubt had a great moral effect in Roumania, but that town changed hands too often to give its transfer very decisive significance. The success of the

Russian drive was credited to artillery, and especially to a new shell with which the Russians were plentifully supplied. Some reports said this shell was made in Japan and was charged with a powerful new explosive. In describing these battles a writer in Hungary [3] said:

"The Russian attacks are preceded by unexampled artillery bombardment of our positions. After the first lines had been totally destroyed by the Russian shells and then abandoned, the Russians were able, owing to the great number of their guns, to pour a curtain of fire behind the evacuated trenches, and thus cut off all retreat. These tactics were followed by the Russians everywhere. The progress of the Russians was rapid almost beyond belief, the destruction and capture of men coming like a lightning-stroke, leaving the staff-officers, whose station is from five to fifteen miles behind the firing-line, with no means of repairing the initial mischief, and so they simply fled."

On July 1 came an announcement that the Russians had captured Kolomea. The importance of Kolomea was obvious. An army which held it not only had cleared the Bukowina of Austrians, but had planted on the flank of the Austro-Germans a force which might make a rearrangement of their line inevitable. By July 5 the Russians had definitely assumed the offensive over another considerable part of their thousand-mile European front. Brusiloff's push continued to make steady progress and the left wing of the main front—that is, excluding the Bukowina and Transylvania—was well west of the meridian marking the forward points on the right wing. The Germans still maintained with concentrated fury their attempts to cut into Brusiloff's position between the Stokhod and Styr. His new line of advance reached a point more than half-way to Sokul. The fighting over all the Russian front indicated that the Germans were occupied with attempts to meet Russia's strategic plan, and had no plan of their own in operation anywhere. In other words Russia had become for the first time master of the situation.

The greatest battle of the series on the Russian front was still expected to occur in the so-called Lutsk salient where

[3] In the *Az Ujsag* (Budapest).

the key to the whole situation was the Kovel junction. Gigantic efforts were made by the Germans to safeguard this vital point; they massed every available unit there to counter the Russian thrust. The Russians late in June had been within twenty-one miles of the junction, but for ten days had been held back. The Germans had made efforts to check an indirect Russian approach to Kovel by the southern flank, where the issues hung in the balance at Lokatchi, the apex of the whole salient. All Bukowina was now in Russian hands. In three weeks Lechitzky had broken through positions fortified as the French front was; had taken over 40,000 prisoners and added 4,000 square miles to the territory controlled by Russia.

Thus had closed the first stage of what was one of the most rapid and spectacular advances in the war. In three weeks a whole province had been reconquered; Lutsk and Dubno retaken. The advance was to within twenty-five miles of Kovel, and within ten of Brody; the prisoners captured numbered 4,031 officers and 194,041 of other ranks; 219 guns and 644 machine-guns, besides vast quantities of war material. On three vital places behind the enemy front toward Kovel, Lemberg, and Stanislau, the Austrian line had been pierced and shattered. Over wide stretches the campaign had been translated from the rigidity of trench-warfare to something like freedom of maneuver. For the first time, as regards artillery and munitions, they were on terms of something like equality with their foe. Brusiloff made brilliant use of newly acquired advantages, and conducted vast operations with the skill of a master. Only the first step had been taken, however, the movement still far from having won a strategic decision; but reverses, vast and irreparable, had come to the waning man-power of Austria.[4]

[4] Principal Sources: *The Literary Digest*, The *Evening Sun*, The *Evening Post*, The *Times*, the "Military Expert" of The *Times*, *The Outlook*, The *Journal of Commerce*, New York; The *Times* (London); The *World*, The *Sun*, New York; The London *Times'* "History of the War," "Nelson's History of the War" by John Buchan, *The Fortnightly Review* (London), *The Independent* (New York).

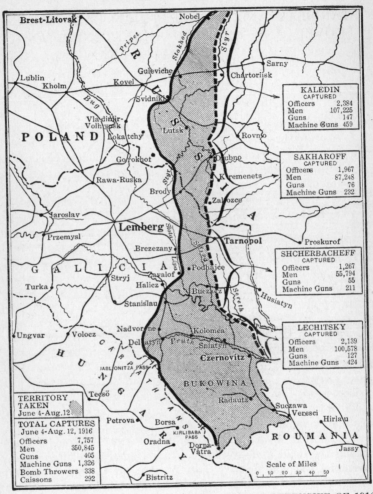

TERRITORY TAKEN
June 4–Aug. 12

TOTAL CAPTURES
June 4–Aug. 12, 1916

Officers	7,757
Men	350,845
Guns	405
Machine Guns	1,326
Bomb Throwers	338
Caissons	292

KALEDIN
CAPTURED

Officers	2,384
Men	107,225
Guns	147
Machine Guns	459

SAKHAROFF
CAPTURED

Officers	1,967
Men	87,248
Guns	76
Machine Guns	232

SHCHERBACHEFF
CAPTURED

Officers	1,267
Men	55,794
Guns	55
Machine Guns	211

LECHITSKY
CAPTURED

Officers	2,139
Men	100,578
Guns	127
Machine Guns	424

Scale of Miles
0 10 20 30 40 50

PRINCIPAL TERRITORY TAKEN IN BRUSILOFF'S OFFENSIVE OF 1916

STANISLAU AND A CARPATHIAN PASS TAKEN,
KOVEL AND LEMBERG THREATENED, AND
THEN A STALEMATE—FRANCIS
JOSEPH DIES

July 6, 1916—January 1, 1917

SUCH had been the progress of the Russians that it was easy to credit the report that both Hindenburg and Mackensen in person had arrived on the Eastern Front in order to stem the tide. That the Teutons were entirely on the defensive was apparent from the lack of any concerted counter-attacks, such attacks as had been made being purely local. Meanwhile, the severance of communications between Bothmer's army and Hungary through the Kirlibaba Pass increased the dangerous position in which that general found himself, besides adding to the menace to Lemberg, while the approach of the Russians to within fifteen miles of Kovel tended to strengthen the line and exert pressure at another vital point. Plainly, if the Germans were to relieve the situation by a heavy blow, the time had come, for Bothmer's position had become perilous.

Nearly half a million Austrians and Germans, it was said optimistically in Petrograd, had been put out of commission since Brusiloff began his advance. The grand total of prisoners to July 6 was in round numbers 235,000, of whom 4,500 were officers. Estimates by military experts placed the dead and wounded at from 200,000 to 220,000. Austrians predominated overwhelmingly among the prisoners; but among the dead and wounded a fairly large percentage were Germans. It was figured that 250 guns of various sizes and upward of 700 machine-guns had been taken and in addition vast quantities of munitions, supplies and transports. Letchitzky's advance west of Kolomea, where he cut the railroad into Hungary at Mikuliczyn, was emphasized as a new blow to the Austrian defense of East Galicia. Northwest of Kolomea his troops on July 6 were within ten miles of

Nadworna, well to the rear of the Austrian right flank, facing Tarnopol, between the Stripa and Zlota Lipa.

By July 10 the Russian armies had crossed the Stokhod River in operations against Kovel, and had captured several villages along the line of the Kovel-Sarny railroad. Despatches from Petrograd said the Stokhod had been crossed at Ugil, which lies a few miles south of the railroad, but an Austrian official statement made mention of fighting at Stobychwa, lying west of the Stokhod, which indicated that the Russians had crossed the river about thirty miles northeast of Kovel. The Russian advance was most promising at two points, near Kovel and in lower Galicia. In the former territory it had gone forward fourteen miles in two days, and crossed the Stokhod, where it was believed that the Germans would offer a most determined defense. It became obvious that if the rest of the Stokhod River line were abandoned, it would hardly be possible for the Teutons to hold Kovel. Mackensen and Hindenburg, if they were really at Kovel, had now to play their trump cards or reform their whole line for a long distance.

The Russians in seven weeks had regained upward of 15,000 square miles—or about twice as much territory as the Germans held in France and four-fifths of the area of all German conquests in the west. Berlin announced that the Russians killed had been officially estimated at 262,000, which would mean a total loss of at least a million. Even if this price had been paid, not even the German authorities could question the ability of Russia to pay it.

Toward the middle of July Linsingen made a sudden effort to regain Lutsk and push back Kaledine's left wing to the upper Styr. Saharoff, in command of the Russian forces on the southern face of the Lutsk salient, turned on the Austro-German army with superior numbers, and not only checked the German movement eastward, but inflicted a severe defeat east and southeast of Swiniuky. German foresight, which had seldom been at fault during the war, was turned to good account when the Sokal-Kovel railway extension was constructed, for by this line, and by the one running from Lemberg to Stojanow, Linsingen was now able to bring reinforcements to any point threatened by the

Russian commander. The Germans were massing enormous forces before Kovel, bringing up every available reserve in the hope of stalling the Russian mowing-machine. A state of comparative calm was announced in Petrograd as a prelude to a resumption of heavy and important fighting. Should the fall of Kovel occur, it would be a staggering blow. Lemberg would then be menaced more than ever, the road to the great fortress of Brest-Litovsk would be opened and the rear of the entire Pinsk region threatened. All this would make necessary a German withdrawal.

The battle for Kovel was marked by extreme violence, Brusiloff having brought up forces from the Stokhod to the Lipa. Southwest of Lutsk and at the bend of the Stokhod River, north of Sokul, Teutonic forces on the offensive against the Russians meanwhile made gains. The menace, with Lemberg as the objective, had, however, assumed substantial proportions. The Russians had crossed the Styr by July 21 and carried their southward advance to the town of Berestechk, two and a half miles from the Galician border. Berestechk was of strategical importance to the Russians. Twenty miles west lies Stojanow, the terminus of a railway running directly to Lemberg. At that point the Russians would be in a position to drive toward the Galician capital from two directions, as soon as they reached the Stojanow-Lemberg railway. At the same time a Russian offensive was in progress against Hindenburg's lines on the Dwina, around Friedrichstadt, against positions west of Vilna and German counter-attacks northeast of Kovel had been repulsed. Russian troops dominated both banks of the Lipa from the Styr to near Mirkow, and in some parts of the line had thrust forward eight or ten miles beyond the river.

This Russian advance beyond the Lipa, by which crossings of the Styr north of Werben were effected, and the pushing of the Russian line south to the heights above Berestechk, practically surrounded the bend in the Styr, so that no line of retreat was left open to the Austrians who occupied it. As the Russian pressure on the circle increased, and the Russian lines were drawn in, the Austrians occupying the salient had nothing to do but surrender. It was in this corner that most of the 13,000 prisoners were captured. The heights in front of Berestechk had not been a sufficiently strong position from which to hold back the Russians who were among the best fighters in Europe when capably led and had now for weeks seen nothing but victory. Altho suffering great losses they had seen one position after another fall into their hands, and knew they were going ahead. Not only that, but they saw Austrian and German prisoners passing through their lines to the rear by thousands, which created in their ranks an *élan* that enabled their officers to drive them anywhere.

In the section south of the Dniester the Russians were also moving. A great battle for the approaches to the pass through the Carpathians at Jablonitza had been in progress for several days, and the War Office in Vienna announced that the Austrians had to retreat to the crests of the mountains. Reports from Petrograd suggested that Austria might now make a separate peace, altho there was no active evidence of any such intention except Austria's plight. After the war there was evidence enough that Austria even then was ready to quit war. She had met with another great defeat, but as yet it was less considerable than her breakdown in August and September, 1914. Nevertheless, her defeat was of the first magnitude. Coincident with it came an abandonment of her Italian drive from Trent toward Verona, and Vicenza, her recall of troops from the Balkans, and the entry of Roumania into the war with the Entente Allies. At this time the terms which the Entente would have been likely to make with Austria were, for Russia, possession of Galicia and the Bukowina, and the cession of Bosnia and Herzegovina, together with the southern end of Dalmatia, to Serbia. Italy would have demanded Trieste, the Trentino, the islands of the Dalmatian coast and probably most of Dalmatia, and that Austria should abandon all claim upon Albania. In sum, Austria would have lost at the least some 60,000 square miles of territory with a population of about 12,000,000, or, roughly speaking, a quarter of her area and a quarter of her population. With slight exceptions this population is wholly Slav—Pole and Ruthenian in the east, Serb in the south, and Slovene around Trieste. The Slavs numbered a little more than half the population of the whole Austro-Hungarian empire. Peace on these terms would have removed about half the Slavs; it would have left only the Czechs of Bohemia as a considerable Slav block in Austria.

An Austrian surrender would, in effect, have changed the whole face of the eastern issues. A century of rivalry between Romanoff and Hapsburg would have ended in a decisive victory for the former. Seated at Constantinople,

ONE OF THE BREST-LITOVSK FORTS AFTER IT WAS
TAKEN BY THE GERMANS

politically supreme in Sofia and Belgrade, Russia would effectually have barred the road of the Austrian and the German to the East. Asia Minor would conceivably have remained an occasion for rivalry between Russia, Italy, France, and Great Britain, but it would have been beyond the grasp of Viennese and Berlin statesmen. Had Austria made peace before Roumania entered the war, then Roumania would not have acquired Transylvania or Bukowina;

the dream of a Greater Roumania would have vanished, and this disappointment of Roumanian patriots would have been difficult to deal with. Perhaps the Petrograd rumor originally was intended only to influence Roumania and bring in that eastern Latin State, which had so much to gain from picking Hapsburg bones. Once more it became necessary, however, to caution observers to put small reliance on rumors of actual Austrian collapse. Austria was the weakest of the great states at war, she had suffered most in losses except Russia, and she had no such resources left in men as Russia had. She had a huge Slav population, which was, in part at least, frankly disloyal; but her financial situation, bad at the outbreak of the war, was probably well-nigh hopeless now. That Austria was beaten to the point of making a separate peace seemed, however, unlikely, because she was in no position to break with Germany—at least, not yet.

The Austro-German defenders of positions before the lower Stokhod had now withdrawn behind the river which had proved Brusiloff's greatest obstacle to a successful advance on Kovel. Less than twenty miles away the Russian right wing was plunging forward until it seemed as if a few more such plunges would make Vladimir-Volynski, Kovel, and Lemberg untenable. The Russians had broken the Stokhod lines at Hulevitchi, almost due east of Kovel. Below this point the marsh-flanked stream juts out in a wide curve to the west, forming a huge salient, along whose inner rim lay the Teuton defenses. The piercing of the front above this salient immediately forced Linsingen's troops to retreat back toward Kovel. As a result, virtually the entire line of the Stokhod passed into the hands of the Russians.

Further south, Bothmer's army, outflanked north and south, was trying to extricate itself from the perilous position in which it had been placed by the Russian blows south of Brody. What had been thriving towns on the steel highway that linked Brody with Lemberg had become deserted villages; busy farms had become isolated stretches of bare land. Hindenburg's troops felt the effect of this Russian *coup de main*. Besides surrendering territory won only at much cost and valuable time, the occasion seemed to have come when he would have to permit his lines to be thinned out and exposed to the growing pressure exerted by Kuropatkin. It was not the extent of territory won by Brusiloff's drive that was important as much as the capture in two days of 20,000 prisoners and more than one hundred big guns. The Russians many times before had extended their lines, but never had they—or any single one of the combatants in the war—struck such a blow at an enemy's means of defense. There was only one conclusion to be drawn, according to high army officers: The Teuton system of defense had collapsed more completely on this occasion than ever before. In Southern Galicia the Russians had again taken up the drive for Lemberg through Stanislau and Halicz, both important railroad centers.[5]

By August 1 the Austrians were still falling back. Lemberg and Kovel were more and more in danger. The first achievement of this month had been the capture of Brody, fifty-eight miles northeast of Lemberg. The Russian advance on Lemberg was now under way from both south and northeast. Having crossed the Stokhod, in Volhynia, the Russians bade fair to reach a position which would endanger the German lines along the Bug. Even south of the Dniester the Teuton forces had been driven back in some places. The capture of Kovel and then of Lemberg seemed inevitable. Unless the German and Austrian armies should move westward rapidly, a Russian wedge might be driven between them. After nearly two months of activity, the Czar's forces claimed they had captured over 350,000 Austro-German troops, while the capture of artillery and supplies had been enormous. In addition not less than 15,000 square miles of territory, including all of Bukowina, had been reconquered. This was an area, as already stated, but little smaller than the combined area of the French and Belgian districts occupied by the Germans. It was thought to demonstrate clearly that Russian reverses of a year before were only temporary, that Russia had mastered herself again, that she had succeeded in transforming herself industrially, and had managed to equip new millions, behind

[5] Arthur S. Draper in The *Tribune* (New York).

which were other millions. In men Russia had always been the richest of the Allies, but the real problem of the war for her was whether she could supply the men with guns and ammunition. That problem she apparently had now solved.

One thing the Russian success had done; it had terminated for the time being the Austrian menace to Italy, for the Austrian campaign in the Trentino had been abandoned. Troops concentrated there had in large numbers been sent to support beaten troops in Galicia. At this time the Russian advance beyond Erzerum was threatening the Turk in Asia Minor, and a new campaign from Saloniki seemed assured. This campaign, if successful, promised to contribute more than either of the great drives to bring about peace, since it would deprive Germany of her only considerable prize of the war, which was Serbia. It would, in fact, eliminate that "place in the sun" so dear to German hearts which had been temporarily achieved by Mackensen's great Serbian campaign in 1915. On August 8 Litchitzky scored a new victory by the capture of Tlumach, ten miles further northwest. This cut the railway between Stanislau, Tysmienitza and Buczacz, which had been utilized by the Austrians for supplying the southern end of Bothmer's front, and gave the Russians another direct avenue of attack on Stanislau, which, having been "pocketed" by the capture of other villages northeast and south, was now being evacuated. Three achievements marked Russia's campaign in the week in which came August 10—the capture of Stanislau, which is eighty-seven miles southeast of Lemberg, and an important "stepping-stone" in Russia's march on Lemberg; the crossing of the Zlota Lipa which made the German army under Bothmer draw back and take a line of defense nearer Lemberg; and an advance in the far south, through the Carpathian pass of Jablonitza and the town of the same name, into the borders of Hungary. It was stated in despatches that the Kaiser had insisted that Kovel, now threatened north of Lemberg, should be held at all costs. Already the Russian offensive had played a tremendous part—undoubtedly the leading part—in the concerted Allied offensive.

On August 9 the Russians had been within six miles of

Stanislau, and were smashing the Austrian line on a twenty-five-mile front. Russian advance-guards were almost on the outskirts of this important railway center, whose fall was then expected at any hour. Brusiloff had not been idle along the Stokhod, altho it was apparent that, for the time being, the drive on Kovel was secondary in importance to greater movements in Galicia. The Czar's troops had attacked at three points on the Stokhod—south of the Stobychva bend, east of Kovel and north of Kiselin, but were rolled back by the furious fire of the Teuton batteries and counter-charges by Linsingen's forces. Apparently a serious break had occurred in the Teutonic lines along the Dniester in the whole Stanislau region. Letchitsky's army was only eight miles southeast of Halicz, and his troops pushed on so rapidly that the Austrians had to blow up storehouses in their haste to get away. The capture of Stanislau then rapidly completed the encircling movement that had been unfolding for ten days.

By August 18 the Russians had advanced three miles into Hungary and were storming Austrian positions on a mountain peak near Korosmezo, at the Hungarian end of Jablonitza Pass. From Korosmezo ran a railroad that led down into the fertile plains. Brusiloff's army had fought its way through the Jablonitza Pass along the line of this railroad by hard work along wooded Carpathian peaks and ravines. At the same time the Russian offensive further north along the Zlota Lipa front had grown stronger. Determined Austrian counter-attacks could not stop it permanently. Gains in several parts of the front were announced. Hungary had been entered at its northeastern corner, not far from the Transylvania border. The point where fighting went on was the summit of the Carpathian range.

The Russians advanced along the railroads from Stanislau and Kolomea, in Galicia, which converge at Delatin and then go through Jablonitza Pass. Once through the pass, running through Korosmezo, the railroad goes southwest, along the line of the Theiss to Szigeth, a distance of 150 miles from Budapest. This railroad and the valley of the Theiss would be the natural line of advance in an invasion of Hungary. Hungary would have been a rich prize for the armies of the Czar and a heavy loss to the Central Powers. Hungary besides being the great wheat-growing, cattle-raising region of the Austro-Hungarian empire, has many valuable mines and ammunition works. Russian occupancy would have cut the Central Powers off from these much-needed and valuable supplies. In the northwest are sheep-grazing lands, and immediately to the south thick forests. About Koloszvar pigs and sheep are raised. The south and east look like Kansas, so wide are the wheatfields. After breaking through the Stokhod line, the Russians made a further advance and captured several positions.

August 29 marked a renewal of the Russian offensive on the Zlota Lipa when the first blow was directed against a salient near Zavaloff. Important artillery positions on Hill 413 were captured and the Teutons were compelled to retire beyond the Zlota Lipa. On the following day the fighting was extended toward the southwest and soon the battle had spread over the entire front from Zavaloff and Nosoff on the Zlota Lipa to Mariampol on the Dniester. On September 3 the struggle reached its culminating point when in the morning of that day the Russians, operating on both sides of the Dniester, captured the town of Jezupol and its surroundings, including wooded heights which dominated that town and the crossing of the Dniester, on the Stanislau-Halicz railway line. Further north, the advance was against the Dryshchoff-Nosoff front, across steep hills and through thick forests. Especially obstinate was the resistance in forests between Horozhanks and Dryshchoff, which were held by picked German troops. Three successive Russian attacks were repulsed. Later in the afternoon the Russians by an advance through forests north of Byshoff, succeeded in turning the right German flank. At 6 P.M. the Russians forced their way into the forest, and bitter hand-to-hand fighting developed. By the end of the day four square miles of forest were strewn with German corpses.

With the piercing of the Nosoff-Deleyoff front all further resistance on that advanced line was rendered impossible. In the ensuing German route, Russian cavalry played a brilliant part. More than 4,000 Austrian, German, and Turkish prisoners were captured. On the following day the advance from the southeast was reinforced by a concentric movement from the east, across the Zlota Lipa. The difficult river-crossing between the village of Voloshchyzna on the eastern and Bozhykoff on the western bank was captured, and the Turks who held that sector were routed. On the same day the Russian advance was prest across wooded heights west of the Zlota Lipa within a few miles of the Halicz-Podvysokie railway. Meanwhile, at the southern end of the line, the Russians had cleared of Teutons the eastern

GERMAN SOLDIERS SIGHTSEEING IN WARSAW

243

corner between the Dniester and the Gnila Lipa, had captured the railway between Vodniki, Siemikovitse and the railway station of Halicz, and were crossing the Gnila Lipa. On the night of September 4–5 the military stores of Bolshovtse were set on fire.

Of this campaign later in September so little was heard that an impression that it had exhausted itself, and come to a full stop before the gathering forces of Austro-Germans concentrated on the roads to Kovel, prevailed even in neutral quarters. But Brusiloff had been continuing his tactics of sharp, unexpected thrusts along the whole front, changing the point of attack with rapidity, with the result that the Austro-Germans were kept in suspense and unable to withdraw troops from one sector to another, where for the moment they were needed. When Roumania entered the war the events came to occupy much of Austria's attention, especially in the Dobrudja and in eastern Roumania. Opposing armies were engaged from the Black Sea to the Danube along a front of seventy miles. On the northern end of their line, near Riga, the Russians began a new undertaking and crossed the Dwina. Repeated efforts were made by the Germans to dislodge them. In eastern Galicia the Austro-Germans were fighting to hold back the Russians from Halicz, southeast of Lemberg.

By September 8 the Russians before Halicz had gone forward several miles along a broad front where the troops of Pflanzer and Bothmer, bulwarked by Turks and Germans, were striving to defend the southern gateway to Lemberg. While Letchitsky and Cherbatchoff were assailing Teuton lines in the south, Sakharoff was continuing his pressure east of Lemberg, where he had pushed to within thirty-five miles of the capital. Russian attacks against Halicz and the railroads radiating from that town beat back all resistance. Halicz was an important bridgehead, guarding the passage of the Dniester, and a railroad center of much value. Here the Teutons effected a great concentration of troops. By September 9 the Austrians began to blow up forts at Halicz and the Russians occupied some of the fortifications. The great bridge across the Dniester was blown up. Official bulletins indicated that the struggle was a desperate one.

Gradually driven back, Bothmer's army was compelled to retire five miles westward of the Zlota Lipa line of defense until Halicz was in a critical position, surrounded as it was on three sides and saved from immediate capitulation only by excellent natural defenses. Halicz was in a Russian noose. With this fortress trapt, the drive on Lemberg was to be prosecuted without delay.

By September 21 the battle for Kovel took on new intensity. Along a twelve-mile front the Russians advanced in heavy formation, while the Germans in turn counter-attacked repeatedly. The Russian Guard, the flower of the Czar's troops, was taking part in this attack, which aimed to flank the Austrian positions at Kovel and so force its surrender. Meanwhile, in Galicia the Halicz battle continued on the same scale with the tide turning slowly in favor of the Russians, altho the advantage fluctuated. The Czar's commander, unable to force a way through to Halicz, shifted the attack to Volhynia in an attempt to weaken the German line in Galicia by forcing a transfer of troops. Altho the Russians still claimed the initiative, it was evident that the German counter-attacks were becoming more frequent and vigorous. In large numbers of reinforcements sent to these regions from other fronts, as well as in the more aggressive character of the German fighting, there were signs that Hindenburg was planning a new campaign to recover his old positions before winter set in.

On October 4 the Russians were almost in the suburbs of Brzezany, an important railway junction on the Zlota Lipa, fifty miles southeast of Lemberg. In a desperate three-day battle, the Czar's troops forced the Zlota Lipa, swept the Teutons from heights dominating the town and then carried out a destructive bombardment. The investment of Brzezany by the Russians promised to compel the retirement of Bothmer's army from the whole line of the Zlota Lipa north of that point. With the Zlota Lipa line entirely in the hands of the Russians, the Teuton forces in Galicia would have been compelled to retreat on Lemberg to escape flank attacks.

Stubborn battles were continuing in Volhynia, west of Lutsk, where Berlin reported the Czar's troops had lost thousands in killed and had won not a foot of ground. Battles of a desperate character were also in progress along all four of the main approaches to Lemberg. While the fighting in the Balkans, and particularly that in which Roumania was engaged, had occupied the attention of the public almost exclusively for several days, the Russians in the second week of October were fighting one of the greatest battles they had yet engaged in. All efforts to take Kovel apparently for the present had been abandoned. The main Russian effort was to be made against Lemberg, which had been made necessary by the entrance into the war of Roumania. Roumania had induced the Russians to localize their attacks at a point where it would do the most good to the Roumanian cause, and this point was Lemberg. Once in Lemberg, the Russians would be able to force the retreat of the Teuton line back to the Stryj-Grodek line and to make the passage of the Carpathian mountains easier, and, once the Carpathians were crossed, Falkenhayn, the discredited chief of staff of the Verdun failure, now in command here, could be taken in flank, the Germans forced to release the pressure they were exerting on the Roumanians, and to fall back, abandoning practically all of Transylvania. The Roumanian situation was giving the Allies not a little uneasiness. The quickest and most effective way of relieving it was by a Russian success north of the Carpathians.

Referring at this time to the battlefields of Galicia, the Berliner *Vörwarts* estimated that, between Gorlice and the heights of Tarnovo, there were no fewer than 419 graveyards, which by the summer of 1916 had been cleared of unsightly surroundings, and whenever possible natural beauties in landscapes had been utilized to lend dignity to these enormous cemeteries. All along the Dunajec these graveyards of soldiers were thickly strewn over the countryside. Russians, Austrians, Germans, Hungarians, to the number of 40,000 were buried in cared-for places, but this number did not include men buried in masses in one grave. In west Galicia alone were 600 graveyards, and in other parts more than 100. From the Dunajec eastward countless graves were to be seen stretching far away to the eastern plains—memorials of Mackensen's great victory in the summer of 1915.

A violent attack on Russian positions in the Stokhod region of Volhynia was made on November 9 by Austro-German forces. After repelling several onslaughts the Russians were compelled to fall back to their second line, and as a result of a German counter-attack in the region south of Dorna Watra, they had to give up some of the heights which they had captured on the day previous. Nevertheless, Brusiloff remained as confident as ever of the ultimate success of Russia in the East. He said:

"The war is won to-day, altho it is merely speculation to estimate how much more time will be required before the enemy is convinced that the cause for the sake of which he has drenched Europe with blood is irretrievably lost. If there remain any Germans still hopeful for their cause, let them realize that to-day, when the Central Powers already have lost the initiative and are finding difficulty in refilling their ranks, Russia has not yet reached the zenith of her power, which will only be approached next year, when we shall have the largest and best army since the beginning of the war. Next year we shall have material on an equality with the Germans, and superiority in human resources which should steadily increase as long as the war endures. The morale of the Russian people has been slowly rising for two years, and it is my absolute personal conviction that, if it were possible to take a vote of the entire population, ninety-nine out of every one hundred Russians to-day would demand the continuation of the war to a definite and final victory regardless of the price." [6]

Amid these events came news of the fall of the pro-German Stürmer, the Russian Premier, and the appointment in his place of a man in sympathy with the Duma. This was regarded as the most important incident in Russia since the Czar took command of his armies after the great defeats of 1915 that began at the Dunajec and ended at the Beresina. The change was regarded as a final answer to the German hope that Russia would make a separate peace. Broadly speaking, the Duma represented the national and popular emotions of Russia, the demand for prosecution of the war against Germany. The proclamation of an au-

[6] Dispatch from Stanley Washburn to The *Times* (London).

tonomous Poland had already been a recognition by Vienna and Berlin that there was no chance of a separate peace with Russia. At bottom this war was a war of liberation for the Russian people who were fighting it with the spirit that marked the French in their own war late in the eighteenth century to protect their revolution from monarchial Europe. Germany, the stronghold of reaction and absolutism, had been the friend of Russian reaction and Russian despotism. Not merely had the German influence in Russia tended to strengthen the bureaucracy, but it had brought about a situation where Russia had been exploited by German industry. The German merchant and the German manufacturer dominated Russia, and by virtue of a treaty, wrung from Russia at the moment of the Japanese war, Germany had obtained a practical monopoly of Russian trade.

An event surpassing in far-reaching importance the actual military operations of the war happened on December 3 with the public announcement by the new Russian Premier that, by an agreement concluded in 1915, and subsequently adhered to by Italy, the Allies had definitely established Russia's right to Constantinople and the strait. The existence of this agreement had been for a long time alleged but never before had it been publicly and formally admitted. Constantinople and the Dardanelles were now guaranteed to Russia by the Allies "in the most definite manner." An arrangement that had been more than hinted at by Sir Edward Grey, and that had been announced with greater certainty by Professor Miliukoff, leader of the Liberal majority in the Duma, was thus formally made public. It became an exhortation to increased energy and greater sacrifice at a moment when Roumania had cast a bleak aspect over the Allied cause. But Premier Trepoff's words were addrest not only to the Russian people, but to Germany and to Russia's Allies. It was explicit notification that all possibility of a separate peace with Germany had ceased. By appealing to the ancient Russian sentiment that clustered about Byzantium, Premier Trepoff gave notice that the pro-German intrigues of the Stürmer Cabinet were at an end. To Berlin's announcement of a reestablished Polish kingdom, the Russian Government retorted not merely that it was determined to keep Poland out of Teuton hands, but that it still held fast to the proudest purpose of Russian policy—the acquisition of Constantinople. Far from considering herself beaten, Russia saw no reason why she should yield a jot from her original program. Hindenburg was reported as saying of this announcement that Russia had undertaken to acquire of "a big mouthful."

The announcement was of great significance, however, and

NEVSKY PROSPECT IN PETROGRAD

came at a time when it should have inspired the armies and people of the empire to their utmost efforts. As Premier Trepoff said, this promised the realization of the "age-long dream, cherished in the hearts of the Russian people" for more than a thousand years, of a "free outlet on the open sea" to the south. The time had come when Russians should know for what they were shedding their blood, and it was "in accordance with her Allies" that the announcement of the agreement was made. "Absolute agreement on this point," the Premier took pains to repeat, "is firmly established among the Allies."

There remained six weeks of good campaigning weather in which to complete the work begun early in June by taking some keypoint like Kovel or Lemberg. The previous two months seemed to have warranted such hopes, while the entry of Roumania into the war promised a grave situation for Hindenburg on his southern flank. But Germany had not been slow to perceive and prepare against the danger that threatened her. The whole eastern command had been transformed. A *de facto* German control, which had existed since the first day of war, was now formally proclaimed and extended to the smallest details. Austrian regiments were moved about like pawns on a chessboard, without regard to the wishes of their nominal commanders. They did not complain, for the Prussian handling was efficient, and that of their own leaders had been chaotic. Moreover, they were now decently fed, and their transport was well organized.

Russia faced the winter with very different prospects from those of a year before. Then she lay weary at the end of her great retreat; now she had behind her a summer of successes which, if they fell short of her hopes, had yet inflicted irreparable losses upon her enemies, and had proved conclusively that, given anything like a fair munitionment, she could break the front of the invader. There were, however, two dark spots in her outlook. The success of the summer had weakened that political unanimity at home which had characterized the darkest days of the retreat. Reactionary elements had appeared among ministerial appointments. The Duma and the Government drew apart. Omens already as to Russian internal politics were not propitious for a harmonious winter. It was clear meanwhile that Germany would struggle desperately to put Roumania out of action; to make her share the fate of Serbia and Belgium, and succor could come only from Russia, for the Allies at Saloniki were too weak and too far away to affect the situation. Could Russia be depended on in such an emergency?

A manifesto of Emperor William and Emperor Francis Joseph again calling into existence the ancient Kingdom of Poland was read in Warsaw on November 5 to Polish repre-

FRANCIS JOSEPH OF AUSTRIA

Sixteen days after he and the German Kaiser proclaimed Poland again a
Kingdom, Francis Joseph died, his reign the longest active one in history

sentatives assembled in the Royal Palace. Outside in the great square before the castle, and in the courtyard of that venerable fourteenth-century pile, inhabitants gathered by thousands to attend what was designated as the rebirth of the Polish nation—a concept the importance and bearing of which were then making their way into the minds of people after a long sleep of more than a century. The ceremony was short and simple. Precisely at noon General von Beseler, wearing decorations granted to him for the reduction of Antwerp and the Polish fortresses, mounted the dais in the ball-room of the castle and read the Imperial manifesto "in ringing, soldierly tones." When he ceased, Count Hutten-czapski, the palace commandant, read from a leather-bound pamphlet to the Polish notables a translation of the manifesto in their own language. Then came cheers from a hitherto silent crowd, and a band in an adjoining gallery struck up the strains of the ancient national anthem. After a few bars had been played, Poles in the hall burst into strains which recited the ancient glories, the fallen fortunes, and the undying hopes of Poland. Twenty minutes saw the end of the ceremony, the participants, excitedly discussing the future, slowly making their way home.

The importance of this declaration would have been less debated had it not contained an uncertain condition—"The exact frontiers of the Kingdom of Poland will be outlined later." The promise of automony for Poland made from Petrograd at the beginning of the war had been a tactical move in the great war game, precisely as this promise of a "national state" from Berlin and Vienna was now a move in the same game. A principle, however, had been laid down on both occasions. The price which Petrograd and Berlin both contracted to pay for the support of the Polish people and for sympathy from the outside world, could afterward no more be recalled than the price that Petrograd and Berlin had to pay for guns and ammunition they contracted to buy. To the outside observer it was enough that, out of the wreck and evil of the war, one solid gain for progress and civilization had emerged; and not the least, because the gain fell to the share of a people that had suffered more than any other in this war. Poland's woes, under the forward and backward sweep of armies, had been heavier even than Belgium's.

The question at once arose, could Germany and Austria refuse after the war to give up their own share of the ancient Polish patrimony in order to rebuild old Poland? In consistency, many held that they could not. One bitter comment was that "a reformed pirate is an interesting person, especially when he returns a former partner's swag and keeps his own." Would the people of any new Polish kingdom remain content to have millions of other Poles still living outside their kingdom under foreign rule? Most observers knew they would not be so content, and that there would have to come a change in Prussian policy in Posen. It was impossible to think of a Polish kingdom living in "intimate relations" with Germany while dragonades in Posen continued. The Teuton manifesto was highly significant in its bearing on a possible separate peace with Russia. Perhaps the manifesto had been a result of Russia's refusal to enter into any separate negotiations.

In any case the Central Powers had obviously abandoned all hope of a separate peace with Russia. Because of Teutonic hopes for such a peace the Polish question had perhaps been adjourned for more than a year. All through the war, in fact, Germany had alternately cherished and put aside this hope. The decision to recreate Poland now definitely closed the way to negotiations, but Russia's offensive spoke volumes for determination to stand with her Western Allies to the end. In restoring a part of Poland, Germany and Austria had raised a new problem for themselves. In Galicia there were not less than five million Poles; in Posen and the Prussias there were nearly four million more. Krakow, in Galicia, was the old Polish capital, and nowhere had the dream of a restored Poland been cherished more steadily than in Polish Galicia. Once the liberation of Poland had begun it would not end until all the regions inhabited by Poles were gathered under Polish sovereignty.

On November 21 Francis Joseph, Emperor of Austria, died. This was the most important death that had occurred among the chief actors in the war drama. An old era ended with Francis Joseph's life. He inherited a great patrimony, kingdoms, and duchies, and he had kept his dominions as might a steward, and transmitted them to a successor almost intact. He had sacrificed the political progress of his peoples and had allowed control of Austrian policy to pass to the Hohenzollerns, all for the sake of his patrimony. His was the longest active reign of which there was authentic record. When he went to Schoenbrunn, he found about him the memories of a Napoleonic occupation not yet remote; he lived to an hour when a new Napoleonic struggle convulsed the world. He was the last great remaining royal figure of the nineteenth century.

When Francis Joseph was young Metternich ruled in Vienna. Other great men of the fight against Napoleon were still on earth. When he came to power the Revolution of 1848 was going forward. He was young when Cavour unified Italy, when Bismarck created modern Germany. William I., Victoria, Louis Napoleon, Victor Emmanuel, these were his contemporaries. The world that he best knew had vanished also. Republican institutions had returned to France. During the threescore and eight years that he reigned, he saw all Europe, save his own realm, made over. The war with Napoleon III. drove him out of Italy; the war with Prussia expelled him from Germany, and from that moment Austria declined; she was no longer one of the dominating voices in European councils; she had become more and more the vassal of that Prussia whose rise she had opposed.

Francis Joseph was not a great Emperor like Napoleon, nor yet a great King like Louis XIV., and he had no wide outlook upon world affairs. He was a typical product of the Hapsburg family, whose reactionary ideas he shared and served. When young, the theories of Metternich ruled and he accepted them. He fought to prevent the unity of Italy and the rise of modern Germany. He sought to enslave the Balkans as his predecessors endeavored to enslave Italy. Francis Joseph resembled Louis XIV. in his fidelity to the task that had come to him unsought. No man ever worked harder; no man ever devoted himself more unsparingly to the business of ruling. He did not create, he did not transform, but he did preserve. Ultimately, by dint of devotion

EMPEROR CHARLES, SUCCESSOR TO FRANCIS JOSEPH, TAKING HIS CORONATION OATH
IN BUDAPEST AS KING OF HUNGARY

The ceremony occurred less than two years before Charles's abdication. Cardinal Czernoch, the Primate of Hungary, is reading the oath to Charles. Near the Cardinal stands Count Tisza, at that time the Hungarian Premier, who was assassinated in 1919 to what he conceived to be the welfare of his people, he built up a tradition, and constructed a legend.

And so the Eastern Front entered upon its winter of rest from war's doings. Between the Russian and the Teuton came a pause, really a stalemate in the fighting, but before spring had dawned, the whole aspect of the war in that field was completely transformed. Russia was in a revolution, the tremendous consequences and frightful aspects of which engrossed all the world till the war's end and long after. [7]

[7] Principal Sources: The *Evening Post,* the "Military Expert" of The *Times,* The *Tribune,* New York; The London *Times'* "History of the War," "Nelson's History of the War" by John Buchan; The *Evening Sun, Bradstreet's,* New York; Associated Press dispatches, The *Evening Post* (New York).

STÜRMER, THE DEPOSED PRO-GERMAN
PRIME MINISTER OF RUSSIA

IN THE EAST, NEAR EAST AND SOUTH

Part IV

THE REVOLUTION, THE BREST-LITOVSK TREATY AND ANARCHY UNDER THE BOLSHEVIKI

THE TRAGEDY OF A RUSSIAN PEASANT SOLDIER

I

THE CZAR DEPOSED AND A REPUBLIC PROCLAIMED

March 15, 1917—April 6, 1917

IT would have been hard to find seven consecutive days within a century (except perhaps those of the signing of the armistice and the German Revolution, or the days immediately preceding the outbreak of the war itself), that were so big with events as that brief period in 1917 between March 15 and March 21. Within that time occurred the revolution in Russia, an event unparalleled since the days of the French Revolution, the beginning of Hindenburg's retirement of German forces on the Western Front, the rout of Turkish forces by British and Russian armies in Persia, Mesopotamia, and Syria; an open confession by Bethmann-Hollweg, the German Chancellor, in his "woe to the statesmen" speech, that Germany must become more democratic; and signs almost unmistakable of the early entrance of the United States into the war as an active belligerent, the President having issued a call to Congress to meet in special session on April 2 for the purpose of dealing with the war-situation—as a matter of fact, for declaring war on Germany, which was done on April 6.

When people said the Russian Revolution came unexpectedly, they ignored a long undermining which gradually had melted away the supports of autocracy, so that when the Russian people struck they struck an empty shell. Persons familiar with Russia had believed since the beginning of the war that a revolution might come any day, with a suddenness characteristic of many movements in Russia, but on the morning of Sunday, March 11, 1917, after some days of bread riots, few people had noticed any real revolutionary spirit in the crowds of people who lightly taunted policemen in the streets and good-naturedly cheered Cossacks. General

Khabaloff's order to police and Cossacks, posted on March 10, had been to shoot if necessary when dispersing crowds. That smacked strongly of serious business, but when the Cossacks refused to use their rifles and, later, when they fired blank cartridges from machine-guns, a revolution still seemed a make-believe affair. It was not until a regiment of soldiers, when ordered to shoot into a crowd of hungry civilians, mutinied and, after shooting their own officers, made common cause with the people, that it seemed probable a new birth for Russia was imminent.

The anger of the people at shortages in ammunition for the army, which was largely caused by the inactivity of the Government, had grown in intensity as Russia had been hampered again and again by deficiencies. The removal in 1915 of the Grand Duke Nicholas as Commander-in-Chief of the armies, the repeated arrogant treatment of the Duma by the Czar and his reactionary ministers, and the appointment of such pro-Germans as Stürmer and Galitzin to the position of Premier, all had goaded the people into a state of frenzy from which there could be only one outlet. Most of all were they aroused by a dawning belief that these occurrences were all part of a pro-German propaganda, headed, it seemed to many, by their German-born Empress, and by the notorious degenerate priest, Rasputin, whose assassination several weeks before should have warned the Government, if anything could have warned it, of an impending uprising.

One of the most extraordinary, as well as one of the most successful, impostors who ever made religion a cloak for ambition, sensuality, and vice was removed in this Russian monk, Gregory Rasputin. Mr. George Kennan, the American traveler, who many years before investigated and wrote on the Siberian-exile system, said[1] that Rasputin's very name meant a "rake, a dissolute, licentious man." It was assumed by its bearer when, in his later life, he "put on a deceptive garb of sanctity," perhaps intending "to suggest the idea that he was a reformed and converted sinner." But he was no real monk at all—that is, he was a member of no monkish order in the Greek Church—but a man of peasant stock, who had received an elementary education in

[1] In *The Outlook* (New York).

public schools, which enabled him to write his name and read the Bible. As a youth, he was "given to drunkenness and dissipation, and lived the life of a common village hoodlum of the peasant class; but, in spite of excesses, developed into a man of powerful physique and not unpleasing appearance, and a man, moreover, who for some reason was particularly attractive to women."

Accounts of how he first met the Czar differed, but the meeting had occurred about ten years before the Revolution. His influence at court became so great that "even nobles, generals and high officers of State who desired promotion or increase of salary sought his intercession and support." But by 1909 his loose moral conduct had become a scandal in Petrograd, and in 1910 Prime Minister Stolpin ordered him out of the city. He disappeared for a time, but at the end of 1911 was back again and "became the favorite, if not the adviser, of the Emperor and Empress." During the next two years, so Mr. Kennan quoted from the Petrograd *Ryetch*, "the life and success of the *starets* were perhaps without a parallel even in Russian history." To Rasputin's influence were attributed the resignation of S. M. Lukianoff, Procurator of the Holy Synod, the overthrow of Bishop Hermogen and the monk Iliodor, with whom he had quarreled; the promotion of Bishop Barnabas; the campaign against the Metropolitan Antonius; and the wholesale dismissal of professors from the ecclesiastical academies. His activities finally created so much indignation in the Duma that they were made the subject of two interpellations.

After the outbreak of the war, Rasputin's influence over the Emperor and the Empress "was popularly connected with many important events, notably the removal of the Grand Duke Nicholas from command of the armies." Rasputin, it was said, favored a separate peace with Germany, and the Grand Duke, when he heard of it, "declared that if the *starets* should fall into his hands he would hang him." Frequent references were made in the press to the "dark forces" that were attempting to control Russia's foreign and domestic policy. These "dark forces" were Rasputin and other adventurers, impostors, or fanatics, "who were apparently influencing the character and sometimes inspiring the acts of a religiously inclined but superstitious monarch." Several weeks before the Revolution broke out, Rasputin was assassinated in Petrograd.

Prince Felix Yusupov made his aquaintance because he was convinced that his removal was essential for the safety of Russia. The scene of the tragedy was the Palace Yusupov, a long building with twenty-six windows on each floor, overlooking the Moika Canal. Prince Felix went himself to fetch Rasputin, who had never before been in the Yusupov Palace. Rasputin, when invited to refresh himself, drank a glass of red wine in which poison had been put. Felix himself drinking no wine, being a total abstainer. The poison had been bought some weeks before, and strength had apparently evaporated, as it failed to take immediate effect. Prince Felix determined, as the night was now far advanced, to shoot the man outright and with the weapon held behind his back, approached Rasputin, who was leaning over the supper-table and shot him at close quarters through the left side, The man reeled and fell heavily on a white bearskin, Felix, believing he was dead, left him lying there. Later, when bending over the body, he was horrified to find the eyes were not only wide open, but gleaming with tiger-like fury. Suddenly the

RASPUTIN, THE SO-CALLED RUSSIAN "MONK"

Rasputin's evil influence at the Russian court and his murder by men interested in better government was an incident that led to the outbreak of the revolution

262

wounded man raised himself on his elbows and struggled to his feet. Springing at the man, Felix seized him by the throat and tried to strangle him. Purishkevich, a member of the Duma, who was called for at once came to the scene and fired four shots at Rasputin. Two bullets hit Rasputin, one on the back of the head, the other in his forehead. His lifeless body was then picked up and placed in a motor-car, and driven rapidly out to Kristovski Island, where it was thrown into a hole in the ice of the Little Neva.[1a] Next.evening the *Bourse Gazette* announced Rasputin's death. That night at the Imperial Theater an audience celebrated the event with wild enthusiasm, as they sang the National Hymn. The whole country applauded the deed less as a murder than as a judicial execution.

The death of Rasputin was the first act in the Russian Revolution. For the moment the autocracy drew the strings tighter. Rasputin was dead, but Protopopov remained, and the censorship was intensified. Alexander Protopopov will remain one of the enigmas of Russian history. Originally a Liberal, he came to Western Europe in the summer of 1916 with a deputation of members of the Duma and the Council of the Empire, and delighted audiences in England and France with his oratory. He had great charm of manner, and a kind of earnest simplicity which deeply imprest those who met him. On his return he fell completely into the hands of the Court party, and more especially of those elements which were represented by Rasputin. His neurotic temperament and restless imagination predisposed him to the influence of the Court and the necromancy of charlatans. Toward the end he became known as the "Mad Minister," It is likely that his wits were seriously unhinged.

The winter had been bitter with heavy snowfalls, and the supply of food was scanty. The Government had no plan to deal with the shortage, and by February the daily bread-ration in Petrograd, small at the best, looked as if it were about to fail. Word began to go around that before the spring came real starvation would be upon them, and there were many—Social Democrats in the factories and mysterious figures at the street corners—to point the moral and ask what was the use of a Government which could not give them bread. Thursday, March 8, was a day of fine.

clear weather. In the Duma a debate on the question of food-supplies was winding out its slow length. Everywhere there seemed a profound peace—the peace of apathy and disheartenment. But in the afternoon a small party of Cossacks galloped down the Nevski Prospect, causing the promenaders to ask whether there was not trouble somewhere across the river. A little later a few bakers' shops were looted in the poorer quarters and a forlorn and orderly procession of students and workmen's wives appeared in the Nevski.

Protopopov's spies reported that all was quiet; but they were wrong—the Revolution had begun. The breaking point had been reached in the people's temper. All Russia was on the tiptoe of expectation, seeking for a sign. Next day, in the same bright cold weather, it became apparent that some change had taken place. The people by a common impulse flowed out into the streets, but it was hard to believe that leaderless crowds could achieve anything worth while. They were unarmed and undisciplined, and in Petrograd there were at least 29,000 police, with many machine-guns. On the following day trams stopt running, altho shops were still open, and the motion picture shows crowded. Streets were more densely packed than ever, and the following morning it was announced that the police had orders to disperse all crowds. Enormous throngs, including women and children, had turned out from pure curiosity, the police patrols much strengthened, and detachments of regulars brought in to assist them. The Nevski Prospect being cleared from end to end, it was put under military guard after some two hundred had been killed. Prince Golitzin prorogued the Duma, under powers received from the Emperor, but the Duma refused to be prorogued and elected a Provisional Committee. Rodzianko's huge figure rose in the winter twilight, and waving in his hand the order for dissolution, announced that the Duma was now the sole constitutional authority in Russia. During that act of defiance to an order from the Czar, Kerensky had made a dramatic speech in the Duma.

Monday, March 12, was a critical day. A movement which had begun by slow and halting stages was about to become a whirlwind. The troops, both the garrison and the

NICHOLAS II AND GEORGE V IN GERMAN ARMY UNIFORMS
Nicholas has on the Hussar uniform, George V the white uniform of the
Kaiser's Cuirassiers

reinforcements, aware what their orders would be, resolved to disobey them. They could not shoot down men of their own class. Before nine o'clock the streets were black with people. On the crust of the volcano much of the normal life of the city still went on, men going about their ordinary vocations. Early next day came the crisis. The Preobrajenski Guards regiments, the flower of the Household troops, were ordered to fire on the mob; instead, they shot their more unpopular officers. The Volynski regiment, sent to coerce them, joined in the mutiny. The united forces swept down on the Arsenal, and after a short resistance carried the place, and provided the revolutionists with munitions of war. Then began a day of sheer chaos. Soldiers having no plans, drifted from quarter to quarter, intoxicated with their new freedom, but still maintained a semblance of discipline. There was no looting, and little drunkenness. No leader appeared. A force of some 25,000 men moved about from street to street. Headquarters of the autocracy fell one by one. At

MICHAEL RODZIANKO

Rodzianko was President of the Russian Duma at the time of the overthrow of the Czar's government. He became head of the provisional government established afterward

11 A.M. the Courts of Law were on fire, then various prisons were stormed, and a host of political prisoners, as well as ordinary criminals, released. In the afternoon the great fortress of SS. Peter and Paul surrendered. All day nests of secret police were smoked out, the chief office raided, and the papers which it contained burned in the street. The Bastile of the old régime in Russia had fallen in a revolution.

About midday came news that the Emperor had wired the Minister of War that he was going to Petrograd. He had appointed General Ivanov to supreme command of the Army, and troops were coming from the Northern Front to quell the rising. In the afternoon the Duma, in secret, chose an Executive Committee of twelve men as a Provisional Government. Outside its walls another committee was formed of workmen and social revolutionaries who speedily obtained great influence over the troops pouring into Petrograd. Close on midnight a shabby man in a dirty fur overcoat spoke to one of the Duma guards. "Take me," he said, "to the Committee of the Duma. I surrender myself voluntarily, for I seek only the welfare of our country. My name is Protopopov."

The Emperor to the vast majority was still sovereign and father. On Wednesday, the 14th, he was going to Petrograd. Ivanov, whom he regarded as the bulwark of his throne, with a battalion composed of Knights of St. George, were to take command of troops in the capital. Ivanov never reached the city. His train came within a few stations of Tsarkoe Selo, where it was held up; and, after wandering aimlessly for some time up and down the line, he received instructions from General Ruzsky to return to Pckov. The same fate befell Ivanov's master. On the 14th he tried to reach Petrograd; but he got no farther than the little station of Bologoi, where workmen had pulled up the track, and he was compelled to return to Pckov. At 2 A.M. on the morning of the 15th he sent for Ruzsky, and told him: "I have decided to give way, and grant a responsible Ministry. What is your view?" The manifesto, already signed, lay on the table. Ruzsky advised him to get in touch with Rodzianko and himself telephoned to the Duma in Petrograd and to the other generals. The replies he received made it clear that there was no other course than abdication, and at 10 A.M. he made his report to the Emperor.

Late on the night of Thursday, the 15th, a deputation, led by Vladimir Lvoff, and including Kerensky, sought out the Grand Duke Michael and informed him that the people demanded that he should renounce the Regency, and relegate all powers to the Provisional Government until a Constituent Assembly should decide upon the future. The Grand Duke bowed to fate, and on the morning of Friday, 16th, there was issued a declaration in his name which rang the knell of the Romanoff dynasty. The sacred monarchy had disappeared, the strongholds of reaction had been obliterated as if by a sponge, and agitators, but lately lurking in dens and corners and dreading the sight of a soldier, were now leading regiments of Guards under the red flag and dictating their terms to grand dukes and princes.

The fall of the Emperor was received among the Allies with mixed feelings. Even those who warmly acclaimed the revolution, and recognized the hopeless inadequacy of his rule, could not view without some natural regret the fate of a man who, since the first day of the war had been scrupulously loyal to the Alliance; who, as was proved by his creation of the Hague conferences, had had generous and far-sighted ideals; and who, on the admission of all who knew him, was in character mild, courteous and humane. A stronger man than Nicholas might have established an efficient autocracy with the complete assent of his people; a wiser man could have transformed Tsardom into a constitutional kingship. Nicholas wavered between the two, and was incapable of the sustained intellectual effort necessary to follow either course. His sympathies were, on the whole, liberal; but he was easily swayed by his entourage, and especially by his wife. He did not blunder from lack of warning. The Grand Duke Nicholas Mikhailovitch had told him the truth the preceding Christmas and was banished for his pains.

The worst influence was attributed to the wife, whom he deeply loved. She was possest of firm ideas about divine right, and her one object in life was to hand on the Russian crown to her son with no atom of its power and glory diminished. Her shallow mind, played upon by every wind of superstition, was incapable of distinguishing true men from false, or of discerning the best means of realizing her ambitions. In the end she had surrounded herself and her husband with charlatans. The revolution succeeded not so much because it was well planned and brilliantly led, as because there was so little opposition. It triumphed in a week, and at a cost of human life in that week far lower than any other movement of the same magnitude had ever produced. What happened was a *coup d'état*, supported by nearly all the troops, and such strokes are usually swift and bloodless. It was not till March 18, that any connected narrative of events appeared in the Russian press, and not till March 21 that something was learned by the outer world of the events that led to the revolution.

The revolution broke out almost simultaneously in Petrograd and Moscow. Kronstadt, the fortress and seaport at the head of the Gulf of Finland, twenty miles west of Petrograd, soon joined the movement. The spark ignited in Petrograd carried enthusiasm over all Russia. In Moscow Cossacks who formerly had attempted to ride down people in the celebrated Red Square beneath the gray old walls of the Kremlin, now, when their intended victims made known news of a *coup d'état* in Petrograd, leapt off their horses and joined in huzzas for the new Government. The revolution in Moscow had cost at first only four lives. By evening of March 12 the last supporters of the Czar in the capital had been holding out in two small groups, one firing from behind barricades around the Admiralty buildings overlooking the Neva, the other sniping stubbornly from windows and roof of the Astoria Hotel at men who sent back a hotter fire from such scant cover as could be found in the square south of St. Isaac's Cathedral. Later in the evening, when the revolutionaries broke into the Astoria Hotel, which had been considered a hot-bed of pro-German intrigue since the beginning of the war, the last organized resistance from loyalists was broken. For two days longer there was sniping.

Resistance to the revolution in Petrograd lasted not more than four days. Long before that time had expired, the streets were filled with civilians and soldiers flaunting the red flag and singing the "Marseillaise." With a few exceptions, the army and navy of Russia stood loyal to the revolution from the first. One of the first acts of the new Government was to pledge Russia's allegiance to the cause of the Allies and her unswerving determination to prosecute the war against Germany to a finish. The war had made the revolution possible. It had taught the people their own strength. United from the outset in determination to defeat Germany, because they realized that a war against

Germany was a war against their own oppressive Government, the people had gradually come to know their powers as they had been forced to take over the management of the war through their provincial assemblies and co-operative societies after their inefficient and corrupt Imperial Government had dropt the burden. Without so long a war, a war which had killed off so many old professional soldiers loyal to the bureaucracy, Russia never would have had new soldiers ready to side with the people in a national crisis.

On March 21 an order was issued for the arrest of the

TSARSKOE SELO

Here the Czar and Czarina were held under arrest before they were
transported to Siberia

former Emperor and Empress. General Alexieff was charged with the duty of guarding them until members of the Duma could arrive with an escort and take them to Tsarskoe Selo. After signing the decree of abdication in Pskoff, Nicholas had returned to headquarters, to say farewell to the army. Wild rumors spread that he had gone to his estate of Lavidia, in the Crimea. On all sides the question was asked, "Why is he allowed to travel about Russia at will?" It was feared that he might use his opportunities in attempts to recover the crown. In view of this popular excitement it became evident that steps must be taken to secure the safety of him and his family on the one hand, and on the other hand to prevent monarchist agitation.

The arrest and the journey to Tsarskoe Selo were replete with dramatic incidents. Four Duma commissioners boarded the Czar's train at Moghilef, after the Dowager Empress, his mother, had bade him an affectionate farewell. A large crowd stood silent outside offering no demonstration. "I am ready to go anywhere and submit to any decision," said the Czar to General Alexieff when informed that the Commissioners were waiting. After finishing his morning cup of coffee in the dining-saloon of the train, he bade farewell to his servants and suite, all of whom kissed him on the shoulder with every mark of affection and esteem. "I thank you all for your services," he said, *"Au Revoir!"* When the train arrived at Tsarskoe Selo, he stept out on the platform calmly, but looking haggard and tired and wearing a Cossack uniform of purple with a dagger at his belt, his only decoration the Order of St. George. Entering a waiting motor-car he was carried to the palace from the station, from which the public had been excluded. In the custody of four members of the Duma he was turned over to the Tsarskoe Selo commander and taken to the Alexandrovsky palace, where the former Empress Alexandra already had been interned. On leaving the train, Nicholas had entered an automobile, accompanied by the four Commissioners and by his adjutant, Prince Dolgorukoff, the only courtier of the first rank who accompanied him. He was met at the door of the left wing of the palace by Count Benkendorff, who was his marshal of the court, and was now under arrest. Nicholas held himself erect, looking calm and indifferent, altho he stept from the automobile with nervous haste.

The palace lies in a large park, surrounded by a plain spiked fence, five feet high, coated with silver paint. From a corner near an old palace the new palace is partly visible through a thick wood, the chief façade, facing the north, being entirely in view. No Imperial standard now floated from its roof. Within the park, over a broad expanse of snow, not a person was visible. Apparently there were no guards within the park, but outside the fence, every fifty yards along the roadway, were double sentries from the Petrograd Regiment in long blue coats, with fixt bayonets. An astonishing circumstance, in view of the former relations of Nicholas with the population of Tsarskoe Selo, which lived entirely upon Imperial favor, was the lack of public interest in his arrival. During a drive of three miles alongside of the palace fence a correspondent saw no civilians, and, with the exception of guards, saw only two of the gigantic black-bearded Caucasians of the famous "Convoy of his Majesty," who, now fallen from favor and destined to be sent to the front, were allowed to peer through the fence. When Nicholas arrived, all five of his children were in bed with the measles. Alexandra had not been outside the palace walls for two days. In a room on the first floor were seventy persons in civilian dress, formerly palace spies and provocative agents. Here were also four Russian officers with German names who had been arrested on suspicion of having sent communications from the former Empress to Berlin by way of Stockholm. In a neighboring room sat the director of the Tsarskoe Lyceum, who was a general in the army and had been a close friend of Rasputin.

Not since August, 1914, had anything come out of Europe to stir the pulse and fire the imagination like this news from Russia. Wherever there were men of liberal minds, wherever belief in Democracy prevailed, people were rejoicing that the Russian autocrat, disgraced by innumerable cruelties and massacres during his reign, had been driven from his throne, and with him a whole band of pro-German intriguers. One had to go back at least to 1848, when Europe was seething in revolt, to parallel the thrill that this news brought to struggling men everywhere. To the ends of the earth the thrill penetrated. It was the first visible sign of that extension of Democracy in the world which had to come if civilization was to profit by the unparalleled bloodshed of this world-war. Men who had dreaded a German victory in the sense that they feared the triumph of the ideas of Bernhardi and Trietschke, believed they could now sleep in peace. The happenings of four days had made it clear that there could be no alliance between the new Russia and the Germany of the Kaiser until Germany began to free herself from the imperialistic hindrances to her destiny.

It was at once widely conjectured that the effect of the revolution on the German people would be tremendous. Germany had been taught to believe that the war was inaugurated by Russia for aggressive purposes. Germany's democratic leaders repeatedly had pointed to Czarism as the evil spirit dominating the Entente, and the object of the Central Powers was proclaimed to be the overthrow of the Russian autocratic menace. Now that Russia herself had removed the menace, Germany was likely to be profoundly moved. Her greatest disillusionment since the war began might occur. Indeed the dawn of Democracy in Germany seemed at once foreshadowed in those very days by a speech from Chancellor Bethmann-Hollweg in the Prussian Diet.

According to the *Reinische-Westfalische Zeitung* of Essen, the speech was evoked by a demonstration from the Socialist members of the Diet against the composition of the Herrenhaus, or Prussian House of Nobles, the membership of which was anything but democratic. Entering the House during the course of a debate, the Chancellor made an unpremeditated speech in which he stated that: "After the war we shall be confronted with the most gigantic tasks that ever confronted a nation." They would be so gigantic that "the entire people would have to work to solve them." A strong foreign policy would be necessary, "for we shall be surrounded by enemies whom we must meet not with loud words, but rather with the internal strength of the nation." Germany could only pursue such a policy if the patriotism which during the war had "developed to such a marvelous reality, was maintained and strengthened." He added that the maintenance of patriotism could be secured only by granting the people in general "equal co-operation in the administration of the Empire," and then proceeded: "Woe to the statesman who does not recognize the signs of the times and who, after this catastrophe, the like of which the world has never seen, believes that he can take up his work at the same point at which it was interrupted."

The effect of this speech in Germany was electric. With

SOAP-BOX ORATORS ADDRESSING OUTDOOR MEETINGS IN PETROGRAD

273

the exception of the ultra-Conservative and militaristic Berlin *Kreuzzeitung,* German papers generally exprest approval of it. A dispatch from Berlin to the Copenhagen *Nation Tidnede* said the speech had "made a tremendous impression throughout Germany." Such an answer to the Diet's attitude was "entirely unexpected." Taken as a whole the incident "had the character of a great political demonstration." What made the greatest impression was "the firmness with which the Chancellor declared that he would carry through his new policy against every opposition." Liberals, members of the Central Party, and Independent Conservatives, stood on their feet while he was speaking and interrupted him repeatedly with prolonged applause. Scarcely more than eighteen months afterwards the storm broke over Germany, and the Kaiser was a fugitive in Holland, from which six months later he was sending to the new German Government for money with which to pay his board-bills at Amerongen.

It was right and fitting that the first formal recognition of the new-born Russian Government should come from the United States which embodied the first large-scale experiment in Democracy of modern times. The American people had been better qualified than any other to understand the aspirations of the Russian people, just as they were specially qualified to understand the evil nature of the system which the Russian people had shaken off. Mr. Wilson seemed to have been speaking with prophetic vision when he told Congress two months before that there could be no lasting peace "which does not recognize and accept the principle that governments derive all their just powers from the consent of the governed, and that no right exists anywhere to hand people about from sovereignty to sovereignty as if they were property." The Russian revolution had affirmed both these contentions. At the same time that it made an assertion of Democracy, it made a protest against the machinations of a court camarilla which had sought to make a separate peace with Germany, that involved the surrender of large sections of Russia. Soon afterward British, French, and Italian Ambassadors in Petrograd called on the Minister of Foreign Affairs and formally extended the official recognition of their Governments to the new Russian Government. Travelers arriving in Copenhagen from various parts of Russia gave glowing reports of the success that had been achieved by the new Government within a fortnight of the overthrow of the old. The greater part of the Russian people, they said, favored a republic and favored a vigorous prosecution of the war. All Russia, including Finland, Turkestan, the Caucacus and Siberia had declared its adherence to the revolution.

After the fall of the Czar, the Petrograd press, no longer under the strict censorship of the old *régime*, published facts hitherto supprest in regard to the assassination of Gregory Rasputin. While the whole nation was breathing a sigh of relief at deliverance from the monk's malign influence, the imperial family had been laying away his remains with great reverence and pomp at Tsarskoe Selo, after his body was recovered from the Neva. It had been taken to Tsarskoe Selo in the imperial car, in which rode M. Protopopoff and General Voyekoff. At the palace a funeral ceremony was held in the imperial chapel. In a silver coffin the body was carried to its resting place by the Emperor, M. Protopopoff, General Voyckoff, and others, followed by the Empress in deep mourning. The affair caused a great scandal at the time and further inflamed the people against the Empress.

It should be kept in mind that almost at the beginning of the war the supply and commissariat departments of the Russian army and navy broke down with great promptness the first time any unusual strain was made upon them for supplying the needs of the mobilized millions of troops. Rail transportation, at no time of the best in Russia, began slowly to grow worse and worse, until finally the only way in which supplies could be brought to Petrograd and Moscow from other places, in quantities sufficient to feed the populations of those cities, was by suspending for weeks at a time the passenger traffic and turning the lines entirely over to the freight trains. There has never been any scarcity of food in Russia. The cessation of exports, owing to the closing of export shipping through the Black Sea, on the Danube, and through the Baltic, left in the country millions of bushels of grain which ordinarily would have gone to Europe. This, added to a succession of good harvests in nearly all the more important crops, had given the country plenty of foodstuffs. The only problem had been to get them from the places where they were grown to the places where they could be eaten. Another reason for shortage in certain places was a lack of common sense on the part of local military authorities. There were large accumulations of grain in some provinces, and these were more than enough for the needs of the people of adjacent districts where there had been some partial failure of crops. In a country as large as the Russian Empire, it had always been impossible to manage transportation problems as in the rest of Europe. In war-time the constantly increasing number of fronts and the necessity of keeping these fronts supplied with men, food and munitions, and the further necessity of taking away from the fronts hundreds of thousands of German and Austrian war prisoners besides the Russian wounded, some of whom could be transferred only after six weeks or more of travel by rail, occasioned a hopeless paralysis of the railway system.

Penetrating into and under the vast prison-like palace of the deposed Emperor, a correspondent of the Associated Press on March 26 obtained from the jailer a statement of the former Emperor's condition, and visited the desecrated grave of Gregory Rasputin. He was told that Nicholas was in all respects a prisoner and treated accordingly, that he was in perfectly good health and in fairly good spirits, except when alone, or with his own entourage, when he had "fits of crying." He was no longer allowed in the park; but twice daily, between eleven and three o'clock, was permitted to walk for recreation in the railed garden between the east and west wings of the palace. Outside the railing were six soldiers, constituting the so-called intermediate guard, another guard being within the palace walls. His chief serious occupation in the first week after the revolution was shovelling snow. He showed boyish interest in what was said and written about him, and did not resent abuse. The former Empress physically was in better health than before. Her real malady was not of the nerves, but of the heart. She was unable to walk any distance and was carried in a chair, even when going from her own suite to her children's rooms.

The correspondent [2] visited Rasputin's ·burial-place "on the edge of a ravine beyond a desolate and roadless plain, covered with deep snow." It was surrounded by an unfinished log chapel, which adherents of the dead impostor monk, with monetary assistance from the former Empress, had planned to raise over his remains. Beside the chapel nave were half a dozen tiny cells for pilgrims. In the ground was seen a ten-foot hole from which revolutionaries had disinterred the body. The chapel was filled with soldiers, some of whom were inscribing ribald remarks on the walls. One of these read: "Here lay Rasputin; foulest of men, the shame of the Russian Church." As the correspondent was reading the inscriptions, he heard loud shouts, and looking down into an open grave saw there a little brown Siberian soldier on his haunches doing the Russian squat dance. Soldiers told the correspondent that someone had offered a large sum to the guards if they would have the grave covered so as to prevent its further desecration. After disinterment the body had been hidden in the private apartments of the deposed Czarina at Tsarskoe Selo. On its silver casket were found engraved the names of the Czarina and her four daughters. Soldiers in searching the palace found the body in a locked room which the former Empress had asked them not to enter as it contained "some silver mementoes and jewels." Army officers had ordered the body removed for burial. One report was that they burned it. For several days afterward the empty silver casket lay in the freight station and later on in a freight car on a siding, where it long stood unguarded. The Czarina was wearing deep mourning for Rasputin.

It had long been a commonplace to predict that the war would bring great political changes in Europe. But they were believed to be now in sight on a vaster scale than anybody had dared to prophesy. The old order was breaking up under men's eyes. More and more openly men were saying that king-craft, with the statesmanship which served it, had written its own doom. It was more than the dawn of

[2] Of the Associated Press.

freedom we were witnessing in Russia; it was the full sun. Not all the swift succession of emotional crises which the world had experienced in three years of war could steel men to the poignancy of the picture of numberless victims of Czarism streaming forth in March and April from Siberia westward toward home, liberty, and a new life. From prisons, convict-hospitals and settlements, from frozen villages on the Arctic steppes, these hapless pioneers of freedom, the youth, conscience and aspiration of Russia, had been called back to the realization of a great dream, to take their places in the upbuilding of a new nation by the side of their comrades from the dungeons of St. Peter and St. Paul. Not even in the French Revolution was there such swift and complete adjustment. Fifty thousand sledges carrying victims of the old *régime* back to freedom were speeding in an endless chain across the snows toward the nearest points on the Trans-Siberian Railway. Their passengers ranged from members of old terrorist societies to exiles who had been banished without trial or specified offenses. It was a race against time as the spring thaw was imminent and the roads, even in the coldest settlements of the lower Lena, would soon be impassable. Exiles who did not reach the railroad within a fortnight would have to wait six weeks or two months until the ice melted and the river navigation began.

By the end of March the liberation of Siberia's prisoners had barely begun. West of the Urals only a handful of returning exiles had yet been seen. The first large party on reaching Ekaterinburg consisted of 150 political convicts and administrative exiles, including twenty members of the Jewish revolutionary band, mostly from the Vorkholensk district, west of Lake Baikal. The exiles were traveling in special cars, and had been on the road continuously from March 24, five days after they first heard of the revolution. The cars were met by a vast crowd at the railroad station, which cheered them tumultuously. The returning exiles were in a deplorable physical condition, shaggy, uncouth, unwashed, and extremely emaciated. Many were crippled with rheumatism. Two had lost hands and feet from frost bites, and one, who attempted flight a week before the revolution, had been shot in the leg when recaptured and was lying in a prison hospital when he learned that the revolution had made him free. The exiles had an extraordinary variety of incongruous garb. Some wore new costumes which had been supplied by sympathizers along their route, some had handsome fur overcoats covering hideous jail-uniforms.

Among the men who wore the latter costume was a young millionaire aristocrat from Odessa who had been sentenced to life ten years before for fomenting a revolutionary mutiny in the Black Sea Fleet. Others of the party wore shaggy sheep- or wolf-skins as a protection against the bitter Siberian blasts. One man from the Irkutsk city jail wore the gold braided uniform tunic of the dismissed Governor of Irkutsk under a ragged and greasy overcoat. The president of the Exile Reception Committee estimated that there were about 100,000 persons in Siberia who had been released under the amnesty measure of the Provisional Government. This number comprised political offenders, including terrorists convicted after trial, persons suspected of furthering revolutionary propaganda and exiled without trial by order of the Secret Police, or the Minister of the Interior, and tens of thousands of peasants exiled without trial by decrees of village communal councils. Many of the latter expected to remain in Siberia voluntarily, where the conditions of life and work would be excellent under the reform Government.

The practical confiscation of the Czar's estate left him a comparatively poor man. Within less than a month after his abdication, he had to ask for an appropriation to cover the family's immediate wants. As "Autocrat of All the Russians" he had possest two-fifths of the registered lands in Russia, amounting to 400,000,000 acres in European Russia. The revenues from them were enormous. In the Czar's name stood titles to a hundred grand palaces and innumerable churches, convents, houses, farms, mines, manufactories and forests. Some idea of his wealth, in addition to the $8,000,000 annual civil list, could be gained by recalling the fact that the small army of Grand Dukes and Grand Duchesses whom he maintained were notorious in all the fashionable resorts of the world as reckless spendthrifts. His vast estates had now fallen to the State, so that his private fortune probably did not amount to more than $500,000 in cash and securities. His wife had about $550,000. Their twelve-year-old son, Alexis, was much richer than either parent, as his allowance had not been used up. He was thought to have saved about $2,750,000. The fortunes of his sisters were estimated as: Olga, $1,750,000; Tatiana, $2,000,000; Maria, $1,850,000; Anastasia, $1,650,000.

The victims of the revolution in Petrograd were solemnly buried on April 5 in the historic Field of Mars. As the coffins, draped in scarlet bunting, were lowered, one by one, into an enormous grave in a corner of the field, a series of salutes—one for each victim—boomed across the ice-bound Neva from the fortress of St. Peter and St. Paul, where the last Ministers of the fallen empire were still confined. Regimental bands flanked the square field and thousands of persons with bared heads joined in a mass for the revolutionary dead. The somber aspect of the city was relieved by innumerable flags and streamers of flaming red, some few of which were edged with black bands of mourning. Banners of every description, bearing familiar devices of the new republic, were carried by each unit in the procession, which gathered from every quarter of the city to march to the burial ground. Each column bore the bodies of victims who had lived in their district.

The tremendous funeral cortège wound its way through a city almost empty of spectators. Apparently every woman and child able to walk was marching in the procession. Perfect order prevailed. Except for the muffled tolling of church bells, dirges played by military bands and slow melancholy chants, the procession proceeded in complete silence. One hundred soldiers from each regiment engaged in the revolution took part in the procession. Girl students from universities formed an enormous brigade, which marched down the Nevsky Prospect at the side of a company of workingmen and was followed by a long column of peasant women and servants, with detachments of officers and soldiers bringing up the rear. The same spirit of quiet reverence dominated all as they united in dirges and strode side

NICHOLAS II CLOSELY GUARDED
The forest in which he is seen is part of the Tsarskoe Selo Imperial estate, where he was confined before he was taken to Siberia

by side to the burial-field. Grim with the memory of the recent struggle, but inspired with new hope, it was a strange army of pale-faced black-garbed people which took its solemn course through the city. One after another the columns bearing scarlet coffins reached the burial-ground. Each stopt a moment while the burial-ceremony was taking place and then passed on in silence over the adjoining bridge. Early in the afternoon when the last group reached the field, 180 bodies had been interred.

Nicholas became to all appearances a model prisoner, entirely contented with his lot. He continued his régime of early rising and plenty of walking, as followed when autocrat, and uttered no word of complaint at his treatment. He spent the greater part of his time in the garden. During Sunday's services in the chapel the first one to kneel when prayers were offered for the Provisional Government was Nicholas.

After the revolution had sent its shock through Europe, the world had many assurances from German sources that there was and could be no revolutionary spirit in Germany. The Germans, we were told, were convinced monarchists, nine-tenths of them. They were satisfied with their government and the Kaiser was the most popular man in Germany. If there should emerge a German republic, he would be elected President by an overwhelming vote. Nevertheless the new spirit and the rising popular demands were such that the Kaiser himself was forced in April to make concessions. Electoral reform in Prussia, which he and his Government and the privileged classes had fought for years, he now declared to be "near his heart," and made solemn pledges to abolish the antiquated Prussian franchise. The result was a burst of free political discussion in the German press and among public men which was fairly bewildering. Conservatives were stunned. They seemed to fear that the Kaiser had entered upon a glissade which could end only in the destruction of all the institutions they had cherished. Liberal newspapers accepted, in general, the Kaiser's promises with joy, but only as a payment on account. They made it evident that nothing would satisfy them except a responsible Government—a Ministry that was answerable to

the Reichstag. Maximilian Harden issued an Easter pro-
nunciamento in which he declared that it was for Germany
to remodel her monarchy on the line of the English system,
which might not be a revolution, but it would certainly seem
so to the Prussian Junkerdom.

Catherine Breshkovskaya, "Grandmother. of the Russian

Revolution," arrived in Moscow on April 5 from Minusink,
Siberia, after having spent
forty-four of her seventy-three
years there as a convict,
prisoner and exile. She had
an enthusiastic welcome. In a
speech she made a moving appeal for ·books and educational
facilities for the masses. Soldiers and members of the committee carried her into the
street after the meeting.
Madame Breshkovskaya was
first imprisoned in the seventies
as a member of the 'Terrorist
Society called "Land and
Freedom." She was dragged
from prison to prison, from
convict settlement to convict
settlement, until, as she observed, she "knew the in-
teriors of thirty prisons as intimately as a monk knows his
cell." Twice she escaped and

© PAUL THOMPSON.

CATHERINE BRESHKOVSKAYA

Madame Breshkovskaya has been
familiarly known as "The Grandmother of the Russian Revolution."
After the revolution, she was released from exile in Siberia, where
she had spent much of her life as
a prisoner. She was 73 years old
at the time of her release. Her
father was a Russian nobleman

finally was freed after the revolt which took place during
the war with Japan. Later she was denounced by a police
spy and again sent into exile.

Against a 'background mass of scarlet tulips, symbol of
the revolution, one of the most poignant and dramatic events
of the new Russia was staged in the second week of April
when Madame Breshkovskaya was more formally welcomed
home. It was no ordinary welcome. It was even more than
a state affair. It was an epitome of the fall of the Romanoff

dynasty and the resurrection of the masses. Madame Breshkovskaya was received in the imperial chambers of the
Nikolaievsk railway-station, reserved under the old *régime*
for personages of royal blood. A government delegation,
headed by Minister of Justice Kerensky, was present to
welcome the aged heroine of the long struggle. But this
welcome was almost swallowed up in a surging mass of
sweeping and shouting ex-terrorists, reformed bomb-throwers,

M. PROTOPOPOFF

Protopopoff was the organizer of
Petrograd's police force under the
old régime, and as Minister of the
Interior had made a surrender to
the Duma

Nihilists without a present occupation and unshackled political convicts. Democrats, Re-
publicans, Socialists and
"Reds" of the most extreme
type packed the vast drawing-
room where great monarchs
had met and empresses had
waited. The contrast was not
lost on the crowd; in fact, it
was Minister Kerensky's deliberate plan to emphasize it.
The walls of the room were
banked with flowers, big floral
pieces and baskets inscribed
"To Our Dear Grandmother,"
"To The Queen of The Peo-
ple," "To Russia's Martyr
Heroine." It seemed as if the
entire city had turned out to
welcome the old woman. It
was an emotional crowd, chanting "The Marseillaise" with a
religious fervor and everywhere waving the red flag.

On August 19 it was officially announced that a new residence for the deposed Emperor had been fixed at Tobolsk,
a western Siberia town, which achieved new publicity in
revolutionary Russia as the birthplace of Gregory Rasputin,
the mystic monk. With him went his wife and their children
of their own free will and certain of their entourage. The
family was to reside permanently. in the former Governor's
palace at Tobolsk, which is a large house with modern im-

provements, but built in the eighteenth century for a local speculator. Nicholas spent one night there in 1891, when returning from his visit to the Far East. Other reports were that the former Emperor would stay at the ex-Governor's palace only one week, and then would be sent to the Apalatsk Monastery in a forest twenty miles outside the town. Tolobsk was by an irony of fate associated with the system of political exile inaugurated by the Romanoff dynasty.

News came from Petrograd on May 24, that Madame Anne Virubova, lady-in-waiting to the former Czarina and the right-hand associate of Rasputin, had been transferred from Tsarskoe Selo, where she had been confined with the former Czar and his family, to the fortress of St. Peter and St. Paul in Petrograd. It was Madame Virubova who had collaborated with Rasputin in his machinations to keep the Czarina constantly under his influence, who had drugged the Czarevitch whenever Rasputin was forced out of court by his enemies, so that the monk's departure would be accompanied by visible effects on the health of young Alexis, and then the Czarina would immediately request the return of the monk, and believe in the imposter more than ever. About this time the former Minister of the Interior, Protopopoff, who had become the leader of the court camarilla after the death of Rasputin, was subjected to a thorough examination by the commission appointed by the Provisional Government to investigate the activities of the "dark forces." The examination lasted more than five hours and took place in the fortress of St. Peter and St. Paul. When he complained of the rigid régime imposed on him in the jail, he was told that he ought to get used to the thought that he was no longer a minister, and to bear in mind that during his career in office he had subjected thousands of Russians to a similar punishment.[3]

[3] Principal Sources: Articles in *The Outlook* by George Kennan and others, The *Evening Post,* The *Journal of Commerce,* The *Times,* New York; Associated Press and United Press dispatches, and especially "Nelson's History of the War," by John Buchan. The Russian Diary of an Englishman (R. M. McBride & Co.).

KORNILOFF'S LINE OF RETREAT IN 1917 AFTER HIS VICTORIES
HAD THREATENED LEMBERG

286

II

CIVIL ANARCHY, ELIHU ROOT'S MISSION, AND THE FAILURE OF KERENSKY'S OFFENSIVE AFTER KORNILOFF HAD TAKEN HALICZ

May, 1917—August, 1917

THUS, to all outward appearances, had ended in success this extraordinary political upheaval, the people contented with it and the new Government, for the time at least, in the saddle. The real revolution in all its horrors was yet to come. Before the end of April, Russia began to loom up as a portentous obstacle to an early ending of the war in a way favorable to the Entente Powers—a far from satisfactory relation having grown up between the Council of Workmen's and Soldiers' Deputies and the Provisional Government, composed of men who were known as constitutionalists, who realized that Russia was in the throes of a great war, and that some kind of stable administration was needed without delay. Their following lay among the professional classes, business men, country gentry, and the bourgeois, the best element in Russia.

They alone in Russia had any understanding of foreign politics and of the main problems of the war. In them, in fact, reposed all of such limited store of administrative experience as the country possest. Worthy, honest, and patriotic, it was they who had held aloft the banner of a reasonable freedom during the darkest days of the old régime; but they had failed in the past to achieve reform, and the memory of that failure still clung to them. They were not by nature makers of revolutions. They lacked the fiery appeal, the dynamic personality, which awes and attracts great masses. There was among them no Danton, no Camille Desmoulins; above all, no Mirabeau. Logical, capable, and intensely respectable, they were also a little dull. They were wholly right in their perception of the needs of their country; but when an excited populace was clamoring for a new heaven and a new earth, it was not greatly attracted by a merely well conceived plan for stable government. Moreover, the blackness of the record of the old régime seemed to demand a sensational and violent reversal.

The extremists of the Council of Workmen and Soldiers represented a far narrower class. They stood for the working population of Petrograd, and in lesser degree for industrial Russia; but Russia was not a highly industrialized country, and the workmen were a mere handful compared with the many millions of Russia's peasantry. The rank and file were profoundly ignorant on all questions of government, and the leaders knew little more. Their strength lay in the fact that they preached a creed which was the antithesis of all that had gone before, and which combined ideals that made at once appeals to a narrow class-interest and to the generous and imaginative side of the Russian mind. Their organization was made up of two divisions, the Social Democrats and a limited number of Social Revolutionaries.

© UNDERWOOD & UNDERWOOD. N. Y.

PAUL N. MILIUKOFF

Leader of the Constitutional Democrats in the Duma and Foreign Minister of the provisional government formed after the overthrow of the Imperial Power. Professor Miliukoff at one time was a professor in the University of Chicago

While they represented only a fraction of Russia, that fraction was in Petrograd, at the center of affairs, where it was vocal, while other sections were dumb. Many of its members were sensible men, who saw that victory in the war was essential in safeguarding their new won freedom, and they had a wider outlook in political matters than the restricted interests of one class. But the best of them were ignorant and inexperienced in public affairs, and it is not easy for men who have long been compelled to work in the dark, to come suddenly into the full glare of responsibility and then act normally. Some were beyond doubt in German pay, but the majority were as honest as they were determined.

By the second week in May the Entente world was startled by news of resignations in high places, including Paul Miliukoff, the Foreign Minister, Generals Brusiloff and Gourko and the Minister of War and Marine, with rumors that the Council of Workmen's and Soldiers' Deputies had called for an armistice. Meanwhile, from the Baltic to the Danubian region of Roumania, Russian and Teutonic forces continued almost inactive in their trenches. Only spasmodic exchanges of rifle-fire and here and there small reconnaissances were reported. That Germany herself was seeking a separate peace with Russia in these circumstances, came to be generally suspected and later the fact was known.

Thus, while both British and French, after Hindenberg's "victorious retreat," were advancing from Arras and the Aisne more rapidly than the year before in the Somme offensive, and along fronts about three times as broad, there remained as a subject of grave doubt this Russian situation. The question of the hour became how much the new turn of affairs would damage Franco-British efforts in France. For the time being the overturn of authority in Russia seemed to have diminished Russian fighting power more than any reverse that Russia had suffered in the field. That unfortunate country had lost not only its Czar but its best commanders, the Grand Duke Nicholas and General Ruzsky, and now its chief ministers of State and military commanders had resigned. Worse still, it had cast off to a great extent the exercise of that authority which the Duma possest and should have maintained. A revolution at the outset may be the work of many; but its establishment is usually the task of one man—a Cæsar, a Cromwell, a Napoleon. Among the extremists there was no such man, for in the nature of things he could not have been extreme. While a master-mind may dream dreams and see visions, it must have an iron hand and a clear eye for realities. In the respectable circle of the Duma, which included statesmen who were competent, honest, and even brilliant, one such man was lacking. ,

As the autumn advanced only one figure seemed to stand out from the others—a young man barely thirty-five, the son of a Siberian schoolmaster, hitherto an obscure Petrograd lawyer, and a somewhat flamboyant orator in labor circles. His haggard, white face and melancholy eyes showed his bodily frailty, and indeed he was one who walked very close to death. From the first day of the revolution, Alexander Kerensky had not wavered. Himself a Red Republican and an extreme Socialist, he seemed to recognize that a country could not be saved by ideals alone, and to gird himself for the rough work of construction. His fervent speeches had kept the new Provisional Government from being wrecked at the start. He had his way alike with elder statesmen of the Duma and firebrands and amateurs of the Workmen's Council. He had the wild courage of one who lives always on the brink of the grave, the magnetism of a man who has one foot in the other world. Here, so at the moment it seemed, was a new "swallower of formulas"—a second Mirabeau. Would he die, like Mirabeau, before he could guide the revolution right? Would he faint by the wayside, baffled by problems too great for mortal solution, and handicapped by the trammels of his old environment? Or would he live to lead his people beyond the wilderness to the Promised Land?

The opinion was strongly held in Germany that the Russian armies were now out of it, at least for the campaign of 1917, that Hindenburg could crush their disorganized forces, if he so chose, but that it was better to let them alone. It was believed that revolutionary and Socialist ferment was still at work, that the soldiers would not fight, and that the Provisional Government might soon be forced to ask for a separate peace. Generous terms could well have been granted by Germany, for the sake of detaching Russia from the Allies, and to this end all the resources of German diplomacy and intrigue were for weeks drawn upon. Even Scheidemann, the Socialist, was made an agent of the Government and sent to Stockholm to confer with Russian delegates, to tell them that their only hope lay in an early and separate peace. How great were the expectations pinned by Germany to this mission of Scheidemann could be inferred later from the abuse which was poured upon him by the German press when he returned with a confession of failure. Scheidemann, a little more than a year afterward, was to become Chancellor of a German republic, only to resign rather than accept the peace terms laid down by the Entente.

There was historic warrant for the German hope that the Allies would not stand united till the end of the war. Frederick II had been able to fight the Seven Years' War to a successful conclusion, only because of the jealousies of confederates arrayed against him. Singularly enough, it was Russia who then saved Frederick when his fortunes looked most desperate. In the very year when Pitt's death had paved the way for a peace between England and France —thus depriving Frederick of his English subsidies and of his only friend in Europe—the Empress Elizabeth of Russia died and her successor, the ill-starred Peter, showed himself at once intensely pro-Prussian, released his Prussian prisoners and actually sent 15,000 troops of his own to strengthen the shattered armies of Frederick. A peace on terms favorable to Prussia was thereafter soon concluded, so that Frederick was raised from the depths of despair and enabled to win the war—all in consequence of the defection of Russia. Beyond all question the German Government hoped that this bit of history would repeat itself in 1917.

The discord that prevailed in Petrograd naturally found an echo everywhere at the front, but the war spirit of the soldiers recovered in time, altho slowly. The army as a fighting force had never actually been eliminated. Kerensky's appointment as Minister of War was received in the army with great enthusiasm. So was the Government's declaration that Russia's defeat would be a great misfortune to all nations. While willing to make a general peace, the Government declared firmly that revolutionary Russia would not consent to the defeat of the Allies in the west. When the German Chancellor, Bethmann-Hollweg, made an offer of a separate peace to Russia on May 15, the "thunderous applause'' that ensued in the Reichstag testified unmistakably as to Germany's great hope, through peace with Russia, to gain a partial victory from the war. When the answer of Revolutionary Russia to this offer was made known in a fairly complete form, it came from a reorganized Government determined on a continued prosecution of the war. At the same time Brusiloff and Gourko withdrew their resignations and returned to the front. What that might mean was clear to those who recalled what Brusiloff had done a year before. Russians in London declared that the breakdown in their army discipline was only temporary and looked to Kerensky, who was young and energetic, to revitalize the force and inspire it to fresh deeds of valor. It was his influence that induced Brusiloff and Gourko to reconsider their resignations and take an active part in another campaign. When at last conditions that 'at one time threatened political dissolution were righted, it became possible to see with some clearness how they had been the natural concomitants of a revolution. A change of government to the popular form called for a reorganization of the army. More than one hundred officers holding high commands at the front had to be relieved because too closely identified with the old régime.

Brusiloff and Gourko now made strong appeals to their troops to stand firm and get ready for a new offensive. The sky cleared almost as rapidly as it had been obscured by storm clouds. Russia had weathered a tempest and the sun of liberty was out again. Alexieff, who had retained his post during the political storm, declared that under the new coalition Government it would be possible to conduct military affairs in an energetic manner, and it was the imperative duty of the Russian army to resume operations on the Dwina and in Galicia. The changes had been a natural reaction from the enthusiasm first created by the revolution. The revolution in itself was a thing so close to a miracle that men had looked for other miracles to follow. Overnight it was expected that a settled revolutionary government would take the place of the tyranny of a thousand years; that the army's allegiance to the throne would change without a jar into allegiance to the revolution; that men

RUSSIAN SOLDIERS IN PETROGRAD

who had suffered in Siberia and the dungeons for fifty years would settle down into sweet reasonableness once power suddenly became theirs. It seemed to be expected that a revolutionary army in Russia would turn upon the enemy much as revolutionary France turned on its enemies at Valmy. Men were disappointed because all this did not happen in two months, or in about the time New York had once taken to impeach a Governor, or investigate a traction company. Men forgot that Valmy did not come until two and a half years after the fall of the Bastile, and that the triumphant march of the armies of France into eastern Europe did not begin till two years after Valmy.

Our Government at Washington in this emergency decided to send an Advisory Commission to Russia. Its personnel, announced on May 11, was as follows: Elihu Root of New York, Charles R. Crane of Illinois, John R. Mott of New York, Cyrus McCormick of Illinois, Samuel R. Bertron of New York, James Duncan of Massachusetts, Charles Edward Russell of New York, Major-General Hugh L. Scott, U. S. A., and Rear Admiral James H. Glennon, U. S. N. Mr. Root was to be "Ambassador Extraordinary on Special Mission," the others, except General Scott, "Envoys Extraordinary." Mr. Root was soon in Washington consulting with the State Department and receiving instructions from President Wilson. One of the members of the mission, Mr. Crane, was already in Russia, and had lived there in former years. The appointment of Mr. Russell, who was a pronounced Socialist, was a concession to the strong Socialistic feeling among many of those who had been responsible for the overthrow of the Russian monarchy. But Mr. Russell was not of the Socialist type which wanted a separate peace. General Scott, as Chief of the General Staff of the United States Army, was the directing head of the organization of the military forces of the American nation. The object of the Mission was primarily political. Mr. Root and his associates were clothed with broad authority, even with plenary powers, with respect to some aspects of their work in Petrograd. The purpose of their going was to save Russia to the Entente cause. Much was left to the decision of the Mission itself after reaching Petrograd. Mr. Root and his colleagues went prepared to deal with any form of authority which they might find in control when they arrived.

Formal declaration was made by the new Russian Cabinet on May 19 that it was a unit against a separate peace with the Teutonic Powers. Kerensky, the new War Minister, declared that he intended to enforce discipline in the army, and was going to the fighting-line to make sure that the military forces would do their duty. The Provisional Government adopted as its peace aim the re-establishment of a general peace which would not tend to domination of other nations or to seizure of their national possessions—a peace without annexations or indemnities. By May 31 Kerensky seemed to be successfully accomplishing his task of spurring Russia's soldiers to fight. At the front a new spirit of determination was apparent after the minister made a whirlwind campaign, and, in a conference with officers and soldiers, made an impassioned plea that fighting men should give their lives to Russia, so that the fruits of the revolution might be secured. Every man rose to his feet after this speech, shouting, ''We swear it!'' and a tumultuous demonstration followed in which Kerensky and Minister Thomas, of the French Munitions Department, who had been to the front with him, were borne from the meeting on the shoulders of soldiers. This new sentiment of patriotism in the army was soon reflected in Russia by a steady, sober undercurrent of feeling among all classes.

On June 13 the American Mission, headed by Elihu Root, arrived in Petrograd and an American Railroad Commission, headed by John F. Stevens, about the same time. Mr. Stevens' commission had for its aim to assist the Russians in railroad affairs, by placing at their disposal America's technical skill and industrial resources. This commission also was strictly official. America delivered a new message to Russia which said, ''We are going to fight, and have already begun to fight, for your freedom equally with our own, and we ask you to fight for our freedom equally with yours.'' In these words Elihu Root addrest the Council of Ministers on June 15. He laid stress on American disinterestedness in the war, except so far as to conserve Democracy was concerned. In Russia, he said, America saw no party, no class, only great Russia as a whole, one mighty, striving, aspiring Democracy. For long years his own country had been striving with the hard problems of self-government. "With many shortcomings, many mistakes, many imperfections," he said, "we still have maintained order and respect for law, individual freedom, and national independence." Under the security of our laws, we had grow in strength and prosperity. "We value our freedom more than wealth," he said. "We love liberty and we cherish, above all our possessions, the ideals for which our fathers fought and suffered and sacrificed, that America might be free. We believe in the competence of the power of Democracy and in our heart of hearts abides faith in the coming of a better world in which the humble and opprest of all lands may be lifted up by freedom and equal opportunity."

News of Russia's new-found freedom, he declared, had brought to America "universal satisfaction and joy." Sympathy and hope went out from America to "the new sister in the circle of democracies." America believed that Russia would solve her problems, that she would maintain her liberty and that the two great nations "would march side by side in the triumphant progress of democracy until 'the old order everywhere had passed away and the world was free." One fearful danger, however, threatened the liberty of both, "the armed forces of a military autocracy were at the gates of Russia and the Allies." The triumph of German arms "would mean the death of liberty in Russia." While no enemy was at the gates of America, America had come to realize that "the triumph of German arms meant the death of liberty in the world; that we who love liberty and would keep it must fight for it, and fight for it now when the free democracies of the world may be strong in union, and not delay until they may be beaten down separately in succession."

Two days later the Duma in a secret session passed a resolution for an immediate offensive by the Russian troops. The resolution declared a separate peace with Germany, or prolonged inactivity on the battle-front ignoble treason toward Russia's Allies, for which future generations never

THE ELIHU ROOT MISSION TO RUSSIA

Left to right—M. Terestchenko, Russian Minister of Foreign Affairs, General Brusiloff, Mr. Root, Gen. Hugh L. Scott

VII.

would pardon the Russia of the present day. The resolution added: "The Duma therefore considers that the safety of Russia and the maintenance of the liberties which have been obtained lie in an immediate offensive in close co-operation with Russia's Allies." On June 21 the Congress of Workmen's and Soldier's Delegates from the whole of Russia voted confidence in the Provisional Government and unanimously passed a resolution demanding an immediate resumption of the offensive and the reorganization of the army. Germany's efforts for a separate peace meanwhile had been made in many directions: in a speech by the Chancellor in the Reichstag, through agents sent to Russia, and at the front where she brought into service alcohol and ink instead of powder. Despite all efforts to stop communication between the two sets of trenches, German liquor appeared on the Russian side. Every morning hundreds of neatly printed, or carefully written peace-notes and letters were deposited near the Russian trenches.

Reports from the front began soon to show an increasing betterment of morale among the Russian soldiers. Brusiloff went on a tour of the battle-front, in order to stir up his soldiers to fighting spirit and to restore rigid discipline, and met with enthusiastic receptions everywhere. General Scott left Petrograd on June 19 for a visit to the front, and Rear-Admiral Glennon visited the battle-fleet in the Black Sea. On June 26, Elihu Root and the whole American Military Staff, accompanied by M. Tereshcenko, the Russian finance minister, arrived at Russia's General Staff Headquarters and held a conference with Brusiloff. The aids of General Scott began a ten days' tour of the front, as far south as Roumania. During this tour a congress of Cossacks listened to a speech by John R. Mott of the American Commission, who described America's war preparations, complimented the Cossacks on their unity and strength, and declared that America would never abandon Russia and the other Allies. The Cossacks passed unanimously a resolution in favor of a vigorous prosecution of the war, and rejected the idea of a separate peace, declaring that the war must be fought in co-operation with the Allies until victory was reached.

IN THE EAST, NEAR EAST, AND SOUTH

By July 10 the American Mission had completed a month's survey of the situation and was confident that the nation in time would successfully emerge from its internal difficulties and redirect its forces toward the energetic prosecution of the war. Its optimistic conclusions were not derived alone from consultations with governmental heads, but were based on the spirit and determination of the people as encountered in public organizations, political and industrial councils, and in delegations properly representative of the temper of the nation as a whole. A feverish conflict of words and ambiguity of terms had been the natural result of a newly acquired right of free speech, but underneath these lay a patriotic purpose not essentially different from that of other democracies at war with autocratic ideas. There was no disposition on the part of the Commission to minimize either the dangers threatened by widespread German propaganda and pacifism agitation, or the practical difficulties in the way of transportation and the reorganization of Russia's economic life. Mr. Root made the following statement:

"The mission has accomplished what it came here to do, and we are greatly encouraged. We found no organic or incurable malady in the Russian Democracy. Democracies are always in trouble, and we have seen days just as dark in the progress of our own. We must remember that a people in whom all constructive effort has been supprest for so long can not immediately develop a genius for quick action. The first stage is necessarily one of debate. The solid, admirable traits in the Russian character will pull the nation through the present crisis. Natural love of law and order and capacity for local self-government have been demonstrated every day since the revolution. The country's most serious lack is money and adequate transportation. We shall do what we can to help Russia in both."

"Tell Americans," said General Scott, "we have found the heart of Russia sound, and we have found the army's heart sound at the core." Premier Lvoff, at this time made an enumeration of the political and economic reforms that had been put through in the midst of the revolution that was little short of astounding. He said that in one hundred days Russia had moved forward one hundred years and minimized the danger of separatists and seditious movements which had given anxiety in other countries because they were spread in flaming headline across newspaper pages. With the very fountains of national life breaking loose, there was still much to admire in the resourcefulness and self-restraint of the men who were in charge of the country's destinies. Amid revolution reconstruction had been going on. Amid outcries and fears concerning the demoralization of the army, Kerensky and Brusiloff had been preparing for an offensive of which the outside world was in doubt, but about which men at the head were not in doubt.

July had been a fateful month in the Russian Revolution. Political and military complications had followed with kaleidoscopic rapidity, forming an intricate maze—separatist tendencies among Finns, Little Russians, and other nationalities, each of whom sought to take advantage of the country's weakness to secure a selfish, if fancied, profit; a short-lived victory in the field, followed by a shameful retreat of troops twice as numerous as the enemy; a serious crisis in the Cabinet, which led to the resignation of Prince Lvoff and the advent of Kerensky to the premiership; and another mutiny among sailors of the Baltic Fleet, which failed lamentably at a later date in defending the country's shores from invasion. Russia had lost nearly all the territory she had occupied during the preceding year in Galicia, and after having had a magnificent harvest. She had been saved from irretrievable military disaster only by the energy of her Allies on the Western Front. The Revolutionary Government, now led by Socialists and dominated by the Soviets (Council of Workmen, Soldiers and Peasants), had neither the independence nor the force requisite for coping with lack of discipline.

Four of the Russian armies that were involved in the disaster had been extricated from a well-nigh hopeless position by the skill of Korniloff. Kerensky and his associates had made concessions to Ukranian demands for autonomy which gravely imperilled the unity of the State and further weakened its armed defenses, already impaired by revolutionary propaganda. Altho nominally a republic, Russia was suffering the consequences of a departure from the monarchial form of government with which her greatness as an Empire had been bound up in the past. Symptoms of disruption obtruded themselves on every side. Autonomies were demanded by Siberia, Esthonia, Georgia, by the Lithuanians, the White Russians, the Letts, and also by Germans and Jews. Even the Asiatic dependencies of Khiva and Bokhara did not escape the general contagion.

Another Russian offensive, and the last, was begun on July 1, under Korniloff. For a few days it revived hopes in Allied centers that Russia might still be saved. Then treachery and want of discipline in the army turned the victory into defeat. A turning point in the revolution had been reached. Kerensky and Tseretelli saw that while Russia had captured the Bastile of autocracy by assault, and had won for herself full liberty in a single week, she had yet to consolidate and stabilize her freedom. The revolution had already undermined the morale of the army, sown a fatal distrust among men toward their officers and taken from soldiers the incentive for fighting. Underneath, however, still slumbered something of the old indomitable spirit which had made Russia a military nation and real encouragement from the right source might yet have induced the flame to rise again. This incentive Kerensky sought to give when he issued a stirring appeal, calling upon the soldiers to fight again, and vindicate the principles of the revolution. His summons called forth an immediate response, and a visit which he made to the front evoked scenes of indescribable enthusiasm. Even the Soviets were carried away by it. All Russia, postponing party interests and considerations, seemed to have risen up awaiting the issue with revived hope. Disorders were forgotten, and when bulletins of victory again reached Petrograd and Moscow, in the early days of July, all classes united in heartfelt joy and praise only to be driven to despair three weeks later when these same armies, after having inflicted defeats upon the Germans, mutinously deserted and fled in panic before an enemy far inferior in numbers and guns, abandoning positions of great strength, leaving behind a vast quantity of arms and supplies, a whole network of railways that had been laboriously constructed at great cost, and a fertile country with wheat ready to be harvested.

It had been the first movement Russia had made since the revolution. The attack began on an eighteen-mile front in Galicia. Fierce fighting set in and showed signs of spreading north and south until the whole battle-front of 100 miles in Galicia and Volhynia promised to become engaged. A renewed drive for Lemberg and Kovel was under way from positions gained in Brusiloff's offensive of 1916. From southeast of Brzezany to north of Zlozhow, along a front of about thirty miles, the attack extended, until the Russian Army seemed about to capture Halicz and Brzezany, the keys to the southern approaches to Lemberg. This advance was begun dramatically in person by Kerensky, who for four days had been continuously at the front, spending every effort in urging troops to advance. He rode forward in person to the first line trenches, placed himself at the head of the line and gave orders to advance, a spectacle which recalled Napoleon at the bridge of Lodi and accomplished what Kerensky's oratory had failed to do. The line swept forward into German trenches, stormed a strong position at Koniuchy, north of Brzezany, and took seven heavy guns and more than 10,000 prisoners.

When Kerensky told his soldiers that if they would not attack, he would himself march along against enemy trenches, soldiers embraced and kissed him. One division that had been especially known for unwillingness to fight, and which became afterward the most militant, was "reborn at this time under men's eyes." Soldiers seemed really to have been permeated with Russia's new political program, convinced as they were by Kerensky that they were fighting, not for imperialism, but for freedom at home and for international peace. Three weeks before, Kerensky had informed our Government that "a big Russian offensive would take place in the early part of July," and it had actually begun on July 1, but no offensive on so large a scale had confidentially been looked for in months. Kerensky's promise had been made somewhere about June 10, after returning from a tour of the front, where he addrest thousands of soldiers and awakened an enthusiasm without parallel. Ground for the advance had been prepared by the incessant labors of

Brusiloff and other generals, but it was virtually Kerensky's work that brought on the attack. What he had done, in the time in which he did it, promised to go on record as one of the historic feats in war operations. When Kerensky risked his life, soldiers begged him to remain behind and spare himself for the sake of the future of Russia, but he would not listen and boldly gave the command. Petrograd was aglow with demonstrations which lasted through half the night. A huge crowd surrounded Kerensky's home singing the "Marseillaise." After the advance was begun, Kerensky watched the fighting from an artillery observation point, attended funerals of the dead, distributed orders, promoted officers and soldiers, and once during the battle, dismissed the commander of a division.

On July 7, violent fighting began near Pinsk, where artillery levelled all obstacles, and continued on the Galician front, the Russians making important advances despite stubborn resistance, and capturing over 1,000 prisoners. The fighting was particularly fierce in the Zlochoff region and near Konichy, north of Brzezany. In the former region the Russians occupied three lines of German trenches, but were forced back again by a series of strong counter-attacks. In the Koniuchy sector six fortified positions changed hands several times. While the Russians lost some of their gains, they maintained their hold on the heights northwest of Preservce and those east of Godov, together with two villages. No one, including the Germans, had believed that Russia could make an attack in such force with any chances of success. Never under similar circumstances had a nation been more completely demoralized. In every department of the Government there was chaos, transportation totally disorganized, munition manufacture infected with strikes, even to a point of complete paralysis. Government, so far as it was able to exercise its function and enforce obedience to its mandates, had ceased to exist. Petrograd was still permeated with German spies, working night and day to keep the air impregnated with civil strife and discontent. But Russia seemed still a force before which depleted, almost exhausted, Austria might tremble; a force which might yet inflict upon Germany the same

measure of defeat by which Hindenburg, in the first year
of the war, had been twice driven back from the gates of
Warsaw to the East-Prussian frontier.

The offensive soon spread north and south of Halicz.
Halicz a year before had virtually been under the guns of
Brusiloff when his advance was brought to a standstill. It
was important as the key to Lemberg, and was about sixty
miles southeast of that city.
Three armies were now en-
gaged on a front of more than
thirty miles along the Nara-
yuvka River. Major-General
Scott arrived at the southwestern front just in time to witness the beginning of the offensive. Standing on a hill
overlooking Russian and Austrian lines near Zloczow, Scott's
party had an opportunity of
observing the Russian artillery
preparation and the charge
which followed. He described
the artillery preparations as
"excellent," and personally
saw the Sixth Corps of the
Eleventh Army take three lines
of Austrian trenches. By July

© HARRIS & EWING.

MAJ.-GEN. HUGH L. SCOTT

3, Austro-German forces were evacuating Brzezany, fifty miles
southeast of Lemberg, and Russian armies had invested
Brzezany from the northeast, southeast and southwest. Units
of four armies were co-operating in the advance, covering a
front of about twenty miles. The Russians had taken prisoners exceeding in number 16,000.

Not alone did the Russians in Galicia make good gains
of terrain, but their captures of men, guns, and material
were enormous. From July 1 to July 13, according to a
Russian official communication, 36,634 officers and men
were made prisoners and 93 heavy guns and light guns, 28
trench-mortars, 406 machine-guns, and 91 guns of other
descriptions were taken. Austro-German forces had with-

drawn beyond the Lommica River, about ten miles west of Jezupol. West of Stanislau toward Kalusz and Dolina, the Russians penetrated Teutonic lines to a depth of nearly seven miles and between Stanislau and Halicz widened their wedge. In their retirement, the Austro-Germans failed to make a stand at two rivers—the Lukovitza and the Luvka. Russians were now within less than eight miles of Halicz on three sides. Only one avenue of retreat toward Lemberg was left open, that between the Dniester and the Lipiza. Meanwhile artillery was hammering lines south of Brzezany. Berlin and Vienna admitted the success of the Russian thrust, but both capitals claimed that the advances had been checked by German reserves, thrown in to save the Austrian positions. The Teutonic line was here formed on two sides of a quadrilateral from Dolina north of Stryj, and from Stryj east to Chodorow. Apart altogether from its moral significance, the capture of Halicz by Korniloff, which resulted from this operation, constituted a menace to the whole front of the Teutonic armies, whose northeastern sector, hard prest before Brzezany and Zhotow, now risked being outflanked by Korniloff's crumbling process.

Russia was now ringing with the name of her latest hero of the war, Korniloff, who had succeeded Brusiloff in the chief command on this front. He was reported to be the most daring, chivalrous, and scholarly officer in the Russian army. Korniloff was born in 1870, in a little village of western Siberia, of humble Cossack parents. Compelled almost from infancy to work hard, he managed by indomitable energy, and self-taught, to enter the Cadet Corps at the age of thirteen. Within six years he has mastered foreign languages and entered the Artillery College at Petrograd, and in 1892 obtained his commission. Everywhere at the head of his class, an excellent mathematician, and an erudite historian, he might, had he chosen, have had an easy and brilliant career in the metropolis, but instead went to Turkestan, allured by prospects of hard work, of expeditions to dangerous fastnesses, and of studying new peoples and languages. Between 1896 and 1902 he carried out a series of daring missions in Afghanistan and Persia, often disguised as a native. As a result he was

GENERAL KORNILOFF

Korniloff was eventually accused of disloyalty to the government of Kerensky, and was arrested and punished. Many held that Russia might have
been saved from the Bolsheviki had Korniloff been supported as head of
of the National Army. In 1918-1919 he was leading troops in Southern
Russia against the Bolsheviki, and in March was killed in battle

able to make important contributions to science. When the Japanese War broke out, he was on a special mission in India. Recalled home, he took command of a brigade, and displayed military talent, winning golden opinions and the Cross of St. George. His capture of Halicz and Kalusz signalized him as a leader of men. His bold and masterful letter to the Provisional Government insisting on the restoration of the fighting efficiency of the army, stamped him with the hall-mark of a soldier and statesman.

Korniloff in this offensive carried out his appointed task in more than full measure. Had his army had suitable reserves he might easily have reached Rohatyn from Halicz, turned the strong Brzezany position and, following up his successes at Kalusz, reached Dolina, south of Lemberg, thereby severing the enemy's communications and isolating some of his forces. Never had the Russian army been so well equipped. Artillery of all calibers, trench-mortars, and machine-guns, had been provided in abundance with plenty of ammunition. There were armored cars, including British and Belgian contingents, posted with every active corps. The roads and railways—a heritage of Austrian dominion—ensured easy and rapid intercommunication. The Russians had repaired them and had laid down field railways to their heavy batteries. As regards numbers, the Russians had a superiority. Enemy lines were thinly held—about one division per seven miles, not counting reserves.

After the capture of Halicz, Korniloff forced the Austro-Germans to continue their retreat across the Lommica and occupied two towns on the western bank of the river. South and west of Stanislau he reached the Posiecz-Karmacz line, the central point of which, Lesiuvka, is four miles west of the River Bystritza. The extension of the fighting line to Zolotvin brought the battle-ground into the foothills of the Carpathians. On July 12 he captured 2,000 more prisoners and thirty guns. A large quantity of machine-guns and war-material also were taken. The fate of the Zlota Lipa line defending Lemberg on the east was now in the balance. The Russian advance west of Stanislau, besides endangering the Austro-German line immediately north in Galicia, was a threat against the line in Roumania.

The new offensive had as yet accomplished nothing remotely suggesting the clear and definite results of the attack by Brusiloff in the previous year. It gained ground, just as all offensives on either sides in the West had gained ground, but it gained less ground, and less important ground, than the British about Arras, or the French between Soissons and Auberive. The fact that Russia had attacked when an attack by the Slavs seemed unlikely, took the world by surprize, and the additional fact that the Russians gained ground and took prisoners served to heighten the impression that another Russian sweep like that to and through Lemberg in 1914 and toward Kovel and Lemberg in 1916 was to occur. It was a great thing that Russia had attacked, but, up to July 9, the attack itself had only minor military value. On the political and moral side, however, the Russian offensive had, even tho a temporary, a clear meaning; for many months the German people, with diminishing hope, had looked toward the possibility of a separate peace with Russia. We had in the Russian offensive only a promise, brilliant, but by no means solid. Nothing, in fact, but evidence that a portion of the Russian army asked by Korniloff, could and would fight.

Until July 18 Austro-German troops had been on the defensive, but German reinforcements now arrived, and on the morning of the 19th a counter-attack, launched against the Russian army operating north of Brzezany, pierced the Russian position east of Zloczow on a wide front, and advanced toward the Strypa. This was the beginning of a movement which ended in the expulsion of the Russians from nearly the whole of eastern Galicia, and the recovery of the Bukowina by the Teutonic forces. The efforts of Russian commanders to arouse men to further duties were fruitless. Kerensky in putting Korniloff in full command acted from military and not from political reasons, for Brusiloff had been the first of Russian generals to accept the revolution and place his services at the disposal of the Provisional Government. He had proved himself one of Russia's best fighting generals, and had acquired high reputation as a strategist. Where he failed was not in the field, but in moral power to cope with the mutinous spirit which had crept into the Russian army during the time he was commander-in-chief. To some extent he was the victim of circumstances. With an army reduced to an armed mob Brusiloff could not have launched a successful offensive. General Gutor, who, under Korniloff, commanded two of the Russian Armies, was unable to get through to Brzezany, and tho he won a tactical victory, had nothing in the shape of a territorial gain to show for the sacrifice his soldiers had made. Thus it came about that when the Germans took the offensive the men turned mutinous and refused to fight.

The German commander, Boehm-Ermolli, pushed his attack with great energy all along the line from the Lemberg-Tarnopol railway to the Carpathians. Advancing astride the railway Austro-German troops, assisted by Ottoman units, recaptured all the positions that were won by the Russians on July 1, and, crossing the Strypa, occupied Jezierna on the 21st and reached the line Tarnopol-Trembowla on the 23d. There the Russians rallied, and a battle lasting three days was fought under Korniloff and in the presence of the German Emperor, who arrived in time to see his troops defeat the Russians and drive them across the Sereth. Tarnopol was occupied on the 24th, and on the 26th Austro-German troops crossed the Sereth. Halicz was evacuated on July 20, and Stanislau on the 23d. Next day the Austrians occupied Nizniow on the Dniester and Nadworna on the upper Bystrycza. On the 26th Austro-Hungarian troops entered Kolomea and pushed advanced guards down the Pruth. The Russians evacuated Czernowitz and fell back, at the same time calling up reinforcements to hold the frontier between the Pruth and the Dniester, but practically the whole of the Bukowina passed into the possession of the Austrians.

While the Russian army had done wonders, its superiority in numbers had been partly discounted by errors of strategy and tactics, and, above all, by the demoralizing influence of no discipline and unceasing propaganda. Had the Russian High Command been in a position to take the necessary measures for restoring discipline, the Austro-German hosts might have sustained a signal defeat and Lemberg been in Russian hands. A Russian victory then would have altered the whole subsequent course of events on all the Allied fronts, but by July 25 it had been made clear that the defection of the army was not confined to the Galician front, but was ravaging other parts of the Russian line. "On the Dvinsk front," said that day's *communiqué*, "whole divisions without attack by the enemy left their trenches and some sections refused to obey commands." The central front also had failed. Tarnopol fell on July 22, Stanislau was evacuated on July 25, Kolomea (recently Korniloff's headquarters) on July 27. Czernowitz, the capital of the Bukowina, had to be abandoned a day or so later. Korniloff was marshaling his armies eastward and Kamieniec was prepared for evacuation.[4]

[4] Principal Sources: The "Military Expert" of The *Times* (New York), "Nelson's History of the War" by John Buchan; The *Sun,* The *Evening Post,* New York; The London *Times'* "History of the War"; The *Times,* The *Tribune,* New York; The *Times, The Fortnightly Review,* London; Montgomery Schuyler in *The Times* (New York).

III

RIGA FALLS, KERENSKY IS DEPOSED, AND THE BOLSHEVIKI GAIN CONTROL

August, 1917—December 13, 1917

UNDER such circumstances it was only for the prophet to suggest what would happen in Russia, and for the historian in the future to say what actually did happen. All that anybody could see was that the prospect of a successful Russian participation in the military operations of 1917 was fast fading. It was no longer possible to represent Russia as fully reorganized and reborn by the revolution. The offensive, which had wakened so much hope, had as its result not victory, but disintegration. Russian soldiers who had fought brilliantly under Brusiloff and won victories under Korniloff were on the run. Anarchy had entered the ranks, with a lack of discipline, lack of organization, and a transformation of military procedure into direct primary and caucus methods. The sole question was as to what amount of Germany's limited man-power would be available for the tremendous military and moral demonstration necessary for an advance on Petrograd and Moscow. Germany seemed once more near to victory. Consciousness of this was the sole factor in silencing domestic tumult in the German home crisis in the later months of 1917.

Advices reached Petrograd late in August that a retrograde movement by the Russians had occurred southeast of Riga, the important Russian port and naval base on the Baltic. Here the Germans had occupied the Ukskull bridgehead, which the Russians had previously evacuated, and by September 11 all the Russians had retreated from Riga. Riga, however, was not a new Tarnapol; the retreat from it was conducted on the whole in orderly fashion. During a fortnight the Russian commanders had prepared for the blow by withdrawing troops from positions along the shore and taking heavy artillery out of the danger zone. Immediately after the Germans forced the Dwina, orders had been given to evacuate the place, and the evacuation was accomplished in two days. The last train, loaded with wounded, left Riga under heavy fire. All witnesses testified to the extreme intensity of the German bombardment, which, with the help of chemical shell and gas-waves, silenced the Russian guns. The Russians left Riga partly aflame, as the result of German shells sent into the town before they departed. Smoldering ruins of small villages marked the path over which the other contingents passed. With the Russian front broken over a distance of about forty-five miles between Riga and Friedrichstadt, the province of Livonia was fast overrun by Germans. Everywhere they prest against the retreating Russians, among whom disaffection daily became more apparent. Altho the Russians fell back with great speed all along the line, it seemed evident that they had not been put to rout and that loyal troops were fighting rear-guard actions. This seemingly was borne out by the fact that the German bag of prisoners was less than eight thousand and their capture in guns only 180.

In ordering a public celebration of the capture of Riga, Berlin made the most of an opportunity that it had long needed. Hindenburg had won no victories in France to set the German capital fluttering with flags. The steady hammering by the French and British since April against Hindenburg's western lines had sorely tried his powers of resistance. The Kaiser's Government had had no pretext since the invasion of Roumania for organizing a festival in honor of the feats of German armies. Riga might have been taken months before when the demoralization of the Russian armies became evident, but toward Russia Germany had been carrying on more of a political than a military campaign. Germany now stood badly in need of such pseudo-victories as mutinous Russian troops had placed within her reach. So Riga served for the moment to help the political situation that confronted the Kaiser's government.

After the crowds had shouted themselves hoarse and the rejoicing had subsided the position of Germany remained no better. The occupation of the Russian seaport did not create any more reserves for Hindenburg's battered lines in France. It did not fill any empty German stomachs or lessen the drain on the empire's resources. There was a hollow and perfunctory sound in the Kaiser's congratulations. A resonant, full-throated roar, swelling with conviction, had given place to a half-mechanical toying with old phrases. He acted now like a weary horse under an insistent spur. He was not half so enthusiastic over Riga's fall as he was over Bucharest. The reason was that the campaign against Riga and Petrograd was a political campaign, not a military one. He could have had Riga long before, but he did not need it until now.

The campaign was, not against an enemy in the field, but against people at home. Need existed for a success that would sound large, that would still the voice of discontent and hearten the people for another loan and another winter of war. Riga was a desperate expedient, undertaken probably with misgivings. As for the capture of Petrograd, even the serious menace of its capture might be the only thing needed to rouse the vast forces of nationalism in Russia into crushing the centrifugal forces of anarchy and so unifying the whole vast country for war. It took the capture of Moscow in 1821 to rouse the whole Russian nation, and the same thing might have the same result in 1917. The Kaiser and his lieutenants were playing with dynamite, but their need at home was great. A German advance far into Russia would have been a dangerous enterprize. Apparently they knew it.

For many months before the Russians collapsed in Galicia, an attack by the Germans on Riga had been foreseen in Petrograd. The place was vulnerable because it was open to attack by naval and aerial forces, as well as by an army. What actually took place was that on August 31 the Russian island bases in the gulf were attacked by numerous airplanes, while naval vessels operated in the gulf. Before retreating the Russians destroyed quantities of stores and burned, or removed to Petrograd, military munitions and valuables, laying waste the country behind them as they retreated to the northeast. One reason for the abandonment of Riga was that it had long been a hotbed of German agitators and Russian anarchists, and was a very doubtful asset to Russia.

in the struggle to recover military efficiency. Within a week there was a considerable slackening in the German advance, due in large measure to the Russians making stands at several points, particularly on the front of the Pskoff railroad line leading eastward from Riga. Here the German vanguard and Russian cavalry engaged in fighting, the result being that the invaders were held back while the Russians prepared defenses in which to make a stand. Thirty-

THE ALEXANDER III CHURCH IN RIGA

two miles northeast of Riga, near Segevold, "a death battalion" forced the Germans to retreat south, while along the Burtnetsk line to the Dekoff railroad rear-guards gave strong battle to advanced Teuton contingents.

Late in the summer and in the midst of these events, the proclamation of an independent Poland, which had been issued by the Central Powers in November, 1916, was withdrawn and a proposed new partition of Poland substituted for it. This act was believed to show, among other things, the utter failure of the Teutonic attempt to win over the Poles and to enlist 500,000 Polish recruits in the Teutonic cause. From the Polish point of view, Poland had to be reconstituted as a sovereign State, this State to embrace the Russian part and Galicia, and above all, the Prussian part, or the Grand Duchy of Posen, with Danzig as a Polish seaport. So it was with horror for every Pole that an agreement was announced between Germany and Austria for a new partition of their unhappy country. Here was indeed a challenge to the civilized world by powers whose arrogant defiance of its opinion had long been difficult to understand.

The act united all Poles, some 25,000,000 of them, as no other stroke or policy could have done, and it made less likely than ever the willing service of any Pole in the armies of the Central Powers. Germany by this proposal was to annex such parts of Russian Poland as she needed "to rectify her strategic frontier," territory which in extent would be about one-tenth of Russian Poland, and Austria was to annex the remaining nine-tenths. The Emperor Charles was to promulgate a decree, uniting Austrian conquests in Russian Poland with Galicia, to proclaim the whole territory thus consolidated as the kingdom of Poland, proclaim himself King of all Poland, and decree that the Polish crown should descend to his heirs in like manner with the crowns of Austria and Hungary. The fundamental purpose of the entire program was the perpetuation of the alliance between the two Central Powers and the continuance of the Austro-Hungarian monarchy in its historic mission of a German outpost in the East.[5]

German forces landed on the island of Oesel, at the head of the Gulf of Riga, on October 14 and captured Arenburg, the capital of the island. Aiding the operations as far as possible were German cruisers and torpedo-boats which shelled coast-batteries and towns. Attempts by the German fleet to enter the gulf, or to operate in the waters between Oesel and Dage islands, met with some resistance from Russian land batteries and Russian naval units, but by October 17 German troops had taken the greater portion of

[5] The *Journal of Commerce* (New York).

the island, altho the aid they had expected from their fleet in putting down the Russian opposition in adjacent waters was still meeting with some check from Russian warships. Next day the Germans were entirely in possession of the island, and Russian forces were cut off from communication with Petrograd. Small naval engagements continued, and German aircraft carried out reconnaissances over other islands in the gulf.

The occupation of Oesel was a Russian defeat, but it could hardly be called a German victory. Russian weakness rather than German strength accounted for Russian reverses. Almost simultaneously with news of this German success, dispatches revealed the fact that six weeks before a mutiny in the German navy had amounted to an organized and widespread revolt. Sailors seized officers, threw overboard and drowned at least one captain, and some of the men were on their way to Norway to become interned, so as to avoid further participation in the war. All news of this revolt had been scrupulously repressed in Germany until it was revealed by Chancellor Michaelis in the Reichstag; but it had become an open secret in Amsterdam and Copenhagen. Admiral von Capelle made use of the occurrence to strengthen the political hold of the war party, laying the mutiny at the door of men whose heads had been turned by the Russian revolution. There had been some loss of morale in civilian Germany, of which this naval mutiny was indication. A navy held in idleness in the midst of a great war gets nervously undermined. Great Britain had been holding Germany's navy inactive, and had thus been working injury upon its men, even if unable to reach and destroy their ships. Repugnance to submarine duty, which so often ended in unrecorded disappearances of German sailors, was one of the factors in the mutiny. Hunger and ill-treatment also had had some effect.

Two German dreadnoughts, one cruiser, twelve torpedo boats, a transport and numerous mine-sweepers were reported out of action or lost in the taking of Oesel, Mohn, and Dago islands, with the adjacent bit of coast at Verder. The loss of six torpedo-boats was definitely established. The German squadron suffered from mines, torpedoes, and the fire of

Russian naval guns and shore-batteries. British naval aid came to the Russian sea forces and helped in the escape of the Russian fleet from Mohn Sound. A British submarine fired two torpedoes at two German dreadnoughts, injuring or destroying one. The German fleet comprised dread-noughts, ten cruisers, several scores of torpedo-boats, sub-marines, trawlers, and transports.

With so much uncertainty as to whether Russia could be again counted on even as a factor in the Allied cause, it was interesting to know what was the state of the Russian cam-paign at this time in Armenia and on the Turko-Persian frontier. Conditions there had varied little. There had been no Russian retreat in Armenia, and a good deal of desultory fighting had occurred, in which the Russians gen-erally had held their own. They seem not to have been touched by the internal dissensions in their own country. Their front began at Elebu, on the Black Sea, west of Trebizond, and passed near Ardassa and Gumishkaneh to the town of Kelkid. They were still in Erzinghan, their point of contact with the Turks in this district being near Kemakh, sixteen miles to the southeast. The line then swerved south-east across a mountain range to the village of Kighi. The Russians had withdrawn from Oghnut and Mush early in May, but still held positions close to those towns. They were not in Bitlis, but occupied part of the district between Bitlis and Lake Van, and also held the town of Van, on the eastern shore of the lake. It was believed that they still held the Persian city of Kermanshah and the country for some distance to the west. Broadly it could be said that they still held nearly the whole of their conquests in Armenia. Small bodies of their troops were scattered along the Turko-Persian frontier from the neighborhood of Lake Urumiah to some unknown point west of Bagdad. The Turks had not seriously fought the Russians since the winter of 1916–17.

By the first week of September the Russian Government was facing a new crisis. Korniloff, commander-in-chief of the army, backed in part by a group of political agitators, sought for himself greater powers, if not the surrender of the Government into his hands. Kerensky refused to comply with his demands and imprisoned in the Petropavlovsk fortress M. Lvoff, member of the Duma, and former Premier, who had acted as Korniloff's intermediary, and under a severe examination had given details of a plot to overthrow the Government. Korniloff was in consequence deposed from chief command of the army, while Lokomsky, when he refused to take up Korniloff's duties, was pronounced a traitor. Meanwhile, martial law was declared in Petrograd and its environs, and the Government took measures to crush the revolt. The situation on September

© UNDERWOOD & UNDERWOOD, N Y.

RUSSIA'S WOMEN SOLDIERS IN CAMP

In the clash between the Bolsheviki and followers of Kerensky, the women soldiers alone, of all the troops in Petrograd, remained loyal to the Premier and suffered heavily for their devotion, many being killed by Maximalist troops

12 had become acute. Korniloff began a march on Petrograd, but was soon checked, as defections from his ranks occurred, and a great majority of commanders at the front adhered to the Government. Next day official reports said that Korniloff's headquarters had surrendered and that Korniloff himself desired conditionally to place himself in the hands of the authorities. The Government, however, demanded his unconditional capitulation. Kerensky was then confirmed by the Cabinet as commander-in-chief of the

army. Russia had apparently surmounted the peril of actual civil war—but only for a brief period, as the event proved. One decisive factor in the failure of Korniloff was the rallying of General Alexeieff to the Provisional Government, and as chief-of-staff to Kerensky Alexeieff was to be the real commander-in-chief.

After the event some observers regretted the fall of Korniloff. Had power come to him, these observers believed, he might have saved the country from the Bolsheviki. The immediate cause of this open clash had been the danger in which Russia stood from a German advance that had so easily captured Riga, and was then seriously threatening Dwinsk. Korniloff and his followers had been greatly dissatisfied with what they considered the temporizing policy of Kerensky. At a national conference in Moscow Korniloff had made a brilliant and forceful speech in favor of the restoration of discipline and aggressiveness in the army, and had particularly urged that the military commanders have full power in inflicting death by court martial, but he had received only lukewarm support from Kerensky, and the recent German advance had led him to feel that nothing but a vigorous administration of discipline by the Government could save Russia.

Politically the clash was one between Constitutional Democrats such as Milliukov and Lvoff, and Social Democrats and extreme radicals who had control of the Workmen's and Soldiers' delegates. The former were urgent in desiring a vigorous prosecution of the war, but the latter wished to establish a Social Democracy, and many of them were so radical in their political views that they regarded the conduct of the war as a secondary matter. The movement headed by Korniloff was not reactionary in the sense that it desired to restore imperialism, but it put vigorous prosecution of war before discussion of political theories. Kerensky held that the movement under Korniloff was an attempt to effect a counter-revolution, which had "the design of robbing the Russian people of hard-won liberties," but Korniloff's adherents declared that a vigorous prosecution of the war was the only question now before the country, that the Kerensky government was "carrying water on both shoulders,'' and that it was unwilling to meet the war issues squarely because of pressure from the more radical Socialists and labor leaders.

Altho he had failed in the attempt to establish a stable government, Korniloff had the satisfaction of knowing that his action for a time had been the means of strengthening Kerensky's hands and replacing a weak administration by what promised to be a strong one. It was understood that the policy and conduct of the war would now be left in the unfettered hands of a ''Council of Five,'' and on September 16 a Russian Republic was proclaimed. To strengthen the organization of the State, it was declared that a change to the republican form was necessary, that a republic had been one of the chief aims of the radicals and the Council of Workmen's and Soldiers' Delegates, and that it had been approved by the Russian Congress at Moscow.

Of the Korniloff demonstration, the proclamation of a republic marked one result, and the new influence of the Council of Workmen and Soldiers revealed another. To Kerensky the lesson of the episode was that a more emphatic need than ever existed for national unity and cooperation. His proclamation was plainly an exhortation to all parties to lay aside their differences for the preservation of the one ideal upon which they all agreed—a free republican government. Common-sense seemed once more to have emerged from a crisis. The formal proclamation brought into strong relief the difficulties in the way of creating a workable system of republican government in a land where the racial and lingual diversity of the people was so profound. This diversity had a lurid illustration when what was known as the ''savage'' division of the Russian army placed itself under the orders of Korniloff and marched to attack Petrograd. The division was composed of Georgians and Caucasians, who did not speak Russian and who in religion were Moslems. It needed the intervention of an officer of their own race to explain to them the enterprise on which they were engaged and to induce them to abandon it.

The next turn in affairs came early in November when the world received the startling news that the Provisional

Government had been thrown out of power by the Bolsheviki or Maximalists, headed by Nikolai Lenine, the radical Socialist leader, whose real name was Vladimir Ilitch Ulianov. Kerensky had fled from the capital and several of his ministers had been placed under arrest. The Winter Palace, the seat of the Government, bombarded by guns from the cruiser *Aurora* and from the fortress of St. Peter and St. Paul, had been forced to capitulate. Delegates from the Black and Baltic fleets declared themselves in favor of the radicals. A congress of the Workmen's and Soldiers Delegates of all Russia convened in Petrograd to discuss organization, peace and war, and the formation of a constituent assembly. A delegation was named to confer with other revolutionary and democratic organizations, with a view to initiating peace negotiations for the purpose of "taking steps to stop the bloodshed." Cossack regiments, meanwhile, were declared to have announced their readiness whole-heartedly to support the Provisional Government on condition that no compromise with the revolutionists was made.

The battle at the Palace, which began shortly after 6 o'clock, was a spectacular one, armed cars of the revolutionaries swinging into action in front of the Palace gates, while from the Neva came shells from the guns of the *Aurora*. The men entrusted with power comprised fourteen Maximalists, or extreme radicals, including Nikolai Lenine, M. Zinovieff, an associate of Lenine, and Leon Trotzky, president of the Central Executive Committee. Some of the excesses of the French Revolution were equaled and often far exceeded in Petrograd in the anarchy that ensued when Kerensky's wavering rule came to an end. While Russia groaned under the rule of the Bolsheviki and was out of sympathy with the idealism that Lenine and Trotzky were attempting to put into practise, there was general submission to the "tyrants of the moment," for Lenine had an iron hand and did not hesitate to let it be felt. The Petrograd correspondent of the London *Morning Post* gave a vivid description of the reign of terror under which the Russian capital groaned. Altho floods of indignation were being poured out daily upon the Bolsheviki, it was beyond

ON THE NEVSKY PROSPECT IN PETROGRAD

From the roof of the Public Library machine-gun bullets are killing and wounding people in the streets

question that they were gaining ground in Russia, simply
because they used a strong hand. In three weeks there were
taken out of the rivers and canals of Petrograd 7,000 naked
corpses of persons whose deaths were not caused by drown-
ing. The corpses of the women had their hair cut off, because it represented marketable value, as had their clothes.
Anti-Bolshevik papers were supprest, but occasionally made
a spasmodic appearance.

As early as November 10 regiments loyal to Kerensky
were marching on the capital and fighting was under way
in the city. An organization which had adopted the name
of the All Russian Committee for Saving the Country and
the Revolution announced that the defeat of the Bolsheviki
movement was a matter only of days. The town of Tsarskoe
Selo, fifteen miles south of Petrograd, where the former
Emperor Nicholas had lived, had been captured, after which
the rebels retired in disorderly mobs as Kerensky approached
Petrograd. Thus a counter-stroke was being delivered with
apparently some chance of success.

It required a long perspective, to estimate the results of
this as of any revolution. Russia was a great, unwieldy,
awakening giant, unconscious of her strength, groping
toward the light, learning by experiment and pain, and was
still a force for good could she be rightly directed. That
the nation as a whole would eventually prove loyal to her
pledges was the sincere belief of many who knew Russia.
Men often forget how slow revolutions are. As had been
remarked by a French statesman, it took eighty-two years
to establish the French Republic; that is, the time between
1789 and 1871. The revolution in England had first developed a dictator in Oliver Cromwell, and then followed
the Restoration, before the real revolution came in 1689. We
easily forgot how long our own revolution was in the making, and at times was held in suspense, even tho the heart
of the English people was not in the fight against us, and
the best men among Englishmen regarded their German
King with contempt. What Russia needed was sympathy
and understanding. To criticize her while in the throes
of her awakening was like criticizing the Gulf Stream or
the Equator. She had to work out her own salvation some-

how; and if, for the moment, her experiments in government leaned to the German side, many felt that they would ultimately go to the right side ·and reflect the true spirit of the Russian people.

The fate of Russia thereafter hung in the balance with the choice between anarchism and democracy left to the decision of war. When the Bolsheviki revolted against the Provisional Government, attacked and seized the Winter Palace, arrested most of the ministers, forced Kerensky into flight, and proclaimed a Government of which Lenine, long since denounced as a German agent, was the head, and Trotzky, a fiery speaker and wild thinker, formerly a Socialist editor in New York City, was the Foreign Secretary, it seemed as if all was lost for the cause of stable democracy in Russia. In a day or two, as the situation became clearer, men began to ask whether civil war itself was not more desirable than the tyranny shown by these anarchists. From Moscow came news that Kerensky was marching with troops against the Bolsheviki, that Miliukov, Korniloff, Alexieff, and Kaledine were combining to establish a real democratic government and to put Russia again on the fighting line. It had become clear that the voice of Russia was not the voice of Lenine. The Constitutional Democrats, the voters in small cities, the great cooperative associations, and the zemstvos, were by no means at the beck and call of German agents, or of theorists so blind as to think that to call grandiloquently on the world to make peace forthwith was the way to get some other kind of peace than German domination.

The most conflicting reports were printed. One account said Kerensky had been arrested in Petrograd and his forces routed; another that Kerensky had been victorious; another that street fighting was going on; another that Korniloff, with twenty thousand soldiers, was approaching the capital. Civil war, however, existed. A large force ·was approaching Petrograd, but for what purpose was unknown, and another was approaching Moscow. There had been fighting in Kakan and Tasskent. In Kief there had been some disturbance of ordinary life and Czech troops fighting for the Government had secured the mastery. Strong protests against the Bolsheviki were made in many provincial towns. When the Bolsheviki deposed Kerensky he appealed to the army, most of which was apathetic or hostile, but he raised a small army and marched on Petrograd. The report of his advance, spread and magnified, induced a handful of military cadets to try, in a moment of ecstatic enthusiasm, to overthrow the Bolsheviki before he could arrive, but they were surrounded, shot to pieces and captured. At the same time riots broke out in Moscow, with disastrous results for thousands of innocent people.

Meanwhile Kerensky advanced toward Petrograd, where the Bolsheviki had hurriedly collected a miscellaneous mob of 16,000 and sent it against Kerensky's much smaller force. In this Bolsheviki army were some soldiers and many sailors, but the great majority were factory hands and boys who had been frantically and feverishly armed and decorated with the title of "the Red Guard." The two forces met at Gatchina where Cossacks confronted the Red Guard for two days, occasionally firing aimless volleys, and finally made a sudden and apathetic charge. The Bolsheviki had sent the Red Guard against Kerensky's Cossacks apparently because they could not get regular soldiers to go and Kerensky had raised only 1,500 Cossacks, obviously because more would not go, and those who did go immediately repented of their bargain. Soldiers would fight neither for Kerensky nor for the Bolsheviki. Then the Russian tragedy for a week seemed to take on the color of a farce. The Bolsheviki were in power, but dispatches became contradictory and confusing. One thing was clear, there was no government in Russia. The great question was whether the moderate elements could gather head and power enough to make Russia a self-governing country, and recreate an army that would offer resistance to Germany.

Kerensky had few if any supporters left among the masses, who were convinced that he had connived at Korniloff's march on Petrograd, which they had regarded as a reactionary movement. The Red Guards, whose formation he had permitted in order to resist Korniloff's cavalry, turned against him, and sailors came in warships to support Lenine. Kerensky in fact was deserted by the troops, except officer cadets and the Women's Battalion who, faithful to their duty, bore the brunt of the Bolshevist attacks and suffered the greatest losses. Kerensky had only one hope, the Cossacks, but he antagonized them when he tried to ride rough-shod over their elective institutions. Moreover, they mistrusted him for "duplicity" in the Korniloff affair, and resented the charges of disloyalty that he had brought against their organization. In July the Cossacks had saved Kerensky and incidentally the soviet

© UNDERWOOD & UNDERWOOD. N. Y.

BOLSHEVIKI SOLDIERS MARCHING IN PETROGRAD

from the Bolshevists, but now in a secret midnight consultation with him, they told him in plain words that they would no longer support him. Thereupon Kerensky secretly fled from the city, hoping to return at the head of troops. He found them at Gatchina, but, as they also went over to the Bolshevists, Kerensky's brief rule was over.

By December 10 a counter revolt against the Bolsheviki in southeastern Russia was gaining some momentum. It was described as spreading fanlike from chosen bases northward, northeastward, and northwestward, while preparations were hastening to extend it southward into the Caucasus. Meanwhile, the Bolsheviki continued to issue manifestoes calling upon their followers to resist the attempt that was being made to overthrow them. From his base in the river Don region, Kaledine, Hetman of the Don Cossacks, was moving toward the borders of the Ukraine, which already had declared its independence of, and hostility to, the Bolsheviki. At the same time was forming a menace to Moscow, where the Bolsheviki were in control, and other forces were making their way northward. From Orenburg, near the Siberian frontier, General Dutoff was moving to capture Cheliabinsk, the junction point of the Trans-Siberian Railway, in order to prevent food and other supplies from reaching European Russia, and especially Petrograd, from Siberian ports on the Pacific. Altho it had not definitely alined itself with the movement, the new Republic of Siberia had issued an order that promised materially to aid the Kaledine forces. This order, in forbidding the shipment of food supplies into European Russia, took the ground that they might reach the Germans.

It seemed for a time that Russia would not perish without a struggle. There were honorable and intelligent elements among her people. That was the meaning of the revolt headed by Kaledine. There was ground for hope in the very deliberation with which he moved. He had been consolidating his position for months, evidently with the determination that his movement should be no flash in the pan. There was every reason to believe that many recent declarations of independence on the part of different portions of Russia had, as a matter of fact, been parts of this great effort of Russian sanity to resume control. The Ukrainian Republic, for example, was working with Kaledine, and the Provisional Government of Siberia was moving in the same direction. In the beginning of his operation, Kaledine held only the Don region, but within a fortnight he had extended his influence over much of Little Russia, the lower Volga provinces and Turkestan. Kaledine was no military adventurer, no upstart. He was the Hetman of the Cossacks, and how well he represented them was shown by

THE RUSSIAN "DEATH BATTALION" OF WOMEN SOLDIERS

the fact that, when Kerensky called upon them to arrest
him for supporting Korniloff, they replied politely that, as
Kaledine was engaged in attending to his official duties as
Hetman, it was impossible to execute the Government's
orders.

Civil war in Russia was at white heat. Kaledine, supported
by Korniloff, had raised the standard of revolt, and Constitutional Democrats and Bourgeois were aiding them. Observers began to think of a possible disintegration in the
empire, with its vast areas and its tremendous resources
and that there might arise a Russian question that would
prove more dangerous to Europe than the Turkish, or
Eastern, question for several centuries had been. For the
twentieth century the Russian question might therefore replace the Eastern question. Like the Turk, the Russian
had conquered many races and like the Turk had failed to
assimilate the races he conquered. Russian unity was
dynastic and governmental, and so when overthrown by the
revolution and succeeded by anarchy, the unassimilated portions promptly began to seek some other unity than the
Russian-Romanoff unity had secured. In Finland, Poland,
Lithuania, and Ukraine these national movements had already begun.

On December 13 the curtain fell on the first act in a
new drama when about twenty Social Revolutionary delegates to the Constituent Assembly attempted to hold a meeting in Petrograd, entrance to the Duma hall being prohibited
and numerous armed sailors guarding all doors. The delegates then entered the library, with the intention of holding
a formal session there, but an officer appeared before them
and read instructions from Lenine which declared that all
meetings would be illegal until the Constituent Assembly
had received permission to meet. Delegates in spite of this
imperturbably proceeded with their business, and made a
protest addrest to the whole world. Another meeting was
then postponed by formal action until a substantial number
of delegates could arrive in Petrograd. Before an adjourn-
ment was reached an officer, accompanied by sailors with fixt
bayonets and cutlasses, appeared and ordered the assembly
to disperse, whereupon the library was slowly emptied. The

© KADEL & HERBERT.

PREMIER KERENSKY

VII.

incident was perhaps trivial, but it was characteristic of conditions in Russia where the bayonet now ruled. A democratic government did no longer exist.[6]

So passed a day for which the original revolutionaries had eagerly waited, but instead of an accredited body of 600 delegates they saw only a little group of forty or fifty, most of them unknown men, not one in the foremost rank—a quiet little meeting of low voices speaking timidly in whispers. One delegate announced that three delegates had been arrested and another, as he walked out, said: "We are all waiting for our turn." Thus the Constituent Assembly of Russia had met under a shadow, not that of a Czar, but that of a worse tyranny, the tyranny of radical class Socialism. The Bolsheviki had determined that it should not meet unless they could control it, and they could not do that because the elections had gone against them. At first their intention was to set the election aside in districts where they had been defeated and to order new ones, presumably under the auspices of the Red Guard. But a simpler method was employed. They adopted Cromwell's old method of a "purge."

Reports as to the progress of operations between the Bolsheviki and Cossack forces for weeks had been much beclouded. Both parties were credited with victories. One report said Kaledine was besieging Rostov-on-Don and that fighting was in progress near that city. Another that a revolt to assist him had set in. Men and guns from the Black Sea fleet were said to be aiding the Bolsheviki; Korniloff had routed the Bolsheviki near Bielgorod; Korniloff had been wounded and was in danger of capture; attempts by Kaledine's followers to cut off food supplies had failed. Reinforcements at this time were being sent by the Constitutional Democrats southward to Kaledine and Korniloff, and eastward to Dutoff. Kaledine had seized Rostov at the mouth of the Don, but withdrew his troops from the latter place when it was attacked by Bolsheviki troops landed from the Russian fleet. Korniloff, who had been imprisoned at Biekhoff, managed to escape and collecting all the Cossacks he could find, reached Bielgorod on his way to join

[6] Cable dispatch from Harold Williams to The *Times* (New York).

Kaledine. There he was met by Bolsheviki troops, who defeated him and compelled his Cossack followers to break up into small parties. Korniloff himself escaped. Kerensky was now in hiding and appeared to have lost his followers.[7]

[7] Principal Sources: The *World*, *The Outlook*, The *Times*, The *Journal of Commerce*, New York; The *Times* (London), The *Wall Street Journal* (New York), The London *Times'* "History of the War."

TIFLIS IN THE CAUCASUS

Here the Grand Duke Nicholas had his headquarters, after he was removed from command of the Russian armies in Europe

IV

RUSSIA PROSTRATE AT BREST-LITOVSK UNDER GERMAN INTRIGUE AND MILITARY FORCE

December 17, 1917—May 3, 1918

REVOLUTION and counter-revolution seemed daily to be plunging Russia into deeper chaos. Little was known of the meetings of the new Constituent Assembly, nor were expectations of it particularly sanguine, seeing that the Bolsheviki leaders threatened to dissolve it, or to annul its proceedings if it ventured to adopt a course contrary to their dictation. Meantime, in advance of anything which it might do, the Bolsheviki decreed the abolition of all courts in the empire, and the substitution therefor of new tribunals arbitrarily created by themselves. At the same time they declared all land the property of the State, and then they entered into an armistice with Germany. The British envoy at Petrograd strongly criticized their course, pointing out that it had been incumbent upon them, first, to discuss the matter with the Allies of Russia and come to an agreement with them before opening negotiations with the enemy.

Germany's artistice with Russia now signed covered a period of twenty-eight days, beginning at noon on December 17. Peace negotiations were at once entered into. One of the conditions of the armistice was that no German troops should be moved from the Russian front while the armistice lasted, but Hindenburg, who had moved masses of troops before the signature of the armistice, continued to move many others afterward. Discussion of a general peace was in progress at Brest-Litovsk by December 19. German and Austrian Foreign Ministers, both astute politicians, had gone to Brest-Litovsk for this purpose while the war-aims of Great Britain were being concretely set forth in the House of Commons by Lloyd George as being a complete restoration by Germany of all invaded territory, with compensa-

331

tion for the havoc wrought. "A joyful Christmas" had been promised to the world by the German press, but instead of holding out an olive branch the Kaiser threw another brickbat. In one of his most frenzied moods he talked about bringing peace to the world through "battering in with the ,iron fist and shining sword the doors of those who will not have peace."

Germany was represented at Brest-Litovsk [8] as expecting to sacrifice certain of her colonies in the interest of a general peace with the Entente. She might even think of indemnities to Belgium, her main objectives being in the East and the Balkans. For the time being, at least, her efforts to dominate the world by crushing France and getting at Great Britain seemed to have been laid aside. She was looking instead for compensation in the East. When a declaration was made that the Central Powers were ready for a "general peace without forcible annexations and indemnities," it failed to stir a ripple on the Entente surface—least of all in Washington, where there was no longer any disposition to take any German declaration as made in good faith. While the German delegates at Brest-Litovsk uttered fair words, the Kaiser had thundered forth his familiar boast that "the German sword and German iron," backed by the old "German God," awaited those who longer resisted German might. The determination of the Allied Governments was fixt and irrevocable that, so long as there existed in Germany a vast military force controlled by an irresponsible Government, they would not think of peace. Before any official, or even semi-official, copy of these German camouflaged terms reached the Entente Allies, Great Britain, France, and the United States had virtually rejected them. Under cover of a formula, giving small races the right to choose their own political allegiance, the Germans had deliberately undertaken to create a land barrier between Slav races and the Baltic; in fact, to erect a German-controlled state comprising all the Russian Baltic ports from Libau to Reval, and including Pernau and Riga.

[8] A more detailed account of the Brest-Litovsk negotiations has already been given in Volume IV, Part XV, Chapter II. That account is here briefly summarized.

If this proposal had become a reality, 150,000,000 Russians would have been deprived of an outlet upon open waters, save on the Arctic and Pacific, and Russia would have been made industrially and economically a slave to Germany. Through Danzig and Königsberg and through her new acquisitions, Libau and Riga, Germany would have controlled all Russian northern roads to the sea, and through mastery of the Turk at Constantinople, would have dominated the road from Russia to the Mediterranean. While

SOLDIERS' AND WORKMEN'S DELEGATES IN SESSION
IN PETROGRAD

Germany proposed to permit the people of certain Baltic provinces in Russia to decide their own allegiance—that is, in Esthonia, Livonia, Courland, and Lithuania—she would have so managed the proposed plebiscite as to have secured possession of the Baltic seacoast of Russia, and in addition the coast of the Gulf of Finland, which was the sea-gate of Petrograd. As Finland was to be independent, Russia would have been completely excluded from the Baltic, and the Baltic would have become a German lake. A state of some six millions of people, with an area about equal to that of New York State, that is, some 50,000 square miles, would have been interposed between 150,000,000 Russians and one of their two natural sea-gates. Of these some three millions would have been Lettish and Lithuanian, that is, Slav; upward of a million would have been Poles, who also are Slavs; perhaps half a million would have been Finns, and the remainder, Slavs, Jews, and Germans. Such a state would have had no real ethnic bond of union, nothing out of which might have been developed a nation, even of Balkan proportions.

The Germans now occupied by force of arms most of this territory; the ruling class in it was German and eager to escape from a Bolsheviki Slavdom to a Prussianized Germany. These Germans were of the same spirit and held the same ideas as those other German minorities who ruled in East Prussia and Silesia over conquered Slavs. Having military control and aided by the ruling class, who were of the Junker order, they demanded that the fate of these provinces should be determined by a plebiscite and that this plebiscite should take place before their troops were withdrawn. The result of such a plebiscite could have been foreseen. Four million and a half to five million Slavs would have been swept into a German-made state, controlled by a tiny German minority, who maintained themselves by German bayonets. Another and even more gigantic Alsace-Lorraine would thus have been created. The German delegation to Brest-Litovsk pretended willingly to accept the Bolsheviki slogan of "no annexations and no indemnities." It appeared later that to their minds this was only to be applied to Russia proper. Germany's desire for peace was known to be acute—but it was not a desire for peace for peace's sake; it was peace for the sake of war gains. Her love of peace had been well indicated during three years—that is, it was a peace which would satisfy Pan-German greed for new territory. Germany declined to give up the Russian territory she had overrun and proposed to garrison the leading towns in it. By a military promenade she had placed herself in readiness for the position she now took, that of blandly informing Russia that the principle of "no indemnities and no annexations" did not apply to Poland, Lithuania, Courland, Esthonia, and Livonia, because the future of these provinces had already been determined— by their own people, as Germany had the cynicism to add— and that she must retain for the present her garrisons in Riga and Libau.

It was quite natural that Germany should exult over the separate peace she entered into at this time with the Ukraine, followed by a collapse of further opposition from the Bolsheviki; but when the bell-ringing and the flag-waving were over, the question of establishing a political quarantine against her new-found friends promised to become as urgent as finding ways and means by which to acquire, on any terms, the surplus stocks of grain, oil, and minerals in the Ukraine. The Bolsheviki government, by February 24, when confronted with irresistible military force, announced their readiness to accept all the terms Germany had laid down. Without further hesitation they yielded to the enemy still more of their valuable western territory, extending from the Gulf of Finland southward, and even agreed to withdraw troops from Finland and give back to the Turks what had been taken from them in Asia. The surrender was thoroughly abject. Russia was at once to send a delegation to Brest-Litovsk to discuss with German representatives the final details of the peace and to sign a compact.

Meanwhile the German armies gave no heed to this peace, but methodically pushed forward their line over more than 500 miles of front from the Gulf of Finland region to Volhynia, and nowhere met with any systematic attempts to hinder their progress. Additional towns were captured, several thousand Russians made prisoners, and nearly 3,000 German and Austrian prisoners of war were liberated. Reval, Russia's principal port on the Finnish coast, was rapidly approached notwithstanding the snow-covered roads, troops were being pushed forward in forced marches, the desire of the German High Command evidently being to capture the port, which would be available, if necessity arose, as a base for operations by a fleet of war vessels against Kronstadt and Petrograd. The internal situation in Russia continued chaotic. So bad had conditions become in Petrograd that a state of siege was declared by the military authorities. Reval, Russia's principal port on the Gulf of Finland, together with its fortress, was soon captured. Pskov, on the railway about 160 miles southwest of Petrograd, fell into German hands, and southwest along the entire line the invaders everywhere steadily prest eastward, and in their southern wing formed a junction with the Ukrainians at Zhitomir, 85 miles west of Kiev, which town it was their announced purpose to take from the Bolsheviki. Since the renewal of hostilities the Germans had taken over thousands of additional square miles of Russian territory, their advance virtually unimpeded.

That Germany considered the convention she forced Lenine and Trotzky to sign as another "scrap of paper" was further shown when Teuton forces reached Jamburg, a town only 68 miles from Petrograd. Further invasion of Russia had therefore not been abandoned. The Bolsheviki at the same time made a futile announcement that they would not permit the revolution to be defeated and exprest a determination to continue a "holy war," even if they were "forced back to the Ural Mountains." The text of a peace treaty signed at this time by Roumania served to show that the Central Powers were loath to forego any conquests they might make. One of the clauses of that treaty bound Roumanians to assist in the transportation of Teuton forces through Moldavia and Bessarabia on their way to Odessa, the "granary of Russia." Germany also negotiated a treaty with Finland by which the latter agreed not to cede to Russia any territory, or grant any territorial rights, without the consent of Germany, who, in consideration for this concession, covenanted to exert her influence to secure recognition of an independent Finnish Government from other nations. The Kaiser telegraphed to Hindenburg: "Our Baltic brethren and countrymen are liberated from the Russian yoke and may again feel themselves Germans." These "Baltic brethren" in Courland numbered less than 9 per cent. of the population; in Livonia they were 8 per cent., in Esthonia less than that, and in Lithuania less than 2 per cent.

The treaty of peace between the newly created Ukrainian

Republic and the Central Powers had been signed at Brest-Litovsk on February 9. The frontier of Galicia remained as heretofore, but the Ukraine received a large portion of the Cholm province, amounting to more than 5,000 square miles, with a population considerably in excess of 1,000,000. This province formed part of the ancient Kingdom of Poland, and tho there were some districts containing White Russian inhabitants, the large majority of the people were of pure Polish descent. Further north the southern parts of the two provinces of Grodno and Minsk, including the

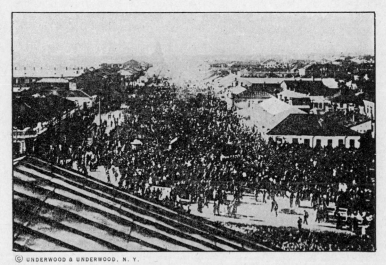

BOLSHEVIKI TAKING POSSESSION OF A RUSSIAN CITY

fortress of Brest-Litovsk, were allocated under the terms of the treaty to the territory of that Republic. This further partition of Poland was at variance with the declarations of Count Czernin, the Austrian representative, who had proclaimed the wish of the Austro-Hungarian Government to create "an independent Polish State which should include all the territories the populations of which are indisputably Polish."

The treaty made no contribution to the solution of the racial problem as between Austria-Hungary, Russia, and Poland,

and left a population of between three and four millions of Little Russians under Austrian rule. Its provisions were in direct conflict with four principles which President Wilson laid down in his message to Congress on February 11 as the basis of a peace settlement, and especially with the President's third proposition that "every territorial settlement involved in this war must be made in the interest and for the benefit of the population concerned, and not as a part of any mere adjustment or compromise of claims among rival States." The British Government took the lead in refusing to recognize a treaty which was opposed to the declared policy of the Allied Powers and the effect of which would be to reduce the Ukraine, with its population of 30,000,000 Russian peasants, to the status of a vassal State under German domination. No treaty could receive the sanction of international law till a stable Government had been established in Ukrainian territory after the inhabitants had enjoyed an unrestricted freedom of "self-determination' in regard to their future government.

What Kühlmann's terms of peace to Russia were, apart from those offered to, and accepted by, the Ukrainian Rada, the world did not definitely know, but he made it clear to Trotzky and other Russian delegates on the opening day of the conference at Brest-Litovsk that he had not come there to negotiate, but to impose terms which had been already fixt by the German Government. The delegates were bluntly told that they were the representatives of a conquered nation, and had no alternative but to throw themselves on the mercy of their conquerors or take the consequence of their refusal. Kühlmann agreed to adopt "self-determination" as the guiding principle of a peace settlement, but it was to be the determination, not of the people concerned, but of Prussian bayonets. Beaten to his knees, Trotzky accepted the terms imposed on his country and agreed to sign the treaty. The Bolsheviki, on February 11, declared the state of war that had existed with the Central Powers at an end and ordered a demobilization of Russian forces on all fronts.

Russia thus stept formally out of the war by act of the Bolsheviki, whose authority at this time seemed virtually unquestioned in northern Russia. The Teutonic Powers had already secured a cessation of hostilities elsewhere along the Eastern Front by imposing a peace on the Ukraine and so isolating Roumania. Altho she had cut little figure in the war for nearly a year, Russia's great and vital part in the conflict in its early years came forcibly to mind as the circumstances leading up to her exit were now reviewed. Since August, 1917, she had figured in the great world conflict as a military factor only by reason that she was still keeping numbers of German and Austrian troops on her frontiers. Whether the culmination of Germany's Ukrainian negotiations for a peace treaty was the determining factor in inducing the Bolsheviki to declare the state of war at an end was not clear, but it had become fairly evident that Germany had no idea of yielding to the Bolsheviki on the question of an evacuation of occupied Russian territory, which had been the sticking point in the negotiations, and that she was preparing virtually to ignore the Bolsheviki, as long as she could make peace with the Ukraine and secure the opening of her frontier to the grain-growing provinces controlled, nominally, by the Ukrainians.

It appeared that the discussions at Brest-Litovsk had been particularly stormy and that they ended in a violent scene which bore all the seeds of a future conflict. Already at the German headquarters the war lords had been discussing "the eventuality of energetic military measures against the Russians." German newspapers noted that three hours after the news came of a demobilization order, another Russian message directed that this order be no longer circulated. The Bolsheviki were said to be energetically forming a Red Guard army out of the remnants of the Russian army, in the hope of raising a million men to establish Bolshevikist power in the border States. Nothing in the way of definite terms, apparently had been accepted by the Russian people or by any authority supported by them. Nor was there any enthusiastic reception of the idea of peace with Russia by the German people. The practical meaning of the change in conditions was a puzzle all around. If it had been brought about with a view to drawing all German forces from the Eastern Front to the Western, there was no assurance that this was a safe thing to do. The Bolsheviki grip was liable to be broken at any time and there was no knowing what uprisings there might be, or what new leader might not arise to save Russia from being a victim of the greedy Teutonic monster. It looked as if the chief result would be simply to prolong the war and add to its cost.

It was plain that in working out common purposes the Russians under the old *régime* in the early days of the war had made earnest endeavors to enact the part which the war had imposed upon them. In 1914 it was they who made the only great offensive into Germany and when driven out they had come back. Of all the Allies they had done the hardest fighting up to the close of 1915. At that time there had been 1,200,000 Russians killed and only 800,000 Frenchmen and 200,000 British. Nothing could be plainer than that, in the early years of the war, Russia had saved the day for France, Great Britain, and all the Allies.[9] Now, however, the Western Powers were left to carry on the war with their own resources and with the help of the United States, for even if there should be a counter-revolution in Russia and a constitutional government should be set up in Petrograd, the belligerent power of the country had been paralyzed by the events of twelve months. As an ally Russia in future would only be an incubus instead of a help to the Western Powers. With her armies beaten in the field and her people demoralized by internal anarchy, she had no alternative but to submit to a German peace, which had placed her under the iron heel of her conqueror until a decisive victory in the West restored the equilibrium which Russia had lost in the East. The situation in Ukraine presented one of the most intricate questions arising from conditions in the East. Dissatisfaction with the peace terms within a few weeks was widespread among peasants and workingmen, and was being aggravated by German requisitions of grain, sugar, and other products. The Rada, the chief legislative body, passed a vote of want of confidence in the Ukrainian Government after the treaty was signed. The high-handed methods of the Ukrainians by the Germans, leading to a conflict with the

[9] Isaac R. Penypacker in *The American Historical Review*, April, 1918.

German commandant at Kief, resulted in the resignation of Mr. Petlura, a member of the Government.

In so far as the Bolsheviki were sincere, they aspired to attain at once to a heroic maximum, and to transpose, at one bound, not only Russia, but all the world into the seventh heaven of the Communist creed. Hypnotized by this hope they shrank from no crime in order to hasten its consummation. Their theory of wholesale expropriation rapidly degenerated in practice into plain brigandage and murder; political opponents were assassinated; the Church was

BURNING THE IMPERIAL EAGLE IN PETROGRAD

despoiled; the treasury was sacked, and the Constituent Assembly, which was to have decided the future disposition of Russian lands, was dispersed by armed force. The masses, devoid of civic sense, hailed with almost delirious enthusiasm a doctrine which they forthwith translated for themselves in the primitive terms of "Bread, Land, and Peace." Even the Cossack proletariat became infected. Kaledine, the Cossack Hetman, seeing his forces melt away, and with them the last hope of restoring in a near future ordered government in Russia, committed suicide. What was left of the Russian classes looked on with the impassive detachment that they had always exhibited in the presence of an accomplished fact. By the so-called treaties Russia lost in the aggregate about one-fifth of her territory in Europe, including Finland, Estland, Livland, Courland, Poland, Lithuania, and the Ukraine, as well as gains she had made under the Berlin treaty of 1878 in the Caucasus; about one-third of her European population; one-third of her railways; about one-quarter of her internal revenues, and over three-quarters of her iron and coal fields. Russia, both north and south, was reduced to a condition of economic servitude, which had no parallel in history.

The Kaiser persisted in an amusing pretense that the downfall of Russia had been a feat of arms on the part of German troops. Germans, he said, "led by ideal generals, had broken the Russian power and won the safety of the empire in the east." German generals had yet to prove, however, that they were ideal leaders somewhere else than in Russia. While a great empire had been torn from Russia and added temporarily to Germany, this had not been done by generalship. Generals had advanced into Russia when they could not have helped doing so unless they had been stricken with paralysis. Against any enemy of her own size, Germany had from the beginning of the war dashed herself in vain. She had never thus far been able to make gains in France after the Marne—not on the Aisne, in Flanders, at Verdun, before Arras, or at the Chemin-des-Dames.

In fact, she had by this time retreated from more than one-half the French territory that she seized in August, 1914. She had won her success at Caporetto, not by arms, but by pacifist and Socialist propaganda, and she had been halted afterward. She had made conquests over little Belgium and, with aid from Bulgaria, Austria, and Turkey, other conquests over Serbia and Montenegro, and again with Austria, Turkey, and Bulgaria to help her, had defeated but not conquered Roumania. Roumania, in fact, had held her in check, until Germany debauched Russia, and so surrounded Roumania with enemies. After Russia fell into confusion, Germany had not dared to advance until the work of demobilization became complete; she would not challenge even Kerensky. The greatest militaristic nation of modern times—the new Assyria—really had had no great military conquests to boast of; her victories had been won against small States and were mainly the product of her propagandists instead of her soldiers.

The streets of Petrograd had never been so quiet as now since the beginning of the war. The turbulent emotions of a year of revolution exhausted, the fever was slackening, the pulse of life low and depression and forebodings had become inarticulate. There had been by March 10 a great exodus. The Government was migrating to Moscow and let fall hints that Moscow would be proclaimed the capital, the Council of People's Commissaries to have its seat in the Kremlin, Lenine to sit in the seat of Peter the Great and Ivan the Terrible. Day after day many thousands waited on the Nevsky Prospect in Petrograd for permits to leave. Overcrowded trains moved off south and east with soldiers in the forefront, dismissed workmen, and a miscellaneous mass of humanity afraid of starvation, afraid of unemployment, afraid of the invader, and of unknown calamities. Many thousands who could not go by trains went on foot through the snow. Many who had ready money to spare hired sledges and went driving off on a pilgrimage into the depths of Russia.

There was no noise, no outward sign of panic, but a strange hush about it all, a sad and patient resignation, as if people were in the presence of an unintelligible, inexorable fate. Those who remained went wandering about streets, vaguely, hopelessly, asking for an explanation of conditions that had grown meaningless. Somehow the city still managed to live from hand to mouth. Refrigerators were emptied and their contents allotted among the population as a parting gift, so that for a few hours they had plenty of flour, dried vegetables and frozen goose. Half the cabmen had gone home to villages, after selling their horses to be killed for meat. Horse-meat now was a recognized article of diet, even in many families that were once well to do. Day after day one saw horses fall in the street and gathering around them were doleful crowds of idle onlookers willing to see them die. The bodies of these horses lay in the snow unburied for days. All sledges, motor-cars, and lorries had already been requisitioned for the evacuation, their movements for the week constituting almost the sole traffic of a once great industrial center.[10]

By March 10 Trotzky had followed another minister with his resignation. Of the Bolshevist triumvirate only Lenine was now left. Whether Lenine was consciously a German agent, receiving money for what he did, or whether he was only a fanatic unconsciously doing Germany's work, was of small consequence, since the work he had done was of the same character in either case. From the beginning Lenine had worked indefatigably, unswervingly, to do everything that Germany needed to have done. He found the army becoming demoralized and he destroyed it; he found the people anxious for peace and he led them swiftly to the most shameful kind of peace that could be framed. If he was only a fanatic, then no fanatic in history ever worked such swift ruin on so vast a scale. The idea of those clown-and-harlequin negotiations at Brest-Litovsk, however, was Trotzky's; that dismally comic figure had conceived a notion that a mouse could safely play with a cat; that he, the prolific and omniscient soap-box orator and newspaper writer of East Side New York, could discomfit the massed militarism of Germany by a negotiation which, on his part, consisted of smart repartees and clever speeches. When Trotzky came to the end of his game of mouse and cat he drew back from its frightful consequences and talked of fighting. Not soon would history forget the brisk, sleek and knowing cockney, jauntily stepping forward to confront the German war colossus and worst it with witty turns of phrase and confident similes. And the nimble adventurer actually got back into office.

While the Entente Allies were "nibbling" at the German line from the North Sea to Switzerland, the Teutonic Powers took another step in exploitation of the East. Their advance guards entered Odessa, the principal Russian port on the Black Sea and the center of a great agricultural

[10] Harold Williams in a dispatch from Petrograd to *The Times* (New York).

GERMANY'S OCCUPATION OF RUSSIAN TERRITORY

In the above map the territory in black is that to which Russia, under
Lenine and Trotzsky at Brest-Litovsk on March 3, 1918, renounced all territorial rights. The German army at that time was also holding territory as
far east as the black line from Pskov to Homel. Kieff and Odessa were
afterward occupied by the Germans and the Ukraine further invaded, the
Crimea being occupied

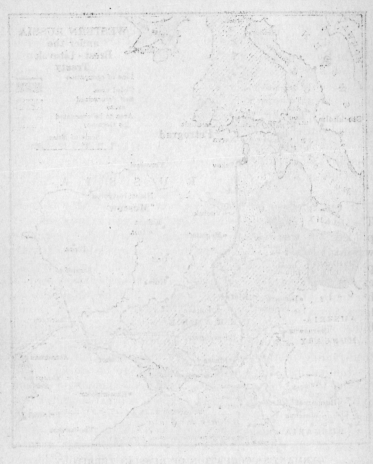

section, the products of which were desired for the hungry peoples of the Central Empires. The capture of Odessa meant to the German imagination something more—an advance over the northern route to Persia, the Persian Gulf and Afghanistan, and possibly to India, in spite of the fact that the British in Mesopotamia had severed the famous Berlin-Bagdad route via Asia Minor. Odessa was the fourth city of Russia in population and the largest shipping point of the country. Its population was 631,040 in 1912, nearly one-third of whom were Jews. Its situation near the great waterways of the Dnieper and the Dniester made it the natural outlet for the exports of the southwestern provinces. Here the Central Powers would be in touch with some of Russia's stored-up wheat, provided any supplies existed; for Odessa was the one Russian city equipped with grain elevators.

It remained to be discovered how much wheat was there. The idea of an unprecedentedly large reserve was soon exploded; it was based on certain absurd trade estimates which pictured Russia, in the face of a breakdown of transportation, a depleted labor market, and the blockade of an export trade which had frequently absorbed one-third of her peace time crops, as raising in all the war years as large harvests as she had raised before. The strong probability was that Russian wheat production had been steadily and rapidly diminishing—a presumption which the known food-famine in the Russian cities quite bore out. Even if production had continued large there were no storage facilities in Russia for more than a moderate amount. Broomhall, the Liverpool grain-trade expert, estimated that northern Russia was bare of supplies and that the Ukraine might have 40,000,000 bushels left, but even this figure was in the nature of the case largely guess work. Supposing it to be correct, only a part could be stored up in Odessa. Chicago, the largest of all grain-storage centers, had elevator capacity for no more than 55,000,000 bushels, and Odessa's capacity was much smaller. Furthermore, we were approaching the end of the grain marketing season of southern Russia, and in a season of famine demand at that. Forty million bushels would not go far toward feeding Russia herself until the

July harvest. The country's own consumption of wheat in a single month in time of peace ran close to that figure. In March the semi-official Berlin correspondent of the Cologne *Gazette* telegraphed a warning against exaggerated hopes of food from Ukraine. He said the country was very unsettled, and it would take a long time to organize a transport system. All the big estates had been wrecked, and all their seed-corn pillaged. The only people who had any stocks were peasants, and they were suspicious of the German soldiery and unwilling to sell except in exchange for the hard cash of the old Czarist *régime,* since they did not trust the new Russian paper currency, or for German products which they might need, but which it would take some time for Germany to provide. The correspondent urged great patience and skepticism about reports of food to be had for Ukraine.

Lenine and his Government reached Moscow on March 11 and thus revived the ancient city's eminence as a capital city, an eminence which Peter the Great had taken from it 215 years before when he went north to build a new city at the mouth of the Neva. Never had any government moved with less pomp, unless it was the government of Peter himself, who, like Lenine, had a genial disregard for non-essentials. After Lenine's arrival the hall of the National Hotel was seen piled up with unimaginable rags and tatters of baggage, bedding rolled into blankets, tatter-demalion baskets and battered trunks. Lenine himself, the man with the most influence over his own followers, dominated this scene—calm, fearless, and without a guard. Moscow had been badly scarred by the revolution. Corner houses, and sometimes the whole side of a street, had been pitted with bullet-holes. The Italian gate of the Kremlin was badly battered by shell-fire. Below a sacred picture on the gate, still hung an inscription declaring that, in the raid of Napoleon in 1812, the picture had survived undamaged as by special provision of the Almighty. Half the shop-windows were boarded up. Many had windows with half a dozen bullet holes; others were patched up with paper. All the Kremlin gates except one were closed. Huge stores of ammunition were deposited inside, and hundreds of ammunition carts, which went far to turn the old fortress of Ivan the Terrible into a new fortress of the revolution.

The All-Russian Congress of Soviets on meeting in Moscow on March 16, by a vote of 453 to 30, decided to ratify the peace treaty with the Central Powers and then dissolved, but the Germans did not cease their inroads into Russia's richest territory in the south. Nikolaiev, the great navy-yard city northeast of Odessa, the headquarters of the High Com-

RUSSIAN SOLDIERS RETURNING TO THE FRONT IN THE
EARLY SUMMER OF 1917

mand of the Russian Black Sea fleet, was taken. Situated at the mouth of the Bug River its capture gave the Germans a water route of value through the rich agricultural country from Volhynia to the Euxine. That peace terms had been offered at this time to Great Britain was inferred from several significant statements. Lord Robert Cecil, when asked if proposals "had been received for a peace at the expense of Russia," answered that "no such proposals are being considered or will be considered." It was admitted that offers of peace had been made to Serbia by Austria-Hungary and Bulgaria, but Serbia had refused to consider them. The attitude of the American Government was directly in line with the statement of Lord Robert Cecil.

Altho the All-Russian Congress of Soviets had ratified the peace treaty, everybody in Russia realized that the agreement was purely temporary. About eighty of the Bolshevik delegates did not vote. The Social Revolutionaries of the Left announced that they "would not share the responsibility of putting the peace conditions into effect." The general character of the meeting at which ratification was decided upon was not that of serious debate, the real work of persuasion having been already done in private factional meetings. Not a single speaker suggested that the peace could be anything but transitory. A prominent Bolshevist said: "Our hope now is in Hindenburg and Ludendorff. If they are puffed up by their success in the east and are refused an agreement in the west, then the war will continue and the eventual victory of the revolution is assured."

Notwithstanding that peace with Germany had been ratified, the German advance in Russia continued, evacuation of Petrograd having served only to change the German objective to Moscow. Germans were moving toward Moscow from three directions, southwest, west, and northwest. The Soviet Government was rapidly disarming and disbanding the old army and eliminating its influence from public affairs, but old soldiers at many places were found unwilling to surrender their arms and return to work. When at Petrograd three regiments refused to be demobilized, the Bolshevik Red Guards entered the barracks, surprized the sleeping soldiers, seized their arms and forced them to leave the city, stating that these regiments were under influences contrary to the revolutionary movement, that they were lazy and undisciplined and refused to assist in guard duty.

In explanation of the evacuation of Petrograd, the Soviet issued a statement saying the commissioners had gone to Moscow to save Petrograd from destruction, believing that the removal would demonstrate the strength of the Russian people's government, and show the Germans that capture of the capital would be useless, as the Government was prepared to fall back constantly before an advance, resisting and slowing down the onslaught. The evacuation of Petrograd began in the second week of March. Trotzky had announced that "the leaders of the revolution were prepared to fall back even to the Ural Mountains." Moscow was to become the new capital, and Petrograd proclaimed a free port. All State institutions would be transferred to Moscow, Nizhni-Novgorod, and Kaza. When the population of Petro-

BOLSHEVIKI SHARPSHOOTERS

grad began once more to quit the city, many transportation difficulties were met with. All roads leading from Petrograd were crowded with all sorts of vehicles.

Roumania was now on the point of effecting a separate peace with the Teutonic allies, meeting hard demands exacted in return for a cessation of Teutonic inroads into the little kingdom, now absolutely isolated from its Allies. A preliminary peace treaty had been signed by March 7, and the armistice extended so that discussion of a formal treaty might begin. Among the chief demands was the cession of the Dobrudja, rectification of the Hungarian-Roumanian border, certain great economic advantages for the Central Powers and unmolested passage for troops through Moldavia and Bessarabia to Odessa.

The anti-German feeling in Ukraine soon showed itself in the difficulties the Germans had in collecting grain. Small bands of revolutionaries sometimes were able to seize and make away with whole trains of food, already on the way to Germany. An endless series of sporadic peasant risings occurred which made it unsafe for the Germans to move except in considerable companies. Arrests were made by various associations of persons who were prominent in helping the Germans. The net result showed the anti-Germanism of the bulk of the Ukrainian population and further that they would look, not to their own bourgeoisie for salvation, but to Russia. The Germans found they had camped in a hornets' nest.[11]

When the Committee of the Soviet Associations declined the humiliating terms offered for acceptance at Brest-Litovsk, General Hoffmann had declared that German troops would continue to advance till peace was concluded. The committee then yielded to *force majeure,* and the treaty was signed on March 2. By its terms the state of war was declared at an end, and the belligerent nations concerned "resolved henceforth to live in peace and friendship together." Russia agreed to evacuate the territories that had been taken from her and refrain from any interference in their internal affairs, leaving "Germany and Austria to decide their future fate in agreement with their populations." The practical effect of this treaty, if its provisions could be finally enforced, so far as European Russia was concerned, was to give Germany military and economic control over Finland, Livonia, Esthonia, Poland, and the Ukraine. The ceded territory amounted to about 435,000 square miles, with a population of between fifty-five and sixty millions. Petrograd was the only port left to Russia on the Baltic Sea, and there seemed a likelihood of this port eventually coming under German control. Russia also engaged not only to complete the evacuation of Anatolia, but to cede to Turkey the districts

---

[11] Moscow dispatch from Arthur Ransome to *The Times* (New York).

of Ardahan, Kars, and Batum. Russia was not to interfere in the reorganization of the constitutional and international conditions of these districts, but was to "leave it to the population of these districts to carry out the reorganization in agreement with the neighboring States, particularly Turkey."

This article gave back to Turkey the whole of the territory which was taken from her in 1878 by the Treaty of Berlin, and had great significance as far as Great Britain was concerned. The Germans now had direct railway access to the Caspian Sea, and German newspapers were talking of "Germanizing" the strategical railway extending from Krasnovodsk to Tashkent along the northern frontiers of Persia, Afghanistan, and Kashmir, with lines to Kushk, Termez, and Marghilan. The Tiflis-Julfa railway was open to Tabriz, and the British position in Mesopotamia was imperilled. A "shorter cut" to India than the route by the Bagdad railway was opened to Germany. In fact, the Russian menace to India removed by the Anglo-Russian Convention in 1908 had been transferred to Germany—so at least Germans fondly assured one another.

"In southwestern Finland we have overwhelmingly defeated the enemy during a five days' battle near Lakhti and Tavasthus, capturing 20,000 prisoners," said the German official communication issued on May 3. This defeat, by the Germans, of the Bolshevist Red Guard with the loss of 20,000 prisoners, coming on the heels of the victory of the White Guard, or Finnish Government forces, at Viberg, on April 1, apparently freed the former Grand Duchy from Bolshevist influence and placed it under German dominance. German influence had always been strong in Finland, due to the fact that before the war thousands of Finns went annually over into East Prussia for the logging season, and returned with marks and German Kultur. Of the entire population, however, of 4,000,000, including 3,000,000 Finns, there were only about 2,000 Germans to 500,000 Swedes and 8,000 Russians. Finland had been the first of the countries of Russia to declare her independence of the Petrograd Government after the Bolshevist *coup d'état* of November 7, 1917. Indeed, independence had already been voted by the Landtag as early as October, when the Provisional Government, then under Kerensky, abolished the legislative functions of the Landtag and ordered a new election. All through the peace game played at Brest-Litovsk, in December and January, a new Government was being organized at Helsingfors with a military force under General Mannerheim. This force, as soon as it came in contact with the invading Red Guard on the road between Viborg and Petrograd, toward the last of January, became known as the White Guard.

Significant facts were cited as showing Russian conditions. In a single day in Kief 1,048 Russian soldiers had been murdered by a Bolshevist mob. Many other murders had occurred in Petrograd, and not a single conviction had been secured for them. Courts had been abolished. There were "rump" trials, where anybody in the audience had the privilege of testifying, asking questions or making speeches. In the streets of Petrograd former generals in uniform could be seen selling newspapers, while ladies in sealskin coats were shoveling snow. Bolshevist soldiers stood by laughing gleefully at such scenes. People who were formerly well-to-do had been reduced to menial employment. Many noblewomen begged food from house to house. The orgies on Russian ships in various ports were said to beggar description. Officers were murdered by their men, and men took possession of the vessels. Former royal yachts were scenes of revels in which the basest passions had free rein. The black flag and the skull and crossbones were flying over the fortress of Peter and Paul.

No sooner was the treaty with Ukraine signed than Germany sent an army into the coast provinces and took over full control of Odessa and Sebastopol. She then fortified her hold by seizing the capital, Kief, and placing the country under German military rule. She arrested members of the Cabinet and Rada, whom she considered unfavorable to her, and set up a government in which there was not one Ukrainian serving in a ministerial capacity. The excuse offered for this severity was that the "Government was too weak." Its weakness, however, as disclosed in the official statement, consisted in its inability to supply

Germany with cereal products. The Central Powers had demanded the entire store of some of the grains and 85 per cent. of the wheat. Peasant farmers refused to accede to these demands and arose in revolt. In repressing these up-risings German troops killed many of the inhabitants and seized all food stores in rebellious districts.

No other sentence in President Wilson's Red Cross Speech in New York on May 18, 1918, was so enthusiastically applauded as this: "So far as I am concerned, I intend to stand by Russia as well as by France." No problem of the

RUSSIANS FIRING ON POLICE IN PETROGRAD
The police at this time were supporting the reactionary element

war had become more intricate and difficult of solution than this Russian problem; and yet, unless it was solved, the war would have been practically lost, because in its opportunity to exploit a broken and helpless Russia, Pan-Germanism had found a prize beyond its wildest dreams of conquest when the war began. It was easy for us to see how we could help France, because France was mostly intact and could help herself. We had only to supply her with her deficiencies in her long battle against Prussianism, to send her men and supplies and provide money to the limit of our ability, all of which was relatively simple. We not only knew what to do, but we were rapidly learning how to do it with the least delay and the greatest efficiency.

But Russia was a problem peculiar to Russia. There was no Government in the country with which we could co-operate. There was no Government that invited, or would accept, our co-operation. If it had been a question of sending troops to reinforce Russian troops, if it had been a question of furnishing supplies to make good Russia's shortage, or if it had been a question of lending money to a people impoverished by bad government and by war, that would have been a simple matter. In dealing with Russia, there was seemingly no place in which to begin. One fact, however, was plain; a defeated German autocracy, a Germany whose military power and prestige had been broken, would not be able to enslave Russia, would not be able to hold vast Russian provinces in subjection, would not keep Russia in vassalage and exploit her population and resources in preparation for another and greater war for German conquest.

There were excellent reasons for believing that Germany's next peace proposal would involve generous terms in the west in exchange for a free hand in the east. Had the Allies been deluded into accepting such terms they would have lost the war. They would have given the future peace of the world into Germany's hands as a hostage. The saving of Russia from the grip of Prussianism had become an essential part of any peace plan worthy of consideration by the Entente Allies. Had it not been for the fighting of Russian soldiers early in the war, Germany might have won on the Western Front. Russia had suffered 8,000,000 casualties, and in the soil of that stricken land were the graves of 2,000,000 Russian soldiers. The Russians had fought when they had no guns, had faced Germans when armed with knives or spades, and they did not give up until they were dead or wounded. When the great collapse occurred, there was only one surgeon at the front for each 4,000 soldiers.

All revolutions have had certain features in common. In

all there was the same blotting out of the past, the same confidence that the world could be started anew with a clean sheet, the same orgy of disheveled idealism, the same dissolution of the structure of society. The future of a revolution depends upon the shaping elements which it may contain of a new world order. Nature will not tolerate a vaccum. The old must be replaced by a new, and the new must be of the same quality as the old—in that it is an organization which will integrate and direct the nation. The fatal weakness of Russia's condition was that there was no such organization. Her revolution had come, not from the burning inspiration of new faith, but from sheer weariness. She had lost nerve and heart; was tired in mind and body. It was instructive to remember how different was the case of France after 1789. There it had been the movement of a whole people inspired by a definite creed of life, a people which knew, however crudely, what it wanted, and was determined to achieve certain positive results. In Russia it was simply an automatic crumbling of old things, leaving the great mass of the population with no object to strive for. In France the leaders of the Revolution had been essentially Frenchmen of that stubborn middle-class which could create and continue to provide a force of social persistence. Some of them were mad, like Marat and Robespierre, but the majority were soldiers, lawyers, and men of affairs who could govern other men.

In Russia there was no such dependable middle-class. The men who alone had a policy were International Anarchists and Socialists, whose creed was one of furious negations. Again, the French Revolution did not come upon a tired France. It broke down old barriers, and released a flood of energy which naturally fell into military channels. Its laws may have been harsh and cruel, but it was an organization and presently it took shape in a formidable army. In Russia war-weariness made each step in her Revolution movements away from the discipline of soldiers, while she was in the midst of a struggle of life and death. France acquired from her Revolution a new and deep consciousness of nationality, but Russia lost what little she had possest. The autocracy had held in formal union elements different in race, speech, religion, and social tradition. With its disappearance the great Empire began to split up like the ice on a lake when the binding spell of frost is withdrawn. The ideals of the new leaders were cosmopolitan, and there was no real nationalism to set against them.

Lenine, otherwise Ulianov, was a scion of a noble house in the Simbirsk district, who, after his elder brother's death on the gallows for complicity in a Nihilist plot, had become an active leader in revolutionary propaganda. From 1900 onward he was in Switzerland, where he created the extreme left wing of the Social Democrats. From 1905 to 1907 he was in Russia, where he found the reform party not yet ripe for his intransigence. His chance did not come till the outbreak of the Revolution, when he was permitted by the German Government to journey overland from Switzerland to Petrograd. He was in his own way the most consistent politician alive, for he had never wavered from the creed of destruction which he had formulated at seventeen, and which now, at the age of forty-six, he had a chance to put into practise. He accepted German assistance and German gold, but he had as little love for the Hohenzollerns as he had for the Romanoffs. He held his somber faith with the passion of a dervish, and, without sense of humor or proportion, set about rebuilding the world after his own crude patterns. But in the nature of things he could not live to see any new structure rise; his part had to be to destroy the old social system everywhere, that the poor and opprest might at least be free of the taskmasters. Such a creed was not without a somber greatness, and beyond doubt Lenine was a single-hearted fanatic, without fear or self-seeking, merciful and gentle in the common relations of life, but pitiless in the service of his cause. He knew that for him there was no hope; sooner or later he would go down in the ruin he had made; but he was content if those who came after him to carry the last fort should find his body prostrate by the wall.

This Russian tale was too pitiful to linger over. The brethren of men who had conquered at Rawa Ruska and Przasnysz, who had carried out the greatest retreat in all history, who had fought with clubs, fists and sword-bayonets when they had no rifles, whose resolution no weight of artillery could daunt, and whose ardor no privations could weaken, who had come in their simple hardihood to the pinnacle of martial greatness—had now sunk into a mob of selfish madmen, forgetful of their old virtues and babbling of uncomprehended pedantries. Most pitiful was the case of those who still remained true to their faith, and were murdered or trodden down by a panic-stricken horde, and of officers who loved their men like children, and saw their life's work ruined and themselves engulfed in a common

© UNDERWOOD & UNDERWOOD, N. Y.

A RUSSIAN GENERAL URGING HIS MEN TO CONTINUE THE WAR

shame. No great deed, it is true, can wholly fail. The exploits of Russia during the first years of the war could never die. Their memory would surely survive to be a treasure and an inspiration for the Russia yet to be. But at the moment, to Brusiloff and his heartbroken captains, who strove during those awful days to stay the rout in the Galician valleys, it seemed that a horror of great darkness had fallen upon the world, and that the best life blood of their country had been idly shed.[12]

[12] Principal Sources: The London *Times'* "History of the War"; The *Times,* The *World,* The *Evening Post,* New York; "Nelson's History of the War" by John Buchan—principally derived from John Buchan's superb narrative.

V

RUSSIA'S EFFORTS TO RIGHT HERSELF—ALLIED
INTERVENTION AND THE CZECHO-SLOVAKS—
BOLSHEVIKI TYRANNY, THE CZAR'S FATE
AND THE ADVANCE OF KOLCHAK AND
DENIKIN'S DON COSSACKS

June 20, 1918—June, 1919

IT was now demonstrated that Russia could not be restored to the independence which Germany, with help from the Bolsheviki, had taken from her, except through an Entente victory. From Germany Russia had nothing to gain, except continued oppression. Nor had Russia anything to gain from a negotiated peace, except further subjection to Germany. Therefore, if the Allies intervened in Russia, either with a military force, or with a purely economic one, or with both, it had to be for the distinct purpose of building up again an eastern Allied war-front. Situated as she was behind a strong natural barrier, from which it was doubtful if the western Allies alone could drive her, Germany wanted and sought peace, and really had to have peace if she was ever to develop the Russian territory she had seized. She could afford to give up Alsace-Lorraine and all of Belgium, including even the iron and coal lands of northern France, provided she could retain enough territory in Russia to get control of Russia's vast mineral resources. In fact, she could afford to pay with one hand an indemnity for having ravished Belgium, if she could take the money with the other hand out of Russia. She sought peace on such terms only—Alsace-Lorraine to go to France, Belgium to be restored, and she to have a free hand in the east. The only course that seemed left for the Entente, under the circumstances, was to rebuild the Russian front through an intervention seeking to restore the eastern frontier, for Germany could not be allowed to have Russia for exploitation after the war.

REVOLUTION, BREST-LITOVSK, AND BOLSHEVIKI

Late in June it became known that a serious revolt had occurred at Kief. Artillery stores had been exploded, there was continuous street fighting, and the revolt spread to the Poltava and Chernigof districts. Forty thousand peasants armed and organized had participated in the uprising. A real revolt of peasants about Moscow and Kief, the chief city of the Ukraine, had long been regarded by friends of Russia as practically the only means of saving the country. The peasants comprised more than 90 per cent. of the population, and if they had been even partially organized and provided with any kind of leadership, they could before this have swept the Germans out of Russia. It was recalled that Napoleon had easy going in Russia until the peasants were aroused by the burning of Moscow. The action of the Germans in taking away land which the peasants had preempted, and in levying upon them forced contributions of grain and other products, had been the best way possible for driving them into revolt.

The Ukrainian Government, set up by the German military pro-consul, von Eichhorn, was finding that to do Germany's bidding was difficult, if not perilous. Obstinate peasants would not empty their granaries to feed Austria-Hungary and Germany, but would instead burn their stores of grain and let their fields lie untilled. There had been mutterings of discontent ever since the mirage of a Ukrainia for the Ukrainians, as conjured up at Brest-Litovsk, had vanished into dreams and a nightmare. The illusions of "self-determination" had lasted only until a German task-master could get installed in Kief and German food collectors could "get busy." Even the government which had sold the Ukraine into German servitude had been overthrown and a new and more pliant government established, propt up by German bayonets, and now this second *régime* was faced by a peasant revolt so serious as to make necessary a demand on Berlin for armored cars and troops with which to tranquilize the country.

Germany, when she no longer had to fight organized Russian troops, had shifted most of her eastern divisions to France, where Ludendorff was making his last gambler's throw in the 1918 offensive, but she now found that she had to fight chaos not only in parts of Russia which she had appropriated, but in the bulk of the old Romanof Empire which she had turned over to Lenine and Trotzky. The order which she had set up in Poland, in the Ukraine and in the Black Sea region could not stand on its own feet, but had to be backed up by military force. And with demands for man-power in the West and on the Italian Front, every new division sent back into Russia represented a dispersion of German energy. At Brest-Litovsk Germany had over-reached herself. She had created a running sore, had fomented a reign of anarchy which she could not safely flee from, and which it would cost her a great waste of military effort to exorcise. Russia was still a peril to Germany. The Ukraine had got into a state of countrywide revolution. The Germans had sent in reinforcements, which reached a total at one time of thirty-five divisions (420,000 men), while the peasants had only several small armies of from 15,000 to 20,000 each. Korniloff, former Commander-in-Chief of the Russian Army, and one of the anti-Bolsheviki leaders, offered what was left of his army to oppose the Germans, making the one proviso that negotiations should be opened with the Entente, who, he believed, would help in expelling the Germans.

Stirring scenes took place at this time during a Pan-Soviet Congress at Moscow, the German Ambassador, Count von Mirbach, occupying one box and representatives of the Allies another. A delegate from the Ukraine rose and denounced German Imperialism and its influence, two hundred and fifty members cheering him wildly, while Mirbach and his suite sat stiffly erect. "The Germans have come to the Ukraine," the delegate said, "to obtain bread, but they won't get it. Whenever the Germans have loaded trains, we have blown them up, and have treated likewise all artillery and magazines in the Ukraine. The Germans sought to transfer huge aviation machinery from Odessa and Niko-laieff to the Krupp Works, but we blew it up. The Germans will be wiped out in the Ukraine. They already have paid in thousands of lives for their tyranny." "Down with Mirbach!" cried other delegates; "Down with the lackeys of Mirbach—the Bolsheviki!" Another speaker charged the recent surrender of the Russian Black Sea Fleet to Germany, as virtual treason, and, turning to Mirbach, said: "Revolutionary Russia and the Ukraine will no longer remain passive. These contemptible dogs of despots are strangling our brothers in the Ukraine." After this the entire audience made an anti-Mirbach demonstration, shouting: "Away with these robbers! Throw them out." Early in July Mirbach was assassinated in Moscow.

What would the arrogant government in Berlin do to Russia now? While all the world was wondering about it, a semi-official announcement came from Berlin that Russia was "doing all that was possible to punish the murderers." Men recalled after this statement that in June, 1914, Serbia had been ready to do all that was possible to aid in punishing the murderers of the Austrian Archduke, assassinated at Sarajevo; in fact, she was prepared to go to any lengths short of abdicating her sovereignty to assist the Austro-Hungarian Government in bringing the criminals to justice, despite the fact that

COUNT VON MIRBACH

Mirbach was appointed German Ambassador to Russia after the negotiation of the Brest-Litovsk Treaty. His tyrannical ways exasperated the Russians and he was assassinated

the actual murder was not committed upon Serbian soil, but upon Austro-Hungarian soil and by a subject of Austria-Hungary. But Serbia's readiness met with no more sympathetic response in Berlin than it did in Vienna, simply because Germany's preparations for a great war were then complete, and the opportunity to strike had come. Murder, and particularly a political murder, had then to be avenged in the name of "Deutschland" and "Weltmacht," and so the world had been plunged into this maelstrom of blood and destruction.

IN THE EAST, NEAR EAST, AND SOUTH

It was different with assassination in Russia in 1918. Altho the German Ambassador at Moscow was killed on Russian soil and by Russians, the Soviet Government was not held responsible, nominally because the crime was committed by political opponents of the Bolsheviki, but in reality because such action did not accord with the military policies of the German Government. The Bolsheviki were in effect Allies, and the difficulties of Germans in holding Russian territory were increasing from day to day. Assassination to the German mind was a crime to be dealt with ruthlessly or not, according to the effect that it might have upon the strategic policies of the German Government. If a war was wanted assassinations could be made to promote war, but if one had more war on his hands than he could conveniently attend to, a political murder could safely be left to the ordinary processes of justice.

Former Austro-Hungarian prisoners, Czecho-Slovaks, who had been interned in the heart of Siberia, had now armed and organized themselves to aid the cause of the Entente. While the Allied Governments had been debating the question of military intervention, these Czecho-Slovaks, driven by necessity, had effectively intervened until they had so far got control of vital parts of the Siberian railroads, as to have made any Allied intervention which might come later more than a mere parade from Vladivostok to the Ural Mountains. Czecho-Slovaks had possession not only of Vladivostok, but west of Lake Baikal were reported in undisputed possession of the Siberian Railroad and to have crossed into Russia proper, taking Ekaterinburg, on the eastern slope of the Urals. In fact, they had carried the frontier from which the Allies could exert military pressure to deGermanize Russia, to points more than 5,000 miles west of Vladivostok with only a relatively short section of the Siberian Railroad—that between the Chinese Border and Lake Baikal—remaining in the hands of the Bolsheviki.

Dispatches from Tokio and Peking announced at this time the creation of a new Siberian State to fight the Central Powers, establish a Constitutional Assembly and restore law and order. The flag consisted of two stripes of white and green, the former representing the vast snow covering of

362

Siberian plains, the latter the verdure of Siberian forests. The program included the liberation of Siberia from the Bolsheviki, the avoidance if possible of foreign intervention, the establishment of provincial councils, and a labor bureau, and the distribution of land among those possessing none, as well as control of economic activities. Siberia was thus to become the first democratic State in Russian history, and would have been set up by foreigners. The new government was to fight the Central Powers. The people to a man sup-

ALLIED SOLDIERS IN VLADIVOSTOK
In this group are American, British, French, Japanese and Czech soldiers

ported the new *régime*. A defeat of the Bolsheviki in Western Siberia occurred late in June, and forced them to evacuate Irkutsk. The counter-revolution, assisted by the Czecho-Slovaks, soon spread over other parts of Siberia.

People occupying the Kola Peninsula on the Murman coast in the north, about this time broke loose from the Bolsheviki, refused to be bound by the Brest-Litovsk treaty, and declared their loyalty to the Allies. Little by little different localities were thus breaking away from the central government and establishing local governments of their own, which they declared independent of the Soviets. These bands of independents, however, were entirely disjointed, with no organization of their own for the purpose of local administration. Kola, bounded by the northern tip of the Scandinavian Peninsula, the Arctic Ocean, and the White Sea, contains the town of Kola on Kola Bay, which port, by virtue of the vagaries of the Gulf Stream, is open all the year round, while Archangel, further south on the White Sea, is open only in summer months. Kola was the terminus of the new railroad, constructed since the war began, to establish direct communication from the sea to the interior by a line open all the year. The Allies here had an open base, giving them local protection, and saving thousands of miles of travel.

The supplies they had sent to Archangel were therefore now under a certain degree of protection. The Bolsheviki had been doing all in their power to seize them, and there had been considerable fighting in the general region of the White Sea port. Since the beginning of the war $750,000,000 worth of materials had been sent from this country to Archangel and Kola. In 1917 shipments to Archangel and Kola totalled $314,630,000, most of which remained there still. Including materials sent to Vladivostok, America had sent goods to Russia, altogether, to the value of $1,080,000,000 since the war began. Fear as to hostile developments in Russia was becoming a palpable thing in Germany. For months no unwelcome news from Russia had been published in Germany, the people being kept in ignorance of the situation. Letters from occupied districts, however, did not hide the feeling that existed against the Germans. The Bolsheviki were becoming more and more isolated, largely due to hatred of the Brest-Litovsk peace. Anti-German feeling had been growing as a consequence of this treaty.

On July 22 news came that the former Czar Nicholas had been shot in Siberia by order of the Bolshevists, who feared that the Czecko-Slovaks were advancing to rescue him. His execution, as contemporary accounts described it, was carried out in a manner that caused regret among people sincerely sympathetic with the Revolution. Shunted from place to place, apparently often maltreated, and at last condemned by a local Soviet, he had suffered the fate of Louis XVI., without that open and reasonably fair opportunity to present his case that was accorded to the French monarch. Late in December, 1918, came a dispatch from Carl W. Ackerman,[13] dated at Ekaterinburg, giving a "detailed account of the Czar's end." An eye-witness represented what was thought to have been Nicholas intriguing with military leaders for the restoration of the monarchy, and that discovery of this plot by the Ural District Soviet had caused an order to

INTERIOR OF A CHURCH IN SUWALKI IN RUSSIAN POLAND

be given for his execution. But whether he was actually shot was "a mooted question in Ekaterinburg which will never be definitely solved until the Czar or his body is found." Meanwhile he was considered dead, altho all the members of his family might be still alive.

This account came from Parfen Alexeievitch Dominin, who for 21 years had served the Czar as major-domo, accompanied him into exile and remained with him until the early hours of the morning of July 17, when the Czar was

[13] Correspondent of The *Times* (New York).

led away by Bolshevist soldiers. Report after report, each different from others, continued to be printed until weeks after the war ended. Early in January, 1919, an account came from an "official" witness who described [14] an Imperial pyre, the ashes of which contained shoe buckles, corset-steels, crosses and diamonds, "but no bones." Doubt rose as to whether the bodies of the Imperial Family had been burned at all, some saying they were buried, others that they were thrown into a lake. Whatever disposition had been made of the body, or bodies, there seemed little conflict in contemporary testimony that the Czar, if not the whole Royal Family, had been put to death. History, however, might have to be content with an inconclusive verdict. Claimants to being Nicholas Romanoff, the former Czar, might rise up just as had been the case with the Dauphin of the Revolution, and Marshal Ney.

From the first the Allies had made it clear that they did not intend to recognize the Brest-Litovsk treaty. It had been forced upon the Russ'ans, was based on the idea of conquest, and distinctly contemplated the dismemberment and exploitation of Russia. Thus it was of the essence of that militarism which the war was being fought to extirpate. If the treaty stood, the whole Allied program for a league of Nations, and for the right of nations, great and small, to self-determ'nation, would be brought to the ground. In Russia itself the treaty was soon stoutly opposed. In May, 1918, the Inter-party Council of the All-Russian Constituent Assembly made a declaration that the treaty was "not recognized," and that Russia was, and continued to be, "in a state of war with Germany." Dispatches from Constantinople in July implied that even Turkey, an ally of Germany, d d not intend to be bound by it.

In Germany itself there were significant admissions that the treaty was a failure and a distinct movement set in to have it revised. One of the reasons why Kuhlmann fell into disfavor in July, 1918, and was dismissed from the Foreign Office, was that the treaty wh'ch he thought such a triumph had turned out unsatisfactory and unpopular. Among Germans there had been steadily growing up a

[14] In a cable dispatch to The *World* (New York).

feeling quite apart from any fear that the treaty, in the hostility which it had stirred up among the Russians, was playing into the hands of the Allies, that it was bad in itself and that it ought to be revised in order to make it more tolerable to the Russians. Signs abounded that it was breaking down of its own weight. Not only were Germans discontented with it, but Austria was restless under some of its provisions, and Bulgaria and Turkey were at loggerheads over it. In fact the golden idol of German annexationists was found to have feet of clay, and it was only a question

THE HARBOR OF ODESSA
Odessa was captured by the Germans after they had made
peace with Russia

of time when they would crumble and bring the idol's torso crashing down.

On July 31 Eichhorn, German commander in the Ukraine, and his adjutant, Dressler, were mortally wounded by a bomb, thrown while they were driving to their headquarters from the Casino in the Ukrainian capital, Kief, and died that night. The bomb was thrown from a cab which was driven close to the Field-Marshal's carriage. The assassin and the cab-driver were both arrested. The crime had originated with the Social Revolutionists in Moscow. The assassin, a youth of 23, declared that he came from the province of Ryazan, adjacent to Moscow, on orders from a Committee of the Social Revolutionists to kill the Field-marshal. He had reached Kief that day, having been supplied by the Committee with a bomb, a revolver, and some money. The assassination gave emphasis to Germany's rapidly developing troubles on her Eastern Front. In the Ukraine, with its population of 25,000,000, small landholders had risen in guerrilla revolt against Eichhorn's troops. The occupation of their farms by German troops had been more than the peasants could stand, and they rose to a man against the German invaders. The assassination of Eichhorn was strong indication of the progress made by this guerrilla war. Later reports were that chaos reigned throughout the Ukraine. Rich crops on which Germany had counted strongly were being destroyed in a wholesale manner, and economic production of all kinds was paralyzed. The entire Ukraine had become a hostile battle-ground for Germany.

Only three months before he was murdered, Eichhorn had arrested Ukrainian Ministers on the floor of the Rada, had declared in the Ukraine, "a state of enhanced protection," which meant that all tribunals were superseded by German courts-martial, had arrested men here, dispersed mobs there, and finished by installing a new government under German protection. Eichhorn's assassination and that of Mirbach were proof that there were men in Russia whose detestation of the German conquest was active enough to make them willing to risk their own lives in killing high German officials. Under Eichhorn the Germans had undertaken to force the Ukraine to deliver up the grain with which to feed the hungry in Austria and Germany. Because it turned out that there was not much wheat, to begin with, and that the peasants intended to keep what there was, Eichhorn had taken strong measures to substitute the rule of the German army of occupation for that of the Rada, installed his state of "enhanced protection," filled jails to suit his own notion, and then forced the overturn of the Rada Government in favor of a dictatorship. What had happened was a striking comment on the German incapacity for getting along with other nations. Assassination and peasant rebellions were the result of three months of Eichorn.

In an agreement, reported in July to have been made between the Allies and the Murman Regional Council, were embodied some of the principles which were to prevail in any general plan to help Russia. First of all was economic relief. Food was to be imported for the needy population. Supplies of manufactured goods were also to be brought in, along with material for construction-work in restoring and

THE HARBOR OF VLADIVOSTOK

Allied warships are lying at anchor in the harbor, and in the distance are seen hills which had been fortified

equipping transportation. Whatever steps were taken for military defense were to be at the request and with the co-operation of the Murman people and their local government, and were to have the sole aim of repelling German aggressions. The Allies formally disclaimed any thought of forcible intervention or conquest, and asserted that their only object was "to guard the integrity of the Murman region for a great, united Russia." The United States Government was understood to be a party to this agreement. London

on July 23d heard from Vladivostock that the Provisional
Government in Eastern Siberia had submitted to the Allies
a request for joint military action. There was every hope
that the situation would be liquidated and the danger of
civil war averted.

In President Wilson's long-delayed announcement of his
policy toward Russia, made known on August 5, a former
scheme for a great military expedition through Russian territory was definitely rejected. Mr. Wilson and his advisers
were against it for moral reasons, and also on practical
military grounds. Army authorities at Washington had long
been opposed to the sending of large bodies of troops to
Siberia. They saw in it, first of all, an unwise diversion of
effort. The great battle for Russia was being fought in
France and Flanders, and why dissipate our forces? Besides,
the problem of dispatching and maintaining big armies
across the Pacific was much more easily solved in a club-
corner, or in a letter to a newspaper, than in the offices of
the General Staff. Only "a few thousand soldiers" were to
be sent by the United States and Japan to act as a guard
at Vladivostock, and by France and England, in conjunction
with this country, at Archangel. Emphasis was laid by the
President upon the predominating aim of giving aid to the
Russians "in their present desperate difficulties." These
were economic as well as political—indeed, the political
crisis would not have been so acute but for impending
famine and industrial and commercial demoralization.

A "mission of rescue" was to be sent to Siberia, and to
comprise not only representatives of the Red Cross and the
Young Men's Christian Association, who were skilled in organizing assistance for the wretched and starving, but experts in trade, agriculture and industry, who would place
their services at the disposal of the Russian people. The
latter were to be assured in the most positive manner of our
disinterested motives. Our Government contemplated "no
interference with the political sovereignty of Russia, no intervention in her internal affairs—not even in the local
affairs of the limited areas which her military force may be
obliged to occupy—and no impairment of her territorial
integrity, either now or hereafter." What we were about to

PADEREWSKI, THE POLISH POLITICAL LEADER AND HIS WIFE
Poland had already been recognized by several Powers when the events nar-
rated in adjoining pages were leading apparently to the salvation of Russia

do had for its single and only object "the rendering of such aid as shall be acceptable to the Russian people themselves in their endeavors to regain control of their own affairs, their own territory, and their own destiny." The Japanese Government was to give similar assurance.

Official announcement was made on August 6 of the landing of Allied forces, naval and military, at Archangel. The landing was made in concurrence with the wishes of the Russian population, and created enthusiasm. American troops were among the forces landed, the first detachment including members of the Russian Officers' League. The British Government on August 12 issued a declaration formally recognizing the Czecho-Slovak armies as an Allied force regularly waging warfare against the Central Powers. Problems, intricate and vital, were raised for Allied diplomacy by the British Government's formal recognition of the Czecho-Slovaks as an Allied "nation," and of the Czecho-Slovak forces in Russia, Italy and France as Allied armies. Such an act went further than the British declaration in favor of a Jewish state in Palestine, because Mr. Balfour's declaration that "the British Government views with favor the establishment of a national home for the Jewish people," might mean either independence or autonomy, conceivably even under Turkish rule. The Czecho-Slovaks had their national home already; their soil was a large part of the Austrian Empire, and to recognize them as a "nation" was presumably to recognize their full independence.

The Czecho-Slovaks were Austria's northern Slavs. They stretched in a belt about four hundred miles long, and an average of one hundred deep, from the western frontier of Bohemia to the eastern border of Galicia, with the Czechs, or Bohemians and Moravians, as the western branch, and the Slovaks as the eastern branch. In smaller numbers they were found in Austrian Silesia. A Czecho-Slovak nation would be approximately ten millions strong. Serious enough as the problem of a separation from the Hapsburg monarchy was bound to be, it was rendered more difficult by the fact that the problem affected Hungary as well as Austria proper, for the Slovaks were almost entirely in Hungarian territory. The ordinary antagonism between Hungary and

the American Government was not only in sympathy, but that formal and practical effect had been given to previous declarations of sympathy by recognizing the Czecho-Slovak National Council as a de-facto belligerent government.

The vanguard of the Czecho-Slovak forces from Verchneudinsk, eighty miles east of Lake Baikal, by September 1, had joined the troops of General Semenoff on the Onon River. General Diedrichs was in telegraphic communication

A CROWD GATHERING IN VLADIVOSTOK TO SEE CZECHO-SLOVAK
TROOPS PARADE

with the Trans-Baikal Czechs. There was now an uninterrupted chain of Allied troops from Pensa, on the Volga in Europe, to Vladivostok. Czecho-Slovak recognition as a belligerent nation by the United States, following that of Great Britain, meant a new certainty of national independence for 10,000,000 Czechs and Slovaks inhabiting Bohèmia, Moravia, Austrian Silesia and Slovakia. For long centuries before these people had had no friend on their borders anywhere, completely encircled as they were by immemorial enemies, the Germans and Magyars. Prussia, Saxony, Bavaria, and the Austrian Duchies surrounded them on the north, west and south, Magyar lands on the southeast. Their only neighbors, the Austrian Poles, were bound by ties of traditional friendship to the Magyars, and for forty years had maintained a tacit understanding with the Austrian Germans. Absolutely unaided, the Czech nation had survived the trials of centuries, and it was of the very irony of history that the common war-aim of all who were fighting on the side of the Entente should be closely bound up with the cause of this most isolated of nations, and that the international position of Bohemia after the war should become the truest test of victory. When once a free Bohemian land emerged in the heart of Central Europe, the world would know that the flood of German-Magyar aggression had receded.

Our recognition of the Czecho-Slovaks was purely a war measure, as Lincoln's emancipation act had been. If we had not been at war with Austria, the recognition of one of the nationalities making up her composite empire would not have entered into the imagination of our Government. Judged by the ordinary tests, the Czecho-Slovaks had shown few of the attributes of sovereignty. They had no government except a National Council *in partibus*—and no capital. But they had an army, and it was largely for the sake of this army that recognition was accorded. Czecho-Slovak troops were the mainstay of the Allied military effort in Russia. By admitting their rights as belligerents, the Allies were in a position both to use them and protect them. The Austrian Government could not now go on hanging or shooting them, when captured, as traitors, without exposing itself to reprisals. As to the form of recognition, the American was somewhat different from the one adopted by England, France and Italy. But the effect was the same. The dismemberment of Austria had been disclaimed in 1917 as an object, but now it was implicitly asserted as one. There could be no independent Czecho-Slovak national Government without an Austrian break-up.

While Berlin and the Bolsheviki Government were signing at Moscow treaties confirming and extending Germany's Russian spoliations, the real Russia seemed to be moving toward deliverance. The shadowy authority of the Soviet régime seemed melting. Czecho-Slovak forces had appeared on the outskirts of Nijni-Novgorod, an ancient town in the heart of Great Russia, only about 260 miles northeast of Moscow. They had reached about 150 miles west of their former north-and-south base on the Volga. For a couple of months they had been holding the Volga line from Kasan on the north, through Simbirsk to Samara. The Soviet

THE KAISER IN THE EAST
He is talking with Gen. Conrad von Hötzendorf, the Austrian Commander

Government apparently had lost control of the whole Volga region. Czecho-Slovaks, cooperating with anti-Bolshevist Russians, were making rapid progress toward the Vologda Junction. Marching east from Lake Baikal, they had captured Chita, the capital of Transbaikalia and the chief Red Guard base in that province. This meant that Transbaikalia was nearly cleared of Bolshevist forces, their only line of retreat northeast from Chita, following the Amur branch of the Siberian Railroad into the Amur Province, where they could be isolated and trapt. Japanese and other Allied troops, operating north from Vladivostok, were pushing down the Ussuri Valley toward the Amur. Allied intervention in Russia had thus produced results. The whole fabric of Teutonized Bolshevism seemed threatened with demolition.

A ghastly picture of Russia was painted by Arno Dosch-Fleurot.[16] "Only here, back in civilization where murder is a crime," he said, "do we begin to comprehend how little the world can understand what Russia has come to." The Bolsheviki had instituted a reign of terror "as the only means to maintain the dictatorship, killing without trial or before inquisitional tribunals." Peasants were in revolt everywhere. Every city in Russia witnessed scenes of terror. Conditions were even worse in the provinces. Every man was at every other man's throat. Petrograd had been burning in twelve different places, and there were indiscriminate massacres in the streets. At least 1,000 British subjects had been imprisoned in Petrograd, or been otherwise deprived of their liberty by the Bolshevists. July and August, 1918, were months of horror which never would be forgotten by persons who had seen Russia's two great cities, Petrograd and Moscow, pass through the mad attempt of the Bolsheviki to shoot or imprison all persons who disagreed with their wild efforts to control Russia. Night had been hideous in Moscow for months because of volleys fired by execution squads in military enclosures where prisoners were kept. Foreigners and Russians alike were searched without warrants. Dr. Karl Helfferich, the new German Ambassador at Moscow, had rushed back to Berlin and reported that Moscow was in such a state of anarchy that the Embassy could not stay there. Two attempts were made on his life while he was in Moscow. Shouts were heard in Moscow everywhere, day and night. Motor-lorries filled with armed soldiers dashed madly through the streets with utter disregard for the lives of civilians. It was absurd to compare these conditions to

---

[16] A New York *World* correspondent who reached Stockholm from Russia early in September.

the French Reign of Terror, which, by comparison, was a mild and well-organized system of government.

The year 1918 continued to be a year of chaos, approximating anarchy, with territorial disintegration, rival governments, civil war, famine, pestilence, and industrial stagnation in which Lenine and Trotzky pursued their ruthless way not yet checked. On August 30 two women of the "intellectual class" attempted to assassinate Lenine, but succeeded in merely wounding him. In consequence of this the Bolsheviki began a savage campaign against the "intellectuals," massacring hundreds of them without the formality of arrest

ST. BASIL'S CHURCH IN MOSCOW
During a bombardment of the Kremlin, St. Basil's took fire, but was saved from destruction

and trial, and for several weeks a reign of terror prevailed at Petrograd. It was finally ended for a time by a proclamation of Lenine's on September 26, after several thousand persons had been killed, but a few weeks later violence was resumed and hundreds of former officers were shot, and prisoners generaly put to death "to save food." There were threats that on November 10 there would be a general massacre of the entire bourgeoisie and intellectual classes, but this monstrous scheme, if ever contemplated, was not then carried out. But great atrocities took place later. John A. Embry, American Consul at Omsk, who arrived in New York in July, 1919, gave an account of what had happened in Siberia and Eastern Russia in the last eight months, during practically all of which time he was in charge of American affairs in Kolchak's capital city. He said no language could picture the atrocities that had marked Bolshevist rule in the territories recaptured by Kolchak, a reign of terror marked by murder, violation of women, theft and arson, perpetrated with cruelty unparalleled in the history of civilization. He had photographs to prove what he said, pictures taken by himself or by responsible American Red Cross officials. Men, women and children had been driven into woods and clubbed to death. Public squares had become shambles. Committees, vested with power of life and death, had held orgies of slaughter, giving no pretense of trial. Jails were opened and criminals invited to work their will.

By the third week in September, 1918, ghastly reports of wholesale executions in Russia at the hands of the Bolsheviki had reached the outer world. Some hundreds, perhaps thousands, had perished as if in a massacre. The most awful figure in this Red Terror, the man with the most murder on his soul, was known as the Commissioner Against the Counter-Revolution, a dapper little blond Lett named Peters. He was described as a crouched little man with pale eyes filled with venom, who sat in the Kremlin at Moscow, "where he signed away daily the lives of scores of men he never saw." So soon as any one was declared a counter-revolutionary by a member of the Soviet, Peters ordered him shot without sending him before a revolutionary tribunal. Peters had absolute power of life or death for hundreds

THE FORMER CZARINA AND HER FOUR DAUGHTERS
Left to right—Grand Duchess Olga, Titiana, Marie and Anastasia

in Russia. He had become a mere furious little animal, signing death warrants all day, often not looking to see what he was signing. Once he was seen to sign an order to shoot seventy-two officers without even glancing down at the paper.[17]

It was evident that the French reign of terror was a mild exercise of authority by a government leaning to the side of mercy when compared with what was going on in Russia. It had been reported that 812 persons were executed in a single week by Bolshevist law in Petrograd alone. In Paris, during the Reign of Terror, the total of lives taken by formal execution in seventeen months was 2,596. There had been about a hundred executions before the Reign of Terror began, but counting these, 2,700 would be the outside limit for Paris alone. The Petrograd tribunal had executed in one week 812 persons as against 2,700 executed by the Paris tribunal in seventeen months. With the whole world aghast at these crimes, the American Government, through Secretary of State Lansing, on September 21, sent a communication to all Allied and neutral governments, urging them to take some immediate action in condemnation of these acts of slaughter. This action was taken at the direction of the President, and followed the receipt of definite information in official dispatches describing the reign of terror in Bolshevist Russia. The note urged "some immediate action entirely divorced from the atmosphere of belligerency and the conduct of the war, to impress upon the perpetrators of these crimes the aversion with which civilization regards their present wanton acts."

Even weak-minded people who had seen in Bolshevism merely a characteristically Russian phase of an upward striving of European Democracy, began to recognize it as an essentially evil, wantonly destructive, and cynically despotic thing. The reign of terror which its leaders had instituted in an effort to save their own skins, was the work of men who lived in abject terror of an impending doom. The sanguinary excesses which provoked the indignant protest of President Wilson were a manifestation of Bolsheviki

[17] Stockholm dispatch from Arno Dosch-Fleurot to The *World* (New York).

despair—of struggle against a fate that had been invited, by men as cowardly as they were cruel. The indiscriminate slaughter of Russian citizens, for which the President invoked the abhorrence of all civilized nations, were rightfully reckoned as an addition to the long list of German crimes, for without German support and countenance they could not have been committed.

Proofs removing doubt that Lenine and Trotzky had been paid as German agents in Russia were laid before the world in September by the United States Government in an amaz-

AT GENERAL HARVATH'S HEADQUARTERS IN HARBIN

ing series of official documents disclosed through the Committee on Public Information. These documents not only showed how the German Government, through its Imperial Bank, had paid Lenine, Trotzky, and their immediate associates, to betray Russia into deserting her Allies, but gave added proof that Germany had perfected her plans for a war of world-conquest long before the assassinations at Sarajevo. Before the war was four months old, and more than two years before the United States was drawn into it, Germany had set on foot plans to "mobilize destructive

agents and observers," to cause explosions, strikes and outrages in this country, and planned to employ "anarchists
and escaped criminals" for the purpose. The original documents, including photographs of some of the originals and
typewritten circulars marked "very secret" or "private,"
many of them bearing annotations by Bolshevik leaders, and
containing references to "Comrade Trotzky" or "Comrade
Lenine," were given. Bolshevik leaders had themselves informed their "comrade" that the German Government required the return of the order of the German Imperial Bank
depositing 50,000,000 gold rubles in a Stockholm bank for
Lenine and Trotzky, and that the accounts of the bank were
audited to conceal the payments.

It became clear that the Bolsheviki had ruled Russia
for Germany. There might be something grand about their
villainy, but they had ruled as German agents. As to what
happened at Brest-Litovsk in the winter of 1917-18, there
was now ample proof that a huge nation of amiable but
ignorant people, had been sold out by men who, with German aid, overthrew Kerensky and his Government. Germany's cold purpose was disclosed as having been to use
Russia after the war as a mere province to be exploited for
Germany's commercial gain. Communications had been sent
to Bolshevik leaders by the German Imperial Bank giving
"a complete synopsis of the terms on which Germany intended to have control of all Russian industries."

One of the most hopeful undertakings for the redemption
of Russia had begun in the first half of 1918 at Archangel
under the protection of military and naval forces of the
Allies and by August was formed the "Government of Northern Russia," with Nicholas Tchiakovsky, a revolutionist and
Socialist, as President and Minister for Foreign Affairs. Its
political program comprised the recreation of Russian democratic power, the re-establishment of local self-government
with universal suffrage, a reorganization of the National
Army and a renewal of the war against Germany, with re-
pudiation of the treaty of Brest-Litovsk. Fierce attacks
were made upon this Government by the Bolsheviki, and
for a time it was all but overthrown, but on October 18 it
became fully re-established. A more extensive movement

had begun in Siberia, where during the month of May General Semenoff, an anti-Bolshevist Commander, and Admiral Kolchak, formerly commander of the Black Sea Fleet, set up an independent government beyond Lake Baikal.

On July 14, General Horvath, commander of the anti-Bolshevik Russian forces, appointed at Harbin a provisional War Cabinet for Siberia, with himself as Prime Minister, and associates from among recognized leaders of the Russian people. Meanwhile another government was formed at Omsk, which on July 26 claimed authority over all Siberia, and for a time there seemed danger of disastrous conflict between it and General Horvath's Government. Horvath, on August 25, declared himself a military dictator, and was supported by the troops. On October 2 the Czecho-Slovaks prevented an attempted *coup d'état* at Omsk, and by October 7 the Horvath and Omsk Governments were amicably merged into one, but on November 19, a *coup d'état* occurred, when three of the five directors arrested their two colleagues and proclaimed Admiral Kolchak dictator and commander of the All-Russian Army and Navy. Against this action General Semenoff vigorously protested, but by December 21 he had agreed to recognize Kolchak as dictator, provided the latter would retire in favor of General Denikin, the Hetman of the Don Cossacks, as soon as a junction of the Cossack and Siberian forces could be effected. The German power in the Ukraine gradually waned, but the country remained in a disturbed and almost chaotic condition until November 20, when a strong anti-German and anti-Bolshevik force of Cossacks, friendly to the All-Russian Government, marched in from Astrakhan, expelled the Ukrainian National Assembly and established a Provisional Government. This hopeful movement was under General Denikin.

Encouraging as the movement was, it had an enemy that was powerfully entrenched. As late as April, 1919, Lenine and Trotzky commanded the largest army in eastern Europe, conservatively estimated at 300,000 men, with as many more in reserve. This army, however, held the inside positions, and thus, tho handicapped by lack of transportation facilities, could strike in any direction, and more quickly than its adversaries. But against these advantages was the fact that at least five of the peoples of Europe were actively engaged in military preparations for defense—Ukrainians, Roumanians, Bulgarians, Poles, and Germans. Besides these there were in southeastern Europe 850,000 Allied troops— English, French, Serbians, Greeks, Roumanians, and Italians, and of these the English and French alone numbered nearly 300,000, which with the Czecho-Slovaks and Poles in the north, made a cordon of more than a million men who could be stretched from the Baltic to the Black Sea.

Most encouraging of all was the advance of Kolchak's army in Siberia. With Allied and Czecho-Slovak support in the rear, heartened by promise of Allied recognition of the Omsk Government, with Allied equipment and military advice at his command, Kolchak began a scientifically planned campaign in March, his army moving forward in three columns. Two columns in the south reached tributaries of the Volga, and were near the main stream. The northern column traversed one-third of the way from the Asian border to Petrograd and was soon to menace Vyatka, commanding the branch line to the Dwina River. What might prove the beginning of a movement that would redeem all northern Russia was the success of the Finns in cutting the Murmank Railway at a point as near Petrograd as New London is to New York. Meanwhile a successful action at Kief dealt the Bolsheviki a violent blow, and Polish and Ukrainian forces administered heavy blows in western Russia. The only offset to these reverses were some successes by the Bolsheviki in the Crimea. For the first time the Russians seemed to be fighting the Bolsheviki successfully and there began to be some semblance of government in Russia. The Kolchak movement had furnished the nucleus around which had grown all that was practical and enforceable for a real Russia as against the dismal tyranny which the minority set up after the overthrow of Kerensky. Outside assistance might have saved Russia earlier, but failing that, Russia had finally risen herself. Resolute men in Siberia had raised the banner of rebellion, and from all over Russia men had flocked to Kolchak's flag. It was nominally a Siberian, but really an All-Russian, army that he was leading in what seemed to be a successful march. Kolchak, by the end of May, had captured the last place where the Bolsheviki could make a stand before Samara.

What was more important, the Archangel Government had recognized the supreme authority of the Omsk Government as the Provisional National Government of All Russia. That completed the political laision between Siberia and Archangel. In other words, all of Russia that was opposed to Bolshevism was now united from the Arctic to the Don, and from Samara to Vladivostok. Russia, thrown back on her own devices, seemed to be working out her own salvation.

The story of the rise of the Omsk Government in Siberia was the inevitable one of the ascendancy of the age-old instinct of self-preservation. The Bolsheviki tore down. The people had begun to reconstruct. The movement for recognition of Kolchak by the Allies and the United States as the *de facto* government in Russia was supported generally in Paris, and by May 26 the Council of Four had unanimously decided in favor of recognition "in principle."

ADMIRAL KOLCHAK
Leader of an anti-Bolshevik army recognized by the Entente

Kolchak assured the Allied and associated Powers that he did not intend to retain power longer than required by the interest of the country, and reaffirmed his intention to call elections for the Constituent Assembly as soon as the Bolsheviki had been crusht. The Peace Conference had practically no alternative but to recognize Kolchak, because peace, lacking Russia, would not have been peace, and the Soviet Government had refused to ''accept the fundamental condition of suspending hostilities.'' There had to all appearance begun to rise solid ground for hope that Russia might be saved—and as many wise men had always insisted that she must be saved—by her own people. Kolchak was a Russian admiral, who, when the Czar abdicated, had supported the Provisional Government set up under Prince Lvoff. When Lvoff's administration was overthrown to make way for Kerensky, a plot was laid to put Kolchak out of the way; but he went to Sebastopol, Odessa, and other cities on the Black Sea coast where he preached not only on shore, but on board various men-of-war doctrines of revolution and perfect equality of all men, even those before the mast as well as officers on the quarter-deck.

Meanwhile, General Denikin, leader of the Don Cossacks, continued to make headway in May and June, 1919, against the Bolsheviki, altho Kolchak suffered at the same time a disturbing reverse. In three weeks a volunteer army had trebled its territory. Along the whole front, from the Caspian to the Sea of Azov, four Red armies had been thoroughly defeated, had lost half their number and were still retreating. Denikin's forces had captured 22,000 prisoners, 150 guns, 350 machine-guns, 4 armored trains, and an immense quantity of other booty. This energetic push promised soon to free the Don country entirely from Red forces. Largely through the action of tanks and the daring raids of General Shkuro's horsemen, the Dontez Basin had been conquered, and the Reds were retiring with such speed that if continued it would threaten the early fall of Kharkoff and Ekaterinoslav.

The camel-shaped front of General Denikin's armies in South Russia had become in June a sort of irregular bulge which continued to swell out in all directions. Enemy forces had been crumbling between Kharkov and the Volga, and Cossack patrols were scouring the country northward and roping in scattered and demoralized enemy units. The Bolsheviki's Hindenburg line seemed broken, its morale shaken by the appearance of British tanks, Russian soldiers in British uniform and the stimulating effect of Denikin's proclamations. Trotzky had made superhuman but futile efforts to stem the advance of the volunteer army, and the late Emperor's train, in which he traveled, had once barely escaped capture by Cossacks. In this train, Trotzky had a suite of expert propagandists, forty typists, a printing press which turned out thousands of leaflets and proclamations, and a newspaper called *On the Road*. The Ninth Soviet Army had now been annihilated, and the Eighth and

CHEERS FOR AMERICAN TROOPS LEAVING TILBURY PIER, LONDON, FOR ARCHANGEL
The date of this scene is April 9, 1919

Thirteenth were in full retreat. In the North, General Petlura had advanced along the entire front and was within twenty miles of Kief. Forces under General Grigorieff, after occupying Odessa, Kherson, and Nikolaiev, were marching northward to establish communication with Petlura and were beginning an offensive along the Dniester.

By July 9 the Crimea had been entirely cleared of Bolsheviki, the advance being over a front of seventy miles; it had deprived the Bolsheviki of communication between their main forces and those in the Crimea. Denikin's volunteers were meeting with success on all parts of the front.

One column had reached a point on the Caspian coast fifty-five miles southwest of Astrakhan, and another was on the banks of the Volga northwest of Tchernoi-Jar. In capturing Tsaritsin, Denikin took 10,000 prisoners and a quantity of guns. He was now only seventy-five miles from Saratov, and volunteers had pushed forty miles beyond Karkov. In the Don country, by the end of the month, the volunteer army and the Cossacks were securing further surrenders and pursuing the Reds westward in the direction of Poltava and Kief. In the governments of Voroness and Sarakoff the Don Cossacks were being joined by peasants in revolt. Red reinforcements had been brought up to Tsaritsin, but Bolshevist railway approaches to the town had been cut off and Don Cossacks had reached the Volga. There seemed nothing now to prevent a break through to Moscow, provided communications could be secured and civilian administration guaranteed.[18] The loss of Ekaterinburg, reported in July, loosened the hold of Kolchak on the Ural mining region, of which Ekaterinburg was the center, but he still occupied Tcheliabinsk, on the main stem of the Trans-Siberian Railway, southeast of Ekaterinburg and east of the mountains. Kolchak's armies had now apparently evacuated the district east of the Volga that had been conquered by the Czecho-Slovaks in 1918, so that the route to Moscow from the east had, for a time, at least, been closed. But there was still a route open from the South, where Denikin had been making steady progress for several months, altho Denikin at Kharkov was still 600 miles from Moscow.

Certain definite deductions were possible from the still somewhat confused situation in Russia. The first was that Russian Bolshevism had entered upon what looked like its final phase. Unless it could again be favored in some extraordinary way, it had exhausted its possibilities. The evidence was cumulative that the populations over which the Bolsheviks had ruled longest had reached a stage of disillusionment and reaction that was ineffective only because the people, disorganized, crusht, and starving had not the means or the strength to rise against them. Meanwhile the

[18] Dispatch by Harold Williams, from Novocherkark, to the New York *Times*.

Bolshevik Government could not cope with corruption and disaffection among its own followers. Nearly every one of its various fantastic administrative schemes had broken down. Its fierce terrorist measures, its encouragement of plunder and mass espionage, its efforts to break up the population into a chaos of warring classes and groups had been nothing more than devices for staving off for a time an inevitable downfall. The Bolsheviks themselves were represented as living in a nightmare, possest by a sort of criminal insanity. Their statesmanship had become the strange diabolical cunning of the madman who seeks to intimidate the sane.

Thus the struggle for the restoration of Russia was beginning to give clear proof of solid achievement. In Siberia, at Omsk, with Admiral Kolchak as ruler, the work of reconstruction had to all appearances really begun, in the face of enormous difficulties, political and material. A real and effective administration had been established, an army had been created, all these in spite of serious lack of munitions and only tolerable means of transport. Kolchak was seen to be an able, resolute man of action, with broad views and a finely tempered character. His Government had made progress in organization, it had a good financial basis, and it ruled over the largest extent of Russian territory outside of Bolshevik Russia.

It was to Denikin's army that the masses of Russian patriots turned with the greatest affection as a symbol of the stubborn continuity of the Russian State in the midst of overwhelming disaster. The story of the desperate struggle of his gallant little army in the southeastern steppes made a thrilling record, even amid the great annals of this war. Its former leaders were dead—Korniloff, who, on the Bukowina front in the early summer of 1917, had won for Russia her last victory over the Central Powers, having been killed by a Bolshevik shell near Ekaterinodar in March, 1919, and Alexeiev, who, under the ill-fated Provisional Government had revived hopes that he might soon have the Russian Army in a state of fighting efficiency, having died in October, 1918, worn out with grief over the fate of his country.

Denikin's army consisted at first almost solely of officers. Its strength in March, 1918, was only about 4,000. Its casualties during many long months of grim warfare had been over 30,000. Its strength early in 1919 had risen to over 10,000. It had fought unaided the enemy, overshadowed tho it was by Bolsheviks and Germans. It had not only maintained its own honor respecting the Allies and Russia, but had vindicated the honor of the Russian name. Denikin was "a clean, strong man, firm and tolerant, a devoted patriot, with every quality of a leader except that of personal ambition." Russia had been the arena of a remarkable and bewildering combination of centripetal and centrifugal forces. She had been in the throes of a struggle for nation-making, extraordinarily varied in character and quality, yet in all its forms it was obscurely tending to one end—her restoration.[19]

[19] Principal Sources: The "Military Expert" of The *Times*, The *Tribune*, The *World*, The *Evening Post*, The *Times*, The *Sun*, The *Journal of Commerce*, New York; Associated Press dispatches, "The American Year Book for 1918" (D. Appleton & Co.), *The Literary Digest*, Harold Williams in *The Edinburgh Review* for April, 1919.